My Secret Life ￼
between 1882 an￼
printed (one is at Yale and another at the Kinsey Institute).
The books record some 40 years in the erotic life of an
upper-class Victorian gentleman obsessed with sex and sexual detail. In his preface to the work, "Walter" (the narrator)
maintains that he kept the diary because the male erotic life
had yet to be chronicled. "I determined to write my private
life freely as to fact, and in the spirit of the lustful acts done
by me, or witnessed," he claims. "It is written therefore
with absolute truth and without any regard whatever for
what the world calls decency."

Here are volumes three and four of the 2,360-page work,
in which Walter, now a young man, experiences misadven-
tures with many willing partners. The women in his life
number in the hundreds; there are girls of fourteen and
married women, child prostitutes and servants, working
girls and their mistresses. It is not clear exactly why Walter
wrote his anonymous diary and paid handsomely to have
it printed. Whatever the reasons, his honest and unsparing
account depicts a society that, while very different from the
traditional image of Victorian England, is unmistakably real.

My Secret Life

Part Two

My Secret Life

Part Two

Anonymous

BOOK-OF-THE-MONTH CLUB
NEW YORK

MY SECRET LIFE

VOLUME III

CONTENTS

PAGE

CHAPTER I. — *Straitened circumstances.* — *Promiscuous whorings.* — *The garden privies.* — *Our neighbour's daughters.* — *Effects of a hard turd.* — *Masturbation.* —*Bum-trumpeting.*—*Seeing and hearing too much.*— *A pock-marked strumpet.* — *A neighbour's servant.* — *Don't wet inside.* — *On the road home.* — *Cheap amusements.* — *Bargains.* — *Watching brothels.* — *Cunt in the open.* — *Clapped again.* — *French letters, and effects.* — *Income improved.* — *Piddle in the by-streets.* — *An uprighter.* — *My pencil-case.* — *A female bilker.* — *A savage frig.* — *A silk dress soiled.*   1

CHAPTER II. — *Preliminary remarks.* — *A dress-lodger.* — *Lucy.* — *Sweet seventeen.* — *An impudent demand.* — *A row.* — *The baud.* — *My watch requisitioned.* — *Exit barred.* — *Bill.* — *Funking.* — *Determination.* — *The poker and window.* — *Vici.* — *Apologies.* — *A cautious retreat.* — *My revenge.* — *Lucy scared away.* —*Brighton Bessie.*—*Washing by fire-light.*—*Friendly intimacy.* — *The house in B°w Street.* — *Lascivious evenings.*   13

CHAPTER III. — *A change in taste.* — *A small cunt longed for.* — *Hunting in the Strand.* — *Yellow-haired Kitty.* — *Her little companion.* — *Oh! you foole.* — *The house in E°°t°r Street.* — *Double fees.* — *Kitty's pleasure.* — *Objections to washing.* — *Have the other gal.* — *Cleanliness.* — *Home occupations.* — *I ain't gay.* — *Kitty's males.*   25

CHAPTER IV. — *Little Pol consents.* — *Arsy-versy.* — *Broached, and howling.* — *Kitty's vocalization.* — *A cheap virginity.* — *Two hours after.* — *Love's money lost.* — *The street-gully.* — *Kitty pleases.* — *Pol tires.* — *Kitty's habits.* — *Friendliness and frankness.* — *Sausage rolls.* — *Confessions of lust.*   36

CONTENTS

CHAPTER V. — *Kitty's antecedents. — The fishmonger's. — Jim the shopman. — Betty the maid. — Females in bed. — Mutual curiosity. — Lechery and frigging. — Educated in coition. — Against the kitchen-wall. — Jim in bed. — Betty's cunt washed out. — A look in the basin. — Cousin Grace, and Cousin Bob. — Bob on the spree. — A scuffle. — Topsy-turvy. — Arsy-versy. — Bob's semen. — A masturbating duet. — Caught in the act. — Kicked out.*   45

CHAPTER VI. — *Sausage-rolls, and consequences. — Kitty's home. — The little ones. — A saucy cabman. — Catamenia. — Fucking economies. — Changing money. — Pol and the bargee. — Kit implicated. — A black eye and bruised rump. — A little boy's cock. — Preparation for travel. — Kit's regret. — Bessie in tears. — Amusements abroad. — Home again. — Kitty a strumpet. — An evening at B*w Street. — Kitty's eight months' doings.*   56

CHAPTER VII. — *Brighton Bessie. — Change irresistible. — Bessie in quod. — Lewed effects. — Spooning. — Her home. — Her cabman. — Reflexions. — Two years after. — Five years later on. — The mouse's promenade. — Bessie disappears.*   62

CHAPTER VIII. — *Washerwomen. — Matilda and Esther. — A peep over a wall. — Eaves dropping. — A girl's wants. — Shaking a tooleywag. — A promenade by a barrow. — Disclosures. — A snatch and a scuffle. — An assignation.*   68

CHAPTER IX. — *Returning home. — In the church-yard. — Two female laborers. — Among the tombs. — A sudden piss. — An arse on the weeds. — Torn trowsers and a turd. — In front of the public-house.*   75

CHAPTER X. — *The washerwoman's lane. — An intention frustrated. — A slap on the face. — Choice language and temper. — A dinner in the Haymarket. — The rocking-chair. — A lucky shove. — Up, and out in a second. — A quarrel, and flight. — An enticing laugh. — The house in O***d*n Street.*   81

CONTENTS

CHAPTER XI. — *Esther meets me.* — *Vauxhall.* — *Ex-harlot Sarah.* — *Esther succumbs.* — *Big-arsed and bandy-legged.* — *Periodic fucking.* — *Matilda invincible.* — *I part with Esther.* — *Her fortune.*   87

CHAPTER XII. — *Preliminary.* — *My taste for beauty of form.* — *Sarah Mavis.* — *Midday in the Quadrant.* — *No. 13 J***s Street.* — *A bargain in the hall.* — *A woman with a will.* — *Fears about my size.* — *Muck.* — *Cold-blooded.* — *Tyranny.* — *My temper.* — *Submission.* — *A revolt.* — *A half-gay lady.* — *Sarah watches me.* — *A quarrel.* — *Reconciliation.*   93

CHAPTER XIII. — *Sarah's complaisance.* — *Mistress Hannah.* — *About Sarah.* — *Sexual indifference.* — *After dinner.* — *Start naked at last.* — *Her form.* — *The scar.* — *Hannah's friendship.* — *The baudy house parlour.* — *The Guardsman.* — *Sarah's greed.* — *A change in her manner.* — *A miscarriage.* — *Going abroad.* — *I am madly in love.* — *Sarah's history.*   105

CHAPTER XIV. — *Poses plastiques.* — *Sarah departs.* — *My despair.* — *Hannah's comfort.* — *Foolscap and masturbation.* — *Cheap cunt.* — *A mulatto.* — *The baudy house accounts.* — *Concerning Sarah.* — *The parlour.* — *The gay ladies there.* — *My virtue.* — *Louisa Fisher.* —*A show of legs.* — *The consequence on me.* — *Effect on Mrs. Z**i.*   118

CHAPTER XV. — *Louisa Fisher.* — *Chaffing.* — *Her form and fucking.* — *A supper in bed.* — *A lascivious night.* — *Meeting afterwards.* — *Hannah's legs.* — *Intruders in the bed-room.* — *Louisa's voluptuousness.* — *Enceinte.* — *Her husband.* — *Her gentleman friend.* — *About herself.* — *Illness.* — *Mrs. A***y.*   130

CHAPTER XVI. — *A friend's maid-servant.* — *Jenny.* — *Initial familiarity.* — *A bum pinched.* — *Jenny communicative.* — *Her young man.* — *An attempt, a failure, a faint, a look and a sniff.* — *Restoratives.*   144

CHAPTER XVII. — *When are women most lewed.* — *Garters, money, and promises.*—*About my servant.*—*The neckerchief.* — *Armpits felt.* — *Warm hints.* — *Lewed sug-*

gestions. — Baudy language. — Tickling. — "Fanny
Hill." — Garters tried. — Red fingers. — Struggle, and
escape.—Locked out.—I leave.—Baudy predictions,
and verification.   152

CHAPTER XVIII. — "Fanny Hill" sent to Jenny. — My next
visit. — Thunder, lightning, sherry, and lust. — A chase
round a table. — The money takes. — Tickling and micturating. — A search for "Fanny Hill." — A chase up the
stairs. — In the bed-room. — Thunder, funk, and lewedness. — Intimidation and coaxing. — Over and under.
— A rapid spender. — Virginity doubtful. — Fears,
tears, and fucking.   159

CHAPTER XIX. — My soiled shirt. — Jenny's account of herself. — Fucking and funking. — Poor John! — Of her
pudenda. — Its sensitiveness. — Erotic chat. — Startled
by a caller. — Her married sister's unsatisfied cunt. —
How she prevented having children. — Doubts her husband's fidelity. — Jenny taught the use of a French letter. — Hikery-pikery and catamenial irregularities.   170

CHAPTER XX. — A Saturday afternoon. — Copulation interrupted. — Retreat cut off. — Under the bed. — Enter
sister. — The new dress. — Heat and sweat. — Undressing. — Jenny's anxiety. — Sweating much, and stripping. — Nature in its simplicity. — Nature in its vulgarity. — Delicious peeps. — A cunt near my nose. —
Erotic recklessness. — Fist-fucking.   178

CHAPTER XXI. — Further undressing. — Slippers wanted.
— Toilet operations. — The effects of hash and beer. —
A windy escape. — Feeling for the pot. — Sisters exeunt.
— A crushed hat, and soiled trowsers. — A narrow
escape. — My benevolent intentions towards Jenny's
sister.   186

CHAPTER XXII. — The Sunday following. — Chaste calculations. — The sister alone. — My embarrassment. —
Ale fetched. — Warm conversation. — Stiffening. —
Bolder talk.—An exhibition of masculinity.—A golden
promise. — Lust creeping. — Baudy dalliance. — Cock
and cunt in conjunction.   191

CONTENTS

CHAPTER XXIII. — *Jenny's bed-room.* — *The money hidden.* — *On the bed.* — *Fears of maternity.* — *Inspection of sex.* — *The use of a husband.* — *Another Sunday.* — *Regrets and refusal.* — *Resistance overcome.* — *Jenny's ignorance.* — *Her master returns.* — *Difficulty in getting at Jenny.* — *Her sister waylaid.* — *Against a fence.* — *Jenny's marriage, and rise in life.*   199

CHAPTER I

Straitened circumstances. — Promiscuous whorings. — The garden privies. — Our neighbour's daughters. — Effects of a hard turd. — Masturbation. — Bum-trumpeting. — Seeing and hearing too much. — A pock-marked strumpet. — A neighbour's servant. — Don't wet inside. — On the road home. — Cheap amusements. — Bargains. — Watching brothels. — Cunt in the open. — Clapped again. — French letters, and effects. — Income improved. — Piddle in the by-streets. — An uprighter. — My pencil-case. — A female bilker. — A savage frig. — A silk dress soiled.

I felt such a void, that I came to the conclusion that I had fondly loved Mary, and missed greatly her kind, sympathetic association. For a long time I could think of nothing but her, even when I fucked other women, and got so miserable about her, that I rushed into indiscriminate cheap whoring again. I had still not money for the best class of women, and did not like baudy houses; but there was no help for it, and so whoring I went, and largely in the Strand, for at that time in E**t*r and C*t*****e Streets there were many and nice brothels at all prices.

But I for some time abstained from women, and had wet dreams. My mind ran constantly on Mary, and when I saw a nice girl, used to wonder if her cunt was like Mary's, and this specially of two girls about nineteen and twenty years of age, daughters of one of our next-door neighbours.

The privies of the houses in our terrace were built in pairs, the garden wall divided them and partly the cess-pool which was common to the two. I used to take pleasure in watching to see these girls go to the privy, and although the idea of a female evacuating revolted me, yet used to try to get to our privy when one of the

1

girls went to theirs, and would stand smoking just inside the passage by the backsteps of my house, tip-toeing to catch a glance of their heads, and stopping myself from bogging sometimes, so that I might get there at the same time. Directly I saw a head off I followed quietly, and if the weather was quite still we could hear footsteps in each other's gardens too well.

The cess-pool had at the time I write of just been emptied, the turds dropping and flopping down could be heard, it was not nice, but it did not shock me. I liked to hear the girls' piddle splashing, and used to push my prick back, and sit back on the seat, so that my piddle might drop straight, and make much noise. It pleased me to hear the joint rattle and splash we made if we pissed at the same time. I did this so constantly, that I could tell which girl was there, for the piddle of one always made twice as much splash as the other's. Up would stand my prick, and often I could not piss for its stiffness, directly I heard the girls splashing.

One day I had a hardish motion, and was randy that morning almost to pain. One of the girls was there. I strained, my cock got stiff, and began to throb violently, and shot out its spunk as I strained. I went back to the house, and just entering it saw the other daughter go towards the privy. Back I went and sitting down frigged myself as I heard her evacuations drop, so randy and charged with sperm was I.

After that I occasionally frigged myself at the privy, and used to picture to myself the girls sitting there, their clothes up round their rumps, and slightly up in front showing their limbs, and piddle squirting, but I always thought of both girls as having cunts like Mary's. After a time we knew a little of the girls, and when talking to them I used to think of the same thing. The idea used to fascinate me, and they used to say (I am told), that I was a strange man, for I always stared at them as if I had never seen a woman before. They little knew what was in my mind when I was staring.

Just after the emptying I could not only see their wax as it fell to the bottom, but the paper with which they wiped their bums, and could hear them fart. Sometimes the two came together. One day by a sudden whim I let a fart as loud as I could, and heard a suppressed titter, they I think never knew I could hear, for usually I tried to be as silent as possible. I never coughed when there, and used to pull open my arse-hole to lessen the noise of my trumpet, and singular as it may seem did this out of a feeling of delicacy. Soon the cess-pool was half-filled with water, and I could only indistinctly hear. Then I grew tired of the fun, and again let off my sperm up cunts instead of spilling it on the privy-floor, for sorrow always came over me as I saw it on the floor. A few months after this I took a dislike to the girls through thinking of what I had seen and heard of them, it seemed to shock my sentiment of the beauty and delicacy of a woman.

A confused number of random whorings and miscellaneous fuckings took place about this time, I cannot tell to a month or two, but it began directly after Mary had gone. I tell of one or two of them.

At the back of the Lowther Arcade one night I took a poor girl seemingly about sixteen years old to a house. She had a nice but thin form, and was as white as driven snow. When I had had her, I wanted to see her face more clearly, but she held a hand-kerchief to it, and half turned it away from the light, her privates she allowed to be inspected as I liked.

She was marked badly with the small-pox, and was nevertheless handsome, but with that sad expression which the pock-marks often give. Gents did not like it, she said. It was a dreadfully sloppy, snowy night. "Don't go yet," said she, "it is so warm here." So I sat a while feeling her quim and talking. "Do me again, I want it now, I did not when you did it before." So we fucked again. "Do I please you?" said the girl putting her hand to my face. "Yes my dear." "Will you see me again? — do." I was always careful about promising that, and hesitated; but at length said yes. Again I rose to go, again the girl asked me to stay, it was so warm. "Pay the woman again and say you are going to stay till ten o'clock." There was such simplicity about her that I consented. The woman put coals on the fire, and we sat by it warming ourselves.

After a time she said, "I don't think you like me." "Why?" "Because you don't feel me about." I laughed, and said I had been feeling her. Time ran on. "Won't you do it again?" "I can't dear." "Let me try to make you." "You may, but I can't." She came to me, knelt down, played funnily, but awkwardly with my cock till it stiffened, and again we fucked. "You won't see me again, though you say you will." "Why not?" asked I wondering at her sad manner. "They all say they will, but they never do, — it's the small-pox marks they can't bear, I know it is, — I'm tired of this life." Then suddenly she laughed and said she was only joking.

I never did see her again. Such a young white-fleshed girl, and so fond of the cock, or else she had had but little of it, I have rarely met with. She said she had only been out two months. "The other girls tell me what to do with men, and the old woman where I live tells me; but I always does what a gentleman asks me, I can't do more, can I?" said she. "Other gals say they have regular friends, I haven't." I shall never forget that poor little girl.

On a cold evening a week or two after this, I saw a shortish, dark-eyed girl going along the Strand. She walked slowly, and looked in at almost every shop. I could not make up my mind if she was gay or not. She was warmly wrapped up, her style that of a well-to-do servant. I passed and repassed her, looked her in the face; her eye met mine and dropped, then she stopped and looked round several times after unmistakably gay women as they passed her, then went on again. Opposite the Adelphi she paused and looked at the theatre for a long time, a gentleman spoke to her, and seemed to importune her, she took no notice of him, and he left her. After walking on for a minute quickly she loitered and looked in the shops again.

Near Exeter Hall my cock which was in want of relief giving me impudence, and liking her looks I spoke to her about the things in the windows. At first I got no reply, and she walked on. "Come with me, and I'll give you a sovereign. You can buy it then." What it was I don't recollect. She seemed uneasy and wavering, yet made no reply. I repeated my offer (it was just then money beyond my means, but I had hot desire on me). She looked up the street in both directions, and asked, "Will it be far?" I took her at the instant for a sly gay one. "You know I am sure, it's close by." "It's getting late, I'm in a hurry." Looking both ways quickly and un-easily she placed her arm in mine, and hanging her head down pressed close to me. We walked quickly, and soon were in a snug room in a house at the back of Exeter Hall.

"This is not a public-house," said she looking round. "No, but you can have drink if you like." "A little warm brandy and water then." I ordered it. "Take off your bonnet and cloak." She hesitated. "Tell me the exact time." I did, and then she took them off, sat down, and soon sipped brandy and water looking at me. Thought I, "You must be a servant after all."

I began to caress her, and got my hand on her thighs asking her to come to the bed. "I must go soon, let me go soon." "I will, but let me see your legs and feel them." She let me pull the clothes up to her knees, then pushed away my hand but I thrust one up, and just felt the cunt. She gave me a shove, and nearly pushed me over, for I had dropped on to my knees, a favorite attitude of mine at such times.

Savagely I got up. "Don't be a fool; if you mean to let me do it come to the bed." She hesitated. "Give me the money first." "Oh!" thought I, "she is a whore diseased, and a bilk," so I refused. "You really will give it me, won't you?" "Of course, but I'm not to be done that way." Then I got her on to the bed, and threw up her clothes. She resisted. "What do you take me for?" "Why a whore," said I savagely. It was a word I rarely used *of* a woman, still rarer *to* a woman. She pushed my hand angrily away and sat up.

"I am not, and wish I had not come here, and would not, only I want money for my poor mother, I thought you a gentleman, — I'm not the sort of woman you say, I'm a servant, I am indeed." "Well if you are, you have been fucked." "That is neither here nor there, but I'm not what you call me," — and she pouted. "Lay down dear, — let's fuck if you mean it, if not let's go, — let me feel you, and you feel me." I pulled her back on to the bed, laying down by the side of her, and put my prick into her hand. It was persuasive, for soon I was having that delicious rub, probe, and twiddle. Then I got a sight of all but the cunt itself, the inspection of that she resisted. A fine pair of limbs, a fat backside, lots of hair on her split I could feel. My friction told, she began grasping my prick like a vice, — she was going to spend.

Nice to her that, but I wanted my pleasure. Again I got savage. At length quietly, and feeling my prick all the time she said, "Promise me something." "What?" "Don't you wet inside if I let you." I promised, and turning on to her belly fucked her, and forgot my promise, even if I ever meant to keep it. We were soon near the crisis. "Don't — now, — oh! — wet." "No dear." "T — aake — care." "I'll pull it out just as it comes dear." "Don't — we — wet, oh! — ah! — wet," she gasped out as clutching her arse my prick went fiercely up her, and spent every drop against her womb-tube, my spend made doubly pleasurable, because she did not wish it in her cunt.

Said she with a long-drawn sigh, "You've done it all inside, — you should not." "I could not help it, you are so charming, I could not pull it out and make your clothes or bum wet," said I ramming on, and keeping my prick tight up her lubricated cunt. "Let me get up." "Not yet." "Oh do, I'm in a hurry." "Lay still dear." "No, I'm in such a hurry, — what o'clock is it? — do tell me what o'clock it is, — it will make me lose my place if I'm very late."

I uncunted, told her the time, and she washed her cunt. "Let us do it again." She was wanting it. "I've such a long way to go." "Where?" She told me, and it was my way home. "I will take you home in a cab." On the bed she got, I overcame her scruples, kissed her knees, her thighs, all the way up to her cunt. The thighs opened widely, a second's inspection of a cunt at that time of my life made me think of immediate pleasure, and after promising not to wet in her again, she reminding me of that, till she lost all care or heed in her pleasures. I spent up her as before.

We went home in a cab, and felt each other all the way. She said she was keeping her mother who was poor, she feared, dying. At the end of the road she got out begging me not to follow her. I did not, and never saw her again. She had hazel eyes, spoke with a country accent, and I quite believe was a servant.

Although soon after this a little better off, I had difficulty in keeping out of debt, and the cost of amatory amusements prevented my having women as often as I otherwise should have done. I used to try the cheap at times, and often successfully. Would walk backwards and forwards between Temple-bar and Charing Cross for hours, looking at the women, thinking which I should like, and whether I could afford one. Sometimes I would follow the same woman, stop when she stopped if a man spoke to her, cross over, and wait till she moved off by herself, or if with the man, would follow them to a brothel, return to watch for her coming out, and wait till she did so. This pleased me much.

Then I began to feel women in the streets; they frequently came out of the E**t*r Street houses, and round by the side-entrance to Exeter Hall. That end of the street then was all but dark.

Stopping a woman, this was a frequent dialogue. "A nice night dear." "Yes." "Been taking a walk?" "Yes." "Been to piddle?" "Yes." They usually when I knew they had come out of a house, said they had been to piddle if I asked them. "A shilling to feel your cunt." "All right, give it me." With the left hand I gave the shilling, with the right I fingered their quims. "Open your legs dear, — a little wider, — let me feel up, — have you been fucked to-night?" "No." It was always no. I delighted in hearing them tell that lie. "Come with me." "How much?" "Give me a sovereign." "No." "Ten shillings then." "I can't afford more than five shillings." "No, not for that"; but they more often said yes. Sometimes I went with them, more frequently not. The lesson I learned was that most women denied that they had fucked more recently than the day before (it was always the day before), and that a little bargaining reduced the price of their pleasures.

If intending to have a poke I waited for a girl known by sight, and then often could not find her, then I saw those so dressed that I could not offer them a small sum. On other nights I went up to the girl with the fattest legs, and made advances. In this way I shagged many of all sorts and sizes, many of them poor creatures, others plump, fine, strong, healthy women, whom I was surprised took the small sum for their professional exertions. The end of this promiscuity was that again I took the clap, which laid me up some weeks, and made it again needful to open my piss-pipe by surgical tubes.

Then I was timid, used French letters, and took to carrying them in my purse again, but always hated them. Often my tool stiff as a boring-iron would shrink directly the wet gut touched it, and compelled me to frig up to near the crisis before I could insert it in the skin. Sometimes it would not stiffen completely till up the woman. I used to drop my tool in a state of partial rigidity into the letter, then thumb it slowly up the lady's orifice; there the warmth, the clip, the buttocks wagging, and the look at the belly and thighs between which I was working brought it to the proper stiffness. I usually had the ladies at the side of the bed, when wearing these condoms.

Sometimes my passions overcame my prudence, and a fair lady for her favours got her price. Then I was filled with regrets, and had to content myself with a feel for some time, or wait days till

I could afford the full gratification of my senses with another woman, because I had not the money. Then I fell again on my five shilling offers. About this cunt-feeling there was something very peculiar in me: unless I liked the look of the woman I did not like to feel her cunt, and after I had been groping used to spit on my fingers, and rub them dry, and the smell off of them on to my handkerchief.

Some little time after my clap however I came into a better income through the death of a relative. It was small, but made a difference to me of great importance. I spent it all on myself, that is to say on cunt, and although some of my country relatives must have known I had come into the property, those most interested in knowing it I believe never did. I now longed for nice women whom I could talk and spend the money with. The rapid business-like fucking in the baudy houses was not to my taste, I had scarcely gone to the Argyle Rooms, then not many years opened, for fear that my taste for nicety of manner and something more than mere cunt might lead me into an expenditure still far beyond my means.

It used to wound my pride to hear a woman jeer at my offer, or say, "What the devil do you take me for?" or walk away wagging her rump with offended dignity when she heard five shillings named, or say she would frig me for the money. Now I could offer more, I was more happy in my mind; but there are a few adventures to be told before the time when an easier pocket enabled me to have better female companions.

[The angle of the street named as leading out of the Strand was dark of a night and a favourite place for doxies to go to relieve their bladders. The police took no notice of such trifles, provided it was not done in the greater thoroughfares (although I have seen at night women do it openly in the gutters in the Strand), in the particular street I have seen them pissing almost in rows, yet they mostly went in twos to do that job, for a woman likes a screen, one usually standing up till the other had finished, and then taking her turn. Indeed the pissing in all by-streets of the Strand was continuous, for although the population of London was only half what it now is, the number of gay ladies seemed double there. The theatre-side of the street from Trafalgar Square to Temple-bar was nightly for some hours one large flock of them, and there was not a street or court on the whole line named, and on both sides of the Strand in which there was not a baudy house. I have been in a dozen.]

I used to prowl about to see the girls pissing, and when I had cheek enough, stand and piss by the side of them. That delighted me much. One night I saw two women go up a court, one directly squatted, and I followed. When one had done I asked her to let me feel her. She did. Randy but poor that night the feel of her wet cunt made me reckless. As I gave her a shilling I remarked how I should like to have her, but that I had but five shillings to give.

"You won't have me for five shillings, but you will get some one who will, — you have lots of cheek to offer it." "I am sorry, but I can't help it if I have not more." Had I not ten shillings? No, only enough for the room. All this time I was feeling her. Then her hand went outside my trowsers, feeling at my cock. I slipped it out, she took it in her hand. "Have you not been a long time in the Strand to-night?" said she. I had, and wanted a woman, only I had so little money. I did not know the form or face of this woman, for we were in the darkest place, and the night was dark and cold, but I felt that she had a silk dress on, lots of hair on her cunt, and a large arse. "You may do it here for five shillings," said she. I had never done it in the open in such a place, but consented. Groping in my pocket I found and gave the money, and then she stepped away from me, — a bilk I thought.

It was not so. She went up to the other woman who was standing at the corner, and telling her look out for the police, came back to me, and again placing her back up against the wall, I fucked her. "Wasn't it nice!" said she dropping her petticoats. And then we stood still and talked.

"Stand a drink," said she, "you've got some silver." I did not mind, and was curious to see her. She called her friend, and all three went to a public-house, the lady with all my emission in her cunt. I found she was a full-grown woman of about thirty with dark hair, dark eyes, and with a bold expression in them. We had mulled port-wine, then something else, and stood drinking till all my money was gone. Her companion left us saying she had not gained a farthing that night, and must do so.

My woman then got pleasanter, and wanted more liquor, my

money was gone, but I had a pencil-case, and asked the bar-man if he would lend me a few shillings on it. He did, and I then spent more in liquor, then we went out together again into the cold street; she pissed, saying the cold and the liquor had made her leaky. "I wish you would let me again," said I. Well she would, and up against a wall again we fucked heartily. With my spunk in her we walked together into the Strand. She said she would like to see me again, but I never did. Whilst fucking her the second time she shoved her tongue almost down my throat, and breathed so hard. I never fucked a woman in the street who did so, either before or since. A few nights after I got my pencil-case back from the bar-man.

One night a nice, strong-built woman about thirty years of age seemingly, took my five shillings, and went to a house with me. She was dressed in black silk, neat but shabby. She sat down on a chair, and pulling up her clothes rearranged both her garters, showing what I expected, and what I had engaged her for; a pair of fat legs. Then down went her clothes. I began feeling her, she pushed her bum back on the chair, but her thighs and the hairy ornaments I could feel. I was awfully randy, my prick was raging. "Let's feel *you*," said she. Willingly I let her grasp it, then she moved her arse forward, and I had the pleasure of just feeling a moist clitoris from which I was diverted by a painful squeeze she gave my prick. She was squeezing no doubt to see if I had any ailment. The effect of the squeeze, which made me call out, was to make me mad with randiness. "Take off your things, and let me do it." "Where is the five shillings?" I placed them in her hands, she pocketed them, and got up. Lifting her petticoats I pressed her towards the bed where she was standing when she had spoken, but she pushed down her petticoats, and moved away.

"Not likely I'm going to take off my things for five shillings," said she as the money slipped down into her pocket, "give me fifteen shillings more, and I will, — I'm a fine-built woman," — and she pulled her clothes clean up to her waist, turned round like a teeto-tum, and after showing both arse and belly, slowly dropped her clothes again.

"Come to the side of the bed." "No I shan't, you've had a feel for five shillings, give me fifteen shillings more, and I'll give you pleasure I know, — I'll do all you want me."

"I can't." "Then I can't." I had not a pound in my pocket, but if I had, am sure indeed I should have given it to her, but I could not. "Give me ten shillings, and I'll pay for the room then," said she. I didn't know what house I was at, but generally they asked at those places the price of the room first.

"Just as you like," I said, though I was dying for a fuck. "Then I will go." "I have paid you, — if you choose to bilk me I can't help it." "I don't want to bilk you, but I never let a man have me for five shillings, and I never will, — give me five shillings more."

"Let me feel you, if you won't let me poke you." "You may do that." Leaning her bum against the side of the bed, I began groping; she complaisantly moving one leg up on to a chair, so as to open her thighs well, got hold of my prick, and began frigging it. "Give me another five shillings," said she coaxingly, and under the influence of the masturbating process I gave it her. She gave my penis the most delicate titillation whilst I was searching in my pocket for the money, but she would not let me after she had got the five shillings. She went on frigging me, repeating that she never let any one have her unless she had a pound given her.

I was annoyed, and hated frigging. Here was a well-formed woman, a cunt at hand, and yet I was to spunk out on to the floor, was being made a fool of. Stopping I said, "You don't mean to let me, whatever I give you." "Yes I do, for a sovereign." "Frig me then." She took my tool in her hand, and frigged. "Let me spend against your cunt." "No." "Against your thighs." "No." "Oh! — ah!" Finding it was coming she left off. "Give me five shillings, and I will," said she, but I would not, began frigging myself, and spite of her pushed one hand up on to her thighs, and frigged away with the other. "Take care of my dress," said she. The savage delight of doing what she wished me not, came over me. Turning my prick I shot my sperm copiously over her silk dress, and finished by flinging from my fingers what remained of it towards her face. "You damned dirty beast, you did it on purpose." "Serve you right, you cheating whore," said I putting on my hat, and leaving her with a towel wiping off my sperm, and cursing me as she did it. I don't know when I felt so spiteful against a woman as I did against her. My discharge was quick and copious, I saw it on her waist downwards. I have been bilked before and since, but have mostly pardoned the woman, for sometimes I have thought the poor things had their courses on, or some ailment or deformity; but I still seem to hate this one.

[I may add that at the time these doings took place there were but three theatres in the Strand.]

CHAPTER II

Preliminary remarks. — A dress-lodger. — Lucy. — Sweet seventeen. — An impudent demand. — A row. — The baud. — My watch requisitioned. — Exit barred. — Bill. — Funking. — Determination. —— The poker and window. — Vici. — Apologies. — A cautious retreat. — My revenge. — Lucy scared away. — Brighton Bessie. — Washing by fire-light. — Friendly intimacy. — The house in B*w Street. — Lascivious evenings.

[I have read through the two volumes in print. There are typographical errors, the names of women and places are once or twice wrongly given or spelt, but the context corrects that, and it matters not. What is important is that owing to the brevity with which some occurrences are told, they almost seem improbable; this is the result of not printing my narrative all through exactly as I wrote it. In the manuscript, items of conversation, and numerous details of the behaviour of myself and female partners in my amours, were written down just as they occurred, and showed how the climax was reached, how little by little man and woman inclined to each other, how one pressed, and the other yielded, how from modest talk and chaste kisses our chastity gradually was lost, how by touch and sighs and yielding to the swooning lust which coursed stronger and stronger through our veins, our genitals inflamed, swollen, and sweating, drove us to contact with each other, till the carnal coupling ensued, and prick and cunt revelling and wallowing in each other's juices, downed both wants and senses in voluptuous oblivion.

These details also gave studies of character, and specially of my own character, and as I now read the narratives in print after the lapse of so many years they seem to me to be needed to explain myself, even to myself. It is too late. The manuscript is burnt, that

13

printed in its stead must be taken as truth or not, as scepticism or faith prevails in the reader, if ever there be one but myself.

Nor can I less abbreviate even now and in the future I fear, for the full narrative would entail too much expense in printing, and prolong the time of completion. Yet what pleasure I had in the wordy veracities as I wrote them, childish, fantastic, ludicrous, as some of the doings and sayings now seem! How unlike the doings of the couples in erotic books which I have since read, books written with no other object but to stimulate the passions, — no object that of mine in writing this.

The narratives were written in the present tense, but in print have been altered to the past, which gives them the air of a studied composition, written as a man might write a novel; but the writing extended over well nigh forty years, and barely a word has been altered, excepting those due to omissions.

There are, however, a few remarks added here and there to explain the circumstances and connect the incidents; these are needful to explain lapses of time, and to show the continuity of the history, for all the amours were written separately; yet often I had two or three women in hand at the same period. So in arranging them chronologically, a few additions and observations were needful to explain, and these are of them.]

One muddy night in the Strand there was an exceedingly well-dressed and very short-petticoated (they all wore them then) girl of about seventeen years of age; her legs especially pleased me, they were so plump and neat, and her feet so well shod. After my offer had been accepted, we went to a house in a court just by Drury Lane Theatre, and to a top-floor front-room very handsomely furnished. She lived there, and was a dress-lodger as I found afterwards. She was beautifully clean, had fine linen, and was no sham in any way; a fresh, strong, plump, well-made young girl with lovely firm breasts, and a small quantity of brown hair on her cunt. Cunt and breasts looked only seventeen years, backside, thighs, arms, calves looked twenty. She stripped, and with but one feel and a stretch of her pretty cunt-lips and a moment's glance, I plugged her, and recollect now my enjoyment of her. Then I dressed, and so did she. Though so young, she was a well-trained whore, had much pleased me by her freedom in manner, even to the way in which she washed her cunt and pissed after her fuck. I was not with her

I should say twenty minutes if so long, my lust for her had been so strong.

"What's this?" said she disdainfully as I gave her half-a-sovereign. "What I promised you." "Oh! no you did not, I expect five pounds." I expostulated. "Look at this room, look at my dress, — do you expect me to let a man come here with me for ten shillings?" "It's all I promised, had you refused I should not have come with you." Then I put on my hat, and moved towards the door; she placed her back against it. "You don't go out of here till you give me three sovereigns." It must be added that I had paid for the room what appeared to me then a large sum.

I was in for a row, had not as much as two pounds about me, and was fearful of exposure, just then a row in a baudy house would have injured me if known.

I gave her ten shillings more, she took it, but refused to let me go, she did not believe I had so little money, — I was a gentleman, let me behave as such, — no I should not go till I gave her what she asked. I tried to pull her from the door, but could not, then sat down on the chair, saying that if I must wait, why so I must.

She tried coaxing, I told her I was entitled to another fuck for my other ten shillings. Well I might if I gave her another twenty shillings. I put hands up her petticoats, and fingers up her quim, thinking she was giving way, — but no. I had forgotten my fears in my randiness which came on again by fumbling about her rump and cunt, and pulled out my prick stiff again. She bent over me, and gave it two or three frigs. That so excited me, that I verily believe I should have given her the money if I had had it, for the pleasure of having her again; but putting my hand into my trowsers, found silver only to something like a pound in value, and told her that. Then losing her gentility she said, "I'm damned if you do go, you bugger, till you have paid me properly."

Fear of exposure came over me, but I hid it, and sitting down looked at her as she stood against the door in her petticoats, her handsome limbs showing bright in their silks, and her plump breasts just squeezing the bubbies over the top of the stays. Laying hold of my tool I pulled it out. "Stand there as long as you like, you look lovely, — as you won't let me fuck you. I'll frig myself." Suiting the action to the word I began fist-fucking, not meaning however to finish so. It was but chaff, for indeed I was funky.

She stood looking till I said, "I'm coming, — I'm spending, — lift up your petticoats, and let me see your cunt." Then unlocking the door and opening it quickly she bawled out, "Mrs. Smith, Mrs. Smith, come up, here's a bilk, come up quickly."

I was not near spending as may be guessed, but buttoning up, went towards the door. She heard me, turned round, came in, shut the door, and stood with her back to it till a woman came in; and then she told her I had given her ten shillings.

The woman was incensed. Was I a gent? she was sure I was, why not pay properly then? — a beautiful young girl like that, — just out, — look at her shape, and her face, — she had written to a dozen gents who knew her house, and they had all come to see this beauty, — all had given her five pounds, some ten pounds, they were so delighted with her, — and much of the same talk. The girl began to whimper, saying she never had been so insulted in her life before.

I told her that I had only promised ten shillings, but had given more; that the girl was certainly beautiful, and the room elegant; but I was poor, and would not have come at all had I known the cost. I had not got the money, and therefore could not pay. Then the baud's tone changed. She was not going to have the poor girl insulted in that manner, she knew better about my means of paying, and I should not go till I paid more.

We went on wrangling until the baud said, "Well if you have not money give us your watch and chain, we will pawn it, and give you the ticket, and you can get it out of pawn."

I had hidden my watch, — nearly always did so then when I went with whores whom I did not know, — but saw in this a threat, and was getting more funky, yet determined to resist whatever came of it; so said I had no watch, and if I had, that I would see her damned first, before I gave it up. "Oh! won't you," said she, "we will see if you won't, — we don't allow a poor girl to be robbed by chaps like you in our house. — Call up Bill," said she to the girl. I saw that a bully was about to be let on me, and my heart beat hard and fast; but give up my watch I made up my mind I would not unless they murdered me. I had an undefined suspicion that they would ill-treat and rob me, and prepared for the worst, — my pluck got up then.

But fear of exposure was before me. "Look," said I, "I have no watch, I have given her twenty shillings, here is every farthing I have about me," and emptied my purse (there was but a shilling or two in it) before them, and put all the money I had loose in my pocket on to the chimney-piece. There was I think about seventeen shillings in all. "Look, it is every farthing I have, — you may have that, you damned thieves, — take it and let me go, — see my pockets are empty," — and I turned them inside out.

"You've got more," said she, "be a gent, give her three pounds, she never has less, — look at her, poor thing!" The girl stood whimpering, she and the woman stood with their backs to the door, I with my back to the two windows of the room which looked out on to the public court; the fire-place was between us, the foot of the bed towards it; the fire was burning brightly, the room was quite light. There they stood, the clean, fresh, wholesome-looking lass, and besides her a shortish, thick, hooked-nosed, tawney-colored, evil-looking woman, — the baud, — she looked like a bilious Jewess.

The woman kept repeating this, for a minute or two. I refused to give any more, and grew collected. "Come now, what are you going to do?" said the woman, "you are wasting all her evening." I took up half-a-crown off the mantel-shelf, and pushing the rest along it, "I must keep this," said I, "but take all the rest, I have no more, — I have no watch, — let me go." The woman laughed sneeringly, and did not touch the money, turned round, opened the door, and called out, "Bill, Bill, come up." "Halloh!" said a loud male voice from below.

I turned round, and with a violent pull, tore aside the red window-curtains, and throwing up the window and putting my head out beneath the white blind, I screamed out, "Police! — police! — murder! — murder! — police! — police!"

Beneath the very window stalked a policeman; heard me he must, the whole alley must have heard me, but the policeman took no notice, and stalking on turned round the corner out of sight. Then the fear came over me that he was bribed, I feared they might be coming behind me, and turned round; the woman was close to me, the girl at her back. "What are you doing?" yelled the woman, "what are you kicking up a row for? — shut the window. — Go if you want, who is keeping you? — This is a respectable house, this is."

A tumult of ideas and fears rushed through my mind, I feared

Bill was close at hand, and pushing the woman back with one hand I seized the poker with the right one. "Keep back, or I will smash you," said I flourishing it, and again I shouted out, "Police! — police!" but not with my head out of the window this time.

The old woman backed and shut the door again, the young one came forwards speaking in a hurried tone, the old one dropped her voice to a whine; she did not want to keep me if I wanted to go. "Shut the window, — let her shut it, — give the poor girl two pounds then, and go." Her house was a respectable house, the police knew it, why did I come to such a house if I had no money? The girl cried, I blustered, swore, and all three were speaking at at the same time for two or three minutes.

"Let me go." "Who stops you?" said the old woman. "Give me the money." "Open the door, and go out first then." "I shan't," said the woman with a snap and a look like a demon. I turned round, and with the poker made a smash at the window. The curtains had swung, the white blind was down, but I heard the glass shiver and crash, a shout of, "Hulloh!" from some one in the court. I raised the poker again against the looking-glass, "Get out, or I'll smash this, and you, and everything else in the room," striking a chair violently, and breaking it. I now did not care what I did, but was determined to fight Bill, or any one else, and not be robbed.

The women were cowed, they cried out. Pray drop the poker, — they meant no harm, — the girl always had three pounds at least, — if I would not, — why I would not? — they never had had such a row in the house before, — to have her twice, and give her ten shillings was shameful. "A lie, you bloody baud, I have only had her once, and she has had twenty shillings." "Well, there's a good gentleman, go, and don't make a noise as you go downstairs, — look at her, poor thing, how you have frightened her, — she will let you have her again, if you like, — won't you Lucy? — Well come along then, but don't make a row, — leave the poker, — what do you want for that?" whined the woman.

I would not relinquish the poker, they should go out first. The woman went, the girl waited behind to put on her frock. As she did so the little bitch lifted her petticoats to her thighs, showed her cunt, jerked her belly, winked and nodded her head in the direction of the old woman. I did not know nor heed what she meant by her nod and wink. "Get out, — get on, — get out, — I won't have you behind me." She made a farting noise with her mouth, and dropping her clothes went out. I followed her, looked at the doors on each landing as I passed, fearing some one might come out behind me, and edged downstairs sideways, looking both up and down. One door slightly opened and closed again; at the street-door the old woman said she was so sorry, it was all a mistake, and hoped to see me again. My blood was roused, I would have smashed woman or man who stood in my way, and eying the girl said, "Look at me well, if you meet me in the Strand again, cut away at once, get out of my sight, or I'll give you in charge for annoying me, or robbing me, you bloody bitch, look out for yourself." Then dropping the poker on the mat I went out, glad enough to be away from the den.

About a fortnight afterwards I saw the girl in the Strand, followed her for a quarter of an hour, saw her speak to various men, saw that an old, common, low servant followed her at a distance, occasionally stopping to speak with her, and turning up a street for that purpose. There was a fascination about looking at the girl; she was showily but handsomely dressed, her legs looked lovely. I longed to fuck her again, but without any intention of gratifying my lust, for I loathed her whilst lusting for her. She turned up C*t*****e Street, stood over the gutter and pissed standing, the old woman talking to her and partly hiding her whilst she emptied her bladder. I waited till she had done. It was only about half-past nine o'clock.

She came towards me thinking I wanted her. I moved back close to a lamp, and raised my hat. "Look at me you damned whore, you attempted to rob me the other night, go out of the Strand, or I'll tell the next policeman you have picked my pocket." She turned on her heels and bolted without uttering a word, the old woman after her, cursing.

A month or two afterwards I saw her again. She was speaking to a group of gay women. Said I, "That bitch attempted to rob me the other night at **** Court." "It's a lie," said she, but again turned round, and ran up a side-street as fast as she could. I don't recollect seeing her afterwards.

I often used to go and look at the house when that way, it was such a needy-looking house outside with a narrow steep staircase starting close to the street-door. No one would have imagined it was

so handsomely furnished inside (although I only saw the top-room).
Two or three years afterwards there was a row there, a man
tumbled down the stairs (or was pitched down), and was picked
up dead. The owner of the house was transported. I don't know if it
was the same man who was called Bill, but suspect it was, and that
many a visitor had been bullied out of his money in that house.

One night about this time I saw a well-grown, stout woman who
looked four-and-twenty. "What a thigh she must have," thought I.
"Can I afford her?" and I felt in my pocket. Ten shillings with the
room besides was too much for me that night. I passed her again
looking her in the face, and longing for her, until she knew me and
smiled. She had a bright laughing eye. Summoning courage I gave
her a signal, and she followed me up a by-street.

"I have only five shillings." "Lord! you do want it cheap, —
make it ten shillings." "I can't." "Well I can't." "Three half-crowns,
and then with the room I shan't have a shilling in my pocket." I used
to speak in that frank way to them. She laughed. "You are an odd
sort of chap, — well come along, — what house are you going to
take me to?" "Where you like, — I don't know them." "Oh! yes you
do," said she, "you know well enough with that eye of yours." We
turned into a house which we both knew, not one of the most
expensive.

I was exceedingly pleased with her manner, and in the house
still more pleased with her face. Her eye was one of the merriest,
she was bright, and fresh-colored, yet the general color of her flesh
was slightly brown. Her plumpness made me so randy I could
scarcely wait to feel or look at her, I wanted to push on to the
fullest pleasures at once.

She eyed me pleasantly, and made some remark about the small-
ness of the sum, which made me uncomfortable. She saw it, and
laughing, showed a set of beautiful small white teeth. I gave her
her money at once, and then began preliminaries. The room I
recollect well. There was a large four-poster bed, a large wire screen
three feet high all round the fire-place, like those in nurseries. The
house-woman flattened the fire down, and took away the poker, —
to prevent the fire being stirred I suppose. (There was but one
candle, and the room was dark, there was scarcely gas in any of
the houses in those days.)

I drew her to me, my hand roved about her bum, belly, and

notch, I asked her to undress, desire increased by the feel of her thighs made me inquisitive. She would not undress, was in a hurry, some other night perhaps, not now. Impatient so that I might begin, I placed her on the edge of the bed, putting a chair for one of her feet. She lifted up her clothes freely, and I saw her cunt.

It was surrounded, though not in great quantity, with fine chestnut brown, soft, thick hair, her thighs were large, round, fat, and firm, the split looked small, was small outside, and I found it to be small inside as well. A large bum squeezed together by the position in which she was lying closed up almost the cuntal opening, so that just where the prick must intrude itself the hole could scarcely be seen, her flesh had the slightly brown tint of her face. How is it that at a glance all this was seen, and remembered ever since? What fascination a cunt has! Strange that a mere gap close to an arse-hole should have such power.

In admiration of her cunt and its surroundings I held a candle for a moment between her thighs. "Hold your quim open, — do, — do." Her hand came down, the fore and middle-finger went on either side of the split, and distended the lips, showed the red lining, a clitoris, small, and nice-looking, and small nymphæ sloping down to the narrow carmine darkness, closing up gradually and tightly between her bum-cheeks, squeezed up and closed by the weight of her body pressing up her bum on the bed.

"I can bear being looked at," said she. "Then open your legs wider, — wider dear." Wider they went. Candle in one hand I pushed the finger of the other up her cunt. Then all delight of the eye was merged in the maddening desire to fuck. Putting the candle somewhere, it fell down and was extinguished; at the same moment slipping my prick to the opening, with a smooth glide up it went. Before I had moved my prick half a minute I was spending, before I had had a wriggle in her, before I had well clasped her buttocks, I was leaning over her sighing, and had finished before I had well begun. I now think I feel my sensation up her as I write this, of the rapturous smoothing of her buttocks as I finished. Some women make me recollect them thus.

"What a bore," said I, squeezing my belly close up to hers, "I hate to be quick." I heard her laugh, but could not see her face. She did not hurry me out of her, but at length nature caused me to withdraw, and we got the candle lighted.

Washing herself whilst I stood talking and regretting my haste, holding my unwashed prick in front of her, she laughing and saying I must take my time another day, emptied the basin, and turning round asked if she should wash me. Years had elapsed I think since a woman had done so to me, then it was by a French woman. The offer comes to me now as having been an unusual one. Delighted I let her. Delicately handling my doodle she soaped and washed it, making complimentary remarks about it as she did so.

The operation excited me, I stiffened. "Oh! I do so want you again, — let me." "No it's late, — if I don't make money before twelve, I never do afterwards, — see me another night, — besides you can't do it again yet." "Let me feel you then only for a minute." She approached me, one hand I put to her cunt, the other thrusting between her fat bum-cheeks met the tip of the fingers on the other hand. "My prick's standing so." "It's not." "Feel it." She put her hand down and felt, I stiff to the utmost kept asking her to let me again. "Well get on the bed then," said she after feeling me quietly for a minute. — "See the candle has burnt down, it won't last long." By the time she had said this she was lying down with her clothes up above her navel.

We were fucking with intensity, the candle went out, I felt her kisses. "Oh! what a lovely cunt you have." "You've a nice prick, — who taught you to poke so nicely?" Our tongues met, — silence, sighs, short shoves, spunk, — and all was over. "Let me wash your cunt." "Very well." "You wash my prick." "Yes." The mutual washing over we separated, I promising to see her again. We had washed by fire-light alone.

Next night at the same time we fucked again. I stripped her, and was enamoured of her body if not of herself. She made no sign of wanting to leave me, but rather wanted to keep me. I had not since I lost Mary tasted a woman's mouth, with this woman I was delighted in doing so, though with the ordinary gay women I could not bear their tongues. Whilst we were fucking they knocked at the door saying they wanted the room. Bessie swore. "Damn her," said she, "for interrupting us, — and the money I have brought her." This increased my pleasure, and Bessie participated in it. After fucking her twice we sat by the fire and talked, she warming her bum, her petticoats up to her knees, my hand on her quim, and airing my balls. "If you want me another night, and can't see me, ask the women about, — ask for Brighton Bessie, — there are two Bessies, so mind, — Brighton Bessie," said she as we parted.

I found I could talk to this woman. Whilst doing so she would sit on my knees and feel my prick, and I feel her privates. I had long wanted such a free-and-easy acquaintance, for nothing annoyed me like the sham modesty of doxies, their shuffling out of showing me their cunts, their hurry to get me up them, and away afterwards. Bessie had none of this. Like Camille, Mary, and all women I ever kept to long, she let me do absolutely as I pleased, and without hurry would copulate, then sit and talk till we were ready again for the exercise. But they did not at the house in ****. Street fancy our staying so long at their busy time; so she arranged to meet me at B*w Street one night, and took me to a house there which was dearer, but where she said they rarely interrupted couples.

It was nearly opposite to the Opera House since built. It had a very large frontage, six or seven windows of a row I think, a dingy-looking building that most people would have passed without noticing, or would have thought it a dwelling-house for poorish people. The knowing ones would have guessed that it meant something hidden and convenient. There was no light outside, but if you pushed the door by night or by day, it opened into a darkish lobby, then passing through a glass door with a glimmer of light at the back, a woman met you, and conducted you to a chamber, big or small, handsomely or poorly furnished according to price. In it there must have been twenty rooms, and there was more bum-wagging, more seed spent, more sighs of pleasure in that house nightly, than in any other house in London, I should think.

It was dearer; but if you stayed for hours no one ever interrupted you. There were in winter good large fires, the rooms were a good size, there was no gas, two candles were given, if you wanted more you paid extra. Wine and liquor of fair quality was got for you. The furniture was somewhat dingy, but all the rooms had sofas on which two could lie, and beds large enough for three with clean linen always. It was one of the most quiet, comfortable accommodation-shops I ever was in, and with Brighton Bessie, I passed there many voluptuous evenings.

I took a bottle of champagne with me there one night, the first time I ever did so to a baudy house when I met a gay woman; but

I wanted that night a long, quiet evening with a free woman, and had one with her quite after my own fashion.

I had Bessie often for about two years, and at intervals for two or three years after that, the last was about ten years after I had first met her. I never had a passion for her, nor did I keep only to her; but through the winter of this year, as nearly as I can recollect, I had few but her. After the next hot weather my lust ran riot, I got also better off, and treated my pego to variety, but we then frequently met at B*w Street. Poor Bessie fell in love with me, and was fond of liquor as I shall tell, but now will only tell of the way our evenings and at times afternoons, were passed together.

If warm enough we used to strip, and lay outside the bed; if not, got into bed. As she was beautifully shaped I first took my delight in contemplating her, then I laid along the bed, my head near her knees, she the reverse way, and again I inspected. Sometimes she twiddled my cock, and I her clitoris, but generally the time was spent in putting her in every voluptuous posture, and fucking in all sorts of positions. She liked it. "It's all my eye," she used to remark when we talked on the subject, saying, "I don't like it, — I like fucking and baudiness, it's the best thing in life, — a short life and lots of fucking is my motto, — women who say they never spend with men are liars, — they all like it as much as I do." She was but twenty-one years old, although her stoutness made her look older. And now I leave her for a time.

CHAPTER III

A change in taste. — A small cunt longed for. — Hunting in the Strand. — Yellow-haired Kitty. — Her little companion. — Oh! you foole. — The house in E**t*r Street. — Double fees. — Kitty's pleasure. — Objections to washing. — Have the other gal. — Cleanliness. — Home occupations. — I ain't gay. — Kitty's males.

I don't know why my erotic fancies took the desire for a young lass, but they did. My taste had for the most part run upon the big, fleshy, fat-cunted, and large-arsed; now, perhaps for contrast, perhaps from sheer curiosity, the letch took possession of me. A small cunt, tight and hairless perhaps, — I wondered how it looked and felt, and if pleasure would be increased by it, and though my prick swelled when spending until I have groaned under the grip, even of a large cunt, I longed for quite a little one. I had never had a very young girl, — excepting the little child. — Nelly and Sophy had both a little hair on their mottes, so I would try for a youthful quim, and one if possible with no hair on it.

I was not versed in the walks and ways of little ones, and looking about at night saw none. Talking about it at my Club, I heard they were to be seen mostly in the day-time, so I looked out in the Strand for what I wanted, and during day-light.

On a blazing hot afternoon in June I walked about a long time thinking of youthful harlots, but saw none, or if I did could not distinguish them. At length I saw two young girls idling about, looking in at the shop windows on the other side of the way. One was dressed all in black, and was taller and stouter than the other. They were not got up in any showy way, but looked like the children of decent mechanics.

They took no notice of any one, nor any one of them, they

stopped at a shop, and I noticed that the biggest one had the largest legs. A plump form had, as said, attractions to me almost superior to face. Crossing to the other side of the way, I passed them, looking them full in the face. The taller one was good-looking, white-faced, and had goldenish hair, a colour I could not bear. They looked at me, but there was nothing to indicate fastness. Returning I met them again, the same stare, the same indifference. Thinking of their little cunts, and getting randy and reckless, I determined to try. They stopped at a sweetmeat-shop; going to the side of them, and looking into the shop, not at them, so as to prevent my being noticed, "I'll buy you whatever you want if you will come with me," I said. The bigger of the two edged away from me after looking up in my face, whispered something to her companion, and they both moved along the street without noticing me further.

I was disconcerted, and went over to the opposite side of the way, again watching them. They went to a print-shop, and looked in; the big one looked in the direction of a lolly-pop shop, and up and down the street. She was looking after me evidently, so I crossed over, met them full-face, and as I passed said without stopping, "Come with me, and I'll give you money."

I turned a corner, and looked, they were at another shop, the bigger girl with her arm round the smaller one's neck. I again passed them, going back to do so, and saying, "I'll give you three and sixpence." That was the exact sum, and then turned up a street which led to baudy houses, and waited at the turning into the street.

The two girls turned the corner, stopped, and talked, the bigger laid hold of, and slightly pulled the smaller, and seemed to be persuading her. Failing apparently, she left her but turned back, spoke to her again, and both came on together. Then I turned into the back-street, the two girls appeared at the corner of that, and then stopped and talked for a minute. Tired of waiting I thought I had made a mistake, and going slowly back heard the bigger one say, "You *are a foole*. Oh! you *foole*. Come he wants us. You *foole*."

"I don't want her," said I, "but you. — Come," — and returning entered a baudy house, the outer-door of which stood open, thinking the bigger one would follow, and sure now that she was a harlot. I then passed through the inner door which as usual then had a glass window covered with a red curtain.

A minute elapsed, the baudy house-keeper had been spoken to, but the girl not coming, I opened the door to look out. The bigger girl was just inside the outer door, and was pulling in the other one. "Come you foole, — you said you would, — he'll give you money as well as me, and I'll give you some of mine too, — well, you are a foole," quite bawling it out. There was not much secrecy needed in such things at those times, in those streets.

"I don't want *her*," said I hurriedly, "it's you, — come in, or I won't wait." She came in, the other girl disappeared, and we were soon in a bed-room together.

It was the first house at that end of the street, had been newly opened, and was furnished in a style not like a baudy house; no show, neat and clean, but cheaply; no bed-hangings (and in those days most baudy houses had bed-hangings), the blinds were new and white, the beds quite clean. The top-floor room where I went for economy was two shillings and sixpence. The woman of the house was tall, comely, and middle-aged. As I paid her I noticed she had fat red cheeks. How curious that I should recollect those red cheeks. She had a white apron on, and was a civil sort of creature.

The girl stood still staring at me. Sitting on the edge of the bed I stared at her, filled with baudy curiosity and the appreciation of novelty. "Why won't you have the other gal?" said she. "I don't want her, nor want two, — and she is a dirty little imp." "No she ain't dirty, she washes herself like me, — let her come up." "No, — you come here." "She is quite clean, — I wash her myself sometimes." "No, — come here, I tell you."

The girl came to me dawdling. I put my hands up her clothes. A fleshy little bum met my hand, then in the front a smooth belly, a motte almost hairless as it seemed. She said not a word, but gave a sort of jerk of her body, and as my hand touched her bum it jutted forwards, and as I drew my hand round to her belly she drew her belly back. It did not seem like shame. She did not utter a word. "Take off your things," said I.

She drew away from me, and took off her bonnet, then stood still. "Off with your things," I said, throwing off some of mine. "I can't take them off, — if I do I can't fasten them again, they are in a knot." "Take them off." "If I do you will have to fasten me." "So I will." Slowly she stripped to her chemise. "Take that off."

"I won't." "Come here then." She came. Laying hold of her I lifted her bodily and threw her with her back on the bed, throwing up her chemise and stretching open her legs quickly. She gave a suppressed "Hoh!" put her hand down to her cunt, and felt her mons nervously.

"Take away your hand, dear." She took it away, then I pulled open her little thing. Such a delicious little gap it was, with the smallest possible quantity of golden hair just showing on it; such a smooth white belly and thighs, and all so plump, that I was wonder-struck at a young girl being so round and fine. I had not expected under that shabby black clothing anything so nice. I was charmed with her head also; in a big black and shabby bonnet I had seen nothing but a white face and large blue eyes. Her hair was golden in tone, bright and flowing.

Whilst pulling off my trowsers, she sat up and asked, "Is it big?" For the instant I did not quite know what she meant. "What's big?" "Your thing, — measure it." I went up to her, pulling out my pego. "It is big," said she. "It's little," said I. "It ain't, — it's big." "No." "Yes, — don't push hard sir, — will you now?" "No my dear I won't. — Is it bigger than other men's pricks?" "I shan't tell yer." "Well lay down and open your thighs," — again I lifted her on to the bed. "Don't you do it hard," said she getting up again, "or I won't let you." "Then I won't pay you." Back she fell, I wetted my prick, put it to the notch, and with a shove or two was well up her. She gave a "Oh! — oooh!" and then laid quiet. Grasping her fat little bum I fucked, then stopping, pulled out my prick, and looked at her cunt. "What are you a goin' to do?" said she in an astonished way.

"Get quite on to the bed dear." Slow at obeying I helped her into the posture, and got on to her, and brought my pleasure to an end, lying on the top of the pretty little girl.

I lay on her long afterwards, and tried by the muscular contraction of my arse-cheeks and ballock-roots to stiffen my pego again. She laid quiet all the time with my prick up her, but I could not manage it, my prick shrunk.

A second erection without uncunting being impossible, I got into a kneeling posture between her open legs, and checked a slight movement on her part saying, "Now lie quiet, — don't move." There was I kneeling between her thighs; looking down I saw her half-opened cunt with the gruelly tide issuing from it, took my prick in hand, half its potential size, flabby and wet, pulled back the skin, and out rolled a large drop of sperm on to her thigh. She lay quite quiet, looking at me, her yellow hair falling all around her head as it lay on the pillow. Now I was astonished at her beauty, I had not noticed it fully before.

"You are very handsome, — how old are you?" "Fifteen and a little." "You must be more." "I don't know, but mother says so." I looked at her cunt, the hair on it was not an eighth of an inch long, scarcely any of it, and of course showing no intention of curling, but her form was so round that I could not believe she was so young. "Fifteen and a little," she repeated, her aunt and her mother had been disputing the day of her birth; her mother was out of her mind when she gave birth to her. "Aunt says I ain't fifteen."

"Give the other gal a shilling, — do," she broke in whilst I was questioning her about age, and kneeling between her thighs. "What are you so anxious about the other girl for?" "She lives over us, and is my friend, — will you give her a shilling? — do." "Why?" "Do, — if you don't I shall give her a shilling of mine, and give her some of mine anyhow, — you said you'd gi'me three and sixpence, didn't you?"

Curiously amused I laughed. "I'll give you a shilling for her, if you let me do it to you again." "Oh! *do*," said she.

It was hot, I had not reposed after my pleasure, so quitting my kneeling position I laid down beside her, and began feeling her breasts. She turned her head towards me. "You have not washed yourself," said I after a minute's amusement with her bubbies. "It ain't no good if yer ar going to make a mess in it agin, — when you've done it I'll wash it all out together." I thought from that speech she was not an old one at the game, yet after all she only behaved as every young girl I have had usually behaved, they have mostly objected to washing their cunts directly after a poke, I think they rarely wash it until requested. There must be some sweet tranquillizing pleasure which a man's sperm gives to a woman's cunt, and makes her undesirous of washing it out. It is only when a woman knows it is good for her health if she be gay, that she ever does it. No married woman washes the sperm out of her cunt, yet

in the morning after a night's fucking you never find the sperm
if you feel in the cunt for it, — where does it go? — it is absorbed,
I suppose.

We lay thus and talked. "How old are you really?" "Fifteen
and two months, as I told yer, — I always was fat, but ain't so fat
as I was though. — Father used to say I should get fat on gruel."
I should have guessed her full sixteen had it not been for the little
hair there was on her motte, and the delicate pink small cut, and
tight prick-hole. "How long have you been gay?" "I ain't gay,"
said she astonished. "Yes you are." "No I ain't." "You let men fuck
you, don't you?" "Yes, but I ain't gay." "What do you call gay?"
"Why the gals who come out regular of a night dressed up, and gets
their livings by it." I was amused.

"Don't you?" "No, mother keeps me." "What is your father?"
"Got none, he's dead three months back. — Mother works, and
keeps us. — She is a charwoman, and goes out on odd jobs." "Don't
you work?" "Not now," said she in a confused way. "Mother does
not want me to, I takes care of the others." "What others?" "The
young ones." "How many?" "Two, — one's a boy, and one's a gal."
"How old?" "Sister's about six, and brother's nearly eight, — but
what do you ask me all this for?" "Only for amusement. — Then you
are in mourning for your father?" "Yes, it's shabby, ain't it? — I
wish I could have nice clothes, I've got nice boots, — ain't they?" —
cocking up one leg, "a lady gived 'em me when father died, — they
are my best."

"Are you often in the Strand?" "When I gets out I likes walking in it, and looking at the shops, — I do if Mother's out for the
day." "Does she know you are out?" The girl, who had been lying
on her back with her head full towards me, turned on her side, and
giggling said in a sort of confidential way, "Bless you no, — she'd
beat me if she knew, — when she be out I locks them up, and takes
the key, and then I goes back to them,   I've got the key in my
pocket, and shall be home before Mother, — she is out for the
whole day."

"Do the children know you're out?" "No, I says to them, 'You
be quiet now, I'm going to the yard.'" "What's the yard?" said I
not reflecting. The girl thought a minute, chuckled, turned her head,
and was silent, she was actually blushing. "What's the yard?" Sud-

denly it struck me, "Going to the privy?" She burst out laughing. "Yes that's it, I say I'm going to the privy, and then I comes out with her, and they can't get out, so they are all right, and we go back together if she's with me; if she ain't I go back by myself, — there," — and she stopped satisfied with her explanation. "They may set fire to themselves," said I. "There ain't no fire after we have had breakfast, I puts it out, and lights it at night if Mother wants hot water."

"What do you do with yourself all day?" "I washes both of them, I gives them food if we've got any, then washes the floor and everything, and then washes myself, then I looks out of the winder." "Wash yourself?" "Yes, I washes from head to foot allus." "Have you a tub?" "No we've only got a pail and a bowl, but I'm beautiful clean, — Mother tells every one I'm the beautifullest clean gal a mother ever had. — I wash everything, Mother's too tired. Sometimes we all go out and walk, but that's at night; sometime I lays abed nearly all day."

She was beautifully clean in her flesh, her linen was clean, its color awful; but what could be expected from a pail, a bowl, and one room to dry things in. "You can't always be washing." "No, I do all the mending and making, — look how my finger is pricked," said she showing it.

I had been smoothing and feeling her all over, her unwashed cunt had come in for its share of my attentions, I had been twiddling it till outside it was dry. Recurring to the never-failing and always charming theme, I got close to her, kissed her, my fingers sought the innermost recesses of her tight little orifice. "Don't you like fucking? — does it give you pleasure?" "It never gived me much pleasure that I know on," she replied. "But you don't dislike it?" "Not if they don't hurt me." "Do they ever?" "One or two have, if they pushes hard, — but I shan't say no more, — there."

There was a frankness, openness, and freshness about this girl which delighted me. Question after question I put, and would be answered; if evaded I put it in another shape, but she seemed willing mostly to reply. I put into her little head things she had never dreamed of, and all the time kept rubbing her clitoris, probing her little quim, distending it, tickling it, and exciting her till she wriggled her little fat bum.

"Do I hurt you?" "Oh! no." — "Let me then." — "Oh! don't sir, — I wish you would not." "Did you never enjoy the prick up you? — never enjoy a fuck! — you shall enjoy it with me." "Don't now," said she, turning herself round as I frigged on. "Feel my prick dear." She did not need a second invitation. "Is it not stiff?" "Yes, and big." "Yes, — yes, — but oh! don't sir, — take away your hand, — ah!" I talked on, frigging and tickling, my prick throbbing, but restraining myself, for instinct told me she was about to enjoy a pleasure she had never enjoyed yet. All at once she relinquished my prick, a slight heaving of her belly, and her eyes closed, then I knew she was ready to discharge.

I ceased my frig, her eyes opened, her thighs which had closed opened again. I joined my body to hers, and we were one. I fucked, — we fucked now, for the little lass in a minute or two was dissolving in pleasure whilst I was pissing my sperm up her, groaning as the tightness of her little cunt squeezed my sensitive prick. If Kitty was not a harlot before, she was from that minute she had her spend with me.

She laid quite quiet till nature dissolved our fleshy union by uncunting me, then I laid by her side, she on her back, her thighs wide open, her eyes closed.

"Don't it give you pleasure?" After repeating that half-a-dozen times, she said, "I don't know." "Yes you do, — did you spend?" "I don't know what a girl's spending is," said she. "Did my prick give you pleasure, — tell me Kitty?" At length she said yes, and she had never had pleasure with men before. (Two years afterwards she repeated that the first pleasure she ever had with a man was with me.) "Wash yourself." "I'll wash when I go home." "Wash now you little beast." "What does it matter to you?" "Wash you little devil." She washed carefully, and whilst doing so, "Piddle," said I. "I can't abear to piddle before a man, — what a funny man you are." "Piddle my dear," and the little dear piddled.

Wiping herself dry she stopped in the middle of the operation and asked, "Why wouldn't you have the other gal?" "What do you want me to have her for?" "She's very poor." "What do you do with your money?" "Buy things to eat, — Mother's very poor, we often ain't got enough to eat." "Then you get a little money by being gay." "I ain't gay I tell you." "Well your friend is I suppose, and gets money." "No she doesn't, — she isn't gay either, — no man ain't

ever done it to her, she's such a *foole*, — but she would a come in
to-day with you, she said she would, and she were just a comin'
when you sent her off, — she promised me she'd a let yer if you
wanted, — but she is a foole though."

"I don't believe that." "It's God's truth though, she ain't, she
says she ain't; she knows what men want gals for, but she's never
let any one, — I know she ain't, she is frightened." "Have you looked
at her cunt?" "Often," said Kitty. "And she's looked at yours?" "Of
course she has, — she lives over us I tell you, I go up to her, and
she comes down to me when Mother's out, — I wash her." "You
seem fond of washing." "I likes things clean." I thought for an
instant, "It may be true, — I should like to see her cunt if she's
never been poked, — what object has this little lass in pressing this
so?" Then said I, "Tell me the truth, and I'll give you another
shilling, — don't lie, — I shall soon tell whether you're lying or not."
And getting up, "Here is three and six (I had it on the mantel-
piece), here's a shilling for her, and there is another. If you answer
truly, I'll see you again; but I'll never see you again if I find you are
making up lies, — come here." And I sat down.

She came forward, I pulled her between my naked legs, her
naked thighs met mine, her little cunt was close on my prick, I
put my hand round her fat little bum, and looked her in the face,
pressing her belly close to mine.

"What do you want me to have her for?" "Only cos she's so
poor, — why she only gets sixpence a day, — she works at sack-
making, — oh! isn't it hard! — and her hands if you seed 'em, are
hard and brown, stained with the string, and what they works with,
— Mother wants me to work at them at home, but I won't. — I
tells her I'd run away first. — She is so little she can't carry the
sacks home as other gals do; so a strong young woman who works
at sacks carries them home for her, and charges her twopence for
it, — they carries them home on the top of their heads; but she
is too little, she is." [At that time women worked at sack-making,
and carried them home on their heads.]

"Can she put her finger up her cunt?" "I shan't tell you all
that," said she, turning nasty. "Is her cunt as open as yours?" "No
it ain't." "Then she can't get her finger up." "Oh! you are a rum
cove, you are," said she, breaking away from me, "I never seed
the like of you. I must go, — tell me what time it is." "Half-past

four." "I'll go, — I give the children something to eat about this
time." "Come here, or I won't give you the shilling." We resumed
our position. "Are you sure she has never had a man?" "Never, she's
such a *foole*, — she says she'd like to, and she'd like the money,
and yet she won't, — she is *such* a *foole*." "How long have *you* done
it?" "Only since we have lived this side of the water, after father
died." "How many men have you had?" "I shan't say, — I don't
recollect, — it ar'n't no business of yourn." — "You don't like me."
"Yes I like you, but I won't tell, — no it isn't a dozen, — I shan't say
who first did it, — I shan't then, — it isn't a dozen, — yes I am
quite sure, I don't think it's ten, but it may be about that, I think
it's eight, — they didn't all do it to me, no they didn't, — one of
em only put his hands up my clothes, and went off in a minute;
another pulled up my clothes, and looked at me, and then he
— ." She stopped, and I could not get her to say what, so promised
her another shilling. "I don't know what he did." "Frig himself?"
"I don't know what you call it, — yes he did that," said the girl,
bursting into a roar of laughter when I showed her the operation.
"I looked at him, and he went away without speaking, — he only
gave me half-a-crown; but an old gentleman one day gave me a
gold bit of ten shillings." She began counting on her fingers. I
thought she was reckoning her gains, she was a long time at it,
doing it over and over again; at length, "It's seven," said she.
"What?" "Gentlemen, — you make eight."

"Your little friend is too young," said I. "She is fourteen, but
shorter than me." "Has she any hair on her cunt?" "You can just
see some coming, and it's black." "She is dirty." "No she ain't, but
she was till she knew me, — she can't help her clothes being dirty,
but she mends 'em, — how I wish I had nice clothes like the gals
about at night, and like gentlefolks!" said Kitty, in a sort of ecstasy,
and then tossed up half-a-crown, and caught it.

I began to long for the other girl, and told her she might
bring her the next day, that she should have three and sixpence,
and her friend the same, and more if I did it. Kitty went off agreeing to meet me with her if their mothers were out, but if not, the
day after, all depended on their mothers' absence. She would listen
to the church-clock, and as it struck three she would leave; it
was only by listening that she knew the time. She would put by
a penny for the bridge-toll; generally she went round by West-

minster Bridge to avoid paying the penny. Then we left. Her little friend I found was loitering close by. They went into a pastrycook's, and I watched them both eating together as they went along towards Waterloo Bridge, Kitty and Pol.

CHAPTER IV

Little Pol consents. — Arsy-versy. — Broached, and howling. —
Kitty's vocalization. — A cheap virginity. — Two hours after. —
Love's money lost. — The street-gully. — Kitty pleases. — Pol tires.
— Kitty's habits. — Friendliness and frankness. — Sausage rolls. —
Confessions of lust.

On the appointed day I saw Kitty, but alone. She followed me
to the house, and soon by my pego her sweet little cunt was distended. I had her all the afternoon, and tailed her to the extent
of my powers. The girl was delighted, her eyes sparkled with
lewdness. Was fucking nice? "Oh! yes, yes," she replied, it was
nicer than she thought, nicer than gals told her it would be. This
was after I had called her at our meeting a little humbug for not
bringing her friend. The excuse was that Pol's mother was at home.
I did not believe it, but was so content with her sweet little form,
the ease with which I handled her, the enticing look of the cunt,
its tightness, and her pleasant, frank manners, that I forgot all about
the other little one, till going away, then said, "Mind you bring
your friend, and I'll give you five shillings, but you know you won't,
you little storyteller." "I will, — I shall, — I'll make her come, —
she wants, but she is such a *foole*, — and she's frightened of her
mother."

Another blazing hot day. The two were looking in at the
pastry-cook's, the taller with her arm round the neck of the other.
I watched them for a minute, Kit often looked round anxiously, and
seeing me moved off quickly towards the street. I followed on the
opposite side of the way, then stopped. The small one stood with
her back against a wall, Kitty was gesticulating. I went on passing
without noticing them. As I passed I heard, "You are a *foole*, —

you're a *liar*, — you said you would." "I shan't then." Turning the corner I looked back. There they still were standing as on the first day I saw them. Thought I, "She can't persuade the little one," so walked on to W**l*****n Street, to the Lyceum portico, and back again in a fever of expectancy. As I got near the house they both turned the corner, so in I went, and waited till both girls appeared, and soon heard two pairs of feet after me on the same staircase, two young voices whispering, the Mistress following us all.

"Why five shillings?" "You have *two* young ladies to-day, double price you know sir." I did *not* know, for it was the first time I had had two women together in a house. Excited and anxious I had got to fucking-heat in anticipation of a small unprobed cunt, paid the money, and there was I with the two little ones face to face, two young cunts at my disposal, a novelty, and a charming one. The woman closed the door, casting a queer look at the girls and me. I locked it.

I put my hand up Kitty's clothes. The other girl, an ugly little imp in a bonnet as big as a coal-scuttle, and with boots which looked as if they were her mother's, stood and stared with eyes wide open, — they were dark, and her hair nearly black. "Come here my dear." "Come to him," said Kitty. The girl drew near, I took her on my knee. "So you are the friend of Kitty's, and we are going to play with each other naked, aren't we? — I'm going to look at your cunt, and you are going to feel my cock." She made no reply. "I'm going to look where your piddle comes out, ar'n't I?" "*No*," said the girl sullenly, after reflecting a minute, and hanging her head on one side, "I shan't."

"Yes he is, you foole, — oh! you *are* a foole," burst out Kitty. "I wish I didn't know you, you are *such* a foole. — She said she would sir, she knows all about it, she does, she knows what she has comed for, she does, — now don't be a foole (in a threatening manner), I won't speak to you agin, nor gi yer nothink (Kitty's English was awful), — you may get yer belly filled, I won't help fill it." All this over and over again, in anger.

The girl looked at Kitty humbly. "Well I will then." I put my hands up her petticoats on to a lean pair of thighs. "Take off your things." "Yes *take* them off," said Kitty helping her off with her bonnet, and to undress. "Are you going to take off yours Kitty?" said she. "Yes, when you have," and without more ado she stripped the girl to her chemise, and herself likewise. I took off all but my shirt and socks. It was a sweating hot day.

The girl was not very inviting, was heavy and lubberly, and looked as if she had not enough to eat; but there was in her a virgin cunt, so I was told, although even then a little sceptical about what a female told me on that point. My tooleywag was standing at the idea, I shook it before them, and calling both to me held them round their naked bums, and made them feel me. The pair of little fists anxiously feeling from the root of my balls to the tip of the piercer soon rendered me impatient for action. I was near the side of the bed facing the windows, and through the white blinds came the strong light of a summer's afternoon. Lifting the fresh one from my knee, I put her on her back on the bed, and lifted her scanty chemise. Close went her legs together, I opened them, she resisted, I grew angry, Kitty called her a foole. Coaxed and bullied at the same time she yielded, I pulled the legs wide open, and kneeling threw one over my shoulder, the other I pressed outwards, and with my other hand opened her cunt-lips wide; then she kicked her legs over me, and turning arse upwards, got up. A little row, again she yielded, again served me the same trick. I damned her for a bitch, and Kitty reviled her. "She is a fool, Kitty, — show her what I want." Kitty hesitated a moment, then throwing herself on to the bed opened her thighs, and pulled her cunt-lips apart. The young one, gradually persuaded, let me do for her what Kitty did for herself, after she had carefully studied Kitty's quim for a minute.

I saw with speechless excitement the girl's cunt, which seemed at first glance as if a prick had entered it; but looking more closely saw that the perforation was too small. I thrust gently my finger up it, — a cry, — a howl. "Don't, — you're a hurting," and again the little devil was arse upwards on the bed. Again I coaxed, promised, lied, and Kitty bullied; again I saw the cunt, that it was not like cunts that had been fucked: the hairless lips, a little black tint just above the notch, a little hole. My eyesight failed me, the demon of desire said, "It's fresh, it's virgin, — bore it, — bung it, — plug it, — stretch it, — split it, — spunk in it," and I had laid hold of her thin backside mad with lust, kissing and sniffling at her cunt.

"Let's lay on the bed, and all strip quite naked, — it's so hot." "Yes do," said Kitty. She stripped the girl of her pea-soup coloured rag, and we both stripped. There we were in a minute all three naked, close together, with but little room, the girl in the middle. I pressed to her, put her hand round my prick, talked baudy. Kitty said, "Now let him." The girl said no. I put one leg over, and worked myself between her little thighs, partly holding myself up on my elbow and pattering baudy which Kitty kept repeating. "It won't hurt dear." "No it won't hurt," said Kitty. "Just let me touch it with my prick." "Yes let him touch it with his prick." Kitty in her anxiety slipped right off the bed, and getting herself up stood by the bedside repeating the baudy words I uttered.

The girl lay quiet, Kitty telling her not to be a foole; but I was a foole, for the notch being small I did not hit it well. Putting my prick down to where my fingers underlied the split, I pushed towards the goal, not pressing her with my body, but keeping my weight off by leaning on my right elbow, for it seemed that if I laid on her I should crush and frighten her, the girl seemed so slim. My tool struck hard at the orifice, she howled. Fearing to miss my game, I then fell with the full weight of my body on her, grasping her thin buttocks, and nearly stifling her on that hot afternoon, determined to have her if I killed her. The girl gave howl after howl, and I rammed with all my might the more. "Hish! — hold your tongue you foole," said Kitty, as the girl wriggled violently, and cried.

"Damn you, if you are not quiet I'll rip your dress into ribbons, and you may go home, and tell your mother what you like, — damn you I'll murder you, — I'll give you ten shillings." "You fool, he'll give you ten shillings." I heard no more, oscillating my arse, and driving with all my force between her legs, I knew not how, I knew not where. Still the girl howled, and Kitty kept hushing.

"The woman will turn us out of the house you foole, — she won't let me come in again, — oh! you foole," said Kitty. In my blind battering I at last lodged the tip well between the lips. The next instant with a cunt-splitting thrust I was up the howling little bitch who wriggled like an eel; but I held her skinny arse up to me like a vice, kept my peg fixed and unmovably up her in spite of her. Her wriggles alone would have kept it stiff enough, and fetched me. "Be quiet, — I am up you, — I can't h — hurt — you — now, — ah!" — and my spunk was up the virgin quim of the ugly little devil.

She laid quiet, but whining, "Oh! you said you would not hurt me, — ho! — hho!" she sobbed, then laid quite still with my prick up her, snottily whimpering, "O — oho!" — and all was tranquil, I nearly asleep.

"Is it in her?" said Kitty in a whisper. "Is it in yer Pol?" Having got no answer from me, "Oh! what a foole you are." "I've done it," said I. "Let her get up," said Kit. I don't recollect having been up such a tight cunt, not that it gave me pleasure, but the extreme tightness was such a novelty. "I will do it again." "Have you done it really?" said Kitty. "Put your hand and feel," said I, opening my legs a little to let Kitty feel under my testicles. "My prick's right up her cunt now, — feel."

"Have you done it really?" "Yes, — feel." "Ri — tol — lural — li — do!" said Kitty, setting off in a hoppy dance all round the room. I went on fucking, keeping the girl quiet. I could pull her little form up to me as tight as wax, and coaxing and promising all sorts of things, I fucked her again without uncunting.

"Have you really done it?" said Kitty again. "Yes twice, — put your hand up under my balls and feel." Kitty, thinking better of the suggestion this time did so, and satisfying herself that my prick was out of her touch, set off dancing again with a "ri — too — ralooral — ledo!" I got off the girl, the hair of my prick saturated with blood and spunk. "She is bleeding." The girl began snivelling worse than ever when she heard that, and began feeling her cunt.

"What are you crying for you foole? — did he hurt you much? — let's look at it," — and Kitty looked at the little quim bunged up with sperm mixed with blood. "Oh! ain't he done it! — ritollooralado, ritollooralado," and she capered again. "What are you dancing and singing for?" I asked. "She's had it done, — oh! look what a mess is on the bed, the woman will kick up a row."

"Get up and wash it you foole, and don't cry." "It hurts." "Wash it." "It will hurt." "No it won't you foole." Here Kitty put a basin on the floor, pushed the girl towards it, and made her wash. Then we got her on to the bed, and both of us took a long, long look at her split. It was bleeding freely, I saw the ragged edge my intrusion had made, and not feeling inclined for more fucking, gave the girl half-a-sovereign in gold, Kitty five shillings, and went off leaving them still naked, Kitty from time to time looking at her friend's wounded orifice, and saying it would soon be all right, that her thing had bled also. I had fear that I might be in trouble through my voluptuousness, although a girl of twelve years is competent to judge of her own fitness for fucking, and many not a month over that age are plugged daily in London.

I had to go to the Temple that afternoon, returning along the Strand an hour afterwards, not thinking of my afternoon's amusement, for I had had a disagreeable interview with solicitors, when just at the end of C**** Street was a slight crowd, in the middle of it the two girls, and the one I had fucked an hour before crying. Some man gave her money. "Oh! Lord," thought I, "here is a row about what I have been doing," so got into a cab, and drove off. When a mile away I began to reflect, and felt more comfortable, but still uneasy, and determined not to meet them the next day as I had promised. The day after I saw Kitty walking by herself, that funked me again, so I cut away without her seeing me. Thought I, "There will be a row about that ugly little lump having been pierced, I will go no more." But the letch was so strong that I could not resist, and on the third day driving past in a cab I saw the two girls as usual looking in at shops. Alighting I winked as I passed, heard one say, "Here he is," and three minutes afterwards we were all in the house again.

To strip the two and examine their cunts was an affair of five minutes, then laying the little one open-legged I looked at hers tranquilly, and saw how the slit was completed. The girl whose name I forget, but will call Pol, put her finger down, and indicated where she felt a difference had been made in the shape. I fucked the lass at the side of the bed, propping up her skinny rump with pillows, Kitty with her face about a foot off admiring the prick as it shoved in and of out the little red orifice. It was a novelty to her to see it done.

Kitty was an odd girl. "Don't hurt her now," she kept saying. The little one had objected to my probing her again with my prick, but saying I should otherwise not give her a farthing, she consented. My delight was increased by the power I found I had of making her howl whenever I shoved vigorously, and I nearly knocked my prick through into her womb I imagine. The more she howled the more I banged my prick up her, the more I enjoyed it.

When it was over I asked how she had spent her money. Out burst the little animal into tears. "She made me drop it, I didn't spend any of it sir, I lost it." "You dropped it yourself," said Kitty. "You lie." "I don't." "She does," — and so on, and I got at the facts when Kitty had vigorously slapped the face of her friend, and called her fifty times a foole.

Going into the Strand, the girl had the money in her hand, Kitty told her to put it into her pocket. She refused. Kitty said she would lose it, and just then she dropped it close by a sewer-grating, down which the half-sovereign went. The girl cried, the two quarrelled, and there was soon a crowd round them. Kitty said that the girl's mother had given her a half-sovereign to buy some bread with, and she had lost it. Some one gave the girl sixpence, the crowd dispersed, and Pol lost the fruits of her first fucking. Never was lost a virginity so poorly rewarded. I did not make up her loss, but gave her half-a-crown with which she was well contented. I certainly was in luck to get all this fun for such trifling sums, I being still in poorish circumstances. Five years before I would have given thirty pounds for the same, and had paid two hundred for Louise.

Giving Kitty three and six, and beginning to put on my drawers she said, "Oh! do it to me, you have done it to her." "Do you want it?" "Yes." "Feel my cock." Kitty grasped it eagerly, we got on to the bed, Pol watched now the graceful manipulation, insertion, and wriggles of pleasure of her friend, for Kitty was fast learning fucking, though quite innocent of the art of frigging. I never knew such a bungler as she was at her first attempt at that.

I grew tired of ugly little Pol when I had bored her a few times, and would not have her again. Kitty I continued to see, she was a most amusing girl. Too young on the town to have learnt the tricks and cunning of a harlot, naturally frank and truthful, with some liking for me (for she looked forward to our voluptuous dallyings), she gave me for a long time much amusement, and I heard the incidents of her short life. She would jabber like a magpie about them when she knew me well, which she soon did, and began to look to me regularly for her supply of money.

She used, directly she caught sight of me, to walk as fast as possible towards the house, and get in before me. She was in the room waiting and grinning when I got there. "Shall I take off my things?" "Yes." Off they went, and on to the bed the plump white-skinned little girl rolled whilst I undressed at leisure. "Open your legs, Kit, and let's see your cunt." How she clutched my prick the moment I was by the side of her. It really was very nice.

She said, "I buy things to eat, I can't eat what Mother gives us, she is poor, and works very hard, she'd give us more, but she can't; so I buys food, and gives the others what Mother gives me, they don't know better, — if Mother's there I eat some, sometimes we have only gruel and salt; if we have a fire we toast the bread, but I can't eat it if I am not dreadful hungry." "What do you like?" "Pies and sausage-rolls," said the girl, smacking her lips and laughing, "Oh! my eye, ain't they prime, — oh!" "That's what you went gay for?" "I'm not gay," said she sulkily. "Well, what you let men fuck you for? Sausage-rolls?" "Yes, meat-pies and pastry too."

"What did you let the first man do it to you for?" "I don't know, he came up to me and told me he'd give me some money, if I would go to a house with him, — he only wanted to talk with me, and I was then so hungry. He took me to No. 4, just opposite here, and did it to me." "What did he give you?" "Five shillings." "You had never had it before?" "Never." "I don't believe you." "I never had, I'm only fifteen and a little. — He met me in the Strand near where you did," she cried indignantly. "Did he hurt you?" "Yes, and made me bleed, — I was upset, and didn't think much about it till I got home and found my shemmy bloody. I washed it, and put it on again quite wet, so that Mother mightn't know."

As she talked she would feel my cock, every now and then raise her head to look at it, fall back again as if satisfied, and go on feeling it and talking.

She was intensely curious about my prick, would lay and examine it for half-an-hour at a time silently. One day after feeling it she asked if she might do what she liked with it. Certainly. She moved on to her knees (we were both start naked on the bed, and had fucked not long before), and began feeling it, skinning, then covering the tip, looking under the balls and smelling it. "How smooth and red it is," said she, — "Does that hurt?" and she rubbed her finger over the tip orifice. "A little, — wet your finger." She did. "Shall I wet it with my tongue?" "Do." She licked it, and bit by bit put it into her mouth, asking me occasionally if she hurt me. I laid amused with the sexual promptings of her nature. She took it out of her mouth, put it in again, then it got stiff, then she laughed. "Isn't it funny?" said she, "how smooth and red it is, — first it's flabby, then it's stiff," — and she relinquished it, laying down across me, and contemplating it quite silently.

"Did you do that to the other gentleman?" I asked. "Oh! no, never, — I didn't think about it, — only one on 'em stopped long," — and she told me about all of their doings. She could never make out but seven, though she always asserted there were eight who had had her before me.

I did not like either cock-sucking or cunt-licking at that epoch, and stopped Kitty who was bent on stiffening it with her mouth. She had no idea, however, of giving me a pleasure that way, it was simply curiosity and novelty. Often she did the same thing, indeed always had a quarter of an hour at it.

I saw her about twice a week, sometimes more, it was all she could manage "in dodging her mother." I gave her three and six-pence each time, which made her quite happy and contented, and it was a very economical pleasure to me. She learnt much from me, in six weeks blushed at nothing, and was impatient to be fucked. "Do that afterwards," she would say if I dallied long in the pre-liminaries. Then quietly, "Oh! ain't it pleasure!" she added in an art-less satisfied way.

Then somehow she persuaded her mother that she might go out if fine for a little time in the afternoon, and she was let out occasionally when the mother was at home, but which rarely was the case; and then I saw the pretty lass almost daily, but always in the afternoon; and her impatience to have the pleasure of fucking became almost comical.

CHAPTER V

Kitty's antecedents. — The fishmonger's. — Jim the shopman. — Betty the maid. — Females in bed. — Mutual curiosity. — Lechery and frigging. — Educated in coition. — Against the kitchen-wall. — Jim in bed. — Betty's cunt washed out. — A look in the basin. — Cousin Grace, and Cousin Bob. — Bob on the spree. — A scuffle. — Topsy-turvy. — Arsy-versy. — Bob's semen. — A masturbating duet. — Caught in the act. — Kicked out.

I questioned her many a time, and put together here consecutively what she did. She was as much pleased to gossip about it as I was.

She was the daughter of a carpenter, had been kept at home to help her mother till six months previously to my meeting her, when growing restive, and I dare say her animal vigor inciting her to go forth into the world, she went into a situation at a fishmonger's who wanted some girl to nurse a little child, his wife being ill.

I believed she had told me most things about herself from the time the doodle had first penetrated her: yet why had not such a big girl been put to earn her living? She said that her mother was always in the family way, or a child was ill, so she being the biggest helped at home.

But she had been in service, about all of which she told me one hot afternoon. Ice was then a luxury, they charged two pence extra for a bottle of gingerbeer iced. She was fond of gingerbeer, we had some iced with sherry, and lay on the bed drinking it as she told me her story bit by bit. This is an account of my doings, and not of tales told me by others, but I must tell *her* tale, for I believed every bit of it, and it is almost part of my own, and this is how it came out.

"If you never spent with a man till you did with me, you had frigged yourself." "I never did till the gal at the fishmonger's did it to me, — we slept together." "Then you had been in service?" "Only two months, I went to mind a little child."

The fishmonger was a little struggling tradesman, in a house with a shop on the ground-floor, and a little back-parlour, and kitchens, and a cellar below where they kept fish-baskets.

Over the shop were two rooms, one was the fishmonger's bed-room, and two bed-rooms above. The wife was confined to her bed, and her husband slept alone in the back-room which was usually the female servant's; so the servant was put into a bed on the top-floor. This maid cooked, cleaned, did everything, and had an eye as well to the shop if her Mistress was ill and when Master and his man were out; but she could not mind the child as well. The fishmonger asked the carpenter if he knew of a strong steady lass, the carpenter named his own girl, and Kitty went for grub, lodging, and one and six a week. She was to sleep with the maid on the top-floor over the rooms where Master and Mistress slept. The servant's name was Betty.

The fishmonger drank. A young man named Jim went with him to market, and sometimes without him if he had been very drunk over night. Jim opened the shop, harnessed the horse and cart, and every night when the Master went to bed, Jim went to the underground kitchen, opened a cupboard, pulled down something called a bed, and slept there.

Jim was up first, and to bed but last, could not go to bed till the maid-of-all-work was out of the kitchen. Jim pissed in the sink, and made his own bed every morning as soon as he got up, which was done by turning it up somehow into the cupboard, and then he called up his Master and the maid. The privy was in the yard.

Kitty took charge of the child, and the first night as she was going to bed and took her things off, Betty said, "Where is your night-gown?" "I ain't got none," said Kitty, "I sleep in my shemmy." Betty tossed up her head. Kitty cried. "Father's a poor man," said she, "but he's respectable, and though I sleeps in my shemmy I am very clean, I washes all over every day, — look at my legs and my neck, — but with my first week's wages I'll buy a night-gown."

"Never mind," said Betty, "you *are* clean, and you're fat, — your dad gives you lots of grub, — don't cry, I only said, 'where's your night-gown?' — Lord you are fat for your age! — how old did you say you were? — why what a big bum you've got for your age!"

Kitty had been staring at Betty, and the hair on the bottom of her belly. "She was so hairy," said Kitty to me, "I had never seen a woman naked before, and the hair on her belly made me look." "Say on her cunt, Kitty." "Well on her cunt, — such lots, and so black, — I had seen gals' things, my cousins used to show me theirs, and I showed them mine to see how our hair was coming; but I did not think a woman could grow such a lot there."

It was a cold night, the girl and the woman were in bed. "Come closer, we will be warmer." Kitty got closer, then Bet began feeling Kitty. How smooth, how soft she was, how plump, and not quite fifteen! — what a bum, — why her thighs were quite large. "Oh! don't mind, I want to warm my hand between your thighs, put your hand between mine, — there, — you've just a little hair coming on your thing, — feel mine, it's like the hair on your head, isn't it? — I am only twenty-five, — but when you are twenty you will have as much, Kitty. Your hand is cold, put it between my thighs, we will warm each other there. What a nice little thing your cunt is," said Betty, feeling the little one's.

So on the very first night they felt each other's flesh, Kitty wondering at the cunt and hair of the grown woman, Betty thinking perhaps of what I can only guess at. Kitty went to sleep with one hand between Betty's thighs, and awaking in the night felt Betty again, who was asleep and snoring. She was a stout, big-built, fat-arsed, black-bristle-cunted woman (that is from Kitty's description), but she must have been older than she said, for the hair was thick and black in her armpits, and she had slight hair on her lips besides.

Betty got more free next night. "You've a sweetheart, and you let him feel this little thing, — the men call it cunt." Kitty said she had not, and had not been felt. "I know better, you let him put his cock up it." Kitty did not. "What, never been fucked? — that is what men call it, — let me feel." "No." Betty felt Kitty's cunt, and hurt her. "Well, I don't believe you have, — you are a stupid, — it's half the pleasure of life, — feel my cunt, — give me your hand,

— there, your fingers are on it, — oh! it don't hurt, you may feel right up."

Kitty was overwhelmed and ashamed. "I did not like it, but yet I felt so curious that I let my fingers go where she placed them, and I felt all about her thing." "Cunt, Kitty." "Well, about her cunt."

So gradually at night the elder led on the younger, by talking, feeling, and telling the little one all she knew, explaining the pleasures of fucking, the male mysteries, and male tastes and habits, although she was what was called respectable, and worked hard for her living as maid-of-all-work.

Betty pushed matters further. "I don't quite believe you are a maid, — let me look, — would you not like to look at me? — show me yours, I'll show you mine." Curiosity to see the cunt of a full-grown woman took possession of Kit .

On Sundays Jim had a holiday, the shop was shut, Allwork cooked the dinner, then the fishmonger had grog, and went to lie down, Betty went up to clean herself, Kitty and the child went up with her, then Kitty showed her cunt, and Betty showed hers. "It was big, and such lots of hair, — I'd never seen one before," said Kitty. "She pulled it open wide, afterwards she pulled mine open, and we looked at each other over and over again. I'd seen my little sister's and cousin's, and two or three other gals' things, but they were all young; I'd never seen a big woman's."

Kitty, getting bolder, asked if she had ever let a man do it to her. Yes, she had been married, and knew all about it. "You never had a child?" "Never you little foole, there are lots of ways of stopping that, — oh! I love it, I wish I had a nice young man with a big prick here. — I wish you were a man." She took Kitty in her arms, and put her on the bed. "There, lay still on your back, open your legs, and I'll show you how a man gets on." Kitty did. Then she pulled Kitty on to her, and made her play the man. "There, move, — push your cunt up against mine, — up and down, — quick, — there, — that's how the man moves when he is fucking till he spends, — then Lord! ain't he quiet!"

Within a week the experienced woman talking to the girl about fucking had described its pleasures, explained its mysteries, acted the mode and manner of the doing, until Kitty felt wild to see, feel, and act it for herself.

"Don't you ever frig yourself?" said Bet. "No." "You know what it is?" "Yes." Betty told of the pleasure a finger could bring her, but Kitty was not forward in sensual wants, and she had not frigged herself or known sexual pleasure in her cunt up to that time, though she had fingered herself.

"I'll frig you," said she. Kitty objected, but the talk of prick, of the delight of the male and female in feeling and rubbing each other upset Kitty, who was growing older, and whose animalism was perhaps rampant that night. She felt a lovely sensation all over her as Bet rubbed her cunt, and she spent. Betty then took Kit's fingers, and rubbed her own cunt. "What, with *your* fingers?" Yes Kitty's fingers, and rubbed them on her clitoris, and frigged herself with them, Kit supposed.

That same night laying sleepless under the excitement of the novel pleasure while Allwork snored, Kitty frigged herself. The next night they frigged together. Betty said, "It's poor pleasure, — I likes a man, and you'll like a chap, — some one will fancy you soon, — you let him do it. When you have a great stiff cock up your cunt poking and poking, and poking away, — oh! it's delicious, and you won't like frigging after that."

One night the fishmonger was out, Kitty put the child to bed (he had the child to sleep in his bed usually). Bet and Kit were in the shop-parlour, and Jim in the shop. Betty went down to the kitchen, Jim soon afterwards told Kit to give an eye to the shop, and call him if wanted, and down he went. Kitty, who had been sharpened in three weeks, who had seen Jim kissing Betty, and giving her funny pokes when he thought no one was looking, went to the kitchen-stairs, and going down a few steps slowly and peeping, saw Betty with her back up against the wall, Jim close up to her and his hands round her, and his bum moving in a funny way. She knew they were fucking, and fearful of being detected came softly into the shop again; but she made a noise. Up came Betty, the Master came home, and told Betty to go to bed, and Jim to shut up. Soon after, Betty washed her cunt. That seems to have been an operation that Kitty never had seen her perform excepting on Sundays. Kitty then felt sure that she had caught Bet at the pleasant exercise, for she had heard how something thick and white came out of the man's cock, and how it was wise to wash the cunt out afterwards.

Betty seems to have been suspicious, for she began asking why she had come down the stairs. To call Jim, a customer having come — but he had gone away, she replied. Betty was too clever to take that in. Did she see her, she asked. Kitty had seen her and Jim standing close up in front of her, "and he was moving about, and I told her," said Kitty.

Kitty, on being pressed, said she thought they were doing what Betty had said men and women did. "Fucking me?" "Yes." He was doing nothing of the sort, that she would swear; but they did it sometimes, for he was going to marry her soon, and after making Kitty promise not to tell, they went to sleep. "If you tell," said the knowing older one, "you will lose your place."

Next night Betty said, "You be quiet, Jim is going to marry me soon, only he don't wish it known, he is coming up when Master's asleep, and going to lay down by the side of me, — you sham to be asleep." Kitty remarked, "He can't lay here all night." No, when he had had his pleasure he would go. Kitty had fear come over her, but promised, then fell asleep, but awakened, and gradually coming to her senses listened, and heard Jim say in a whisper, "She sleeps like a top." Then was a rustling and rumpling about, and Jim cried, "Oh! cunt." Betty said, "Hush!" They kissed, sighed, and Jim crept softly away, Betty got out and washed her cunt in the dark, and found Kit was awake.

This went on for several nights, Betty had oiled the lock and hinges of the door, and when she heard the Master go up to bed, would softly open the door, and leave it ajar. When Jim had emptied his ballocks, he would leave and close the door gently, Bet would light a candle, and wash her cunt. One night she said to Kitty, "Come and see the stuff that comes out of a man's cock." Kitty jumped out of bed, saw the seminal sediment that Betty had washed out of her, and stood looking at Jim's spendings at the bottom of the wash-hand basin. "Look how thick it is," said Bet. "We have no thick stuff, have we?" Then she felt it. "You are a beast," said Kit. "Wait till you have a sweetheart," said Bet.

"Why," said I to Kit, "I asked you before if you had seen any one frig, and you said only your cousin." "Yes," replied she, "my cousin Grace. You didn't ask me about any one else, but I did see a young man once do it to himself," added Kitty, "it was my cousin Bob."

I made her tell me all about that. She had cousins male and female, one named Grace, her friend, and a cousin Bob, who used to go and see them; he was a favourite of Kitty's mother, a lad of sixteen, a carpenter. Grace must have been about a year older than Kitty.

Kitty's parents lived in two rooms, and had the right to use a wash-house. I am sure from all she said they were steady working-people. The mother went out sometimes charring, leaving Kitty at home to mind the children. She was useful at home, mended and made their linen. Grace often used to help her at needle-work.

Before Kit went to the fishmonger's she was at home one day mending, and Grace with her. Grace was always talking about what she knew, and had frigged herself before Kit. Kit had tried to frig, but got nothing but a pleasant sort of feeling, nothing approaching the luscious crisis that she felt when Betty tried her middle-finger on her clitoris.

A knock at the door. "Who is there?" "Bob." Kitty had been forbidden under pain of having her ears boxed to let Bob or any one else in when her parents were out. "You can't come in," she cried. "Let's in for a minute, I've got something to tell you." "Tell me through the door." "No, they will hear upstairs." "No." Bob began rapping a tune with his fists on the door. Grace said, "The lodgers will tell your mother." Bob, who seems to have been a little fresh, said, "Oh! won't you be sorry," and tramped downstairs.

A noise outside. "Why, there he is again." "Is that you, Bob?" No reply. "See if it's someone else." There was a shuffling outside. Grace got up and cautiously opened the door, peeping. A big foot was thrust in, and she couldn't close it. Then, pushing the door wide open and himself into the room, comes Bob. Probably with the instinct of what might follow, Kit had thrust the two children into the bedroom. Females are strange and cunning animals; even at an early age, cunt is always ready, always inciting and preparing them for cock, knowingly or unknowingly, whether for intrigue or objectless, or for the delight of doing what is forbidden, cunt is always inciting the female to help the male, for "cock and cunt must come together," as poor Fred said.

Bob was taking a half-holiday, had had enough beer to elevate him, and was of an age at which a prick has a habit of getting inconveniently stiff. If you can't afford to pay for cunt, or don't know a cunt which will take you up it for love, your prick is a restless article which will insist on the buttocks pushing it somewhere or somehow, till the stiffness is taken out of it.

A frisky youth with restless ends was in the room with two girls, one of whom was also frisky, and the younger inquisitive. They got joking, he kissed them, they tickled him, till he threw himself on the floor, and rolled about as the girls tormented him and thought they were getting the best of him. He suddenly caught hold of them both, pulled them on the floor in a heap, one on top of him, one by his side, and holding one one way and the second another way, managed to put his hand on to one's cunt, turned the other over, lifted up her clothes and slapped her naked backside; they struggling and crying out at the attack on their sacred privates, he fighting, overturning and exposing the limbs of the lasses until, as Kitty said, "he'd seen all we'd got to be seen over and over agin."

This quieted Kitty and Grace. When released, they called him a blackguard and told him to go out of their room. "I'll tell my mother," said Kitty. "Tell her," said Bob, "tell her you saw this," putting out a stiff prick. "As stiff as yours," said Kitty, who was laying at the side of the bed feeling my cock about whilst telling me.

"We turned away, then turned round; it was still out, he had got it in his hand and was grinning. Grace said, 'Let's go to the children,' and burst out laughing; so did I because she did." Kitty stopped her saying, "Don't let the children see him, they may tell Mother." After a time they turned around again, the fascination of the prick was on them, both wanted to see it. Grace winked at Kitty. "Go away Bob," said Grace, "you'll get Kitty's ears boxed if it's known you have come in." "Don't care," said Bob, "show me your cunts, and I will. Cocky, cunty, cocky, cunty," he sang out, "Look here, — come and feel it."

"I don't know what you mean," said Grace, turning round again. (Kitty said that Grace told her afterwards she wanted to see as much of his thing as she could.) "Show us the crack between your thighs." "You beast, I've a good mind to hit you," said Grace. "Come on," said he. "You go." "Feel my prick first." "I won't." "You Kitty?" "I won't you beast." "But," said she, "I was curious like to feel it for all I said 'no' to him, and so was Grace."

Bob ran at Grace and catching her, pulled up her clothes, and felt her; then running after Kit, he did the same, the whole three were yelling, Bob with his prick out, promising to go if they felt him, they frightened of the mother coming home.

They were much agitated now, the children in the bed-room were crying at the row, and both girls threatening to call the lodger upstairs. "Let me," said he, "let me put my cock just on your naked thighs, — do, — do, — do, — only for a minute." "Shan't you beast." "Oh! I must do it," said Bob, "I must, — hooo," and then sitting down on a chair, Bob closed his eyes, frigged away, and saying, "Oh! it ought to be in your ck — ck — cunt," spent, the two girls looking at him and at the sperm jetting out on to the floor.

They stood looking, never uttered a word, and fear came over them lest Kitty's mother should come home, and catch him there with his cock out, and his sperm on the floor. "Go, there is a good young man, — mother will be home directly, — oh! that's her foot-step, — run upstairs, and wait till she's in." Bob, whose nervous system was I dare say a little shaken by his frig, buttoned up his trowsers, and ran out of the room. The girls locked the door and listened, — it was not the mother. Then they began to talk.

"That's it on the floor, — that's what comes out of a man's cock when he puts it up a woman's thing," said Grace, " — it's that which gets a woman in the family way, — it's that which gives them both pleasure when they do it together, when *his* thing is up *her* thing."

Grace told all she knew, that when her mother was "lying in," she once peeped through a key-hole, and saw her father frig himself. They talked of the pleasure they had heard it gave the woman to have that warm injection up her. Grace frigged herself, Kitty tried but got no pleasure, they sat opposite each other on chairs, Bob's spunk still on the floor. That was the only time she had ever seen spunk till she saw Jim's in the wash-hand basin. "Should you like to see mine Kitty?" "Shouldn't I!" said she. "You shall some day," and one day she frigged me.

Kitty was quite artless when she told me this, she had taken a liking to me, though I did not then know it, and was delighted to tell me all, it seemed quite a relief to her to do so. She had never spoken to any one else about it. To a man? she should think not, — it was not likely, and though I asked her often and often about it at times, she never varied the account. I believed it implicitly, and that is why I narrated it here.

Several nights Jim served Betty so, till one night Kitty sneezed. "The girl's awake," said Jim. "Who is that?" said Kitty shamming, though she knew full well. "It's Jim, — you won't tell, will you?" said Betty. "I have told her you are going to marry me, — have I not Kit?" Jim went on tailing his mistress, but now that he knew Kit was awake he put out his hand and felt Kitty's bum whilst fucking. "Did you tell Betty that?" said I. "No," said Kit laughing.

Next night Betty, who seems to have taken delight in debauching Kit, made her feel Jim's prick, she pulled her hand to it. "I thought I liked to feel, but I shammed that I did not." "Was it big?" "It seemed bigger than yours, but I didn't see it."

This went on for a fortnight or so, Kitty feeling always afraid that they would be found out, and so it came to pass. Illicit fucking in a house not your own is sure to bring trouble.

The Mistress' sister came to nurse her, and slept in her room. Betty said the sister gave a lot of trouble, and was always poking her nose where she had no business to poke it. Jim did not come up for one or two nights, he had heard some one moving either in the Master's, or in the sick woman's room. Kitty was glad of it. Jim, I suppose, at last randied out of his prudence one night, and Betty reckless for want of fucking, told him to come, and up he came. Then a violent knock at the door came just as he was fucking Betty.

"Who is that?" "Me." "Wait a minute sir." "Open it, or I will break the door open." "Wait sir, I'm not dressed." In came the door with a crash. Jim was just by the bed, Kitty standing by Betty, for both got up. At the door was the Master and his sister-in-law. "You damned whoring bitch," said the Master to Betty, "at day-light out you go from my house."

The sister-in-law turned down the bed, looked at it, and then at Kitty. "Please Ma'am, it's no fault of mine," said Kit. "You dirty little hussy, why did you not tell what was going on, — your father shall hear of this." "Dress yourself," said the fishmonger to Betty. "Leave them alone till the morning," said the sister-in-law, — and both left the room. Jim half-dressed, without speaking a word, had crept downstairs whilst the talk was going on. The Master did not speak to him at all.

"They will sack us both," said Betty. Kitty began to cry. "You are a fool, there are lots of places. I hope old Vinegar-chops liked the look of it," said Betty lifting up the towel (there were the drippings from Betty's cunt on it), " — I dare say the sour-faced beast knows what it is, — don't you cry, you will get a living if your father does turn you out, any girl can so long as she has a good face, and something warm between her thighs." That was Betty's comfort to Kitty.

After breakfast the Master put Betty outside the door, Kitty's mother was sent for, who boxed her ears all the way home, and the father knocked her down when he came home. "If I thought you'd turn a whore," said he, "I'd murder you." She told her mother the truth entirely, but only got her ears boxed still more, — she should have told her Master, the mother said. After this she was again kept at home. A short time after her father died, her mother changed her quarters, keeping her indoors to take care of the children, and had no idea that her daughter was getting fucked to enable her to buy sausage-rolls, as well as for the pleasure of having a male.

CHAPTER VI

*Sausage-rolls, and consequences. — Kitty's home. — The little ones.
— A saucy cabman. — Catamenia. — Fucking economies. — Changing money. — Pol and the bargee. — Kit implicated. — A black eye and bruised rump. — A little boy's cock. — Preparation for travel. —
Kit's regret. — Bessie in tears. — Amusements abroad. — Home again. — Kitty a strumpet. — An evening at B*w Street. — Kitty's eight months' doings.*

One day I took some sausage-rolls to the baudy house. She clawed hold of one directly. "Ain't they prime!" said she, and never ceased till she had finished them all — such a lot, — then she turned pale. "I must go home," she said. "Why?" She began putting on her things. "What is your hurry?" "I can't wait." "Are you ill?" "Yes, — yes, — I must go." "Then I won't pay you." "I'm not well." "How, — you want to go to the privy!" "I do," said the girl hanging her head. I rang the bell, told the woman to show the lass where to ease herself. When she came back I could not get her to look me in the face, and thinking of her operation gave me a distaste for her that day, so I let her go without doing anything. Ridiculous that of course, but I tell things just as they occurred.

When it rained and she could not meet me, how angry she was. "If I buy an umbrella, Mother will wonder where I got it." Once she nearly got wet through, and I did not see her that time, because I did not expect her to be out.

She told me where she lived, and I arranged that if it rained I would go to the front of the house in a cab. I did that once only, and the cabman insolently demanded about five times his fare when I got down at E****r Street, saying I had enticed a young girl into the cab. "Yer haught to be glad to be let orf with ten bob," said cabby. "Think yerself lucky a peeler don't drop on you for taking a young gal like that, — yah! you're a swell, ain't yer? — yah! — yah! — poop!" — and off he drove.

She began to deplore her poor dress, bought a pair of white stockings, and I kept them for her, because she was afraid of taking them home. "Oh! ain't I kept under," said she, "I hate it, — I have a good mind to bolt." "Then you will turn gay." "Well I would like to dress nice, and do as I like, instead of minding children and working." I persuaded her not.

"Have you had no other man but me for the last two months?" "Only one," she said, "but I'm never out if it rains, and I can't get out of nights cause of Mother, and I wash and mend, — so how can I?" "I'll go and ask for some one else at your room, to see if you're in or not." "Do, — if I don't open the door Mother will, on Monday I'll take the brats into the Waterloo Road for a walk." She did, and I saw her. How short her clothes were! A carman as he passed stooped down and gave her legs a pinch. Her mother was at home.

The girl grew fast, each week she seemed bigger than the week previously, the sausage-rolls agreed with her, the hair on her cunt lengthened, — she was so pleased when I remarked it, — her desire was to have as much hair on her quim as Betty had. Then she began to get heavy, dull, and drooping. One day I had her on the side of the bed, just for variety's sake, for sometimes I found it delightful to see my prick up its roots in her, and the next instant its tip. Her cunt felt very wet, looking at my half-uncunted prick it was covered with blood. I pulled it out, a red stream followed running all over her chemise. I had never seen such a sight before when fucking, and only once I think since, though I have poked women in that state.

"What is the matter?" said I startled for the moment, "you're poorly?"

"Oh!" cried out the girl, "I must go to Mother, — oh! let me go." I tried to comfort her, she took no notice of me, but dressed and ran out of the house quickly, white with terror and without her money. That night I had Brighton Bessie, and told her about it. Bessie said the dirty little bitch ought to be flogged by the hangman; if she had her way all such young bitches should be sent to prison, and the men who had them ought to be punished as well.

Kit's first poorliness had come on, that accounted for her dullness, she had no idea of what was taking place in her, her mother
had not warned her. Of course the girl knew of the ailment common to her sex, but her monthlies had taken her by surprise. I never
knew a girl more unaffectedly modest than Kitty was the next time
she met me after her accident, as we called it.

Said she one day, "Give me a sovereign for this silver (savings
out of the money I had given her), I don't know where to put it,
it jingles in my pocket, — I am afraid of dropping it, and Mother
finding it out."

She had put it in a crack between the skirting and the inside
of a cupboard lining as near as I could make out, until it was a
pound's worth. "What a pity I can't buy some nice clothes, is it
not?" said she. Poor Kitty was amusing, but I saw she was brewing
mischief after she had had her monthlies, or was what she called
"a full woman." Several times as she took my money she said it
was no good to her, as she could only buy things to eat. She was
getting restless. When I told her I should be in the Strand one day,
if it were not wet, "Oh! do come, if it's wet or not, — I *will* meet
you." "But your mother?" "Don't care, — if she says anything I'll
tell her I'll run away."

Said she one day, "Hasn't Pol got it? Her mother has nearly
murdered her, — oh! Lor she is bruised all over." Then she told
me that the little dark girl I had had was caught in the privy with
a man, — oh! such a big un, he is much taller than you, — she was
standing on the privy-seat with her legs wide open, and he was
trying to do it to her. The mother had suspected, had the little imp
watched, and caught the man in the act. "How he could do it I don't
know," said Kit, "but he is a bargeman, — such a big man! — and
the little beast stood on the privy-seat too." Kitty was scandalized
at that.

It was some days before I saw her again, then she was slovenly
and had a black eye, and began to cry. "It's mother," she sobbed,
"look here." she pulled off her things, and showed me wales and
bruises. "Mother did it," said she sobbing, "my bottom's bruised, —
she held me down, and hit me with a brush, — look," said Kitty
turning up her lily-white arse for me to see.

Her young friend who had not long before had my prick up
her cunt, and then the bargeman's, had sought to excuse herself

by saying Kitty was as bad. Mother told mother, Kitty was battered
by her mother, and had been locked up, there had been row after
row, till Kitty would not eat, nor wash, nor mend, — she fought
her mother, she threatened to run away, and to turn gay. Said the
mother, "Your father always said you would, he would turn round
in his grave if he knew what you are saying."

"I made my brother's cock stiff," said she one day as she was
playing what we called cherry-bob with my prick, *i.e.* taking the
tip in her mouth when it was limp, and shooting it out again, just
as you see children do with cherries. "Your little brother?" "Yes, —
I washed him, pulled it backwards and forwards, as if I were washing him, so that he should not know what I was about." "Did it
get stiff?" "Quite, and he seemed to like it," said she, "he asked me
to go on doing it."

During all this time I had occasionally seen Bessie, for a youthful cunt never did give me full physical enjoyment, nor fetch me
like a full-grown one, although as an occasional letch it was delicious. After her monthlies had arranged themselves, I fancied Kitty
was more luscious, and her discharge more copious, yet I often used
to think of the spanking posteriors and full crisp-haired cunt of
Bessie whilst operating on Kit. A light-haired quim I also never
liked it, it was the artlessness, frankness, and freshness of Kitty
which kept me to her so long.

I was going abroad. When I told Kitty this she broke into tears.
"Oh! what shall I do! — don't go," said she. The little lass was fond
of me; a thing I never had dreamed of. She promised me to go to
service, and leave off fucking; but she never did.

Then I told Bessie, and she began to cry, and said, "It's always
the way, — directly I like a man I lose him." I thought she was
shamming, but the last night I had her she would take no money,
said if I gave it her, she would throw it into the streets.

Glad to be from England, alone, — alone, I hoped to be sent
to ***, but got no further than ***. There I had women enough.
All women there were examined by medical men weekly, just as
they are at ***, and many a fine Spanish woman and coarse but
well-built English woman, I had for half-a-crown a piece. I was
recalled after seven months, and within a few days was in the
Strand, but saw no Kitty until one night in early summer. "Oh! it's
you, — I'm so glad," said a female. It was Kitty, delighted. I did

not know her for the instant, but in ten minutes we were fucking. How glad she was to see me; she was a well grown young woman, and lovely, her breasts were well developed, her calves and bum as well, although she was not seventeen.

She had quarrelled with her mother, left, and set up as harlot. It was wonderful what harlotry had done in giving her taste in dress, deportment, style of walking, and even in language. She had learned the value of her cunt, it was no longer three and six, but twenty shillings. "I don't want *your* money," said she, "let's talk of old times." We spent several evenings together. One man almost kept her, she thought he was going to keep her altogether, and hoped so.

I had taken her to the house in B°w Street, quietly there we talked all things over; we laughed over the affair of Pol and the coal-heaver, the sausage-rolls, the lost ten shillings, the afternoon her poorliness came on. "So you are gay, — do you like the life?" She really did, got lots of money, and now kept her mother who had been disabled by rheumatic fever. I saw her daily for a week or two afterwards, and we fucked to our hearts' content. Her motte was delicately hairy now, and of dark golden colour, slightly brownish. Then I went to the sea-side. When I came back to London, looking for her everywhere, I could not find her, and though I longed for her very much, was obliged to render myself happy with others.

To complete her history I must go forward two or three years when I had been madly in love with a gay woman as I shall tell, but had quarrelled with her for presuming on my love, and resolutely abstained from seeing her, doing however great violence to my affection and inclination. I used to go to the baudy house in J°°°s Street (not yet mentioned), and cry to its Mistress who would ask me to let her send to the lady of my affection (Miss M°°°s), — but of this more presently.

[After reading over this part of my narrative relating to Kitty written full thirty years ago, I add these few words.

My secret life was written for my own pleasure, and to be a narrative of what I myself saw and did, and nothing else. I have pretty well adhered to that, but my fun with Kitty took place within a few years after I began to write and describe the amatory episodes as leisure inclined me, and as they seemed to me unusually amusing or illustrative. I arranged them in order afterwards. Nothing at that time had been so piquant in my acquaintance with harlots as Kitty had been. I had not then had much to do with lasses as young as she was, the novelty therefore I suppose made me write out her narrative intermixed with my own, at the length it has reached.

Besides, Kitty was really quite original, her freshness, frankness, and truthfulness impressed me much, and after much experienced since in the ways of frail ones, I believe now that what she told me was mainly true, and am sure she was delighted to get a confidant in me, to whom she could unbosom herself unreservedly.]

CHAPTER VII

Brighton Bessie. — Change irresistible. — Bessie in quod. — Lewed effects. — Spooning. — Her home. — Her cabman. — Reflexions. — Two years after. — Five years later on. — The mouse's promenade. — Bessie disappears.

I met in the Strand one night Bessie, who put her arms round me. I repulsed her, she saw her mistake, and followed me to a baudy house. Inside she began kissing me excitedly, and said she was so glad to see me back, that she did not know what she was about. It was not our usual house, I was in a hurry, so after I had fucked her was going away. "What one fuck only! — you have not had me for a year nearly, — I'm damned if you go till you have given me another, — that dear old prick, I've thought of it fifty times when I have been poked." So I fucked her again, and afterwards resumed seeing her, for she was much to my taste sexually. I had many voluptuous amusements with her which she liked and invited, although I have no recollection of playing any of those curious erotic tricks which gratified me later on in life, nice attitudes being then for the most part enough for me. My balls were running over with sperm in those days, and if I could control myself for a few minutes when my prick was stiff, it was as much as I could do. Bessie was full-blooded, and loved to take her fucking with me, kissing me furiously as her pleasure came on. We used again to pass hours at the house in B°w Street, reading, drinking, talking, and copulating at intervals.

Yet I went after other women for all that, for fresh cunt was irresistible. Once when I had been away I missed her for a few days, then I saw her coming out of a public-house. "Oh! I'm so glad, — I've been locked up, — it's a damned shame," she cried out, "I was marched off without having said a word by a policeman, — blast him! — and all because I would not let the bugger fuck me one night up in **** Street, — I'd never let a policeman touch me, — damn them all." She spoke loud to a man and two or three sympathizing women, a mob began to gather round her, so noisy was she.

I turned as quickly as I could up a side-street, she following me. "Oh! come my dear, come, — how glad I am to see you, — I did nothing but think of you whilst I was locked up, — oh! God I'm dying for a fuck, — a whole fortnight I've not had it, and I did nothing but think of you when I frigged myself." There was a roar of laughter from half-a-dozen women who had followed her. "Shut up," said some one. "Ain't she a letting out!" said another. "Ain't you ashamed of yourself?" said a third. "It's one of her men," said another. "She is a nice woman," said some one else. "It was a damned shame," said another. "I know him," said a voice, "he wants every woman in the Strand, and if he don't get them he walks them off." "Yes, the bugger." "She is just out." "Yes, and he quodded Mary Summers last night." "And he is a married man with a large family," — and so on. I felt overwhelmed, and inclined to run away. She turned into the first house which had a door open, and I was glad when the friendly red-curtained door closed behind me, she galloping upstairs in front of me, showing her fat calves. I followed Bessie into a bed-room.

"Five shillings," said the woman to me. "It's all right, — you go, — he's an old friend of mine, — don't bother," said Bessie, pushing the servant out of the room, and slamming the door. Then throwing her bonnet on a chair she caught hold of me, gluing her lips to mine. Feeling at my trowsers front, she cried out, "Let's fuck, — come and fuck me, — I'm dying for you, — a fuck from you, — oh! put your prick up." She had got it out, threw herself on the bed opening her thighs wide, and showing her cuntal beauties, calling on me to fuck her. I mounted her immediately, it was impossible to withstand her randy impetuosity; contagious lewdness coursed through my veins.

"Oh! my God," said she as my prick drove home, "I'm coming,

— oh! my God, — fuck, — fuck, — oh! I'm spending, — oh! my
darling, — fuck, — spend, — oh! — oooh!" I never had a woman in a
higher state of randiness, she would not let me go till I had fully
eased her passions, she lavished expressions of love and tenderness
on me. "Don't pull it out, — there, dear, there, — lay still on me,
I'll keep it up, it will be stiff again, — there it's stiff now." I stopped
with her some hours. A policeman on the beat she said, had taken
a fancy to her, and had asked her to let him do it to her up against
the dark wall at the back of E****r H**l. She would not, he
threatened, still she refused, so he took her to the station one night
on the plea of her annoying gentlemen, and the magistrate gave her
a fortnight in prison. She had come out that very day, and was
rather tight.

In a few weeks Bessie got more and more friendly. I was the
first to leave, and she to ask what was my hurry. When I thought
I had been detaining her too long for my moderate compliment,
she would say, "Oh! never mind, I'll make ten shillings do, — I'm
not in debt, — before the theatres are over I dare say I'll get engaged." It was impossible to avoid seeing she was getting affectionate. She would sit or lay talking, feeling, or kissing me for hours,
whilst her expressions of pleasure when I was stirring up her vitals
equalled those of any woman who has ever loved me or enjoyed my
embraces.

One night I was charged twice for the room for stopping long,
and said something about not being able to afford it. That brought
forth a proposition, one of the most curious I ever had in my life.

Said she, "It's a lot of money to spend on the rooms, — come to
my rooms; they would be too humble for you, but they are clean
and nice, — drop me a line, and I will always be at home, — and
you would be more comfortable than at these houses, and have
nothing to pay." Then after hesitation, and as if reflecting, she said
she lived in the New North Road where she had either a small
house or rooms in one, I don't quite recollect which. "It's paid for
by a friend of mine, he gives me ten shillings a week. Now don't
think little of me because I tell you this, — he is only a cabman,
he sleeps with me nearly always, he's a nice clean, steady man, and
behaves well to me; but I don't like him since I've known you. You
can come when you like, and sleep with me when you like, — I'll

give him up, he shall never come near me again, and I'll always be there for you, — you will see what a large comfortable bed I've got, — but you must pay for the rooms, I must feel sure of a roof over me, — I don't care about anything else, — then you can see me when you like, give me what you like, — nothing if you have not got it, — I don't want your money, I'll get that as I now do."

She said all this in a humble way looking at me, tears half filled her eyes, her tone was sad; it was in its way a clear but simple declaration of affection for me. I saw it, felt it, but shunned it; for a strange dislike to a gay woman loving me came over me, some sort of undefined idea that I should be a species of fancy-man, a man whom I always thought at that time was a baudy house bully; and the offer of Bessie oppressed me.

I told her she was very kind, that I appreciated it, but it was a long way off, — I would think of it, — I did not wish her to give up a friend for me, — that there were obstacles to my accepting which I could not tell her of, and so on. I scarcely knew what to say in refusing without wounding her feelings.

"I am sorry I told you, for you won't think as much of me as you did, — it's the simple truth, — you don't believe me? — only come up and see me." But I could not think of displacing a cabman, I did not even like to think of my prick having taken its pleasure in the cunt which had wriggled the prick of a cabman. My experience in life might have told me, had I thought about it, that the possibility was that my prick might have rubbed up the same channel that a burglar's had. I only saw that I was asked to displace a common man in the affection of a street-doxy, I appreciated the affection which prompted the offer of exchange, felt gratified and sorry at the same time, especially when I saw tears in the poor woman's eyes.

I again said I would if it were not such a long way off, but perhaps I would, and so on. I never did go to her house, but saw her from time to time, until I fell madly in love with a lady of pleasure, and would have given almost my life for her to have loved me. So Bessie was avenged, for I had fallen in love with a doxy after all.

When this infatuation occurred, I ceased seeing Bessie. Then in my trouble a year or two afterwards I sought her again, and told her my trouble. "Ah! you would not love me when I was fond of you, but you love her, and she plays on it, — don't you let her fool you," said Bessie, "she has got a man, — all you give her he will get, I know it from what you tell me." Bessie was right, but Sarah after a time as I shall tell, did not deceive me about the matter.

Then I missed Bessie for a year or two, then found her again in the Strand, she was much altered. "I don't think I ever liked a man to fuck me as I do you," said she one night as she enjoyed me, "if you had but come up to my little home you would have saved me a lot of trouble." But I could not get out of her what she meant by that.

Full five years afterwards, when roaming about not far from the Haymarket one night, I met her, and scarcely knew her. She stopped short, "You, Bessie!" "Ah! yes it's Brighton Bessie, but I'm sadly altered, sure enough." "And you knew me?" "Know you! — I should know you by your eyes, if I saw nothing more of your face but your eyes, — I should know you to the last day of your life," said she. She was always talking about my eyes. She had seen me several times, but had not dared to accost me she said. I told her she always might.

I took her to what had become my favorite baudy house. It was a hot night, and we fucked on the sofa. She had become flabby, and said she had ill health, but I could glean nothing from her about her career, excepting that for some years she had not been gay. We stripped naked, and had just finished fucking her on the sofa when I felt something running over my legs, bum and back over my shoulder, on to hers. It was instantaneous. Then I saw a mouse which had run over us and went fast up the wall into some red curtains where it was lost, — it made her shudder, and me too. That is one of the odd events by which I shall always recollect the last time I had Brighton Bessie. "You won't see me again I dare say," said she in a plaintive tone, and a tear in her eye as we parted. I said I dared say I should. "No you won't, — good bye, dear." With a sigh the poor woman left me, and I never saw her again.

It was whilst I was frequenting Bessie and occasionally other doxies that the following adventure occurred.

I was frequently now at my mother's house, my brother was away, and both my sisters married. I used to stop with her for days together, finding that a relief from home misery, and also agreeable company to her, who was now so much alone. I also at times stopped with one of my sisters whose husband I liked; the other lived some distance from London.

CHAPTER VIII

*Washerwomen. — Matilda and Esther. — A peep over a wall. —
Eaves dropping. — A girl's wants. — Shaking a tooleywag. — A
promenade by a barrow. — Disclosures. — A snatch and a scuffle.
— An assignation.*

I went to see my mother one day in summer, and after luncheon
walked to the end of the garden often mentioned. At one side of
it was a road which gave access to a gentleman's house, and on
the other to my mother's. There the carriage-road stopped, and a
foot path began. At the junction was a mews wide enough for a
cart, which ran at the end of our garden and those adjoining. Our
entrance to it had been long disused, *we* having one in the side-
wall opening on to the road, and the neighbours rarely used their
back-entrances. The mews was grass-grown. On the opposite side
to our garden-walls was the wall of a very large grounds. A gate
not locked, formed of open bars, was at the end of the mews next
to the road.

The footpath mentioned passed between walls of large gardens,
and then between fields, until it joined a road on the other side
of which was the village church-yard, through which the footway
passage continued till again a high-road intervened. This continuous
footway formed a short cut to a distant part of the parish. It was
not much used excepting on Sundays, and by lovers who walked
there on summer nights. I had found out years before that the mews
at the back of our house was an occasional pissing-place, it being
round the corner and out of sight. I used to peep over the wall in
hopes of seeing a female at that operation, mounting to do so by
the gardener's ladder. When I saw a woman piddle, it was a great

delight to me, but I more frequently saw men whose cocks had no attraction for me. On Sunday nights after church, the splash and rustle of petticoats could be heard but not seen; the sight was how-ever rare at any time, for few people had the boldness to push open the gate, and enter the mews.

I never saw copulation, the greatest fun I had was once seeing a female bogging, who turned round and gathered two or three of the largest leaves from the lime-trees in our garden which overhung the wall, wiped her arse with them, and left them sticking on the top of her turds; but she never noticed a youth peeping just over her head. One reason why I was never detected watching was that women always turned their bums to our wall, and so I was at the back of them. Charlotte and I have both looked over the wall.

The wall was mostly covered with our ivy, which fell down in thick masses on the mews side; lime-trees at intervals completed the screen. Any one peeping down from above could be sufficiently hidden if he put his head carefully above the wall at places, and pushed aside the boughs. On the day I speak of, I walked round the garden thinking of old times, of how Charlotte and I used to see if the cook was talking to the gardener before we began our amourous play, of the pranks Fred and others played there, and all the occurrences of my youth, which had taken place in the house and garden.

The gardener was away. I thought I would look over the wall; so, placing the ladder, got up and looking down saw two girls sitting on the handles of a barrow on which were baskets filled with linen. One looked about sixteen, the other a little older. It was a dread-fully hot day, the barrow was at the angle of the mews. They were talking, and I moved the ladder to get a place near to them and not to be seen; for to watch and hear women who thought them-selves unobserved and unheard was always a delight to me. If you ever hear two women talking on amorous subjects, their disclosures you will find are always charming to a man.

At the angle of our garden, and just where the road joined the mews, a large notice-board had been put up for some purpose since I had lived there; it was just outside and higher than our wall. Between the back of it and the wall was a space of a few inches. Our ivy had grown up it at places, and filled up most of the space, but enough was left at the angle to let me look down on the barrow which was just outside the mews-gate, out of the way of what small traffic there was, the gate of the mews being wide open. Then of all my eaves dropping, I have never yet heard anything so amusing as I did then. The air was solemnly quiet in the hot summer's afternoon and though the girls spoke quite softly, I heard them well.

"I should like to feel what it is like," said the youngest, whose face was towards me. There was a mixture of fun, audacity, curiosity and lewedness on that girl's face. "Hish! some one will hear you," and something else I could not hear, said the other. "*Fuck*, — there then," said the young one saucily and laughing. The elder gave her a slap. "Now you may take the things home alone, — I won't help." "If you don't I'll tell Mother." "Don't care." "Yes you do, — what did you say it for?" "Didn't *you* say it?" "I didn't bawl it out, you fool." "*Fuck*, — there, — there," said the younger, going off. "There it may stay then," said the elder angrily, and she moved also off round the corner. They were both out of sight in a second, but I heard their voices quarrelling, the barrow and clothes-baskets were unattended just outside the mews-gate.

A labouring man came along in the opposite direction. Seeing the barrow, he stood and looked round in all directions, turned into the mews, and I think he was going to steal, but thought better of it. I had peeped quite round the board, but had dropped into the old place again, the man turned to the wall, and pissed just under me, his head turned, and looking at the clothes-baskets all the time, then he drew the foreskin backwards and forwards when he had finished, till his prick was standing, an article any man might have been proud of; he played with it, and might have been going to frig himself had he not been interrupted.

The girls came back round the corner just then, still wrangling. They stopped as they came on the man, who turning round shook his tooleywag at them, and moved out of sight, but not out of my hearing. "This is the sort of thing that would please you," said he wagging it. "Go along you beast, I'll call a policeman." "You wouldn't call out if it was up your cunt," — and he walked off laughing. The girls were quiet for an instant, and then laughed. "Hish!" said one, "he is not gone." The other looked round the corner, and said he had; then they laughed loudly.

"Was it not big!" "Did you see it?" "Yes, and stiff, — ha — ha — ha." "He — he — he." "It looked as if it would split any one," said the little one, who sat down on the barrow-handle again. "Sarah says the bigger it is the better it is," said the other, and then they laughed. "Hush!" said the bigger one, "some one may hear us." Turning her rump to the wall she pissed just where the man had. The little one did the same, then off they went, one trundling, the other holding the baskets steady. They took the heavy work in turns, I found.

I rushed to the house, then out, and followed the girls, a desire to show them *my* prick was on me. As I followed, my intentions cooled, fearing they might tell a policeman. I had not the experience then that I now have, or should have feared nothing of the sort, for girls tell no one but each other if they see a man's prick. I overtook them in the churchyard (they were resting again on the barrow-handles), and entered into conversation with them, delighted at their demure faces, knowing that they had just seen a prick, that one had said "fuck," and that I had seen both piss. A notion of getting the younger one by herself restrained me from blurting out what was in my mind, but my delight really was in looking at, and talking with them, thinking that fucking might and probably was in their minds at the moment I accosted them.

They were coarse, middle-sized, well-fed, sturdy-limbed, dark-eyed wenches, unmistakably sisters. Excepting for one being shorter than the other, you would scarcely have known there was a difference in their ages; both had bare arms, one had her frock well pinned up behind over her petticoats, both had short petticoats, thick ankles and strong boots, a washerwoman was then not ashamed of showing what she was, and they always wore dazzling white stockings, — and these girls did. I asked where they lived, they answered readily. I knew the lane well, all the washerwomen in the village were there.

In my lewedness I forgot everything but the pleasure of speaking to the girls. A middle-aged lady passed us accompanied by two or three very young women, who stared hard at me. The barrow-girls stood up and curtsied as they passed, and naming them. I knew them, and a few years before had romped and played with the young ladies, then children. The last time I had seen them there

was not a hair on any one of their cunts; I expect that now their
cunts were full-wigged, and well frigged into the bargain. They
had recognized me, as I heard from my mother afterwards. I did
not recognize them, they having grown from children to women.
I was seated on the barrow-handle as they passed.

"So you wash?" No, their mother did, they ironed, took home,
and fetched the things. What was their name? — would they meet
me? and so on. They would perhaps, — where did I live? — they
did not know me. Getting friendlier and friendlier, I learned all
about them, it was done in a joking, chaffing way. I told them I
lived far off, and was only on a visit at a house close by.

They must go on really, — would I get up? No, unless they
gave me a kiss. I chivied one after the other, and caught and kissed
both, they were not difficult to catch. Then they trundled on the
barrow, I walking with them, the people we met (very few) staring
at a dandy walking by the side of two wash-girls; but I took no
heed then of any one who passed us, nor cared.

We crossed the high-road into another part of the lane, and
again we stopped; more and more randy got I. "What do you think
of when you iron the tail of a man's shirt?" "Nothing." "You know
it wraps round something different from that which a chemise does."
"Does it?" said the little one, who had twice the cheek of the elder.
"Yes, — it makes you think when you iron them." No it did not, —
what did I mean? — they did not know in the least.

[What delight some girls have in their randiness in declaring
they don't understand a man's baudy chaff, the "What do you
mean?" "I don't understand" are only incitements to the man to
declare his meaning in broad, strong, baudy words; and then it's,
"Oh! oh! the beast!" but their cunts tighten with a squeeze of lust,
they go off and think of it all, and perhaps frig themselves under
the recollection. But this is a reflection the result of matured experience, and was not written at the time this part of my narrative
was.]

They turned up the high-road, and at their earnest request I
fell behind, they left the linen at a house, and brought back other
baskets, then I recommenced chaffing. Then we were in the lane
bounded on one side by a wall, on the other by a ditch and corn-
field. They stopped and begged me to go, for so many people knew

them on the road. Prudence told me we had better separate, but my mind full of the idea of getting the younger girl, I asked them to have a drink. No, — they would be seen. Would they meet me? Yes. When? They could not say, — but I had their address.

I am not clear why, but up till then I had not said what I had heard and seen, but I kept it to myself, although dying to let it out. I again sat at the edge of the barrow, and refused to get up till they both kissed me. They could not go without the barrow, and after a little sham I kissed them both. Then the devil took all control off of me, and as I kissed one I felt outside her till she wriggled away from me. This in the open lane.

"Now," said she, "Mr. Impudence, I've a good mind to slap your head for doing of that." "I'm sure you like it," — and I went towards her. She ran ahead, and took up a stone. "I'll heave this at you," said she, looking as if she meant it. I desisted, and went back for the barrow. "What's he done?" said the sister who had been standing a little distance off. "I'll tell you by and by, — come on." The younger began to handle the barrow, but I sat down on a handle, some one came along. "You will do us harm," said one of the girls.

"Tell your sister what I did." "Shan't, — get up." I then, forgetful of my intention, blurted all out, imitating their voice and manner. "Fuck, — hish! some one will hear," — a slap. "Fuck, — there then."

The younger stood like a statue, her mouth opened wide, her lower jaw almost seemed dropping off; the elder stared at me, her eyes nearly out of her head. "Sarah says the bigger it is the better she likes it." Their faces got blood-red, they stared at each other, then one said, "I wish you'd get up and let me have my barrow."

"I saw you both piddle," — then I looked up and down the lane in both directions, I was bursting. "Look," said I, pulling out my prick, "it's as thick and stiff as his, isn't it?" No one was in sight still.

"I wish there was a policeman," said the elder, "Oh! you beast, — we'll tell the police." One appeared just then in the lane, but the girls appeared to be in no hurry to tell him, but I rose, they wheeled off the barrow as fast as they could, I walking with them. I was a little afraid of the policeman.

We had got to a spot where the lane was crossed by a village-road in which were many good houses. "Oh! pray leave us, we go down here, we have customers in the road." "Will you meet me?" "Yes, — but don't follow us." I did not want to be seen, so we parted, after some arrangement about meeting.

CHAPTER IX

Returning home. — In the church-yard. — Two female laborers. —
Among the tombs. — A sudden piss. — An arse on the weeds. —
Torn trowsers and a turd. — In front of the public-house.

They went off, I crossed the road into the church-yard, through
its posts at the entrance to prevent cattle passing, and over which
with difficulty the girls had got their barrow and baskets. It was
a huge church-yard, half of it mere field; at one end the rich were
buried, and there were rows of tombs and monuments, the rest was
only partially filled with tombstones of all sizes. As I entered it two
women passed me; they were tall, stout, and dusty, had very short
petticoats, and thick hobnailed boots, dark-blue dresses hung over
big haunches, little black shawls no larger than handkerchiefs over
their backs. They had big black bonnets cocked right upon the tops
of their heads, and seemed women who worked out of doors, agri-
cultural laborers perhaps, or perhaps the wives of bargemen, for
there was a canal through the village. They had the strong steady
walk and the body well balanced from the hips that you see in
women engaged in out-door occupations; perhaps they carried
strawberries to the London markets in large baskets on their heads,
and they walked as firmly as soldiers.

They went past me towards the monuments, both looked at
me, and they quickened their pace as they went off. I was dying
with want of a fuck. "They are going to piss," I thought. I knew
the spot. We, when boys and when youths years before, had laid
in wait to see nursemaids and their little charges turn up among
the tombs to ease themselves, so I stopped and looked after them.

They heard my footsteps cease, turned round, looked at me,
and walked on again. I followed slowly, they walked slower, so did

75

I; they stopped, so did I; one turned round. "Well, young man, what do you want following us?" This abashed me for the instant, but my prick standing give me confidence.

"You are going to piddle, and so am I." They burst out laughing, then checked themselves, and one said, "Well I'm blessed if you ain't well cheeked young man, ar'n't you?" "It's no business of yourn what we're a going to do, — go your way, and we'll go ours." "I'll piddle by the side of you, — I like doing it where a woman does it," I replied. I was baudily reckless now.

"I'm damned! — did you ever hear such cheek! — go on, young man, — or let us." On they went, I followed; they stopped, so did I; they muttered together half-laughing, and turning their heads round every minute, — and I went on chaffing about piddling.

They had got to a spot where there was a break in the row of tombs, and a length of turf with grass a foot high, burnt up, and almost made hay in the summer sun. "I'd give each of you a shilling to piss before me," said I. They had turned into this cross-passage between the tombs, and no one could see them from the footpath through the church-yard.

"Oh! Lord," said one, before I had got the words out of my mouth, "I can't wait," — and squatting she began pissing whilst I made my offer, and laughing said, "Well if ever I heard the like, — well young man, give it, — I'll never be paid again for getting rid of my water, I'll bet, — you do it Sarah." Sarah said, "I shan't." "Don't be a fool, take his bob." The other looked at me, the splash of the other woman's piddle fell on her ear. When any one wants to piss, and hears another doing it, the desire to piss becomes strong. Down Sarah squatted laughing, and her splash began, before the other had finished pissing.

I wanted to piss, but the rigidity of my prick prevented me; it wanted to evacuate its sperm before it got rid of the thinner liquid. I pulled it out in front of their faces as they squatted side by side, stiff and red-tipped; it throbbed, and knocked up and down in its randiness under every effort I made to turn on the water. One said I was a blackguard. "I want a fuck so bad, — let me have you, — I'll give you five shillings." To which of the two I don't know, for I had no choice, one cunt was as good as another to me at that moment, and I pushed my prick towards one of them, who laughing put it aside with her hand.

"There is a chance for you," said one to the other (they were both up then). "What do you take me for, young man?" said the other, "if my man were here he'd knock your bloody head off." But both stood looking at my prick and me. I kept on asking, and offering the money, — no one would see us, — one could watch, — and so on.

"Do you live about here?" said one. "No, I am going to see a friend at ****" (naming a place about two miles off). "Weren't you never up here before?" "Never in my life, — here is your shilling," — and I gave it her. "Here is yours." She would not take it. "Take it, Molly." She took it. "Oh! let me have you," said I, selecting that one now for my addresses.

"This is a bloody lark," said she, "*What do you take* us for young man?" "Let me fuck you." Both stood still looking at me and my prick. "Some one will catch us," said one, moving out from the tombs, and looking up and down the pathway to see if any one was near, and then came back. I had got close to the other. "Now Molly," said one anxiously, "what are you about?" "Oh! he's made me all overish." "Well if you'd been three months away from your old man as I have, there would be some excuse." "Never mind, — you won't blab, — you stand there, and call if you see any one." "The grave-digger will catch you." "No I saw him right over by the church." "Come away." "No, — you go and watch." And so we talked for a few seconds, but I never put my prick out of sight.

"Well," said the other, moving out of sight into the narrow path between the monuments, "you'll get into a mess." "No I shan't, — I'll let him for the lark of the thing."

The instant she had gone round the corner the selected one laid hold of my prick. "Do it quick, — some one may come," said she as she grasped it. "Lie down." "No I won't, — it's dirty." "No it's dry, — the grass is quite hay." I stripped off my coat, made it into a bundle, and placed it for her head. "There, — there," I said, and pulled her down. She made no resistance. I saw white thighs and belly, black hair on her cunt; and the next minute I was spending up her.

"Shove on," said she, "I was just coming," — and she was wriggling and heaving, — "Go on." I could always go on pushing after a spend in those days, my prick would not lose its stiffness for minutes afterwards; so I pushed till I thought of doing her a second time; but her pleasure came on, her cunt contracted, and with the usual wriggle and sigh she was over, and there were we laying in copulation, with the dead all around us; another living creature might that moment have been begotten, in its turn to eat, drink, fuck, die, be buried and rot. Suddenly she jerked up her arse, and pushed me.

"Oh!" said she uncunting me, "there is some one," — and up she jumped. There stood the other woman. "How you frightened me," said she. "There was no one coming, — well it's a rum afternoon's job this," said she. "Don't you blab." "Not I."

I had hidden my prick, but now my bladder insisted on its requirements being attended to, and I went to the spot which the two ladies had moistened, and pissed on it. The woman who had watched us fucking had dark eyes, she had looked at me without ceasing from the time I had got off from the other, and began pissing. My prick nearly at fucking size still, was pouring forth a copious stream whilst I was feeling its stem which the moisture from the other's cunt had saturated. Seeng her looking I pulled out balls and all, and finished by shaking my tooleywag. She laughed a low laugh. "I feel alloverish myself now." Her eyes looked like fire at me, fierce, lewed. "I'll give *you* five shillings, — let me fuck *you* too, — she will wait and watch for us."

"Oh! — o!" said the one whom I just had fucked, twitching about, and suddenly pulling up her petticoats, and looking up them, "there is something crawling up me." She felt up her petticoats, shaking them, and flourishing them about. "Oh! — oh! — just lift them up, and look Sarah."

Her companion lifted her clothes. "Go away young man, you've had your game, I think." "Oh! not there, — oh! it's biting." "Don't make that noise." "Oh! it's here, — there, — just there." Slowly the companion lifted the petticoats, first one side, then the other, showing thighs and rump, and a great ugly crawling black thing dropped; it had crawled up her petticoats whilst she was lying on the ground. I had drawn near, and was gloating over the display of charms. "Ain't he had a treat Molly!" said she.

This sight finished me by making me as stiff as I had been five minutes before; the other one still kept looking at me. "I'll give *you* five shillings," said I. "I've a good mind," said she. "Lor let him, — who'll know?" "How stiff it is!" "Let him." "Feel it," said

I. The woman put her hand on it. "I'll go and watch," said the other, moving away. "I shan't." "Don't be a fool," — and she moved out of sight, leaving us two alone.

Not a word more was said, I pushed her up against the upright railings enclosing a monument; a slight stone-ledge going all round the monument put her about an inch above me, I lifted her clothes, for an instant only saw another dark-haired cunt, and drove my prick up it. She felt pleasure the very first shove that I gave her. "Oh! — oh! — did she do it with you? — did she spend?" she gasped in whispers, looking me full in the face. "Yes she spent."

That fetched her. "Oh! I'm coming, — oh! it's a coming," she gasped, and laid her head over my shoulder. I felt her bum and belly wagging, and a perfect torrent of cunt-liquor ran down on to my balls. I had not long begun my fuck, so was slower than with the first woman, and had fetched her a second time before I had finished her standing up against the railings. Then we stood, pressing our bellies together, keeping our genitals coupled, and looking in each other's faces without speaking, one or two minutes.

"You don't know these parts?" said she whilst we still were coupled. "I've never been here in my life before," I replied. "How hard your bum is, — are you married?" "Yes." "Is she?" "No, — let me go, she is coming." Down flopped my tool, and down fell her petticoats.

The first-fucked came round the corner, then we talked. I had given the first woman her five shillings directly after I had done her, and before she found the reptile in her petticoats; I forgot to pay the other. "Well young man, you've made a pair of us go crooked," said one. "Aye that he have, — we've played high jinks." "Give us a buss," said one. I kissed them both, and off they walked. "Hulloh!" said I, "I forgot the five shillings." "Lord so had I," said my creditor, — and I gave it her.

"Don't come our way, the grave-digger knows us, — go straight across there, and round the church." I watched them going along with their steady step; who could have known from their look and manner, that both had just been fucked! Who can tell the state of any woman's cunt, whom you may meet anywhere!

I went to my mother's, the hair on my prick was gummed flat on my belly and balls, I found I had torn a hole in the knee of my trowsers, and a lump of turd was sticking to my coat, that I had made her a pillow with, the ground must have been hard and flinty, and some one had shit in the high grass.

What were the women? — certainly not gay. Did they fuck with me for fun, for letch, or for money? I often have thought of it, and came to the conclusion that both were lewed, that my baudy suggestions made them worse, my prick upset them, and the money finished it, but that wanting a fuck was the main cause; that one whose old man been away three months, how she looked at me and at my doodle, after I had fucked the first one!

Towards dusk I went to meet my washerwomen. Near the corner of the lane in which they lived was an old-fashioned public-house well back from the road, in front of it were two large elm-trees, beneath them seats where poor people sat drinking and enjoying themselves in summer. I stopped and looked. Quite at the back sat the two women whom I had fucked; they had pewter pots in front of them, and recognized me at once. Both got up, and rushed inside the public-house rapidly. Funk was on their faces, they seemed to struggle who should get inside the door first. I never saw them afterwards, but at the sight of them my cock stood rigidly, and I would have had them again had it been possible. Many a time since I have been to that churchyard to look at the place among the tombs where we three had our pleasures, and my prick always stiffened when I was there. Such impromptu copulations have a wonderful charm.

CHAPTER X

The washerwoman's lane. — An intention frustrated. — A slap on the face. — Choice language and temper. — A dinner in the Haymarket. — The rocking-chair. — A lucky shove. — Up, and out in a second. — A quarrel, and flight. — An enticing laugh. — The house in O***d*n Street.

Down the lane was the washerwoman's cottage, it had a little garden in front of it. Through the window I saw the girls ironing by candle-light. I walked about till quite dark, then knocked at the door. The short one opened it, and seeing me shut the door saying, "Oh! you mustn't call." So I went away.

Then I wrote asking them to meet me, and got no reply; but I persevered. I was constantly thinking of the girls' baudy talk when sitting on the barrow. I went to the house again, after writing to say when I would be at the end of the lane, and found them standing there, — by accident they said, and they declared they had not had my letter. That was a lie I knew. I began a smutty talk, which they cut short by both going to their cottage.

I wrote letters to the short one again, asking her to meet me, but nothing came of that. At the end of their lane were market-gardens, I saw Esther one evening at that end which joined the high-road, and was close to the public-house where I had seen the women sitting whom I had poked in the village church-yard. It was dark. I asked her to come for a walk, she promised in a few minutes to come to me by the market-garden. "If I don't," said she, "it will be because Mother is at the door." But she came.

I swore I was in love with her, which was true to the extent of her cunt, and wanted her to meet me elsewhere, — we would dine, and go to the theatre together. No, she could not be out late

81

without a row. I kissed her, which she took to in the darkness kindly enough. I whispered, "I should like to fuck." "If you say that again," said she, "I'll slap your chops." I did, and she gave me a slap in the face, and ran off. I was hurt, and so annoyed that I did not follow her, but bawled out, "You'll split your cunt into your arsehole if you run like that." Directly afterwards a voice like as of an oldish female in the darkness said, "Get along you drunken blackguard, the likes of you ought to be locked up." Insulting the girl by foul-mouthed remarks had not improved I feared my chance of broaching her, and for a while I desisted.

But the letch was strong on me, I went to stay with my mother to be nearer my game, and passed my time in playing billiards at the public-house, and nightly I hunted the girl; so that at length under promise to take her to Vauxhall, she agreed to come and dine with me, or as she said, have supper at eight o'clock with me. I usually then went to Vauxhall at ten o'clock.

I went to a French restaurant in the Haymarket, ordered a sitting and bed-room, and a good supper. Thought I, "With a feast and champagne with you by myself for a couple of hours, my cock and your cunt will make acquaintance."

To my annoyance she came with her sister. "I could not stop out late without her," said she. I made the best of it, though very angry on the quiet at seeing my game baulked.

"I'll kiss you at once because you have brought your sister unasked, and you, Matilda, because you came unasked," — and I kissed both to my heart's content. They liked it. They were dressed in the vulgarest style of their class, and I felt ashamed of going to Vauxhall with them, — and did not they gorge! Champagne they had never tasted before and they lapped it up like milk. "It gets into your head, don't it?" said one. "No my dear, champagne gets into your tail, — you'll want to piddle soon." "Oh! for shame!" "Never mind there are plenty of chamber-pots in the bed-room." "If you talk that way we'll go," said they laughing, but we went on talking and drinking.

Supper over, the waiter out of the room, both girls half-screwed, half-screwed myself and wholly lewed, they both came and sat by me on the sofa. Sisters again, — what fatality!

The conversation was soon suggestive. Which did they like

best, washing a shirt or a chemise? They let out, checked themselves, checked each other. "Lord, Esther what *are* you saying?"
"Well Matilda I'm ashamed of you." "Well that's pretty conversation for a gentleman, — let's go, — promise you won't say anything
like it again." "I won't, — but tell me one thing, — how did you feel
Esther, when you sat on the barrow and said, '*fuck*'?" "You're a
blackguard, I never said anything of the sort, — did I Matilda?"
"We'll go if you keep on so."

Matilda got jealous. "It's my turn now," said she after I had
been kissing Esther. The wine got more into all our heads, and
we laughed and shouted. "Why did you come Matilda?" "Mother
don't let Esther out alone, — besides I didn't know what you two
might be up to alone." "What did you think we might be up to?"
"Oh! that's tellings." This talk went on for a time, gradually getting
warmer and more suggestive; all were thinking about fucking,
though no one said so.

By the sofa was an American rocking-chair, the first I ever
recollect having seen. Matilda began rocking herself in it, I rocked
the chair violently for her and then as far as it would go back and
held it there, then rapidly I pushed one hand up her petticoats.
Her legs were distended somewhat as legs usually are when people
are rocking, and my fingers went on to her cunt. She lay back for
the moment, helpless, then managed to close her legs, but being
almost on her back she could not get free; she struggled to get up,
and yelled out, "Oh! pull him off, Esther, — don't you beast."

Esther was on the sofa. She got up, pulled me back, and the
chair came forward, but not till I had lifted Matilda's clothes far
above her knees. She sulked, my blood was up, and pulling Esther
down on the soft kissing her, I pushed my hand up her clothes, and
on to *her* cunt. She screeched, then Matilda pulled me away. There
had been much laughing and yelling, but now they sulked. "We will
go," said they. "I've felt both your cunts," said I.

Their bonnets were in the bed-room, and I would not let
them get them, put both fingers to my mouth, and kissed them saying, "That's touched your cunt Matilda, that's touched yours Esther."
Then I pulled out my prick, and putting both fingers on its tip said,
"That's nearly the same as if my prick had touched your cunts."

"Call the waiter, Esther," said Matilda angrily. I had gone too far, so I desisted, begged pardon, promised never to do it again, to give them both new bonnets, and I dare say anything else, and they sat down, but for a long time sulking, and almost silent.

But my humility and regrets overcame them, there was more chatting, more laughing, more champagne. I got smutty again and now they laughed at it. "What nice legs, and what beautiful white linen you have Matilda." "Mine is as white," said Esther. "Your legs are not as plump." "Yes they are." I pinched their arms, then their legs, we all kissed, they were both as randy as the devil, and incited me to smutty talk, though affecting not to understand me. Then the champagne overcame us all.

"You want to piddle?" "Ooh! — oh! no." "Really? then you want to see if your bonnets are all right, that's all, — I want to piddle though." Saying that I went into the bed-room, pissed, and came back, taking the key out of the door. Laughing, the girls then went into the bed-room, and closed the door. They were very noisy, and groggy, the eldest worse than the other.

I listened at the door. "Lock the door Ess." "There's no key." "Stand there, and hold it, — I'm bursting." "Don't he go on! — make haste, or I'll pee myself." I pushed open the door suddenly, one was pushing her clothes against her quim to dry it, the other on the pot, she let a loud fart just as I opened the door. "Oh!" said she, rising with difficulty. "I'll wait till the music is over," said I going out, — but I returned the next minute, and pulled out my prick again. "I'll fuck you both," said I, and tried to put my hands up their clothes; when I got one, the other pulled me off, then I turned to her, and so on. We upset chairs, we shrieked with laughter, it was bedlam broke loose. I caught Matilda, and threw her on her back on the bed. "Leave off now, — pull him away Essie, — you're a going on too far, — oh! don't tickle, — oh! I can't bear tickling." But I kept on.

The tickling made her screech. I threw up her clothes, for she was still on her back on the bed, I didn't see her cunt, for I was between her legs, and bent over her, lifted her legs, and pressed hard down on her belly, her clothes on it which met mine, I gave a shove, having no thought of doing anything but lewd mimickry of the act of copulation, whilst Esther was tugging at my coat. Matilda shrieked, for my prick went up her cunt, and out again before I knew where it was, — another furious shriek. Frightened, I had let go of her, she rolled off the bed, and sat on the chair maudlin and crying.

"What's the matter?" said Esther, "what's he done?" "Oh!" sobbed Matilda, "where's my bonnet? — let's go, — I will go." "Stay, — be quiet." "I won't. — I will go." The waiter just then came into the room begging us not to make so much noise, as people were noticing it. Matilda crying and angry, Esther questioning, Matilda telling Esther to put on her things, or she would go without her, whilst there stood the French waiter and a chambermaid, wondering what the row was all about, — if they had not heard, and did not guess it.

The girls were frightened, and I could not stop them. They had their things on, and were out of the house in a few minutes, I went down with them saying we would go to Vauxhall. The landlord stopped me. "Your bill sir." I paid it, and when I got out could see the two girls nowhere. I took a cab, drove here, and there, and everywhere, but they were gone.

I came back towards the Haymarket, took the first woman I met, and went to a house in O***d*n Street. Half-an-hour afterwards I went with another; whilst with her I heard a merry-voiced woman in an adjoining room, and without seeing her took a fancy to her. I dismissed my second woman after fucking her, and enquired of the servant how long the lady who was laughing had been in the adjoining room. She knew nothing, so I waited, door ajar, till I saw the woman leave, followed, and brought her back, fucked her, and had not enough money to pay for riding home.

The more I think of that adventure the more extraordinary it seems; from the time I threw Matilda on to the bed, till my prick had entered her cunt, and got out again, I don't believe it could have occupied more than a few seconds. She was heavy, I only just could lift her, and her petticoats seemed but half-way up. She laughed loudly as I did so, and when I leant over her with my prick out, I had not the remotest idea of broaching her, nor that my prick might touch even her thighs; but she must have been in the exact position, and her struggles brought her notch down to the level, and my prick by mere chance drove a little way up the hole; then her bum-wriggle threw me out instantly, and her yell frightened me.

Whether she was a virgin or not, or whether I hurt her or not, I cannot say; could not even swear that my prick had entered her cunt, but it felt like it; and why did she yell, then sulk, and go away in a temper, if I had not somehow touched that slippery orifice?

CHAPTER XI

Esther meets me. — Vauxhall. — Ex-harlot Sarah. — Esther suc-
cumbs. — Big-arsed and bandy-legged. — Periodic fucking. — Ma-
tilda invincible. — I part with Esther. — Her fortune.

I wrote to Esther, who met me in the lane, she was in her
airs. I had quite forgotten myself, she said, and had made them
both drunk purposely, — it was not like a gentleman, — I had acted
very improper; she would not recollect where my hand had been,
did not believe I had felt her thighs, she was tipsy. That was the
line the cunning jade took in a dark lane. "Now don't be foolish,
and run away when I tell you." "Well I won't." Then I said something suggestive, and she got cosy with me. "What was it you really
did to Tilda?" "Nothing." "You did." "Ask her." "She won't tell me,
and she will never speak with you again." Truthfully or not, Esther
declared she did not know what I had done to make her sister
hollow out so.

"I'll give you a bonnet, and we will go to Vauxhall, — don't
let your sister know." I gave her the money, she agreed to meet
me again, and did, and again asked me what I had done to her
sister. I would tell some night when I slept with her. Then she
would never know, for she would never be in bed with me, or any
one else, till she was married.

I progressed in the usual way, praised her big bum, guessed
she had fat thighs, &c. "You know I did feel them." No, she did
not recollect. After talking thus one night my prick was in stiffish
form, and I put her hand round it. She laid hold of it innocently,
then snatched her hand away violently. Then I did the old, old
trick, promised a pair of garters if she would let me put them on,
— in the dark of course. "No, — no." "So help me God, I won't do

87

more than put them on." Two minutes after that my finger was
on her split. This was all in the dark lane.

I wonder what a girl of that class thinks of, hopes, expects
when she meets a gentleman on the sly. Does she expect he will
fall in love, and marry her? — does she know that he wants to fuck
her? — does she like to meet a man who has that intention, and
long to hear smutty suggestions, and baudy talk? — does she like
the lustful feeling creeping over her, as she stands by a randy man
who is making lewed remarks? I imagine that like the man she is
randy and wants to hear his baudy talk, to feel his lips on hers, to
hug him, to feel his hand wandering about her hidden parts, that
she meets him really for that purpose, just as much as he meets her
for the purpose. But they differ in this: he means to get her if
possible; she has made up her mind that whatever she may permit,
he shan't fuck her, — but she generally makes a mistake in that.

We went to Vauxhall, she told her mother she was going to the
theatre with Sarah and her husband (the woman who had said the
bigger it was, the nicer it was), I was to take her to Sarah's when
Vauxhall was over. I gave her a lobster and champagne supper,
she got spoony, I talked baudy, she said it was abominable, this
was all in the Gardens. At length her modesty broke. "Don't you
want to piddle?" "I really do bad," said she without hesitation. I
took her to the ladies' place, and soon we left. There were nice little
houses not far from Vauxhall. I had been in the afternoon, and
paid for a room for the night to be sure of it, and took her there.
She would not go in till I said it was only to have another glass of
wine; but I believe she guessed what she was going in for. Then I
persuaded her to stop all night, the woman of the house was to
call us at six o'clock, so that she might get home early. She had made
up her mind to consent, and had no sham about it. I undressed her,
tore my own things off, threw myself on her, and with the first shove
or two had finished her virginity, — my prick went up with but
little difficulty.

We fucked all night, I revelled in her cunt. She was healthy,
full-blooded, randy-arsed, and spent like fun; we did it several times
before sleeping, then in the night, and awakened about eleven
o'clock next day. "Oh! my God," said she, "what will Mother say, —
I'm ruined." "Well it's no use crying, you are in for it." A few tears,
then a fuck, a piddle, a wash, — and then refreshed we go through

the ceremony of inspecting privates, and so fucking, looking, smelling, frigging, and finger-stinking we lay till devilish hungry. Then we got up, and after going to a chop-house and having food, I put her into a cab to go home. I enjoyed myself much that night, a fresh cunt is always charming, and there is such delight in killing modesty in a woman who has never been fucked before; the struggle to get her to open her thighs to let you see her cunt is in itself a delicious treat.

On the bed spunk lay in all directions, and over her chemise as well, and there was the least smear of blood. I had pushed through something tight to get into her, but it was an easy business, so easy that I thought she had had cock before; but she was large cunted, the very jagged, ragged tear was full size; her cunt-hair was dark, her bum was one of the biggest for her height I have seen, it was out of proportion. Her privates did not fascinate me, and when I had had her two or three dozen times I grew tired of her. She was also bandy-legged, a thing I never could bear in a woman.

She went to Sarah's that day, and remained there, her mother sent to know why. Sarah said that Esther had had a bowel attack after they came home from the theatre, and her mother then went to see her. A girl always looks ill after her first poking, and Esther had been fucked out, so her mother was taken in. Her sister Matilda said she did not believe it.

Sarah, I found, had been gay, and said she now was married; they did not believe that, though they kept their disbelief to themselves, and only Esther knew she had been gay, although all knew she had run away from home. Sarah got her living by washing for Esther's mother. I heard some funny things about her afterwards.

I could not get Esther to stop out again all night, but she met me often enough, and became a baudy little bitch whose cunt much wanted feeding. She told me the awful state of mind she and her sister were in at my first overhearing them with the barrow; they had been talking of fucking all that day, Sarah had begun it. Taking hold of some linen, "Oh! my," she said, "look here, ain't they been a doing it! — here is waste." There was spunk on the linen. I heard a good deal of choice washerwoman's talk from Esther afterwards, and found that it was not an unusual thing for laundresses to joke about the semen they found on the linen of their customers, and that if they found suspicious signs on the man's linen, to give the

lady of the house a hint to look after her husband. Many a husband
has I am sure been discovered to have had illicit pleasure, or to
have the ladies' fever, through the hints of an officious laundress.

I made Esther liberal presents, but didn't take her much to
Vauxhall or theatres, although she was constantly asking me to do
so. I had taken her to Vauxhall one night after I had first had her,
and saw some one there whom I should have been sorry to have
seen me with Esther. We went to the little snug, quiet accommodation house which had been the scene of the slaughter of her virginity, and there fucked; sometimes we walked instead of riding
home, and when near the village, turning down a secluded street
or lane, I set her back up against a fence, and had her; then with
her cunt buttered, home she went alone. I took her once or twice
to the theatre, and for fear of being seen had a box; but I could
not afford those extravagances. Although not a bad-looking girl,
and one who would stir up sensations in a man's ballocks when he
looked at her, she was vulgar in appearance; and neither bonnets
nor dress made any improvement in her, — she was a washerwoman
all over.

After she was well acquainted with two or three baudy houses
I grew tired of her, and quarrelled with her. One night I went to
my mother's who was ill; and as I passed the end of the lane where
Esther lived saw one or two young men and women larking. She
and her sister sometimes came to the end of the lane when their
work was done, to see the people going along the high-road, and to
chat there with neighbours. The men were chivying the girls, and
Esther was one of them. I watched them from a safe distance, heard
laughing and screeching, and every now and then one of the girls
chased by a man darted down the dark lane, and I heard a shriek.
There was no light in the lane, and not much even in the high-road
from the feeble oil-lamps. I thought also that I saw Esther kissed,
she yelled and got away, but it seemed to me she much liked it.
For some reason all the wenches suddenly disappeared, and the
men, who were of the laboring class, leaned against the railings of
the public-house, and talked. I walked slowly by them, and heard
one say, "I felt her cunt the other night, so help me God." I did
not know who he spoke of, but I made up my mind it was Esther.

I wrote Esther to meet me, and then told her she had let a
man feel her cunt, and what I had seen and heard. She denied all

cheekily, but got confused when I told her what the man said. "I was in the lane," said I afterwards, "and quite towards that end where I have felt you often, — I hid, and I know he was feeling you there." It was a bare-faced lie of mine, because I had gone away; but it was a hit. "He didn't," said she, "though he tried." "I heard him say you felt his prick," said I, lying away again, "he went up the lane, and told that tall young man that, 'so help his God,' you had." "He wanted to make me, but I didn't, — he is the greatest liar in the place. It was sneaking of you to be hiding like that, and watching me," said she.

I wanted to fuck her, but she would not let me. She slanged me, said I had deceived her, had said I would keep her, and lots of other things, — and off she went. I took no notice for a fortnight, then went to the lodgings of Sarah, and had a talk with her. Sarah said that Esther was mad with me for not writing nor going to see her, and blamed me for not "behaving handsome." "No other man has ever touched Esther," said she, "you don't seem to care about her, — but there's plenty who do, — there are two or three gents about who would be glad to be in your place."

I had her again, then had a desire to get into her sister, and tried several times to see Matilda, caught her standing with Esther in the lane once or twice, but she bolted off directly I went up to her. Once she opened the door to me at her cottage, and slammed it in my face, I had not told Esther what had made Matilda cry out till that day, and then I did. "It's a lie," said she, "you went up my sister Matilda? — what a crammer!" She might tell her sister, and she did. Matilda said I was a liar, and that what I had done was to shove my finger violently up her, and hurt her very much. Esther believed her sister. Matilda was going to be married to the potman at the public-house close by, I then heard.

After that Esther met me a few times, her sister seemed much on her mind; for she unvariably after she had felt my prick for a minute would say, "And you mean to tell me it went right into Tilda?" "Yes right in." "Oh! what a story, — it could not have been." I grew tired of her, and she of me, — probably some other man had taken a fancy to her, so I gave her ten pounds one night, told her I was going abroad, and would see her on my return, but I never did. I saw her near my mother's house two years afterwards with quite a genteel well-dressed young man, she looking nice and fresh, but very vulgar. She saw me. Her eyes had a painful expression in them, partly like fear, partly as if she were going to cry; and then she dropped them. They passed me, I of course not taking the slightest notice, but had a cock-stand, and felt jealous, — such a funny thing is male nature. I never saw her afterwards, but saw Sarah the washerwoman and ex-harlot, and gave her five shillings for a chat about the two girls. Esther had gone off with a gent, Matilda had married the potman, who had taken to drink, and used to "whop her." And that is the end of my acquaintance with the two girls.

I had great difficulty in keeping Esther from knowing too much about me, and used a false name, had letters sent to a post-office, and had to do much lying. The oddest thing was that though so near my mother's house, and though I passed her one day when walking with one of my married sisters, she did not know I was often living there, and close by her home; but she found it out just before I parted with her. She knew quite well that the conversation when sitting on the barrow could only have been heard from one of the garden-walls close by the barrow; but I would not at first tell her which. My real name I don't think she ever knew, though I am not sure of that.

Curiosity made me call on ex-harlot Sarah, who lived in one room, and whilst talking I put my hand up her petticoats, on to her cunt. She laughed, opened her thighs wide, and said, "I knowed yer would," and looked as if a fuck would have gratified her, — but I did not attempt it. This was after I had quite done with Esther.

CHAPTER XII

Preliminary. — My taste for beauty of form. — Sarah Mavis. — Mid-day in the Quadrant. — No. 13 J***s Street. — A bargain in the hall. — A woman with a will. — Fears about my size. — Muck. — Cold-blooded. — Tyranny. — My temper. — Submission. — A re-volt. — A half-gay lady. — Sarah watches me. — A quarrel. — Re-conciliation.

[I must go back a year or more before the night when I last had Kitty with the yellow hair and yellow motte, to tell the story of my acquaintance with a woman of whom I have little to tell, considering that she more or less is included in the history of my amours for nearly four years, and who will appear more than once some years after that. A word about my sensuous temperament first.

[I had early a taste for beauty of female form. Face had for me of course the usual attraction, for beauty of expression always speaks to the soul of a man first. A woman's eyes speak to him before she opens her mouth, and instinctively (for actual knowledge only comes to him in his maturer years) he reads in them liking, dislike, indifference, voluptuousness, desire, sensuous abandonment, or fierce reckless lust.

[All these feelings can be seen in a woman's eyes alone, for they express and move with every feeling, every passion, pure or sensual. They can beget in the male pure love as it is called, which is be-lieved to be so till experience teaches that however pure it may be, it cannot exist without the occasional help of a burning, throbbing, stiff prick, up a hot, wide-stretched cunt, and a simultaneous dis-charge of spermatic juices from both organs. The rest of a woman's body, the breasts and limbs, can move lust unaccompanied by love, and if once admiration of them begins, lust follows instantly. A small foot, a round, plump leg and thigh, and a fat backside speak to the prick straight. Form is in fact to most more enticing, and creates a more enduring attachment in men of mature years, than the sweetest face. A plain woman with fine limbs and bum, and firm, full breasts will (unless her cunt be an ugly gash) draw a man to her where the prettiest-faced miss will fail. Few men, unless their bellies be very big, or they be very old, will keep long to a bony lady whose skinny buttocks can be held in one hand. I early had a taste for female form, it was born with me. Even when a boy I selected partners for dancing because they were what I called crummy, and admired even at one time a fat-arsed middle-aged woman who sold us bull's eyes, because I had caught her exhibiting her large legs when squatting down to piss.

[For years I had had at the period named, two friends, one of whom was a sculptor, who alas! drank himself to death; and one a painter still living as I write this. I had been in their studios, seen their naked models, heard their opinions on both male and female beauty, and had the various points of female perfection shown me on the lady-sitters. I had them explained in two instances by the ladies themselves, in private sittings, and with them I had sexual pleasures which they said the artists had neither got out of them nor given them. I had myself sketched from the nude, and was thought a not bad hand at it, and had therefore by training, instinct, and a most voluptuous temperament become a good judge of the beauty of female form.

[I did not write the above paragraphs, when I wrote what follows about Sarah Mavis. They are added now many years afterwards, when I am wondering at what I did in those early days, marvelling at my judgment in selection, and seeking the reasons which guided me then in getting for my sexual embraces as many models of female beauty of form as perhaps any one Englishman ever had, — short of a prince.]

One summer's morning about midday, I was in the Quadrant. It had been raining, and the streets were dirty. In front of me I saw a well-grown woman walking with that steady, solid, well-balanced step which I even then knew indicated fleshy limbs and a fat backside. She was holding her petticoats well up out of the dirt, the common habit of even respectable women then. With gay ladies the habit was to hold them up just a little higher. I saw a pair of feet in lovely boots which seemed perfection, and calves which were exquisite. I fired directly. Just by Beak Street she stopped, and looked into a shop. "Is she gay?" I thought. "No." I followed on, passed her, then turned round, and met her eye. She looked at me, but the look was so steady, indifferent, and with so little of the gay woman in her expression, that I could not make up my mind as to whether she was accessible or not.

She turned back and went on without looking round. Crossing Tichborne Street she raised her petticoats higher, it was very muddy there. I then saw more of both legs, my prick stood at the sight of her limbs, and settled me. I followed quickly, saying as I came close, "Will you come with me?" She made no reply, and I fell behind. Soon she stopped again at a shop, and looked in, and again I said, "May I go with you?" "Yes, — where to?" "Where you like, — I will follow you." Without replying a word, and without looking at me, without hurrying, she walked steadily on till she entered the house No. 13 J°°°s Street, which I entered that day for the first time, but many hundreds of times since. Her composure, and the way she stopped from time to time to look at the shops as she went along astonished me: she seemed in no hurry, nor indeed conscious that I was close at her heels, though she knew it.

Inside the house she stopped at the foot of the staircase, and turning round, said in a low tone, "What are you going to give me?" "Ten shillings." "I won't go upstairs then, so tell you at once." "What do you want?" "I won't let any one come with me unless they give me a sovereign at least." "I will give you that." Then she mounted, nothing more being said. Asking me the question at the foot of the stairs astonished me, I had been asked it in a room often before, and in the street; but at the foot of a staircase, — never.

We entered a handsome bed-room. Turning round after paying for it, and locking the door, I saw her standing with her back to the light (the curtains were down, but the room was nevertheless light), one arm resting on the mantel-piece. She looked at me fixedly, and I did at her. Then I recollect noticing that her mouth was slightly open, and that she looked seemingly vacantly at me (it always was so), that she had a black silk dress on, and a dark-colored bonnet. Then desire impelled; I went close to her, and began to lift her clothes. She pushed them down in a commanding way saying, "Now none of that."

"Oh! here is your money," said I putting down a sovereign on the mantel-piece. She broke into a quiet laugh. "I did not mean that," she remarked. "Let me feel you." "Get away," said she impatiently, and turning she took off her bonnet. I then saw she had thick and nearly if not quite black hair, and recollect that I noticed these points just in the order I have narrated them. Then she leaned her arm on the mantel-piece again, and looked at me quietly, her mouth slightly open, and I stood looking at her without speaking, my sperm fermenting in my balls; but I was slightly bothered, almost intimidated by her cool manner, — a manner so unlike what I usually met with in strumpets.

"You have beautiful legs." "So they say." "Let me see them." She laid down on the sofa, her back to the light, without uttering a word. I threw off coat and waistcoat, and sitting at the foot of the soft threw up her dress to her knees; higher I tried, but she resisted. Then my fingers felt her cunt, and the delight at the feel and sight of her beautiful limbs overwhelmed me. "Take off your things, — let me see you undressed, — you must be exquisite." My hands roved all about her bum, belly and thighs, and just seeing the flesh above her garters, I fell to kissing it, and kissed upwards till the aroma of her cunt met my nostrils, and its thicket met my lips and mingled with my moustache, which I then wore, though so few men then did. I fell on my knees by the side of her, kissing, feeling, and smelling; but she kept her thighs close together, and pushed her petticoats over my head whilst I kissed, so that I saw but little of her beauties. Then excited almost to madness by my amusement I rose up. "Oh! come to the bed, — come." She lay quite still.

"No, — do it here, —leave me alone, — I won't have my clothes pulled up, — I won't be pulled about, — if you want it have me, and have done." "Well get on to the bed." "I shan't." "I can't do it on the sofa." "Well I'm going then." "You shan't till I have had you, — only let me see your thighs." "There then," — and up went her clothes half-way. "Higher." "I shan't." Now my prick was out. "Get on the bed, — I won't do it here, — take your things off." "I shan't." "You shall." All was said by her in a determined way, but without signs of temper.

She rose without saying another word. I think I see now as I write her exquisite legs in beautiful silk stockings as they showed when getting off the sofa, and getting on to the bed. "But I want your clothes off." "I won't take them off, I'm in a hurry, — I never do." "Oh! you must." "I won't, — now come and do what you want to do, — I'm in a hurry." She lifted her clothes just high enough to show the fringe of her cunt, and opened her thighs a little. I thrilled with lewed delight as I saw them, and mounted her, laid between them, and inserted my prick. Ah! at my first shove almost I was spending in her.

"Oh! lay quiet dear, I've only been up you a second." "No, — get off, and let me wash." I resisted, but she uncunted me, and got off the bed quickly. "Now don't come near while I wash, — I can't bear a man looking at me washing myself." I insisted, for I was longing to see the form I had scarcely yet had a glimpse of. Putting down the basin, she pulled the bed-curtains round her to hide her whilst she slopped her quim. I would not be rude, and saw nothing. Then on went her bonnet. "Are you going first, or I?" said she. "I shall wait as long as you will." "Then I will go first," — and she was going away when I stopped her.

"When will you again meet me?" "Oh! when out at all, I am up to one o'clock in Regent Street." "Where do you live?" "I shan't say, — good bye." "No, — wait, — come to me this afternoon." "I can't." "This evening." She hesitated. "I can't stay long if I do." "Well, an hour and a half." "Perhaps." "Will you take off your clothes then?" "No, — good bye, I am in a hurry." "Meet me at seven o'clock to-night, — do." "No." "At eight then." "Well I will be here expecting you, — but I shan't stop long." "Will you let me see your form up to your waist?" "Oh! I hate being looked at," — and off she went, leaving me in the room.

I dined at my Club, and was in a fever of lust all day. "Will she come?" for she had only half promised. Half-an-hour before the time I was at the house, and had the same room again. It was handsome throughout, had a big four-post bed with handsome hangings (this was thirty years ago mind) on one side of the room, on another side by a partition was a wash-hand stand of marble, against the wall on the opposite side a large glass just at the level of the bed; at the foot of the bed a large sofa opposite to the fire; over the chimney-piece a big glass sloping forwards, so that those sitting or lying on the sofa could see themselves reflected in it; in the angle of the room by the windows a big cheval-glass which could be turned in any direction, two easy-chairs and a bidet, the hang-

ings were of red damask, two large gas-burners were over the
chimney-piece angles. It was the most compact, comfortable baudy
house bed-room I have perhaps ever been in, although by no means
a large room. They charged seven and six for its use, and twenty
shillings for the night. Scores of times I have paid both fees.

I noticed all this, and that a couple could see their amatory
amusements on the bed, on the sofa, or anyhow in fact, by aid of
the cheval and other glasses. I was delighted with the room, but
in a fever of anxiety lest the lady should not come. I walked about
with my prick out, seeing how I looked in the glasses, laid on the
bed, and noticed how it looked in the side-glass, squatted on the
sofa, glorying in the sight of my balls and stiff-stander. Then I
had a sudden fear that she would think my prick small; what put
it into my head I never could exactly say, I used when at school
to fancy mine was smaller than that of other boys, and some remark
of a gay woman about its size made me most sensitive on the topic.
I was constantly asking the women if my prick was not smaller
than other men's. When they said it was a very good size, — as
big as most, — I did not believe them, and I used when I pulled
it out to say in an apologetic tone, "Let's put it up, there's not much
of it." "Oh! it's quite big enough," one would say. "I've seen plenty
smaller," would say another. But still the idea clung to me that
it was not a prick to be in any way proud of, — which was a great
error. But I have told of this weakness more than once before, I
think.

I recollect well that night fearing she would think my prick
contemptible, and it pained me much for I was hooked, although
I did not know it. I brushed my hair, and made myself inviting
with a desire to please her, without thinking that I was taking the
trouble to do so for a woman who was going to be fucked for
twenty shillings, and whom I now know did not then care how
I looked, or who I was, long as she got her money as soon as she
could, and got rid of me to make way for another man, or to go
and spend what she had earned.

She did not keep her time. I kept listening, and peeping out
as I heard footsteps and saw couples bent on sexual pleasure going
up the stairs, and heard them overhead walking about. This and
the excitement at the recollection of my instantaneous spend be-

tween her magnificent thighs, my pulling about my prick and contemplating it in the glass, the moving about of the various couples,
made me in such a state of randiness that I could scarcely keep
from frigging. A servant who had noticed my peeping, came in and
begged I would not look out, for customers did not like it. Did
they know where my lady lived? and would they send for her?
They did not. Then the servant came to say I had been an hour in
the room, — did I mean to wait any longer? I knew what that
meant, and was about to say I would pay for the room twice, when
I heard a heavy, slow tread, and the lady's face appeared.

I grumbled at her delay, she took my complaints quietly, she
could not come earlier, was all she said. She pulled off her bonnet,
put it on the chair, turned round, leaned her arm on the mantel-
piece, and stared at me again in a half-vacant way with her mouth
slightly open, just as in the morning. I gave her very little time to
stare, for I had my hand on her cunt in no time, and nearly spent
in my trowsers as I touched it. She tried the same game, — she
would not be pulled about, — she would not let her cunt be looked
at, — if I meant to do it, do it, and have done with it. My blood
rose. I'd be damned if I would, — nor pay, nor anything else, unless
she took her gown off. So she took it off laughing, and laid down
on the sofa. No, on the bed. No she would not. Then damned if
I would do it (though I was nearly bursting). Again she laughed,
and then got on to the bed. I saw breasts of spotless purity and
exquisite shape bursting out over the corset, threw up the petticoats, saw the dark hair at the bottom of the belly, and the next
instant a thrust, a moment's heaving, — quietness, — another thrust,
— a sigh, — a gush of sperm, — and again I had finished with but
a minute's complete sexual enjoyment only.

"Get up." "I won't." "Let me wash the muck out." "No," — and
I pinned her down, squeezed to her belly, grasped her haunches.
"I've not done spending." "Yes, you have." A wriggle and a jerk,
and I was uncunted and swearing. She sat down on the basin, I
stooped down, tore aside the curtains, and put my hand on to her
gaping cunt. She tried to rise, and pushed me, — I pushed her. She
tilted on one side, her bum caught the edge of the basin, and
upset the water.

"Damn you," said she, — then she laughed and got up. I pushed her against the side of the bed, and again got my fingers on the cunt, — slippery enough it was. "You're one of those beasts, are you?" said she.

"I've never felt your cunt properly, and I will." "Well let me wash it, and you shall." She did so, I felt it, and then begged for another fuck.

"You are not in a hurry." "Yes I am." "You said you would give me an hour and a half." "Yes, but you have done me, and what is the good of keeping me?" "I mean to do it again." "Double journey, double pay." "Nonsense, — you so excited me, that I've never had a proper poke yet." "Well that is no fault of mine." She laughed, and turned questioner. "Do you often have the women from Regent Street?" "Yes." "Do you know many?" "Yes, I vary so." "Ah! you are fond of change, — I thought so," — and she got talkative after that. I had thought her almost a dummy.

Meanwhile I was gloating over her charms, her beautiful arms, the lovely breasts I now played with, the lovely limbs I saw, for she had sat down in the most enticing position with the ankle of one foot resting on the knee of the other leg. I wanted to pull the clothes higher up the thighs, she resisted, but I saw the beautiful ankles, the tiny boots and feet, the creamy flesh of the thigh just above the garter, thighs thickening, folding over, squeezing together, and hiding her cunt from view when I tried to look up.

I had hid my prick, the fear had come over me of her thinking it small, and that prevented it standing again. An hour ran away. "I'm going," said she rising. My prick stood at the instant. "Let me." "Make haste then." As she stood up I put my hand up her petticoats. She put her hand down, and gave my prick a hard squeeze. I hollowed, — she laughed.

"I've a good mind not to let you, — you've been so long, — but you may do it." She got on to the bedside. "Oh! for God's sake don't move, — that attitude is exquisite." One leg was well on the bed, the petticoats were squeezed up, and the leg on the ground from the boot-heel to about four inches above her garter was visible. She was half turning round, her lovely breasts, or rather one of them, showed half-front, and with her head looking round at me as she was moving, it altogether made a ravishingly luscious picture. I put my hands up from behind between her thighs. That broke the spell, she moved on to the bed directly, — I on to her.

"Oh! God you are heavenly, lovely, — oh! God my darling, — ah!" I was spending and kissing her too quickly again; lust almost deprived me of my pleasure. In a dozen shoves I was empty. It was all over.

"How quietly you stood in that attitude," said I. "I can stand in an attitude nearly five minutes without moving, almost without showing that I am breathing, without winking an eye." I thought nothing of this at the time, excepting that it was brag.

"Give me five shillings, for I have been a long time with you, — I've a reason, — I won't ask you again." I gave it her. "Shall you be in Regent Street to-morrow morning?" "Yes."

I was in Regent Street, met her, and had her you may be sure, and repeated these meetings for a week daily, and sometimes twice a day; but got no more than the shortest time with her, the quickest fuck, a rapid uncunting. She did not spend with me, and showed no signs of pleasure, scarcely took the trouble to move her bum, would not undress, would not let me look at her cunt. I submitted to it, for I was caught, but did not know that then, — she did. That is, she knew that I was damnably lewed upon her, and used that knowledge to suit her convenience. I had no right to grumble at it, I need not have had her, had I not liked, upon those terms. But I did. At length I grumbled, and at last almost had a quarrel. "I won't see you again," said I. "No one asks you," said she.

As my means were not large, and my purse grew rather empty, I was glad to keep away a few days. Then again I saw her in Regent Street; and after giving her the wink, followed her. She walked on, but instead of going to the house, passed the end of the street. On she went, I went close to her, it was the second time I had spoken to her in the street. "Oh! I did not understand you," she said, "besides I'm in a hurry." "Oh! do come." "Well, I can't stop five minutes." "Nonsense." "Well then I can't, — and she went on walking. My prick got the better of my temper. "Well, come back." She turned round and bent her way to J°°°s Street, saying, "Don't let us go in together."

When in the house, she got on to the bed without a moment's delay. I had her, and she was out of the house again in less than ten minutes, leaving me in a very angry state of mind; but she promised to meet me the following night if she could, and to stay longer with me.

She came an hour late, and found me fretting and fuming in the bed-room. They did not hurry me now at that house, I being already known there, and gave me whenever they could the same chamber. "I'm in a great hurry," were the first words Sarah said. "Why, you told me you would stop longer." "Yes, — I am sorry, but I can't." "You never can, — but take off your gown." "I really can't, — have me at the side of the bed, — you wanted it so the other day." "No I won't." "Then I'll get on the bed," — and on she got. I tried to open her legs, to turn her round to see her bum (I had never seen it yet properly). No, she would not undress, she would do nothing, — I might have it her way, or leave it alone and go. How green it was to submit to all this.

I lost my temper, for my delight I see was in her lovely form, in her physical beauty; whilst she seemed to think that the only joy I could have was to spend in her cunt as fast as I could. "I won't have you at all," said I getting resolute at last. "All right," said she getting off the bed, "I'm really in a hurry, — another night I will." "Another night be damned, — you are nearly a bilk, — there," — and I threw the sovereign on a table, and put on my hat. "Are you going?" "Yes, I'm going to get some woman who is not ashamed of her cunt." "Go along then." Off I went. When half-way down the stairs I heard her calling to me to come back, but savage, I went off.

I walked up Regent Street savage with her, and with myself too, for not having had my fuck, even if she had gone away a minute afterwards. Randy as the devil, I saw a woman at the corner of the Circus, and accosted her, she turned away, I accosted her again. "Will you come with me?" "Yes, if you like." "Do you know a house about here?" "No, I'm a stranger." Then I took her to J***'s Street, had her two or three times and toyed with her a long time, stopping till she would stop no longer, saying she should be locked out if she was not off. She was only half-gay I think, and wanted a fuck. I had just offered myself in time. She was a biggish woman of about thirty years of age. After I had fucked her the first time, we laid on the bed together; she played with my prick till it was stiff again, and then turning on to her back said, "Come on, — let's have it again."

I thought much of my fine-limbed Sarah Mavis, but it was with anger. A fuck for ten shillings was all very well when randy, but even when in a hurry I never was satisfied till I had pulled the cunt open, and given it a general inspection, although it was generally but a rapid one in those days. If I had the same woman again another day, it was because I liked her and liked to talk to her, for I always found them more complaisant the longer I knew them. But here had I been having a woman daily, and sometimes twice a day, mainly because she was so exquisite in form (for I had some idea even then that her cunt was not a good fit to my prick); yet I had never seen her cunt, nor her backside, nor her bubbies, nor her arm-pits, nor her navel, nor anything properly, and so I determined not to have her again, and to dismiss her from my mind. But I was hooked.

To economize I again went with cheap women, and seemed to get just as nice women for ten shillings as I did for twenty; but I had taken a liking for the house in J***'s Street, which was an expensive one, and liked the best room, and took my cheap women to my dear room. One woman said, "Well you might give me a little more, and have a cheaper room, — the room gets nearly as much as you give me." And I saw a woman there one night pocket the comb, and a piece of soap, — she stole them. I heard in pleasant conversation afterwards, that soap and combs were often stolen by the women, — especially the soap.

About a fortnight afterwards I saw my Venus again, and again was closeted with her. I could resist my desire for her no longer, having never ceased thinking of her even when fucking other women. She was just as calm, but there was a little, quiet spite about her. When she had taken off her bonnet, and looked at me for a minute with her mouth open as usual, she said, "I suppose you have been having other women." I can't tell why it was, but I lied, and said, "No." "What did you go upstairs with one for?" said she, "the night after you left me, — I was in the parlour, and peeping through the door saw you and the woman who stumbled at the foot of the stairs" (which was the fact). "Well I did," I replied, "and saw her cunt, — and that's more than I ever saw of yours." "You've seen as much as you will." Putting on my hat in a rage, "Then I may as well go, — here is your money," — and I turned towards the door. "Don't be a fool," said she, "What *do* you want? — what *do* all you men want? — you are all beasts alike, — you're never satisfied." She was angry. "Don't be in a hurry, and let's see your precious cunt." I recollect saying that very distinctly, being angry, — and that up to that time I had been chaste in my remarks. I was at that time of my life not at all lewed or strong in word with women when we first met, but was somewhat less so so soon as I warmed, and only when randy to the highest degree or by fits and starts, spiced my conversation highly with lewed expressions.

CHAPTER XIII

Sarah's complaisance. — Mistress Hannah. — About Sarah. — Sexual indifference. — After dinner. — Start naked at last. — Her form. — The scar. — Hannah's friendship. — The baudy house parlour. — The Guardsman. — Sarah's greed. — A change in her manner. — A miscarriage. — Going abroad. — I am madly in love. — Sarah's history.

She laughed. "Well I will, — but don't make me undress, — I'm in a hurry." "Of course, — you always are." She laid on the sofa, and pulled up her clothes, — she was yielding. "No, — come here." She came, and laid on the side of the bed. At length I saw those glorious thighs open wider, the dark-shaded crack with the swelling lips showed itself more freely than I had ever seen it before. I dropped on my knees, and propping up one of her feet with my hand, lifted the leg so that the thighs distended, and a large bit of crimson nymphæ began to show, the faint but delicious odour of her cunt stole up my nostrils, my lips closed on her gap, and kissed it lecherously, my brain whirled as my nose rubbed in the thicket of dark hair, and my lip touched her clitoris. I know nothing more excepting that I was up her as she laid there, and spending as quickly as ever, before I had in fact well plugged her. "Are you satisfied?" said she as she looked up from washing her cunt by the side of me. "No, it's so quick, — you fetch me so quickly." "That is no fault of mine." She had said so often before. I recollect all these apparently trivial, these various feelings and circumstances as well as if it were yesterday, for she had made her mark on me.

I had partly conquered, and saw my victory. "I like seeing you so," said I, "but won't see you, or any other woman who won't let me see her charms, and who is always in such a hurry, — it would

105

be all very well if I saw you for the first time — ("Why you have a new black silk dress on." "Yes, I bought it with your money," said she), — but for a regular friend as I am, it is unsupportable." I conquered more, and subsequently told her that I might be in Regent Street one day, but I did not go there (I had made no promise). She said she went out against her will to see me, — could I write to say when she was to meet me? No, — but I could write to the baudy house, and they would send on the letter. I called there one morning, and left a letter. The Mistress was a shortish sandy-haired woman about thirty years old, with a white face who looked very fixedly at me, and smiled. She would send on the letter to Miss Sarah Mavis which I found was the name she went by; but Sarah never came to my letter, and I paid for the room for nothing. Then I sent for the Mistress; had a bottle of champagne with her, and she opened her heart a little, she was soon a little screwed, and this was what she told me. Her name was Hannah.

She had not known Miss Mavis long, — only a month or so before she had come in with me, — did not often see her now excepting with me. Mavis had been asking if I had been seen in the house with any other woman, "and of course I did not tell her," said Sandyhead. She thought her a nice woman, and had struck up acquaintance with her. Now she often came into the parlour to chat with her when I had left, or before she came upstairs to me, when I was at the house before my appointed time.

Things went on thus for a little time longer, Sarah doing much as she liked, but certainly becoming more complaisant. She stopped longer, we began to talk; I was of course curious about her, she about me. I dare say she got much out of me, I but little out of her. What I mainly learned was that she only came on the streets occasionally, and from about eleven to one o'clock in the day, — never afterwards; and when she had sufficient money to "go on with," as she said, she came not out at all. "I hate it," said she, "hate you men, — you are all beasts, — you're never satisfied unless you are pulling a woman about in all manner of ways." "It pleases us," said I, "we admire you so." "Well it does not please me, — I want them to do what they have to do, and let me go." "Why don't you go out in the afternoon or evening?" "No, I get my money in the morning, and have other things to do the rest of the day."

She had not been gay long, — not more than a month before

I had met her, — was taken to the house in J***'s Street by the first man who met her in the streets, and had been there often since. No, she never had been gay before she would swear, and often wished she were dead rather than have to come out and let men pull her about, and put their nasty muck into her, — "nasty muck" was always the pleasant way in which she spoke of a man's sperm.

"One would think you never cared about a poke, — I wonder how often you spend." "Oh! it's all the same to me whether I have it, or whether I don't, — if I do it once a fortnight it's as much as I care about, — you beasts of men seem to think of nothing else, and you leave us poor women all the trouble that comes from putting your muck into us." "What the devil do you care about?" said I, after a chat with her one day in which she had just said what I have narrated. "Oh! I don't care about anything much."

Another day she said, "I like a nice dinner, and then a read in an arm-chair till I go to sleep, or a nice bit of supper, and to get into bed, — I'm so tired of a night, I like to get to bed early if I can." We went on talking about eating and drinking; she told me what she liked and what she disliked with much gusto and earnestness. "I'll give you a good dinner," said I, "and we will come here afterwards." "Will you?" "Yes, — but I won't unless I have you three hours here." "Impossible, — I dare not be out after half-past ten." "Come early." "I can't come very early, for I must be home in the afternoon." There were all sorts of obstacles, — so many that I gave it up, not going to be humbugged. But *she* would not give it up, and it was arranged that if she might name the evening, she would be with me at six o'clock, and stay with me till ten, — an immense concession, — it was the dinner that did it. I saw she was fond of her stomach, and that made me offer the dinner as a bait.

She would not come in after me to the restaurant, I was to meet her at the corner of St. Martin's Lane in a cab, and go with her, — and so it came off. We went to the Café de P**v***e in Leicester Square, I had already ordered a private room, and a nice dinner. My God how she enjoyed it! "It's a long time since I've had such a good dinner," said she, "but never mind, better times are coming again for me, I feel sure." She ate largely, she drank well, and to my astonishment when I got up to kiss her, she kissed me in return, and gave my piercer the slightest possible pinch outside my trowsers. "Let's feel you," said I. Equally astonished was I when

she said, "Bolt the door, the waiter may be in," — and then I had
a grope, and she felt my prick. "Let's go, — let's go, — I am dying
for you." Off we went arm in arm. Directly we were well away from
the Café she let go my arm. "You go first, and I will follow." I
thought she was going to cheat me. "I dare not be seen walking arm
in arm with a man, — but I will follow." In five minutes we were in
the room together. Sarah Mavis was just in the slightest degree
elevated, and perhaps more than slightly lewed.

To pull off my things, to help her off with hers partially, was
the work of a minute. "I must piddle first, — champagne always
makes me want to piddle so." "Does it make you randy?" "Oh! Lord
it does sometimes; but it's such a time since I tasted it before to-
night, I almost forget." "Are you so now?" "Oh! I don't know, —
come on the bed," said she. She opened her thighs wide, she let me
grope and smell, and kiss, and see. "Come on, — do." Instinct told
me she wanted it, I embraced her, and was enjoying her, when
she clasped me firmly, sought my mouth. "Oh! my darling, I'm
co — com — h — hing," said she, spending as she cried out, and
fetched me at the same instant. It was the first time she had ever
spent with me.

We laid in heavenly quietness, prick and cunt in holy junction,
distilling, slobbering, and bedewing each other's mouths and privates, whilst the soft voluptuous pleasure was creeping through our
limbs, bodies, and senses. She was in no hurry to wash out the
muck. "Oh! I'm choking," said she after a time, "get off." "I won't."
"Oh! do, — my stays choke me when I lie down after food, — I'm
almost suffocated." I held fast. "If I get off, you won't let me do it
again." "Yes, — yes I will." She jerked my prick out of her cunt,
I got to the side of the bed, she sat up, and was about to get off,
when I stopped her, and together we undid her stays, and took
them off. "Let me wash now." "No, you shan't, — I've never yet
fucked with my first sperm in you, — let me now, there is a darling."
She laughed, and fell back; then for a few minutes we kissed and
toyed. Her magnificent breasts were now free, I buried my face
between them, and kissed them rapturously; her moistened quim
I felt, and it drove me wild with desire; so gluing my mouth to hers
I mounted her, and we were soon in Elysium again, Sarah enjoying
her fuck in a way I thought from her cold-blooded manner previ-

ously she was quite incapable of, — and there we laid, nestling cock and cunt together, till a slight sleep or doze overtook both of us.

In a minute or two Sarah sprang up, and rushed to the basin. I lay still, contemplating her, and saying I would not wash my prick for a week, so that I might retain in the roots and its moistened fringe our mixed juices, the remnants of our first spend together. When she had washed, she laid down by the side of me. "Let's have a nap," said she. The wine seemed to be getting into her head more and more, though she was but in the slightest degree fuddled.

I could not sleep. The sight of her breasts relieved from her stays, the free manner in which she let her petticoats lay half up her thighs, the delight at finding her take pleasure in my embraces exulted me beyond measure. I joked and tickled her. "Let's see you naked." "You shan't." "Well, stand up, and let me see your limbs naked, — take off your petticoats, even if you keep your chemise on." She was yielding, took petticoats off, but would do no more. I had seen more than any other man, and she would do no more, she said. The wine had evaporated, and she was herself again, quiet, composed.

Maddened with desire, "I'll give you a sovereign," I said, "to take the chemise off." "Will you!" "Yes." "No, I won't." "I'll give you two." "What can you want to see more for?" "Hang it, take the money, and let me, or I'll rip it off without paying." I closed with her, and struggled, pulled the chemise up above her haunches, pulled it down below her breasts, tore it. "Now don't, — I won't have it," said she, getting angry, "it won't please you if I do, — you will not like to see me half as well afterwards, I tell you." "Yes I shall, — here is the money, — now let me see you naked, — I'll give you three sovereigns."

She pushed me away, and sat down. "Where is the money?" said she. I gave it her. "I've got an ugly scar, — I don't like it seen." "Never mind, — show it." Slowly she dropped the chemise, and stood in all her naked beauty, and pointing to a scar just below her breasts, and about four inches above her navel, "There," said she, "is it not ugly? — does it not spoil me! — how I hate it!"

I told her no, — that she was so beautiful that it mattered not. Yet ugly it was. A seam looking like a piece of parchment which had been held close to a fire and crinkled, and then glazed, star-shaped, white, and as big as a large egg lay between her breasts and her navel. It was the only defect on one of the most perfect and beautiful forms that God ever had created.

"There," said she, covering it up, "you won't want me naked again, — now I dare say you don't like me as much." Yes I did. "Do you?" "Yes." She came and kissed me. I often had her as naked as she was born afterwards.

"What is the time?" "Ten o'clock." "I must go." "Another poke." "Make haste then." We had it. "Oh! now don't keep me, — if I'm not home by half-past ten I shall be half murdered." She had let expressions like that drop more than once; but I got no explanation excepting that she lived with her father and mother, — and at that time I believed it.

At the next meeting she had her old quiet manner, her old "keep your distance" was attempted; but it was impossible. A woman must always give again what she has once given, she cannot help it. Then came more dinners, but she was more cautious now in what she eat and drank, less reckless in her embraces of me; but we were closer acquaintances than we had been; she let me pull her about more freely and as a matter of course, washed her quim without hiding herself for that operation, and so on, — yet still she held me at a great distance, and was reserved. She conquered me, in a degree.

In fact she did pretty well what she liked with me; saw me when she liked, stopped with me as long as she thought proper, let me fuck her just as often as she liked and no more (and it was rarely she let me do that more than once a day), see to her knees, or to her cunt, or pull her about just in the degree she for the time thought fit to permit. I grumbled, said I would see more complaisant women. Well I might if I liked, — but I did not. Her indifference to sexual pleasure chilled and annoyed me and for a reason I never could understand, her cunt never seemed quite to fit me, nor fetch me with the voluptuousness that scores of other women have done. Yet I saw her almost exclusively for three years, and when she gave herself up to pleasure with me, my delight was unbounded; when she let me have her with her cunt unwashed after our first copulation, I thought of it for days afterwards. Altogether she had her way with me in a manner I did not see, and have only comprehended since.

This went on for some months. Whether she had other male friends or not I don't know, but I never found her in Regent Street or other places where I had once been able to find her, after I began to see her regularly, and have reason to think that she ceased casuals after she had me, and perchance another, that is all. Hannah said often at a future day that I was her only friend.

I have not yet described her. She was of perfect height for a woman, say five feet seven, her form from her chin to her toe-nails was faultless, if anything inclining to too much flesh, and to too great a backside; but then I liked flesh, and a woman's bum could not be too big for me. I used to rub my lips and cheeks over her bum for a quarter of an hour at a time, when she condescended to turn it upwards for so long a time for that worship. Handsome her face certainly was, but it was of a somewhat heavy character: her eyes were dark, soft, and vague in expression which together with the habit of leaving her lips slightly open, gave her a thoughtful, and at times half-vacant look. Her nose was charming and *retroussé*, her mouth small, with full lips, and a delicious set of very small white teeth, her hair was nearly black, long, thick, and coarsish dark hair in large quantity was in her armpits, and showed slightly when her arms were down, her arms and breasts were superb. Her cunt was thick-lipped, and with largish inner lips which showed well on nearly the whole length of the split; her mons was very plump, and covered well, but not widely, with crisp black hair. She looked twenty-six, yet was not more than twenty-two, and she looked most handsome when lying asleep.

If I were asked the most perfect thing about her, I should say her feet and legs up to her notch — they were simply perfect; I have seen them as handsome in smaller women, never in one of her height. I must add that her cunt was large both outside and inside, and that she was not a voluptuous poke to me, but why I can only guess at now; I did not know it whilst I was acquainted with her.

"A little of that satisfies me," she would say of poking, "once a week, — once a fortnight, excepting at times, — you men are beasts, all of you." She at first refused my mouth, never moved her bum, and laid like a log. "Here I am, — do what you like, — do it, and get it over, — or leave it," was her common mode of meeting my grumbling. Her first sexual pleasure with me was, I believe, the night she dined with me; afterwards she took pleasure with me

more frequently, but uncunting me and rushing out of bed to wash
the instant I had spent, before I had indeed done spending; until
a sudden change in her took place which I shall tell of, and then
she was kinder, more lustful, or perhaps I might say more loving,
and more reckless; letting me enjoy her after my own fashion, and
abandoning herself to enjoyment as much as it was perhaps in her
nature to do so.

I found that she often now was with the keeper of the house,
or rather she who represented her, — Hannah. So I got acquainted
more closely with Hannah, would go into her parlour, and talk
with her before Sarah came. This began one day when I was awaiting Sarah by her asking me if I would cast up a column of figures,
nearly the whole of which was in five shillings and seven and sixes.
I did it once, then I did it a second time. Going in one day just
afterwards, she stepped out from her parlour and thanked me. I
stepped into the parlour, and got into the custom of doing so, — if
ladies were not in there, — but there was a good introduction business done, as will be seen, and often-times ladies were waiting there
till their swains arrived.

One day she cooked a luncheon for me, once a breakfast, the
latter was during the time I had quarrelled with Sarah, and took
another woman to sleep with me there. I complimented her on her
cooking, she was half groggy (as she often was), and was very
talkative. "Lord," said she, "you have tasted my dinners many a
times." "Nonsense." "Yes you have." "Where?" "Do you recollect a
ball at ****, where all the servants were allowed to look at the
table before supper, and your coming down with Mr. ***, and we
all scuffling back?" "Perfectly." "Well, I cooked that supper." Then
it turned out that she had been cook at a house where I was a
constant visitor, she had recognized me at once, but did not recollect
my name, or so she said, — indeed it was not probable that she
knew it. She had been caught with a soldier in the house, and had
been kicked out.

Now by chance of fortune she was keeper of a baudy house,
and her soldier visited her there when in London, — he was a
Guardsman, — and she supplied him with money, and lots he had,
for she robbed her Mistress wholesale of the baudy house profits.

Hannah had two sisters, one a married woman with a bad
husband, and several children. She often came and assisted at J***s

Street. sometimes acting a chambermaid, — and about two years
after this period of my history a second one appeared who had
been a housemaid, and who had I suppose also lost her character.
A pretty blue-eyed girl about twenty years old with a cast in her
eye, and a lovely leg up to within a few inches of her cunt. I never
saw higher, and shall have more to say about her hereafter. Her
name was Susan — a sailor was said to be in love with her.

Sarah at the end of some months asked me to give her five
pounds, and soon afterwards ten pounds. She was going to make up
a sum of money to buy a business for her father. She had been
dressing very shabbily I noticed, and said she knew I did not mind
that, and it was all because she was trying to save money, — to
quit that life she hoped, — and I believed it. I could not get her
for several days, yet could have sworn I had heard her voice one
day in loud altercation with a man in the parlour when I was waiting for her upstairs. I rang and asked for her; the servant came, and
asserted that Miss Mavis was not there, and I never saw her that
night. Next day I made an appointment (through Hannah) for
eleven a.m., and waited a long time before she came up. She looked
ill. "You've been crying." "I have not." "Yes you have, — your eyes
are red, — aye, and wet now." She asserted she had not, and then
burst out sobbing saying she was unwell. I was distressed, and sent
for wine. Hannah came up and comforted her (I saw Hannah knew
all about it). Then we were left to ourselves. "I've never been a
bed all night," said Sarah. "Come to bed now." To my extreme
astonishment *into* bed she came, after looking at me in a very
earnest manner.

I had often asked her before, and she never would; saying she
never had been in bed but with one man, and never meant. I was
enraptured, stripped to my skin, and was soon pressing every part
of her body to mine. She gave herself up to me entirely, her tongue
met mine as we spent. "Don't throw me out now dear." "Very well."
Oh! miracle, I thought, and there we lay, prick and cunt soaking
together, till we had another fuck, then she dozed off in my arms,
and I soon afterwards. We slept more than two hours, then my
fingers sought her cunt directly and awakened her. I told her the
time, she sighed saying, "It's no matter, — it serves them right."
It was a day of miracles, Hannah sent up food, we eat it in bed,
we fucked again and again. I was delighted with the spunk we left

on the sheets; then we dined at the Café, and went back to the
baudy house, — more fucking, no cunt-washing, all was free, baudy
abandonment.

Hannah came up to us about the time Sarah usually left me,
and told her it was time to go. Sarah said she did not care a damn,
Hannah begged her to go, — she would go home with her. She
agreed to go, kissed me, and said I was a kind fellow. I waited outside, and tried to dodge her home; but was unsuccessful; the two
discovered me, stopped, and upbraided me, and came back to the
baudy house. Then she made me promise not to follow her, and
went out to piddle as she said. Hannah followed, I waited five
minutes for them, and then called to the servant. She came in with
a demure face, and said, "Lor sir they have both gone out five
minutes ago."

For weeks after that Sarah was changed, and with the exception of not stripping entirely, did as freely as I wished, she did
everything I wanted but sleep with me all night; she kept out later,
but away at night she went; she embraced me, enjoyed her fucking,
and in fact treated me like a husband. Then she said one day, "I'm
some months gone in the family way." "Who's the dad?" "You perhaps." "No I'm not, — it's some man you are fond of, not me." "I
am fond of no man," said she. Then she was ill, and away for three
weeks, she had had a miscarriage. I was in despair, and sent her
money all the time of her illness, but could learn nothing from
Hannah, excepting that Sarah was a dear good woman, and too
good for him. That was said before the sister, who cried out, "You
shut up, Hannah." So I came to the conclusion there was some other
man in the way.

Another day I pumped Hannah, but she was an old bird, and
not easily caught. "She is fond of a man," I said. "She is not a fond
sort, — if she is fond of any man at all it's you, — but she has got
her duty to do." "What's that?" "Ask her, — I don't know her business. Now you get out, there are some ladies coming here directly,
and Miss Mavis won't like your being here with them." "I'm not
her property." "Pretty nearly you are, — at all events go, there is a
good gentleman." Whilst Sarah was away I did get acquainted with
three or four ladies, and two of them I had. Sarah had then either
gone abroad, or I had had a desperate quarrel with her.

When Sarah met me again she was still miserably ill, and

thanked me for my kindness warmly. We resumed our meetings, and again she was cautious, but no longer bounced me. She spent with me, enjoyed me, but entreated me,"Oh! let me wash out the muck, — now do pull it out, — I am so frightened of being ill again." So I let her have her way. She refused to say anything about her illness, excepting that it was I who had caused it; but I did not believe her. She usually now gave way to pleasure with me; at the end of the month I gave her twenty pounds to make up a sum, then she got still more exacting about money. "Oh! I do stop a long time with you, — give me more money, — do, — I want to make up a sum," &c., &c., — and then of course came a lie. At length she said (one bright sunny morning it was, I had poked her, and was laying on the sofa afterwards, she sitting on the easy-chair, her lovely breasts out, one beautiful leg over the other showing slightly the flesh of her thighs), "You won't see much more of me, — we are going abroad."

I started as if I had been shot at. "You? — nonsense, — never." "I am indeed, — I'm sick of this life, and will go anywhere, do anything to get out of it."

I sank back on the sofa sobbing, it came home to me all at once that I was madly in love with her. I was dazed with my own discovery, — I in love with a gay woman! one whose cunt might have had a thousand pricks up it! who might have sprung from any dung-hill! — impossible! I felt mad with myself, — degraded! — impossible, — it could not be, — and for a time I conquered myself. I tried then to draw her out about herself. It was useless. Her quiet way of asserting that she *was* going at length brought home the conviction that she spoke the truth. Then I laid and sobbed on the sofa for half-an-hour. "Oh! you will soon get another friend," said she. "No, no, — I can get a woman, but not one I shall like, — Sarah my darling, Sarah I love you, — I dote on you, — oh! for God's sake don't leave, — come with me, — you shan't lead this life, — we will go abroad together."

"That is impossible, — if I did you would leave me, and then what should I do? — come back to this life, — no." "You are going with somebody else, — who?" "I can't say, — I'll tell you when I am gone." "When are you going?" "Perhaps in a fortnight, perhaps a little later on."

I calmed for a time, a fortnight might give me a chance of

persuading her, and I began it at once; but it was all, "No, — no, — no, — it's all for the best for both of us," — and again I fell into deep despair, my heart felt breaking, I had been so happy with this woman for months, she had so filled my thoughts, so occupied my spare time, that I had half forgotten my home life. Now I felt alone again, I had told her some of my troubles, — not all, — now I poured them all out, and offered everything, — all I had, — to go that next day abroad, and never return; that I would make her love me though she did not now, I promised all man could promise, — and meant it.

"No, — no, — impossible," — and again I fell back on the sofa sobbing like an infant. I have almost the deadly heart-ache now as I write this. She sat looking at me for some time, then she arose, stooped over me, and kissed me. I turned round, and — how strange that in my despair I noticed it, and now recollect noticing it! — as she stooped her chemise opened, and as I put my arm round her, her breasts touched my face, and as I moved to kiss them I saw her whole lovely form down to her feet, the dark hair of her motte, the bright white scar; and all in the soft subdued light which is on a woman's body when enveloped in a thin chemise, — and my prick stood whilst kissing her and sobbing, and she was soothing me.

"It's of no use your loving me," she said, "and it's of no use my loving you, — don't take on so, — perhaps when I am gone you will be happier at home, — I can't love you, although I like you very much, for you have been a good, kind man to me, — I nearly do love you I think, — if I were with you I'm sure I should, — but it's of no use, for I am a married woman, and have two children, and am going with them and my husband."

I was amazed, and doubted it. "I'll bring you my children to see," said she, "it was to get them their dinners and tea that I always left you at times as I have." "And at night?"

"I always go home before he comes home." "You always go home to your husband?" "Yes."

How I loathed that man! — my loathing rose to my lips, "That miserable contemptible cur lives by your body, — a dirty vagabond." "No he's not, — poor fellow, he would earn our living if he could, but he can't." "I don't believe it, — a man who lives by a woman is barely a man, — I would empty cesspools to keep a woman I loved, rather than another man should stroke her, — no good can come of it, — he'll leave you for some other woman some day." Sarah turned nasty, said she was sorry she had told me so much, that all I said against him only made her like him the more; and so leaving me in sorrow she went away.

Now that I felt sure she was going away, I could not see too much of her; morning, noon, and night I had her. She brought her two children to me, and very proud she was of them. How it was I never noticed the marks of childbirth on her before I know not, but I never had. I spoke of that now. "I took good care you should not," she said smiling, and I recollected that when I had her by the side of the bed, when I looked at her on the sofa, it was nearly always with her back to the light; when laying on the bed, and I tried to gratify my passion by opening her thighs and gazing on her hidden charms, she nearly always half-turned towards the window, and her belly was in shadow. "I don't like to be pulled about, — I won't have it, — if you want me have me, and have done with it, — get another woman if you like who will do it, or allow it, — I won't." These and similar answers always settled me, and I submitted, for I was under her domination, and in my folly I had actually feared that if I persisted, she would not come to see me.

She brought her children in the morning to me at J***s Street, and I had her that afternoon. Now she was free enough, pointed herself to the marks of childbirth (very slight they were), and voluptuously held her cunt lips open, — she had never done so before. From that day and afterwards she allowed me to see her in every way or manner, if not to let me do what I wished. The mystery was over, I knew most if not all, — certainly all about her person.

CHAPTER XIV

Poses plastiques. — Sarah departs. — My despair. — Hannah's comfort. — Foolscap and masturbation. — Cheap cunt. — A mulatto. — The baudy house accounts. — Concerning Sarah. — The parlour. — The gay ladies there. — My virtue. — Louisa Fisher. — A show of legs. — The consequence on me. — Effect on Mrs. Z**i.

I dined with Sarah repeatedly until her departure. She was now often in low spirits, and drank very freely of champagne; then would fuck with a passion and energy which did not seem natural to her, for by look and general manner one would have sworn she was even tempered, and without much passion, — had I not found that out by experience? One night soon after she had brought her children to me, she seemed wild with lust. What was the matter with me I don't know, but I had no desire for her, and could scarcely stiffen for the embrace; yet she was in ecstasies with me as I fucked her. "Do it again," said she. "I can't." "You must do it, — I've not washed." "I can't." "Yes, — yes, — I'm mad for you," said she, — and we kept on fucking till early the next morning. "I am in the family way again I think," said she as she left, "and if so will jump over Westminster Bridge." But she was not, and after that night she persuaded me not to spend in her, but to withdraw just as my emission took place. "It will spoil all my plans if I am in the family way," said she, "all I have done will be of no use if I cannot act." "Act?" "Yes, I am an actress." "Does not your husband spend in you?" "No one has spent in me but you since my miscarriage, — I won't let him, and he doesn't want me in the family way."

"You an actress!" "Yes, — have you never see me?" "No." "Are you sure?" "Yes." "Did you ever see the *Poses plastiques* and Madame W***t*n?" "Yes, two or three years ago." "Well I was one of her troupe." "Good God! — and what do you do now?" "Nothing, — but we have a troupe going on the Continent, — I am the principal, — I am Madame W***t*n now."

Then she told me she had in her youth been a model for artists, had sat to Etty and Frost, hers was the form which had been painted in many of their pictures, — and then she would say no more.

I grew sadder and sadder as the time came for her departure; so did she. She said I worried and unsettled her; she wondered sometimes if she were doing the best thing for herself and children, or not. She was so frightened lest she should get in the family way that as already said she made me withdraw before the critical moment, spending my sperm on her thighs or on the crisp hair of her motte. I got an idea into my head (a stupid one enough), that if she were to get in the family way by me she would stay in London; and one night after we had dined, and she had had pleasure in my groping, and as usual had said, "Now don't do it in me," I plunged my prick up, and spent a full stream in her cunt. "I hope to God that sperm's all up your womb," said I. Her own pleasure had so overcome her that she could not move for a minute; then jumping up she washed herself with a sponge, — she recently had used one. I never had a spend in her again for months afterwards.

Then for hours I used to look her over and over from head to foot, as if I wished to recollect every part of her person for ever afterwards: the roots of her hair, her ears, the way the hair grew on the nape of her neck; the way it grew on her cunt, and in her armpits, and every other part I used to look over as if searching for something; the only part of her which escaped my investigations was the bum-furrow, which was to me an uncomfortable part in all women, and in my wildest sexual ecstasies and aberrations I neither felt it nor saw it, and don't know whether the hole was round or square, red or brown.

After she had told me she had sat as a model, she brought me a small oil-painting of herself made by an artist of some rank. She was proud of it, and so was her husband. I offered such a price for it that placed as she was she could not resist, and I bought it. She gave me one day a photograph of herself; both had the characteristic opening of the lips well shown. It is only recently that I have destroyed these mementos of a dead affection.

When I saw that nothing would keep her in England, I did my best to help her enterprise, gave her money freely, paid for dresses, boots, travelling cloaks, children's dresses, and in brief, for every-thing. During the nine months I had known her she in fact ran me dry, and in debt. I spent upon her more than I could have lived on for four years at the rate I lived at just before I met her. But I was now in better circumstances than I had been for years, and the money was my own.

As the time approached, I could neither sleep nor eat, and used to be at J***s Street hours before I knew she could come; would wait any time for her, treating Hannah and the ladies, and doing nothing but talk about Sarah. Sometimes I used to think about fol-lowing her abroad. When she came to the house, I used to spend my time in crying, and she after telling me not to be foolish, would cry too. Then, "Oh! let me see you naked." "There then." Then came kisses all over her body. "Oh! now for God's sake don't spend in me." Then came a delicious fuck; then crying and moaning recom-menced. She left a week at least before she had said she should, and did so to prevent me the pain of parting with her, — I must give her that credit. Hannah told me so.

I had arranged to meet her one morning, and was as usual there before my time. Hannah stepped out from the parlour. "Has Sarah come?" She beckoned me into the parlour. "Why, they all sailed this morning, — my sister went to see them off, — did you not know?" I staggered to the sofa dizzy, speechless, then senseless. When I came to myself, Hannah was standing beside me with brandy and water and a spoon with which she was putting it into my mouth.

"Don't take on so," said she, "don't think any more about Sarah, — she is a fine woman, but there are lots as good, — I know a dozen, and any one would be glad to know a man like you, — have some brandy and water," — and she took a great gulp herself. "There now," said she, bending over me, "would you like to see Mrs. ****, — she who met you the other night in here with Sarah, — she has taken quite a fancy to you, — don't cry. Sarah will come back, and if she don't you'll get another woman whom you will like as well. There is Mrs. ****, a splendid shaped woman who only sees one gentleman here, — she took quite a fancy to you, though she only saw you once." But I was desperate, and rushed out of the house. Where I went to, I don't even recollect, but went home at last very drunk, — an extraordinary occurrence for me.

For some days I was prostrate in mind, and almost in body, but at length recovered sufficiently to attend a little to my affairs which had gone altogether to the bad for a month, and had been going bad for many months. I resolutely set myself against going to J***s Street, and would not have women; indeed scarcely knew where to lay my hand on a shilling, so necessity had perhaps as much to do with my virtue as anything else; but I was generally in a weak, low state of health, and really believe, though it seems to me almost incredible now, that it was well nigh three weeks before I touched or saw a cunt after Sarah left.

Then one Sunday I had erections all day long. After dinner lust drove me nearly mad, so I went to my room, took a clean sheet of white paper, and frigged myself over it. My prick only slightly subsided, I frigged again, and then as the paper lay before me covered with sperm-pools I cried because it was not up my dear Sarah's vagina, laid my head on the table where the paper lay, and sobbed with despair, jealousy, and regrets, for I thought some one would fuck her if I did not, that it would be her hateful husband whom she had helped to keep with my money.

I may say here that on several occasions of my life I have frigged myself over a clean sheet of foolscap paper; it was mostly done for curiosity, to see what my sperm was like, whether it was as thin, or as thick, or as large in quantity as at the last time I previously had masturbated.

I could not after that Sunday keep away from J***s Street, and went there the next day. "I don't expect she'll write to you," said Hannah, "even if she said she would, — what will be the use? — it will only make you miserable." But I felt sure she would; and kept away from women still for some time after that, — I was stumped for money among other reasons. Then I began to spend involuntarily in the night, which to me was more hateful than frigging myself; so one night I went out for a bit of cheap quim. Whether I saw Brighton Bessie or not I can't say, but I think I did, and did later on.

I went first into the streets near a large well-known tavern at a spot where several big thoroughfares meet, and where there is a large traffic, and picked up my cheap women there. But the women,

their chemises and petticoats, and their rooms shocked me more
than they used, and kept me chaster than I otherwise might have
been.

One night I went home with a tall straight woman who would
not take my fee. "No," said she, "I've got two nice little rooms of
my own." If you get a woman for five shillings you have to pay
for the room besides, and ten shillings is only a small sum; so I
went with her for ten shillings, and saw her at intervals for a few
months.

She was about five feet nine high, was not stout, was as straight
as a lath, yet not thin, had very firm but quite small breasts, and
a biggish bum. She had mulatto blood in her veins she told me,
and was brown-skinned, had a large mouth and *very* thick lips, the
Negro blood showed there plainly; her hair was dark, and so were
her eyes; her cunt was a pouter: it was small, but the lips pouted
out more thickly I think than those of any woman I ever yet saw,
yet they were not flabby, but protruded largely like two halves
of a sausage; the hair was black, short, and intensely crisp and
curly; it felt like curled horse-hair. I used to think her a plain
woman, one of the plainest, but she was a glorious fuckster; her
cunt was tight inside, and yet so elastic as not to hurt or pinch
(and I was at that time when just at spunking point as often said
before tender-pricked). The hair of her head was coarse yet straight,
her large mouth was filled with teeth of a splendid whiteness, and
when she smiled she showed the whole set. It was seeing her large
white teeth that first attracted me before I could distinguish any
other feature of the face; you could see them at night right across
a road, they were dazzling, and almost made one forget the great
thick-lipped orifice which opened to expose them. I have before
told of women who attracted me by their teeth, and particularly of
a creole.

This *mulatto* as I called her, amused me with her lecherous
postures; she was as lithe as a willow branch, and was willing to
please. I was fond of making her kneel on the bed with bum towards
me, and her legs nearly close together, and then the backward pout
of her cunt was charming to me, so much so that I took to poking
her dog-fashion.

One night when I was full of sperm I made her remain in the
exact posture until all my spunk had run out of her cunt, and sat

holding a candle towards her rump till I was satisfied with the sight; and more than once I kept her in that position, looking at the gruelly lips until I fucked her a second time.

She had such a very remarkable steady walk that she scarcely seemed to move, she glided, her feet were so nicely carried forward, and her body so evenly balanced from her hips. In this respect she resembled a talk dark woman named Fletcher, whom I knew quite recently. There must have been something in the arrangement of their thighs and hips which caused this. Women who are accustomed to carry heavy loads on their heads always walk straight, and never roll from side to side as most people more or less do; but I don't know that either of the women named had carried baskets on their heads, — I knew the walk of that class of women, having been born in the neighbourhood where they worked.

She, I imagine, had a liking for my doing it naked with her, for she was always suggesting that we should strip, but she could not bear my fucking her dog-fashion. When I stripped and got into her on her belly, she would twist her legs right into mine in quite a snaky fashion, and sometimes lift her legs up till her heels were almost up to my blade-bones. She also, like a few others I have poked, seemed to have the power of holding my prick in her cunt quite tightly after I had spent, — perhaps because she had not spent herself, for about her pleasures in the copulation I am not sure, though she always impressed me as being a hot-cunted one.

After I had once been to J***'s Street again I went more and more frequently. Hannah was always nearly screwed, — champagne or brandy pleased her best. When she was so, she would at times gradually let out much that she knew, — and this is what she let out one day.

"Bah! her husband indeed! — she is not married, — he's got a wife besides, and Sarah knows it, — he's blackened his wife's eyes more than once when she has been annoying them; but that don't pay, for she is his lawful wife, so he allows her something, and it keeps her quiet, and she won't last long, for she is drunk from daybreak till night. Sarah's a real good one to keep the lazy beggar, — she keeps them all, poor thing, ever since he could not get any engagement; there's she, and their children, and her sister, who lives with them, and then there is her old mother who she keeps, and his wife as well, — she has enough to do, poor thing." This came out one day after Hannah had dined; I had brought her a bottle of specially fine brandy, and we were sitting in the parlour drinking it together, mixed with water.

I had long been getting into Hannah's good graces. I stood wine and brandy, was always respectful to her and the gay ladies I met in her parlour, and never used coarse, rude language to them, nor in speaking of them or of ladies of their class. Hannah told me I was a great favorite with several of them, as indeed I found to be the case. I may say that all my life I never spoke disrespectfully to or of gay ladies, so long as they behaved themselves; they have been mostly throughout my life, kind and true to me after their fashion, they gave me pleasure, and I treated them as if I was grateful for it.

But I was moreover serviceable to Hannah. Once or twice as told she had brought me some figures to cast up, and when Sarah had left, she brought me others on various little scraps of paper. She asked me never to mention my having done so to her sister, and I did not. I became curious at finding the items were all in five shillings, seven and sixpence, ten and twenty shillings; at last it struck me what it was, and taxing her with it found it was the takings of the baudy house. She told me so with a laugh. She could not write herself.

The takings were put on slips of paper by the servants, and by some process of her own which she could not explain, she got a rough sort of check on the servants to prevent them robbing her. She had to account to the real owner of the house, — and how she did it she alone knows. This is certain (she once admitted it), that from the takings she put a pound a day into her own pocket. Whether she robbed the owner to that extent, or whether it was her admitted share I never knew. She was well dressed, had excellent food, allowed her Guardsman money, her sister's husband money, and others too I rather think. But after she had taken her three or four hundred pounds a year, there was a splendid income handed over to some one. This house had but eight rooms and two mere closets, to let out for fucking; they often took twenty pounds a day, and sometimes much more.

I did this arithmetic pretty regularly, and she became my fast friend. She told me all about Sarah that she knew (what Sarah at a future day told me agreed with it), and much about the habits of other loose ladies which will be partially narrated in due time, and a good deal about baudy house management.

And now more about Sarah's antecedents. A new species of entertainment had sprung into existence a few years before this time, called *Poses plastiques*, in which men and women covered with silk fitting tightly to their naked limbs and made quite white, placed themselves on stages in classical groups to the sound of music. Women and men of great physical beauty formed these groups, they were in fact actors of that class. Madame W***t*n, known as a splendid model, first got them up; her husband was a splendid man, Sarah was her niece, and also had the beautiful form which ran in the family; she was poor, and Madame W***t*n took her to live with them, and at seventeen years of age she appeared as Venus.

At nineteen she had a child by Madame W***t*n's husband, at twenty a second. Madame found out the father, and kicked Sarah out. Mr. W***t*n then kicked Madame out, and went to live with Sarah, rows ensued, other companies of *Poses plastiques* came into competition, the thing got overdone, he could not get his living; he knew a trade, but was I expect too lazy to work at it; so Sarah took to letting herself out as model, and that being poor pay, to letting out her cunt to get their bread; she had just begun it when I first met her. They seem during a year or more to have parted with all their goods, before she took to showing her belly-parting for money.

So beautiful a form of course succeeded, and for a time I became the principal milk-cow. Then a proposition was made to form a troupe to go to the Continent; there seemed to be a grand opening, and with Sarah's money (most of it got from me), the apparatus, costumes, properties, and troupe were got together. Off they had gone. She and her husband were the exhibition-managers, speculators, and chief actors.

Hannah made a mouth when I asked what sort of a man Mavis was. She did not think much of him, — why did he not work? — he had a trade? — No, because he was no longer able to get on as an actor, he preferred to let Sarah get the living for the whole of them. "Ah! you'll see her back, mark my words, — they won't succeed, — and then what will take place? — you'll see, — is she, poor thing, to work and do everything, that he may lay a bed, dress as a gentleman, and do nothing but take her out for a walk on a Sunday; she is as proud of his taking her out for a walk on a Sunday as if he kept her a carriage." After much reflexion I came to the conclusion that Sarah had only just turned harlot about the time I had first met her, that she did it to keep her man and her family, and he got accustomed to his woman getting his living for him.

I kept on calling at J***s Street, always expecting to hear of Sarah. Hannah was glad to see me, for now I cast up her accounts weekly. I got acquainted with two or three ladies there who came at intervals to meet their friends. They were very nice women, none were ever to be seen in the streets, they had either their own acquaintances whom they met at J***s Street, or Hannah had introduced them to gentlemen there. They were not a bit like whores in dress, appearance or manners, and my acquaintance with them opened my mind to the fact that there is a large amount of occult fucking going on with needy, middle-class women, whose mode of living and dressing is a mystery to their friends, and who mingle with their own class of society without its being suspected that their cunts are ever wetted by sperm which lawfully may not be put there.

I began to stand wine when I met them, and was introduced as a friend of Miss Mavis who had gone abroad. I was, I found, well known by name and character for kindness, and I expect also for being a fool. All the women were shy at first, Hannah's sister (the servant), I overheard telling Hannah that the ladies did not like my being in the parlour. Hannah at times would ask me to leave, as a lady wanted to come into the parlour and wait there, and so on. But gradually Hannah would say, "Who is it? — oh! she knows him," — or "Oh! she won't mind, — let her come in." So by degrees I became intimate with these privately gay ladies, and several of them on more than one occasion joined their sweet bodies to mine in the game of under and over.

I had never had a woman in the house since Sarah had gone; firstly because I did then not pay more for the girls than I did for the room alone at J***s Street, and because I feared if Sarah came back Hannah would tell her, — as if it would have mattered to Sarah in any way excepting that another woman would get the money she might have had. Still I had that stupid idea about the matter, and although I had longed for one or two of the other ladies, and although they had looked languishingly at me, I never had then proposed a private interview upstairs.

One day Hannah said she had heard from Sarah who had asked after me. "They are (Sarah and the troupe) getting on well," said Hannah. "If she says so I suppose they are, — but we shall see." Suddenly, "Have you had another woman since she left?" The question startled me. "No." "Oh! I don't believe it, — if you haven't you're a nasty man." Then I confessed, and told her what I had done. "Why don't you have Mrs. Fisher?" said she. "I'm poor, and can't, — I'm not going to do what I did with Sarah." "Lord she won't mind, — she'd like you, I know, — but don't say I said so, — she's got a lovely leg, — she's a fine woman, — nearly as fine made as Sarah Mavis, and she is taller, — she never gets it done at home." Hannah was unusually muddled with liquor that day, and let out, — her sister was not there to check her with "Now then Hannah you'd better shut up," — and Hannah described Mrs. Fisher's hidden charms till my cock stood.

I would pass hours sketching from recollection Sarah Mavis' limbs and form, her bum and cunt being the most favorite subjects; then so randy that I did not know what to do with myself, I would rush out into the streets to prevent my frigging myself, — and erotic night-dreams were frequent.

"Why don't you see Mrs. Z**i," said Hannah to me, "she likes you, and would come up any day if I wrote to her (I had supped two or three times with that lady), — I would not fret about Sarah, although she is a fine woman, — you let her see you have another woman, and she will come round if she comes back." But I did not for a time.

One afternoon, however, being in the parlour, Mrs. Z**i was there, a splendid woman about twenty-six years old. Also was there a young woman who had two children by a man with whom she was about to go abroad, and she was a lovely woman. The two ladies had just had a two o'clock dinner with Hannah, I had just come from my Club after luncheon, and sent for champagne. All our talk got frisky, — all knew Sarah, my love. If I could get any one to talk with me about her, I was delighted, and began at it. Said the Mistress, "Well, she is a splendid-formed woman certainly,

— splendid, but there are lots of others, — I've a good leg to my knee, so has Mrs. Z**i, and Mrs. ***" (meaning the other whose name I forget). "Show us your leg," said one. "There," said Hannah, pulling up her clothes, "now show yours." They all showed their limbs, one after another. "You might fancy you had Sarah's legs round your thighs, if you had Mrs. Z**i's there," said Hannah. I was nigh bursting for a fuck. Mrs. Z**i pulled her clothes up higher, and stood up to show the leg better; the other ladies did the same. I felt my pleasure coming, and objecting to wet my shirt, began to unbutton. "Oh! I can't bear it," I cried, "oh! my God I'm coming," — and the instant my prick was free from my trowsers I spent copiously, the three women their petticoats still up nearly to their cunts, looking and laughing. I had not frigged, it was fullness, and the voluptuous delight at seeing the limbs of the three fine women which fetched me. "There is lots of stuff in him," said one. Ashamed of myself, I begged their pardons, and sent for more wine. "He had better have given one of you ladies that good spunk," said the Mistress. I overcame my bashfulness, they laughed about what Sarah Mavis had missed, one professed to feel annoyed at my behaviour. "Oh! you are damned modest," said Hannah.

Mrs. Z**i soon afterwards went upstairs into the bed-room to a gentleman she had come to meet, the Mistress said she should lay down, — she always did after her dinner, and slept for two hours, — she was fuddled, and indeed always was. The mother of the two children and I were alone; from the instant I had spent she had never taken her eyes off me, — never. I recollect the look of her dark eyes and their expression quite well. Hannah snored almost directly. "Let us have a kiss," said the lady to me, "I know you are fond of a well-formed woman," — and she pulled up her clothes a little. She was sitting on the sofa, my prick rose, I bolted the door, and we fucked whilst the Mistress kept snoring.

Mrs. Z**i came down. "What, you here still? — What have you been doing?" The mother replied, "He has been smoking, and talking about his dear Sarah." The woman was actually sitting at that very moment with a flood of my sperm up her cunt, for she had neither wiped, nor washed, nor pissed since I had fucked her. Then they talked about Z**i's friend who was a clergyman. Z**i was the wife of a man who lived with her, but never had her (so she said); she hated him, he had clapped her once.

The mother went out of the room, and came back, Hannah awoke, we had tea, I paid, it was my rule then to pay for everything for the ladies whenever I was in the baudy house parlour. I rose to go, shaking hands with the two ladies. The one whom I had embraced put a bit of paper privately into my hand. Outside the house I read it. "Wait outside," it said. I had been delighted with her pleasure, and did so. She came out, we walked quickly off. "You go to the top of the next street," said she, "and I'll meet you," — and she went another way, and met me at the top. "I did that in case Z**i came out," said she, "let us go and have dinner together." "I have not enough money," said I. "Never mind, I have." We went to the Café de P**v***e, and dined; I fucked her again and again on a sofa. She was a charming woman. As we sat on a little sofa dallying after dinner, she said she had not had it for a month, her friend had gone to Germany where they were going to live, to make arrangements, he would return in a few days; then he, she, and the children were going to Germany with him. "I liked you," said she, "but when I saw what you did before us this afternoon, I could scarcely stop myself, I wanted it so badly, — I dare say I'm in the family way, — oh! don't look, — it's full, — it's dirty, — you shan't." The next instant I was up her again; afterwards she washed, and I saw her cunt. I paid for the dinner partly, she the rest, — I had not a sixpence left. "I'm sorry," I said to her, "that I have no more money." "I did not come here for money," said she. "Let me leave you half a dozen pair of gloves at No. 11." "No, I've lots of gloves." "Then give me a kiss." She stood putting her tongue in my mouth for a minute, then giving me a hearty kiss off she went. I never saw her, nor had her again. Hannah told me she was in Germany, and very happy there.

CHAPTER XV

Louisa Fisher. — Chaffing. — Her form and fucking. — A supper in bed. — A lascivious night. — Meeting afterwards. — Hannah's legs. — Intruders in the bed-room. — Louisa's voluptuousness. — Enceinte. — Her husband. — Her gentleman friend. — About herself. — Illness. — Mrs. A***y.

I began to meet a Mrs. Fisher at the house very frequently; why she was more frequently there I did not know, and knew it was but of little use asking questions why.

I rather liked this lady. She came usually at one o'clock, and had dinner with Hannah. At three o'clock she went upstairs, was there about two hours, then came down and went away. At times she waited, had tea, and sometimes early supper; this was when she was expecting some one who did not come. I was told confidentially by Hannah it was a rich middle-aged clergyman. The lady's name was Mrs. Louisa Fisher, — her Christian name I have written truly, the surname not. I do this lest she be alive still, and should read somehow this result of my doings with her at J***s Street; she can't mistake if she reads these pages who it was.

After what Hannah had told me I could not help taking a great deal of notice of this lady, and began to lust for her, and of course took to talking to her about Sarah. She was nothing loth, and asked me curious, and at last downright indecent, questions about her, but not in smutty language. Hannah when there used to laugh at the questions and my replies; they made my cock stand, which perhaps was what Louisa intended, or it may only have been curiosity without any hidden intention.

I imagine that the erotic incident in the parlour had been told to a good many gay ladies; it certainly had to Louisa Fisher, for one night after that I had been to enquire if Hannah had heard again from Sarah, and Hannah had mentioned Louisa, the following occurred. I had dined early, it was about half-past six, Louisa Fisher was there. "Stand us a glass of wine," said she. "Do," said Hannah. "Do," said another lady. "Have you had dinner, Miss Fisher?" said I. "No, my friend's not been, — I'm hungry, and Hannah is just going to cook me a chop." I myself fetched a bottle of sherry, the chop came, Louisa eat it, and drank sherry; then I sent for brandy, we drank it mixed with water, and Hannah took some neat. I began about Sarah as I always did. "Well, she was a beautiful model," said Hannah, "but Mrs. Z**i's leg was better to my mind." "Look how he's blushing," said Louisa. "Why should I blush?" They both laughed. "Oh! oh! oh! don't I know what you did when you saw her legs." I was then that odd mixture of baudiness and modesty, that I was just as likely to be bold as to be shamefaced, when a woman spoke to me about anything carnal; and now was confused and half-ashamed. "Lord how he's blushing," said Hannah, and she left the room to look after business, she usually put her head out when the street-door opened if a servant was not in the way on the ground-floor.

Louisa laughed. "I know all about it," said she, "she was a fine woman." After I had got over the stupid bashfulness which I had for the moment, I went (as usual with me) to the extreme of baudy boldness. "Yes," said I laughing, "I wish it had been spilt in her cunt instead of on the carpet." "Oh! for shame," said Louisa. "Well it was waste, was it not, — it might have made two people happy, — did you really spend without frigging it?" "Yes I did."

I got close to Louisa on the sofa to speak with her about the event, to hear from her lips what had been told her. She said not a word, but my face was close to hers, we looked into each other's eyes for a minute, lust was on both. I put my arm round her, pulled her towards me, and kissed her. She returned it, our lips were glued together. "You've got a fine leg, Hannah says." "Does she?" "Yes, — let me see it." "No." "Yes." "You only care about Sarah." I made no reply, but went on kissing lecherously, put one hand down, and going on kissing pulled her clothes up to her knees. She stopped me there. "Oh! how round, how nice, how lovely your leg is." "Now be quiet, Hannah will be in." I ceased looking, but my hand slipped higher up, my fingers were inside the satiny wet lips, and my mouth was glued to hers, as Hannah came back.

We resumed a decent posture, Hannah laughed. "Lord why don't you two go upstairs?" said she, "you want each other, — why don't you go? — the first-floor front's empty." "Come," said I to Louisa, pulling her. She rose instantly. Hannah was a really good soul, she liked to make people happy, and to set them fucking; I have seen it in a dozen instances.

Without another word we went upstairs, I threw her on the bedside, pulled up her clothes, and opened a magnificent pair of thighs. "Let's go to bed," said she. "Very well." We both undressed like lightning without a word passing, and stood, she in chemise, I in shirt, in a trice. "Let's get in naked." Without reply she drew off her chemise as I pulled off my shirt, and the next minute naked in each other's arms we were fucking in a warm bed, not a word of conversation passing till we had spent, those moments are so soul-absorbing in their lasciviousness.

"Oh! how quick we've been, — lay still." With mutual consent we kept together in fleshy conjunction, I nestled my balls up her, she tightened her cunt to stimulate my shrinking organ. But little stimulus was needed, our spend had only made us want it again, we had scarcely rested ere we recommenced fucking, and again we spent before my prick had uncunted. How lovely, how exquisite is the reminiscence! what equals the pleasure of a man and woman pleased with each other, thrilling with lust, when prick and cunt are joined, and they spend in each other's arms!

Still she would not let me out of her, crossing her limbs over my thighs, drawing me closer to her by her hands, grasping my arse-cheeks, pulling the cheeks almost open, squeezing her cunt up to me, she kept me up her, kissing me, shoving her tongue towards mine, and saying I was a lovely poke, the first baudy words that dropped from her, I rubbing my belly up against hers till my balls almost lay between her fat cunt-lips, swabbing up the oozings of the sperm which ran out from her. And so we lay, kissing, tongue-sucking, and talking the stinging words of love and lust.

Then as repose became a pleasure, and nature severed us, "Oh! my God how wet you have made me," she said, "it's all on the sheet." "Let me feel." I felt on my side, she turned on hers towards me, and threw one leg over my haunch, I placed my hand on her cunt, and felt the sperm wetting my hand, whilst she grasped my slippery prick. "Feel how wet your prick is." I put my hand there, and every hair on my prick was plastered against my belly; then hand on cunt, and hand on prick we both dozed off.

When I awakened we were still face to face, Louisa asleep with a hand under my balls. I pulled down the clothes to look at her naked body, the gas was burning brightly, I saw splendid breasts; down went my hand to her cunt, I groped it, she awoke, and without a word turned on to her back, and I on to her belly. Whilst couched easily on to that broad belly, and lying between her ample breasts, and steadied by her large thighs, my prick lying down against her gap, kissing and sucking each other's mouths, she glided her hand down, and introduced my pendulous doodle to her randy cunt, and again we fucked. We were mad for it, neither of us uttered a word, till she cried out, "Oh! I'm coming, — my God, — ah!" And then we spent, and went fast asleep again, exhausted with the pleasure.

We were awakened by a knock. "Who's there?" "Hannah." "What do you want?" "Are you going to stop all night?" "No," said I jumping out of bed, "what o'clock is it?" "It's half-past twelve." "Come to bed," said Louisa. In I jumped. "Oh! I'm so hungry," said she, "how I should like some oysters." "So should I, — get up, and we'll go and have some before the shop closes." "No, stop here, Hannah will get them." I agreed, ordered them, and we went on twiddling each other's privates. I recollect the feel of hers at this very moment, — it was like a paste-pot.

I had never seen her person yet. The throwing her on to the bed and lifting her clothes, her stripping and jumping into bed had been so rapid, and so randy had both of us been, so anxious to copulate, that I had had no time to look, to contemplate, to enjoy her with my eyesight. Now off went the bed clothes. "Let's look at your cunt." "I won't till I've washed." "No, now." I pulled one thigh. "No you dirty dog, — it's not nice." She jumped out of bed, and washed her quim, I my prick, we pissed, and then she threw herself on the bed, and delivered her body up to me. When I had had a quarter of an hour's investigation, she amused herself with looking and pulling my prick about, waiting for our supper.

She was a very fine tall woman, stout, and well-built. She said she was twenty-four, but I believe she was thirty. She looked less stout with her clothes on than when she was undressed, for I was much surprized to see how very big she was when naked. She had a very big arm, her thighs and legs were very big as well. Hannah was right about it, the entire legs were grand, but had not the exquisite curves of Sarah Mavis'. Her bum was proportionate to her thighs, her waist was not nearly small enough, her breasts were very large, and beautifully placed, and beautifully solid; her face was large and common place, she had grey eyes, and lightish auburn hair — immense in quantity — which completes the description of her head, which was pleasing though not handsome; it was not a face which in the streets would have attracted me. Her teeth were good.

The hair on her cunt, which was thick-lipped and pouting, was also of a lightish auburn, not by any means a colour to my taste when between the thighs, — so many women's cunts are furnished with that colour. It was thick, longish, soft in feel, large in quantity, and spread half-way up to her navel, and square across her belly to the line of her thighs. I guessed it a thirty year old cunt from that. She was a lovely fucker, and though her cunt was a large one inside and out, the prick was well clipped by it, and kept in when its business was done. There was such room to lie on her between her thighs, and all seemed so well placed to hold a man, that I often thought of her in after time when fucking Sarah, who was the very reverse, who always made me bend my back when fucking, and from whose quim my prick would always slip, unless we both made some effort to retain it after I had spent. She rarely did that, hating the muck. Indeed, when Sarah was randy, and wagged her arse as she did violently all of a sudden just before she spent, she often threw my stiff prick out, which set me off damning and cursing till it was up her again.

The oysters came, and champagne with them, we went to bed again, and sat in chemise and shirt to eat them. Said I, "Let's have another fuck naked again," for the touch of her large fleshy body to mine had entranced me, and thus we fucked. Another doze. "Ulloh! why it's three o'clock, — I must be off." "Don't go dear, — stop all night." "I can't, — they will think I am ill." "So they will me, but I can't go home, I live too far off, — do stop all night with me, there's a darling," said she.

Instead of a doze, we had slept two hours. I at times stopped out all night, and never without saying I intended to do so, but I was tired and sleepy. "Oh! don't go." I put on my shirt. "Well let's have another poke before you go, — the champagne has made me so randy." It had also operated on me. I looked, there were her breasts naked just peeping above the bed-clothes, one arm out, the hand under her head, the big white fleshy arm, and the thick sandy brown hair in the armpits. "Come," said she, uncovering to her knees. Off went my shirt, and jumping into bed the thighs received me, the voluptuous tongue and round, soft, wet lips glued themselves on to mine again, and heaving gently we were already on the way to another spend. My God what work, what prolonged pleasure! — I forgot Sarah Mavis, and every other woman that night, in the arms of Louisa. In baudy amusement we passed the whole night together, and I awakened at ten the next morning with the need of going as fast as I could to shit.

I came back, washed, and we fucked again; then she went as she said to speak to Hannah, whom I knew was a bed at that time; she went I knew to empty herself, but I asked no questions. We had ham and coffee in bed, and more fucking, and about one o'clock we rose and left. My finger must have smelt of cunt I should think for twenty-four hours afterwards, for I had scarcely left Louisa's cunt for eighteen hours; if my prick was not up her my fingers were, when not asleep. Whether spunk was in it or not was all the same, there was no objecting, she gave way to my insistence, and we lay, at intervals, she feeling my prick, one of her legs placed over mine, and my hand between her thighs, both of us kissing, tongue-sucking, and scarcely talking. I barely recollect our talk at all, — it was one long baudy night; how many times we fucked I can't say, but it was one of my great exercises. She was tired, and so was I, yet at the last moment, "Let's try it again," I said. "No, I'm sore, and in pain," said she. I sometimes think my prick must have been nearly a dozen times up her, and when ramming stiff for a long time without spending she murmured, "Oh! pray dear, leave off."

We fucked in no other fashion than belly to belly, we were naked the whole night, and did nothing outside the bed. When I had paid for the room, supper and breakfast, I only had a few shillings left. I told her. "Never mind," said she, "you shall give me some money some day when I am hard up." So I paid her nothing then.

I recollect all this distinctly, I always do the incidents of a first night with a female. When I am accustomed to them, the more striking circumstances of our acquaintance remain in my memory. It seems to me that first night's incidents will always remain fresh in my recollection, excepting the number of fucks; I recollect up to about half-a-dozen, then I lose count, there my memory of a first night alone fails me.

I took a liking for Louisa. For nearly a year I had borne with the frigidity of Sarah and her tyranny, "You shall only do it once, — I won't, — I can't wait, — well go," were commands I had got accustomed to obey, had bowed to refusals to allow her secret charms to be looked at time after time, to have my prick ejected before the last injecting throb had been given. I liked the woman, doted on her exquisite form, liked the domesticity of sitting and reading to her, and at the same time just feeling her cunt whilst she laid on the sofa. Because I liked her conversation, and because I was at times rewarded by rapturous delight when she abandoned herself body and soul to me, I submitted to all this. But I often rebelled, wished it was otherwise, and made up my mind to leave her for other women, yet did not. I have said all this before.

Now to have a splendidly made woman, who had as much pleasure with me as I had with her, was overwhelming. I forgot Sarah for a time, and longed for the repetition of the baudy, voluptuous hours I had had with the big-armed, big-thighed Louisa, and counted the days till we met again. The instant I set eyes upon her we went upstairs. "Let's get into bed." Then it was a race who undressed the first. "Naked?" "Yes, naked." She laughed. "Look at your thing," said she, as sitting down she pissed. I was stiff as a poker; the next minute I was laying bedded on that soft fleshy form, and we were spending. What a fat, luscious, and grand cunt she had, though three fingers went up it easily.

Then to my delight she threw up her limbs a little, and crossing them over me pressed her cunt close up to my willing cockroots; and there we lay, my prick in her, my balls covering her arsehole; whilst now and then she gripped my prick by muscular cuntal action. When her tongue touched mine, she sometimes ran her lithsome tongue over my teeth, or under my lips, and along my gums, — it was a peculiarity of hers. Then she would glue her wet lips to my wet lips, till our salivas mingled and ran profusely, stimulating our lusts. Thus we enjoyed each other's bodies, till another fuck dissolved us, and separated our spunk-soaked genitals; and she got up, washed, and went away oftentimes in a great hurry.

Soon I grumbled at her going so, and she promised to stop a longer time. "Have a shoulder of mutton," said she, "and onion sauce, — I love it, — Hannah will cook it beautifully, — we will dine at two o'clock, Hannah with us." So it came about; we three sat down to a shoulder. Louisa liked sherry, Hannah brandy; I brought both of fine quality, we gorged, Hannah got slightly tight, observing Louisa and I caressing. "Ah!" said she, "I envy you, you two going to bed." "Why, where is Jack?" "Oh! at Windsor, and I shan't have a bit for a month at least." "You'll have to frig yourself," said I, joking. "That's better than nothing, but I like the wetting best." Louisa laughed, and used afterwards to say to Hannah, "Has Jack given you a wetting?" Later on some other free ladies took up the joke, and Hannah's "wetting" became a bye-word among the circle of free, mercenary lovers.

Dinner over, we hurried upstairs, and we went naked to bed. This was about half-past three; there we lay till eleven o'clock at night, and had an oyster supper in bed. Hannah came up, and eat oysters with us whilst we were in bed together. We eat them out of the shells, and drank champagne, heard happy couples over head, and joked about it, talked about fine limbs, about Sarah's fine legs. "Show us yours, Hannah," said Louisa. Hannah without a word cocked one leg up against the bed, and drew up her petticoats to the top of one thigh. "There," said she, "I am not ashamed of it." She had a fine leg, but was a very plain woman. She had shown her leg to me on the day of the leg-show, when I had spent un-voluntarily, as I have already told. We laughed and praised her leg. "Oh! I'm ashamed of you both," said Hannah, dropping her petticoats, laughing, and hurrying out of the room, "I know where his fingers are." She was right, Louisa was sitting up in bed, her legs half up, but covered, I half reclining by the side of her, had thrust my hand under the thighs, and was feeling her cunt.

Hannah left the room. We began fucking, I was on the top operating when the door opened, and a couple showed themselves. We heard a voice crying out, "Not there Ma'am, it's occupied," and Hannah's sister rushing in ejected a man and woman who had entered before they saw a couple were in the bed. We were too far advanced to mind. I uncunted with the object of closing the door, but the servants having done so, we consummated and dozed off; nor was it till the servant came to say we ought to be careful that I got up and bolted the door.

Then began a regular meeting once a week, and sometimes twice. Money seemed no object to Louisa, she took what I gave, and never asked for more; once or twice she said, "I want a bonnet dear, — give me one," — or a new pair of boots, or was hard up for a trifle, and then I gave her all I could; but she had not in a couple of months as much as Sarah had from me in three days, at the last period of my acquaintance with her. But she let me spend money in oyster and champagne suppers, and early dinners there, and encouraged me to let other ladies partake. At last I think that after our early dinners, Guardsman Jack who had come back from Windsor used often to get his fill. I once saw Jack in bed with Hannah, and his scarlet uniform on the chair; he turned himself round with his face to the wall when I entered. He had a thick head of black hair, which is all I saw.

Louisa was a voluptuous poke, and enjoyed the fun as much as a woman could. I think (but recollection on that point is not clear, when I come to comparison), that she was the nicest woman to lay on I ever had. I was slim, though far from a skeleton, and as I laid naked on her between her large breasts, and between her thighs slightly elevated (for she usually raised her legs after we had fucked and she had recovered from her pleasure, or when I mounted her for preliminary dalliance), I could scarcely roll off of her without an effort. She had also when her pleasure was increasing, a movement of her whole body, and not of her cunt and backside alone; her breasts quivered with a gentle, perfectly natural motion, and I could feel her flesh moving and rubbing against mine from belly to neck in a way which stirred lust in me from the hair of my head to the soles of my feet; I seemed to feel all over her body at once, and it was most delicious. She had a lovely lasciviousness with her tongue. If my tongue was in her mouth when she spent, she almost sucked it out of me, and the clipping of her cunt after my prick had been relieved from its stiffness I have already mentioned. Her length of arm enabled her to squeeze my balls when in various positions, and no woman ever let me pull her about and look at her cunt, whether it was clean or spunky, more freely than she did. With many it is evidently business, with her it seemed pleasure. She took a delight in all I did, even when I washed her cunt.

[My pleasures, however, with her were of a simple kind. I had none of the varied erotic pleasures that I now know, the bum-hole and mouth were reserved for the enjoyment of my more matured years.]

I should have seen her more frequently, but she would only come at the outside twice a week. No it was impossible, — she lived too far off. I tried to get out of Hannah some knowledge about her, but could not. One day only when fuddled she asked if I had heard she was married. "You mean," said I, "living with a man." "No, really married, and been so for years, — oh! don't you tell her, — she'll cut the house if you do."

At the end of perhaps three months I was in bed with her; we had poked, reposed, and were in amorous dalliance, lying face to face, she with one limb over my haunch, so that I could feel her cunt well, she twiddling my somewhat exhausted prick. "I have a surprize for you," she said. "For me, — what?" "I'm in the family way." "The devil, — whose fault is that?" "No one's fault, and perhaps no misfortune, — would you like a child?" "I? — why?" (I had a presentiment of what was coming.) "Because it is yours." "Nonsense." "It is, my dear, — I have felt certain of it for some time past, but waited to be quite sure before telling you." "Are you quite sure?" "As certain as I am that I shall die."

I was flabbergasted, felt distressed, as if I had done her some harm that I could not repair, that I had injured her, and should cause her pain and annoyance. It was succeeded by a fear that I should have trouble through it, and expense that I could not afford. Then came the idea that she was selling me, putting a plant on me; that if she were with child it was another man's, not mine. Then came a belief over me that what she said was true, that her pleasure in my embraces was so real, so unlike that of the ordinary gay women, that the result might be due to me. Overwhelmed, I laid quiet, confused with the tumultuous thoughts and feelings which rushed through my brain.

At length I said, "Are you sure?" "Yes." "It may be your husband's" (for Hannah's hints came to my mind). "He! — he! — the miserable, contemptible little wretch! — he?" she left off feeling my cock, raised herself on her elbow, and looking at me said, "Who told you I was married?" "No one." "Some one has." "No one, — but I have more than once fancied you were married by the difficulty I have in getting you to come to meet me when I want." "Some one has told you." "No one has." "I'm a damned fool," said she, "I dare say you know more than you say, — what do you know?" "Nothing." "It's your child, and no one else's, — I'm sorry I have told you, — say nothing more about it," — and she turned on her back. "Are you married?" "Of course not, or I should not be in bed with you." "Some man is keeping you perhaps." "No one is keeping me either," said she.

I could not keep quiet, so much was I excited, and thought of the man she met at J***'s Street still, although she tried to hide that. I did not like to suggest it, for I had found out that any reference to him annoyed her, and I always avoided giving pain to any woman I had connection with; but the matter seemed so grave that I could not keep what was on my mind to myself, and as delicately as I could suggested him.

"It's not," said she fiercely, "it can't be." "Why?" "You are the only man who has spent in me for years." "What," said I incredulously, "no one had you?" "No one has spent in me but you, for years, — no one." I was staggered, but returned to the subject. "Nonsense, Louisa, — how can you tell?" "I've told you why." "Why, if you've a husband, and if you have a friend who meets you, how can you be sure it's me?"

"I have no husband, and it's no friend, — if you don't believe it, I tell you on my oath, on my body and soul, and may I go to hell when I die if it be not true, that no man has spent in me for years but you." "No man has fucked you! — what do they do then?" "That's no concern of yours, — but no man's stuff has ever been up me for quite two years but yours, — I'm not going to say any more about it, — my business is not yours, — nobody has asked you to keep the child, — you need not trouble yourself, — I'm sorry I told you." She turned her bum to me, and began to cry; I tried to comfort her.

"That will do," said she, "give me some oysters and champagne." I ordered them, then wanted another fuck. "No you shan't have it," — nor would she let me. The oysters and champagne made her more complaisant, but she was angry and snappish. After another fuck she got up and left me before her usual time, and I went away wondering at this, and at the number of women who had been, or who said they had been, with child by me.

Soon after she was loving, sad, and serious, was sorry I would not have liked the child, for it was certainly mine, but she would get rid of it. Then in the familiarity of a lewed man and woman naked in bed together, she told me a lot about herself.

She *was* married, she lived with him and her mother, but loathed her husband. "He, — he the miserable wretch, — he touch *me* the dirty beast! — I'd sooner die than let him," she cried, "if he wanted even, — but he does not want *me*. — What he wants he gets elsewhere, not with *me*," said she with strong emphasis. If she left him, she would have to support her mother alone, — perhaps it would come to that some day, — she was quite prepared for it. They ate and drank together when he was at home, but had not slept together for years. He kept the house comfortably enough, — perhaps he would so long as she took trouble about it; for he did not care so long as he got his food good. Yes, she did meet a friend. It got her luxuries she could not get any other way; her husband knew she got money elsewhere, for she dressed in a way he must know his money would not enable her to do. He asked no questions, and did not care nor heed, nor seem to notice. That was pretty well all I ever got out of her. Hannah drunk and talking to me one day, said he was a very little man, and a brewer's clerk, "a hop o' my thumb," she called him.

"Never mind what my friend does," said Louisa, "I've known him some years, — he does something of course, he does not meet me for nothing, but I tell you he has never spent in me, — no man has spent in me for years but you." "Do you frig your friend?" "If you like, anything else you like, it's all the same, — I'm not going to say; but neither he nor any one else has spent in me, — no man's seed has been up me for two years or more. The first night you had me I spent first, you spent after; the next time as your seed touched me, I felt a shiver run right through me, and I got in the family way at that very instant, I'm sure." Louisa was particular in her language, she never said "spunk," — thought it a nasty word, — she always said "seed" or "stuff" when she spoke of my sperm, — Sarah called it "muck."

Though I had had such lots of women, and had heard of most things, yet simple, straightforward fucking had engrossed me, I rarely had out-of-the-way lusts and letches, and I never thought to ask if her friend buggered or sucked her, or if she sucked him, or what little amusements they were up to. At all events she must have satisfied him some way, for he had known her, she said, some years. A man was likely to stick to Louisa, for she was a magnificent piece of flesh, from her neck to her ankles.

So I believed Louisa, and felt interest in her belly beginning to swell, but did not want the young one, or the troubles of paternity, or to get her into trouble; besides I had no affection for her, though I liked fucking her better and better.

Louisa then was away ill; I saw her again when her womb was cleared out, and we took to fucking as usual. One day in baudy vagaries we had been posturing, and she straddled across my face, bringing her cunt right on to my mouth, and my nose to her bum, she had been asking me if I ever kissed Sarah in any way but the straight one. She began kissing my pego as she lay on the top of me, I kissed her buttocks, but took no hint, if any were intended. She was very heavy, and I noticed for the first time a strongish odour from her cunt which annoyed me; afterwards I used often to fancy she had a strong smell about her quim, and was fool enough to tell her so, which offended her; but we made it up.

After a little time she began asking me if I had not forgotten Sarah, — did I love her as much? — did I long to have her again? — did she (Louisa) not give as much pleasure as Sarah? I had then got over my desolation a little, and only thought of Sarah and her exquisite form with a sigh, was annoyed that she had not written to me, and I began to confess to myself that for fucking, Sarah was not to be compared with Louisa. Then I began to wonder at my having been so infatuated, and let it out to Louisa one night. She said she wished I would keep *her*, — three pounds a week, and she would make it do, and so on; and I began to think seriously about the matter, for the expenses at the baudy house were nearly that amount; and although my delicate senses had begun to revolt at the strong smell of Louisa, yet her voluptuousness was enticing, and was making me actually constant to her. I had quite left off my mulatto, Brighton Bessie, and one or two other of my queens.

Louisa was again taken ill, — the consequence of her miscarriage, and of the measures taken to bring that on, I was told. She got worse and worse, and was in great danger; she never wrote to me, but often to Hannah, and her letters which I saw always referred to me affectionately; above all she wanted to know what ladies I had at J***s Street. Hannah winking at me used to say, "I'd like to know where you put it away now, — it's put somewhere." I had taken no women to that house; but laughing said I was chaste. Hannah did not believe that, so I said I frigged myself. "You don't spill it about in that way," said she, "let me feel it," — and she put her hand outside my clothes on to my tool. "Oho! — oho! — oho!" said she, for I stiffened. Then she brought me her accounts to cast up, and when it was done, "I shall take a nap," said she, "you go now, for I expect Mrs. *** and a strange lady" (I had looked in casually that morning), — and getting on to the bed she laid down showing her legs liberally, and looking at me all the time. "Good bye," I said, and left; but have thought since that Hannah wanted me to have her. She never before or since looked at me in that way, nor behaved with such freedom when we were alone.

Her bed was, as I have I think already told, in the front-parlour in J***s Street, and in an alcove, as many beds are in French hotels and houses; and when the curtains were drawn across it, the bed was entirely hidden.

And then when without a woman at my command, and with a frequent need for one, another piece of luck befell me. The way had been paved for it before Louisa was so ill.

CHAPTER XVI

A friend's maid-servant. — Jenny. — Initial familiarity. — A bum pinched. — Jenny communicative. — Her young man. — An attempt, a failure, a faint, a look, and a sniff. — Restoratives.

I knew an elderly couple who were childless and lived in a nice little house in the suburbs with a long garden in front, and one at the back as well; they were in comfortable but moderate circumstances, and kept two servants only. Every year they went to the seaside, taking one servant with them, and leaving the other at home to look after the house; and usually some one to take charge of it with her. This year they asked if I would, when I passed the house (as I frequently did), call in and see if all was going properly, for the housemaid left in charge was young, and her sister, a married woman, usually only stopped the night with her, leaving early each morning for work in which she was daily engaged. She was an upholstress.

I knew the servant whose name was Jane. She had been with the family some months. I often dined at the house; and once or twice when she had opened the garden-gate (always locked at nightfall) to let me out, I had kissed her, and tipped her shillings. She was a shortish, fat-bummed wench. Not long before this time I gave her bum such a hard pinch one night, that she cried out. A day or two afterwards I said, "Was it not black and blue?" "I don't know." "Let me see." "It's like your imperance," she replied.

After that I used to ask her when I got the chance, to let me see if the finger-marks were there, at which she would blush a little, and turn away her head, but nothing further had come of the liberty.

When I called at the house I had no intention about the girl, as far as I can recollect. She opened the door, and heard my errand and questions. Yes all was right. Did her sister come and sleep there? Yes. Was she there now? No, she would not be there till nearly dark. I stepped inside, for then I thought of larking with her. "I am tired, and will rest a little," and stepped into the parlour, sat down on a sofa, began questioning her about a lot of trifles, and in doing so thought of the pinch I had given her bum, and my cock began to tingle. Then I thought she was alone in the house. Oh! if she would let me fuck her! — has she been broached? — she is nice and plump. Curiosity increased my lust, and unpremeditatingly I began the approaches for the attack, though I only meant a little amatory chaffing.

"Is it black and blue yet, Jenny?" She did not for the instant seem to recollect, for she asked me innocently enough, "What sir?" "Your bum where I pinched it." She laughed, checked herself, coloured up, and said, "Oh! don't begin that nonsense sir." I went on chaffing. "How I should like to have pinched it under your clothes, — but no I would sooner kiss it than pinch it." "Oh! if you're agoing on like that I'll go to the kitchen." I stood before the door, and stopped her going out. "Now give me a kiss." I caught and kissed her, then gave a lot, and got a return from her. "I won't, — Lor there then, — what a one you are," — and so on. "Well, Jane one kiss, and you may afterwards kiss whenever you want, you know." And so she seemed to think, for I got her to sit down on the sofa, and we gossiped and kissed at intervals, till my cock got unruly. "What a fat bum you have," said I. Then she attempted to rise, I pulled her back, we went on gossiping, and kissing at intervals. She got quite interested in my talk as I sat with one arm round her waist, and another on her thigh, outside her clothes of course.

So for a while; but I was approaching another stage, was getting randy, and reckless. "Lord how I'd like to be in bed with you, to feel that fat bum of yours, to feel your c — u — n — t," spelling it, "to f — u — c — k it I'd give a five-pound note," said I all in a burst, and stooping, got my hand up her clothes on to her thigh. She gave a howl. "Oh! I say now, — what a shame! — oh! you beast." I shoved her back on the sofa upsetting her, got my lips on her thighs, and kissed them. Then she escaped me, and breathing hard, stood up looking at me after her struggle. "Oh! I wouldn't

have believed it," said she panting with the exertion. What a lot of
women I have heard say they would not have believed it, when I
first made a snatch at their privates. I suppose they say what they
mean.

Begging her pardon, "I could not help it," I said, "you are
so pretty and nice, — I'd give ten pounds to be in bed with you an
hour." "Well I'm sure." "Think what it is not to have a woman you
like." "Well I'm sure sir, you are a married man, — you've got a
partner, and ought to know better, — missus would not have asked
you to call if she'd a know'd you, — she thinks there's no gent like
you, — what would she say if I tell her?" "But you won't my dear."
"She thinks you a perfect gentleman, and most unlucky," the girl
went on to say, "and she is sorry for you too."

"Oh! she does not know all, but you've heard, have you Jenny?"
I tried to make her sit on the sofa again, and promising that I
would not forget myself any more, she did so. We kissed and made
it up, and talking I soon relapsed into baudiness.

The quarrelsome life I led with the oldish woman at home was,
I knew, well understood by the old couple. "I lead a miserable life,"
said I. "Oh! yes I know all about it," said the girl, "master and
missus often talk about you, — but you're very gay, ain't you?" Then
I told this girl a lot. "Think my dear what it is not even to sleep
with a woman for two months, — for two months we have never
slept together, — I've never seen her undressed, — never touched
her flesh, — you know what people marry for, — I want a woman,
— you know what I mean don't you, — every night what am I to
do? — I love laying belly to belly naked with a nice woman, and
taking my pleasure with her, — so of course I can't keep from having other women at times, — you don't know what an awful thing
it is to have a stiff prick, and not a nice woman to relieve it." She
gave me a push, got up, and made for the door at the word prick.
Again I stopped her. She had sat staring at me with her mouth
wide open, without saying a word, all the time I had been telling
the baudy narrative of domestic trouble, as if she were quite stupe-
fied by my plain language, until she suddenly jumped up, and made
for the door without saying a word.

I was as quick as she, caught her, put my back against the
door, and would not let her go, but could not get her to look me
in the face, I had so upset her. There we stood, I begging her to

sit down, and promising not to talk so again, she saying, "Now let me go, — let me out." "No, — sit down." "No." But in about a quarter of an hour she did, and then again I told her of my trouble, avoided all straightforward allusion to my wanting other women, but hinted at it enough. She got interested, and asked me no end of questions. "Lord, why don't you separate? — if I quarrel with my husband so, I'm sure I will, — I tell my young man so." "Oh! you have a sweetheart." Yes she had, — a grocer's shopman, — he lived at Brighton, came up third class to see her every fortnight, starting early, and going back late. She was flattered by my enquiries, told me all about him and herself, their intention to get married in a year; and I sat and listened with one hand outside her clothes on her thigh, and thinking how I could best manage to get into her.

"He goes with women," said I, to make her jealous. "He don't I'm sure, — if he did, and I found it out, I'd tear his eyes out, and break off with him, though he says Brighton is a dreadful place for them hussies." She got quite excited at the idea. "When he comes up, you and he enjoy yourselves, — his hands have been where mine have to-night." "No he hasn't, — if he dared I'd — now I don't like this talk, — you said you wouldn't, — leave me alone, — you keep breaking your word." Another little scuffle, a kiss, and a promise. "Why should you not enjoy yourselves? — who would know anything about it but yourselves, — it's so delicious to feel yourselves naked in each other's arms, your bellies close together." "Get away now," — and she tried to get up. I got my hand up her clothes, pulled her on to the sofa, and holding her down with one hand, pressed myself sideways on her, and kissed her, pulling out my prick with the other.

Then she cried out so loudly that I was alarmed, for the window at the back was open. "Hush, — be quiet, — there, — I've touched your cunt." I pulled one of her hands on to my prick. "Oh! for shame Jane you touched my prick." Again she got up, and made for the door; so did I, and stood there with my back to it, and my poker out in front of me. "Come and open the door my dear, and you will run against this." She turned her head away, and would not look. "Why don't you come on? — if you run up against it, it won't hurt you, — it's soft though it's stiff." "I'll write to my mistress tonight," said she, and turned away. "Do my pet, — tell her how stiff it was, and the old lady will want to see it when she comes back." "It's disgraceful." "No, my dear, it's to be proud of, — why you're looking at it, I can see."

Then she turned quite away. "That's right dear, — now I can see where I pinched your bum, — it was not far from your little quim, — oh! if that could talk, it would ask to be introduced to this, — it's hot, isn't it Jenny?" I said, this and a lot more. She had walked to the back window, and stood looking into the garden whilst I rattled on. "You're laughing Jenny." "It's a story," said she, "I'm insulted," — and turned round with a stern face. I shook my tooley-wagger. "How ill-tempered you look, — come and feel this, and you'll be sweet-tempered at once." She turned round to the window again.

"I *will* write my missus, — that I *will*." "Do dear." "My sister will be here directly." "You said she comes at dusk, — it won't be dark for three hours." "I wish you would go, — what will people say if they know you're here?" "Don't be uneasy, — they will know no more than they know of your doings with your young man." "There is nothing to know about, but what is quite proper."

So we stood. She looking out of the window, and turning round from time to time. I standing by the door with my prick out; then I approached her quietly. "Feel it Jenny, — take pity on it." "Oh! for God's sake, sir, what are you doing?" She turned, and pushed me back, then retreated herself, keeping her face to the window as she stepped backwards. "Oh! there is Miss and Mrs. Brown walking in the next garden." Sure enough there were two ladies there; they could have seen everything close to the window over the low wall which separated the gardens; and had they been looking, must have seen Jane, me, and my prick. "Oh! if they have seen, they will tell my missus, and she'll tell my young man, and I shall be ruined, — oh! — oh! — oh!" said she sinking back into an arm-chair with a flood of tears, half funk and shock, and perhaps randiness, causing it.

I was alarmed. "Oh!" she sobbed, "if they saw you, — hoh! — ho! — and it was no fault of mine, — you're a bad man, — oho! oho!" She sat with her hands to her face, her elbows on her knees. I dropped on my knees imploring her to be quiet, was sure no one had seen me, and tried to kiss her. The position was inviting, I slid my hands up her clothes between her thighs, she took no notice, was evidently in distress, not even conscious of the invasion. A bold push, and my fingers touched her cunt. I forgot all in the intensity of my enjoyment, at feeling my fingers on the edge of the soft, warm nick. No repulse! I looked up, she sank back in the chair, seemingly unconscious and deadly white.

I withdrew my hand, then came a mental struggle; my first impulse was to get cold water, the next to look at her cunt. I went towards the door, turned round to look at her. Her calves were visible, I ran back, and lifted her clothes, so that I could just see her cunt-hair, gave her thighs a kiss, and then rushed downstairs, got water, and as I entered the room she was recovering. She knew nothing, or next to nothing of what had occurred, nor that my fingers had touched her clitoris, though she had not actually fainted.

"I wish I had some brandy," she said, "I feel so weak." "Is there any in the sideboard?" "No." "I'll go and get a little." A few hundred feet from the house down a side-street, was a public-house. As I was going, "You will let me in again?" I said. "If you promise not to touch me." She looked so pale that I fetched brandy, but put the street-door key in my pocket as I went. "If she don't let me in," I thought, "she shan't have the key, — and what will she tell her sister about that?" It was a key almost as big as a shovel; she never noticed that I had taken it away. She thought by her dodge that she had got rid of me, and told me so afterwards.

I brought back the brandy and knocked. "Let me in." "I won't." "Then you shan't have the street-door key." This was spoken to each other through the closed door. A pause, then the door opened. "You are coming Jenny." We went downstairs into the kitchen, she had brandy and water, and so had I. It was a hot day, the pump-water was deliciously cool, I made hers as strong as she would take it, — it was an instinct of mine. She got her colour back, and became talkative, we talked about her fainting, but she tried to avoid talking about it, and did not want me to refer to what had led to it. I did, and was delighted to think that it was owing to what is called "exposing my person."

"I don't think the ladies saw it, so you need not have been so frightened Jenny, — but you saw it, did you not?" No reply. "I saw you looking at it." "It's a story." "Why did you faint?" "I always feel faint if I am startled." "What startled you?" "Nothing." "You saw it, and you put your hand over it to hide it, and you touched it." "It's a story, — I wish you'd go." "You ungrateful little devil, when I've just fetched you brandy." "It's through you that I felt ill." "Why?" No reply. "Don't be foolish, — it was for fear that the ladies should have seen my prick so near you, — now look at it," — and I pulled it out, it was not stiff. "It was twice the size when you saw it, — feel it, and it will soon be bigger."

The girl rose saying she would go and remain in the forecourt till her sister came, if I did not leave, but I prevented her going out of the kitchen. She began to cry again, and had a little more brandy and water. My talk took its old channel.

"Do you know how long you were fainting?" "I didn't faint, but only a minute or so." "Do you know what I did?" She was sitting down, then got upright, looked at me full in the face, her eyes almost starting out of her head. "What did you do! — what? — what? — what?" She spoke hurriedly, anxiously, in an agitated manner. "I threw up your clothes, kissed your cunt, and felt it."

"It's a lie, — it's a lie." "It's true, — and the hair is short, and darker than the hair of your head, — and your thighs arc so white, — and your garters are made of blue cloth, — and I felt it, the dear little split, — how I wish my belly had been up against it! — what a lovely smell it has!" (putting my fingers to my nose).

"Oho! — oho! — oho!" said she bursting into tears, "what a shame to take liberties with a poor girl when she can't help herself, — oho! — oho! — you must be a bad man, — missus had no business to send you to look after me, as if she could not trust me, — she don't know what sort of man you are, — and a gentleman too, — oho! — and married too, — it's a shame, — oho! — oho! I don't believe you though, — oho — o — o." And when I told her again the colour and the make of her garters, she nearly howled. "You mean man, to do such a thing when I was ill."

I kissed her, she let me, but went on blubbering. "I've a good mind to tell my young man." "That will be foolish, because you and I mean to have more pleasure than we have had, — and he'll never be any the wiser but if you tell him, he'll think it's your fault."

This had occupied some hours, it was getting dark, but it seemed only as if I had been there some minutes, so deliciously exciting are lascivious acts and words. The charm of talking baudily to a woman for the first time is such, that hours fly away just like minutes.

I got her on to my lap and kissed her. She was so feeble that I put my hands up her clothes nearly to her knees before she repulsed them. Then I feared her sister coming home; she promised to hide the brandy, and we parted. She kissed me, and let me feel to her knees, to induce me to go. "Oh! for God's sake sir, do go before my sister comes." My last words were, "Mind you've felt my cock, and I've felt your cunt." "Pray go," — and I departed, leaving her tearful, excited, and in a state of exhaustion which seemed to me unaccountable.

Probably had I persisted a little longer I should have had her, such was the lassitude into which she had fallen; but I felt that I had made progress, and went home rejoicing, and forming plans for the future. When I had had some food, and thought over the matter, I came to the conclusion that I had been a fool in leaving her, and that had I pushed matters more determinately at the last moment, I should have certainly fucked her before I had left. I was mad with myself when I reflected on that, and the opportunity lost, which might not occur again.

Jenny had not fainted quite, but though unable to speak, resist, or indeed move, she must have been partially conscious. I think this from what I knew of her nature afterwards.

CHAPTER XVII

When are women most lewed. — Garters, money, and promises. —
About my servant. — The neckerchief. — Armpits felt. — Warm
hints. — Lewed suggestions. — Baudy language. — Tickling. —
"Fanny Hill." — Garters tried. — Red fingers. — Struggle, and es-
cape. — Locked out. — I leave. — Baudy predictions, and verifica-
tion.

I have a confused recollection of thinking myself the next day
an ass, for having missed a good opportunity of spermatizing a fresh
cunt; yet for some reason or another it must have been three days
before I went to try my luck again.

I had about this time of my life begun to frame intentions, and
calculate my actions towards women, although still mostly ruled
by impulse and opportunity in love matters. My philosophy was
owing to experience, and also in a degree to my friend the Major,
to whom some years before I had confided my having commissioned
a French woman to get me a virgin. He was older, poorer, and more
dissolute than ever. "He is the baudiest old rascal that ever I heard
tell a story," was the remark of a man at our club one night. Ask
him to dinner in a quiet way by himself, give him unlimited wine,
and he would in an hour or two begin his confidential advice in
the amatory line, and in a wonderful manner tell of his own adventures, and give reasons why he did this or that, why he succeeded with this woman, or missed that girl, in a way as amusing
and instructive to a young listener as could be imagined.

"If you want to get over a girl," he would say, "never flurry
her till her belly's full of meat and wine; let the grub work. As long
as she is worth fucking, it's sure to make a woman randy at some
time. If she is not twenty-five she'll be randy directly her belly is

filled, — then go at her. If she's thirty, give her half-an-hour. If
she's thirty-five let her digest an hour, she won't feel the warmth
of the dinner in her cunt till then. Then she'll want to piss, and
directly after that she'll be ready for you without her knowing it.
But don't flurry your young un, — talk a little quiet smut whilst
feeding, just to make her laugh and think of baudy things; then
when she has left table, go at her. But it's well," the old Major
would say, "to leave a woman alone in a room for a few minutes
after she has dined, perhaps then she will let slip a fart or two,
perhaps she'll piss, — she'll be all the better for the wind and water
being out. A woman's cunt doesn't get piss-proud like a man's
prick you know, they're differently made from us my boy, — but
show any one of them your prick as soon as you can, it's a great
persuader. Once they have seen it they can't forget it, it will keep
in their minds. And a baudy book, they won't ever look at till you've
fucked them? — oh! won't they! — they would at church if you
left them alone with it." And so the Major instructed us.

About three days afterwards, taking a pair of garters, two small
showy neckerchiefs, and *Fanny Hill* with me, I knocked at the
door. "Oh! you!," said she colouring up. "Yes, — is everything right?"
"Yes! all right, what should be the matter sir?" She stood at the
street-door holding it open, though I had entered the hall. I turned,
closed the door, and caught hold of her.

"Now none of that pray sir, you insulted me enough last time."
"I could not help it, you're so lovely, it's your fault, — forgive me,
and I won't do so any more, — here is a sovereign, take it, kiss me,
and make it up." "I don't want your money," said she sulkily. "Take
it, I give it with real pleasure, — what I had the other day was
worth double."

"I won't be paid for your rudeness, if that's what you mean."
"Lord, my dear, I've no occasion to pay for that, I took it without
pay, — I wish I could get what I told you yesterday, — I'd give
ten times the sum." "You are going on again." "Don't be foolish, —
take it, buy a pair of silk stockings." "I don't want silk stockings."
"Your plump legs would look so nice in them," — and I forced her
to put the money into her pocket.

Then I got her to the parlour, to sit down, to allow me to kiss
her, and then to talk about me and my "missus," as she called her,
a subject which seemed to excite her, for she began asking me

question after question, and listened to all I said with breathless
attention about my daily habits, rows, and fast doings. Once I
stopped at some question. "I won't tell you that." "Oh! do, — do."
"No it's curious." "Do, — do." It was about a pretty servant-girl
whom I had noticed in my house. "It will offend you if I do." "No it
won't." "Well give me a kiss then."

She kissed me. She had stood up a moment, now she sat down
again by me on the sofa. I went on with my story, every now and
then I stopped till she kissed me, it came to a kiss every minute, as
I sat with my arm round her waist, talking.

Said I, "It was a servant whom my wife turned out at a day's
notice, — a pretty girl, — I had taken to kissing her, and then I
nudged her somewhere you know. One night when she opened the
door, I saw by the light that my wife was in our bed-room. 'Is your
mistress upstairs?' 'Yes sir.' 'And the cook?' 'Yes.' Then I closed with
her. 'Don't sir, missus will hear.' I hugged her closer, shoved her up
against the wall, got my hand on to her cunt, felt her, and gave her
half a sovereign. How delicious it was to get the fingers on to the
wet nick of that pretty girl, and say, 'How I should like to fuck
that, Mary.' " I told it in words like that to Jenny, as she sat listening.
At the word "fuck" up she got.

"You are a going on rude again." "You asked me." "Not for
that." "But that's what I had to tell, what you kissed me to tell." "I
didn't think you would say rude things." "Sit down, and I'll tell you
without rude words." And so I did, telling all over again with additions, but instead of saying "cunt," "fuck," and so on, said, "I got
my hand you know where," — "and then she let me you know
what," — "she was frightened to let me do, you guess what I
wanted."

"Luckily, though she foolishly told her fellow-servant, she did
not say who had been feeling her. That sneak told my wife, who
told me about it, or she knew, and said she could not keep such
an improper girl in the house as that. 'But the other servant may
have told a lie to spite her.' 'Perhaps, but I'll turn her out too,' — and
so she did, both left."

Thus I talked to Jenny till I expect her quim was hot enough;
then said I, "Here is a pretty neckerchief, — put it on." "Oh! how
pretty." "I won't give it you unless you put it on." She went to the
glass and unbuttoned the top of her dress, which was made to

button on the front. I saw her white fat bosom, she threw the kerchief round the neck, and tried to push it down the back. "Let me put it down, — it's difficult." She let me. "You are not unbuttoned enough, — it's too tight." She undid another button, I pushed down the kerchief, and releasing my hand as I stood at the back of her, put it over her shoulder, and down in front, pushing it well under her left breast. "Oh! what a lovely breast you have, — let me kiss it."

A shriek, a scuffle. In the scuffle I burst off a button or two, which exposed her breast, and getting my hand on to one of the globes began feeling and kissing it. Then I slid my hand further down, and under her armpit. "Oh! what a shame, — don't, — I don't like it." "How lovely, — kiss, kiss, — oh! Jenny what a lot of hair I can feel under here." "Oh!" — screech, — screech, — "oh! don't tickle me, — oh! — oh!," — and she screeched as women do who can't bear tickling. I saw my advantage. "Are you ticklish?" "Yes, — oh! — (screech, — screech). — Oh! leave off."

Instead of leaving off I tickled harder than ever. She got my hand out, but I closed on her, tickling her under her arm, pinching her sides, and got her into such a state of excitement, that directly I touched her she screeched with wild laughter; the very idea of being touched made her shiver. We were on the sofa, she yelling, struggling, whilst I pinched her, she trying to get away from me, but fruitlessly; I buried my face in her breasts which were now largely exposed, and she fell back I with my face on her, holding her tight. Then I put one hand down, feeling outside for her notch; that stopped her screeching, and she pushed me off as she got up.

I soothed her, begged pardon, spoke of the hair in her armpits, wondered if it was the same colour that it was lower down. Now she shammed anger, boxed my ears, and we made it up. I produced the garters. "Oh! what a lovely pair." "They're yours if you let me put them on." "I won't." "Let me put one half-way up." "No." "Just above the ankle." "No, my stockings are dirty." "Never mind." "No." Then she made an excuse, said she must see to something, and left the room. I thought she was going to piddle.

She came back. I found afterwards she had been out to lace up her boots, they were untidy. It was coquettishness, female instinct, for she wanted the garters, and meant to let me try them on, though refusing. "Where do you garter, above knee?" "I shan't tell you." "I've seen, — let me put them on below the knees." "No."

"Then I'll give them to another woman who will let me." "I don't care." I threw the garters on to the table after some fruitless attempts. I was getting awfully lewed with our conversation.

"Do you like reading?" "Yes." "Pictures?" "Yes." "I've a curious book here." "What is it?" I took the book out, *The Adventures of Fanny Hill.* "Who was she?" "A gay lady, — it tells how she was seduced, how she had lots of lovers, was caught in bed with men, — would you like to read it?" "I should." "We will read it together, — but look at the pictures," — this the fourth or fifth time in my life I have tried this manœuvre with women.

I opened the book at a picture of a plump, leering, lecherous-looking woman squatting, and pissing on the floor, and holding a dark-red, black-haired, thick-lipped cunt open with her fingers. All sorts of little baudy sketches were round the margin of the picture. The early editions of *Fanny Hill* had that frontispiece.

She was flabbergasted, silent. Then she burst out laughing, stopped and said, "What a nasty book, — such books ought to be burnt." "I like them, they're so funny." I turned over a page. "Look, here she is with a boy who sold her watercresses, is not his prick a big one?" She looked on silently, I heard her breathing hard. I turned over picture after picture. Suddenly she knocked the book out of my hand to the other side of the room. "I won't see such things," said she. "Won't you look at it by yourself?" "If you leave it here I'll burn it." "No you won't, you'll take it to bed with you." There I left the book lying, it was open and the frontispiece showing. "Look at her legs," said I, for we could see the picture as we sat on the sofa; and I began to kiss and tickle her again.

She shrieked, laughed, got away, and rushed to the door. I brought her back, desisted from tickling and lewed talking, though I was getting randier than ever. "Now have the garters, — let me put one round the leg, just to see how it looks, — just half-way up the calf." After much persuasion, after pulling up my trowsers, and showing how a garter looked round my calf, she partly consented. "Promise me you won't tickle me." I promised everything.

I dropped on one knee, she sat on the sofa. "Put one foot on my leg." She put one foot there, and carefully raised her clothes an inch or two about the boot-top. "A little higher." She raised it holding her petticoats tight round the leg, and I slipped the garter round it. "It's too loose, raise a little more." "I won't any higher, — I can see how it looks." "Won't they look nice when they are above the knee! and won't your young man be pleased when he sees them there." "My young man won't see them any more than you will." "Let me slip on the other." The same process, the same care on her part. She bestowed all her care on the limb I was gartering, lest I should slip the garter higher up. The remainder of her clothes were loose round her other leg. Then I pushed my hand up her clothes and herself back on the sofa, relinquishing the leg I was gartering.

Rapidly my hand felt thighs, hair, cunt. How wet! What is this which catches my fingers? — what is it they are gliding between? With a yell she pushed me away, and got up as I withdrew my fingers. She had a napkin on, my fingers were stained red. "Oh you beast," said she bursting into tears. I caught hold of her, and began to tickle her; she pushed me violently away, and escaping, rushed downstairs, slammed the kitchen-door in my face, and locked herself in. I have been accustomed to this behaviour on similar occasions.

I stood outside begging pardon, talking baudiness, I tried to burst open the door, and could not. I was not fond of poorliness in women, had a keen nose, and oftentimes could smell a woman if poorly, even with her clothes down; how it was I did not smell *her*, considering how near my nose had been to her split and her breasts, I can't say, but suppose randiness overcame my other senses. I played with my prick which was in an inflammatory state, feeling it made me much randier, I called through the door how I wanted to fuck her, how my prick was bursting, how I would frig myself if she did not let me. "What a hard-hearted girl, — I'll give you ten pounds to let me, — who will know it, but you and me?" and a lot more; but it was of no use, and at length I went upstairs, determining to wait, and thinking that in time she might follow me.

On the sofa I sat thinking of what I had done. There lay one garter, I took it up, and rolled it round my pego, I rubbed the tip with it, thinking it might be a spell. I took up *Fanny Hill*, got more excited by reading the book, looking at its salacious pictures, and feeling my prick at the same time. Then the sense of pleasure got beyond control, and laying down the book on the floor just beneath me, where I could see a baudy picture, I turned on my side on the sofa, and frigged till a shower of spunk shot out.

Then down I went. The door was still locked, my senses were calmed, but I talked baudy, and offered her money without a reply; growing tired I bawled out, "I'm going, — you will let me in a day or two, and get the ten pounds towards the new shop, — you won't be so unkind when I come again." "I'll take good care never to let you in," said she. They were the only words I could get out of her. I went upstairs, took a slip of paper, and wrote on it, "I have wrapped the garter round my prick, it is a charm. Directly you put it on I shall know, for my prick will stiffen, — you will put it on I am sure; and directly my prick stiffens, your cunt will long to have it up it, even if I am miles away. You will put the garter on, for you can't help doing so, — I'm sure to fuck you, neither you nor I could avoid it if we would. Why should we deny ourselves the pleasure, — no one will know it, and you will be ten pounds the richer." I wrote that or something nearly like it, and charmed with my own wit, rubbed the garter over the top of my prick till I left the smell on it, then laid it on the table over the paper I had written, and went away, taking *Fanny Hill* with me.

It is a positive fact, that about two hours afterwards I had a violent randy throbbing in my prick, and found out later on that just at that very time she had put that garter on.

[And now for the complete understanding of what follows, it it must be stated that the house was in plan nearly like that which I inhabited when I had my beautiful servant Mary. Kitchens in the basement, two parlours with folding doors between them, nearly always open; and rooms back and front over the parlours; and that my absent friend did with those rooms whilst absent at the seaside, what was not unusual with people of their class in those days, lock most of them up, leaving only sufficient for the servant, or care-taker, to inhabit.]

CHAPTER XVIII

"Fanny Hill" sent to Jenny. — My next visit. — Thunder, lightning, sherry, and lust. — A chase round a table. — The money takes. — Tickling and micturating. — A search for "Fanny Hill." — A chase up the stairs. — In the bed-room. — Thunder, funk, and lewedness. — Intimidation and coaxing. — Over and under. — A rapid spender. — Virginity doubtful. — Fears, tears, and fucking.

I waited a few days to ensure her poorliness being over. I had not left her *Fanny Hill*, but why I cannot tell, for I knew how baudy books excited a woman. The night before my next attack I wrapped up the book, directed it to her, gave a boy sixpence to deliver it, hid myself by a lilac which was in the front-garden close to the road, and saw the boy give it to her, and go off quickly as I had told him. It was just dusk, and too dark inside the passage of the house to see; for Jenny stepped outside the house so as to get light, and stripped off the envelope. I saw also that she opened the book, closed it, looked rapidly on both sides, then stepped inside, and closed the door. I expect that her cunt got hot enough that night. I saw her sister who slept with her nightly, going through the front-garden soon afterwards, and Jenny open the door for her. I had then moved off to a safe distance, the other side of the road.

Jenny was fond of finery, and I had heard the old lady of the house declaiming about it. Her pleasure at the showy neckerchief and garters was great, so I bought a pretty brooch, and filling my purse with sovereigns determined to have her at any cost, for my letch for her had got violent. The next day I had a good luncheon, went to the house just after her dinner-time, and took with me a bottle of sherry. I recollect the morning well. It was a sultry day, reeking with moisture; it had been thundering, the clouds were

dark and threatening, the air charged with electricity. Such a day
makes all creation randy, and you may see every monkey at the
Zoological Gardens frigging or fucking. I was resolute with lustful
heat, the girl was, I expected, under the same influence, and taking
her as I did after a lazy meal, everything was propitious to me. How
shall I get it? — if I knock she may not open; and if she sees me
go up the front-garden she won't open. But I had to try, so walked
up to the door, and gave one single loud tradesman's knock.

There was a little porch and a shelter over the street-door.
Standing flat up against the door, so that I might be hidden from
her sight if peeping, I heard an upper window open. She looked out,
but where I was she could not see me. There was delay, so again
I knocked, and soon the door began to open, I pushed it and stepped
in. The front-shutters on the ground-floor to my wonder were closed.

"Hoh! sir, — you," said Jenny amazed, "what do you want?"
I pushed the door to, and caught hold of her. "I've come to have
a chat and a kiss." She struggled, but I got her tight, and kissed as
a randy man then kisses a woman, it is a magnetizing thing. "Oh!
there it is again," she cried as a loud thunder-clap was heard, "oh!
let me go, — oh! it do frighten me so." "Where are you going?"
"Oh! into the parlour, — I've closed the shutters." The girl was in
a panic, and did not know what she said. The parlour-door was
open, the room nearly dark, which suited me. She went just in, and
then turned round to go out, but I pulled her to the sofa. A flash
of lightning showed even in the darkened room, the girl cowered
and hid her face with her hands. I took her round the waist. "Shut
your eyes, and lean your head against me." Mechanically she did,
she was utterly unnerved. I felt down with my right hand the form
of her thighs and haunches through her clothes. My prick began
to stand. Pulling it out, and taking her near hand I put it round my
prick just as the thunder roared. She kept her hand unconsciously
on it for a time, then with a start took it away and jumped up. "Oh!
it's wicked," said she, "when God Almighty is so angry," — and just
as she got to the door a terrific flash made her turn round again. I
caught her, and sitting down on a chair pulled her on to my knee;
she hid at once her face on my shoulder in terror.

Coaxing and soothing, and exciting her, in her fear she listened,
at times twitching and oh-ing. I was sorry I had touched her cunt
the other day I said. "Oh! now don't." "Feel my prick again, — do

dear." "Let me go, — you've no business here." Another flash came, I put my hand up her clothes, the tip of my fingers just touched her quim. She struggled and got away, and in doing so upset the chair which fell down and broke. "Oh! now what will my missus say!" said she. Then a screech, and she got to the other side of the table.

This went on a little longer, a gleam of sunshine came through the shutters. Then she opened one shutter, and said if I did not go she would open the window and call out. The light showed my pego, stiff, red-tipped and ready. "Look what your feeling has done for this Jenny," said I shaking my tooleywag at her.

But her resoluteness daunted me, so I promised not to do so again. "Here is some sherry that I was taking home to taste, — let's have a glass, — it will do both of us good after this thunder, — you look white, and as if you wanted a glass." I had got out of her on a previous day that she liked sherry. "I'll go and get you a glass," said she. "No you shan't, — you will lock the door," said I, — I knew that was in her mind. No she would not. "We will go together then."

We did, and returning to the parlour under my most solemn promise of good behaviour, down she sat, and we began drinking sherry. One glass, — two, then another she swallowed. "No I dare not, it will get into my head, — no more." "Nonsense, — after your fright it will do you good." "Well half a glass." "Isn't it nice Jenny?" "It is." "Does not your sweetheart give it you?" "At Christmas, but only one glass." The sherry began to work. "Only another half-glass," — and I poured it out nearly full. Soon after I got up after filling my own, and standing before her again filled up hers which she had sipped without her seeing me. "Finish your glass dear." "No I can't, — it's making me so hot." "Just another half-glass." "I won't." But she began to chatter and told me again all about her young man, of their intending to open a grocer's shop when they had two hundred pounds; that he had saved a certain sum, and when he had a little more his father was to put fifty pounds to it. She also had put money in the savings bank. I got closer to her, and asked for a kiss. "Well! I'll kiss you if you promise not to be rude again." A kiss and a promise. She was one of the simplest and most open girls I have ever met with, and once a half-feeling of remorse came over me about my intentions, whilst she was talking on quite innocently about her future; but my randy prick soon stopped that.

"What nonsense dear, your young man won't know that I have

felt your thighs, and you my thing, nor any one else what we do, —
I have thought of nothing else since I touched you, — kiss; — now
let me do it again, — just feel it, — only where my hand's been
before, — I swear I won't put my hand up higher, just above your
garters, — have you got those garters on?" "No." "Oh! you have."
"Well I have." "Let me just see." "I shan't." "I'll give you a sovereign
to let me." "Shan't." I pulled out the sovereign, put it on the table,
and spite of her resistance pulled up her clothes just high enough to
see one garter; then clutching her round the waist I pushed my
hands up, and touched a well-developed clitoris. She struggled, but
I kept my hand there, kissed her rapturously, and frigged her; her
cap fell off in her struggle. "Oh! I — can't — bear — it — now —
sir; — I — don't — oh! — like it, — oh!" Then with a violent effort
she got my hand away, but I held her fast to me.

"What a lovely smell your cunt has," said I putting the fingers
just withdrawn from her thighs up to my nose. I have always
noticed that nothing helps to make a woman more randy than that
action; it seems to overwhelm them with modest confusion; I have
always done that instinctively to a woman whom I was trying. "Oh!
what a man, oh! let me pick up my cap." Just then I noticed her
hair was short, and remarked it. She was annoyed, her vanity hurt,
it turned her thoughts entirely. "Yes," she said, "I had a fever two
years ago, — but it's growing again." "Well it has grown enough
on your cunt dear, — did it fall off there?" "Oh! what a man! — oh!
now what a shame!" My hand was on her thighs again, and I
managed another's minute frig, and kept her close to me.

The heat had become excessive. What with struggling, and the
excitement, sweat was on both our faces. Her thighs by her crack
were as wet as if she had pissed them, her backside began to
wriggle with pleasure, which I knew I was giving her; but again
with a violent effort she freed herself from me, and as I put my
hand to my nose she violently pulled it away. The sherry was upsetting her wisdom.

"There is the sovereign," said I as she stood looking at me,
"that will help you." "Don't want it." Seeing where her pocket-hole
was I pushed it into it. "Oh! what a lucky sovereign, to lay so close
to your cunt Jenny," — and pushing my hand into her pocket I
touched the bottom of her belly through the linen. Again a struggle,
a repulse, then she put her hand into her pocket. "You're feeling

your cunt Jenny," said I. "O — oh!" said she taking it out quickly, "I was feeling for the money, — I won't have it."

Then I kissed her till the sweat ran off my face on to hers. "Oh! my goodness," said she as it grew darker, "it's going to thunder again." "Have another glass." "No it's gone into my head already." But she took a gulp of mine. "Let's fuck you Jenny dear." "What?" "Fuck." "Shan't." "Oh! you know what I mean." "No I don't, but it's something bad if it's from you." I pulled out my prick, and tried to push her on the sofa. She got away, and then with my prick out I chased her round the table "Leave off," said she, "a joke's a joke, but this is going too far." She was getting lewed, and was staring at my prick which showed above the table as I chased her. Quick as me she managed to keep just on the side of it opposite to me.

"I'll swear I won't touch you again if you will sit down." "I won't trust you, — you've been swearing all the afternoon." "So help me God I will," said I, and meant it. "Well then not when you are like that." I pushed my prick inside my trowsers, and then she sat down. What a long time this takes to tell, what repetition! but there are not many incidents I recollect more clearly.

Then I took out ten sovereigns, all bright, new ones, laid them on the table, and then the brooch. "Do you like that Jenny?" "Yes." "It is for you if you will let me, and those ten sovereigns also." "You are a bad man," said the girl, "and would make me forget myself and be ruined, and without caring a bit," — and she began rocking her head about, and rolling her body as she sat beside me, and looking at the money. "Who will know? — you won't tell your young man, — I shan't tell my wife, — let me." "I shan't, — never, — never, — never, — never, if it was fifty pounds," said she almost furiously. "He won't find it out." "Yes he would." "Nonsense, — half the servants do it, yet marry," — and then I told her of some I had had who had married. "No, — no, — no," she kept repeating, almost bawling it out, as I told her Mary So-and-So who married a butler, and Sarah So-and-So who married my greengrocer, though I'd fucked them over and over again. "No, — no," looking at the money; then suddenly she took up the brooch, and laid it down again.

Before running round the table after her, I had thrown off my coat and waistcoat. "It's so hot, I've a good mind to take off my trowsers," I had said; but I had another motive. She seemed weaker, and was so, for gradually she had got inflamed and lewed by heat,

the electrical condition of the atmosphere, the titillation of my finger
on her seat of pleasure, and the sight of my stiff penis. She had I
expect got to that weak, yielding, voluptuous condition of mind and
body, when a woman knows she is wrong, yet cannot make up her
mind to resist. Just then it came into my mind to tickle her; and
then followed a scene which is one of the most amusing in my
reminiscences.

She shrieked, and wriggled down on to the floor. I tried to
mount her there. She kicked, fought, so that though once my prick
touched her cunt-wig, I could not keep on the saddle. She forgot
all propriety in her fuddled excitement, and whilst screeching from
my tickling, repeated incoherently baudy words as I uttered them.
"Let me fuck you." "You shan't fuck me." "Let's put it just to your
cunt." "You shan't, — you're a blackguard, — oh! don't, — leave me
alone, — well I will feel it, if you'll let me get up, — oh! — he! hi! hi!
— for God's sake don't tickle, — hi! — I shall go mad, — you shan't,
— oh! don't, — oh! if you don't leave off." "I shall, — I must." "Oh!
pray, — you shall if you leave off tickling then, — oh! don't pray, —
oh! I shall piddle myself, — he! he!" She was rolling on the floor,
her thighs exposed, sometimes backside, sometimes belly upwards
with all its trimmings visible. "Oh! it's your fault," and as she
spoke actually piddle began to issue. I had my hand on her thigh,
and felt and saw it.

Randy as I was I burst out laughing; and she managed to get
up, began to push in her neckerchief which I had torn out of the
front of her dress, and arranged her hair.

"Oh! look at me, — if any one came, what a state I am in,"
said she looking in the glass, and there she stood her breast heaving,
her eyes swollen, her mouth open, and breathing as if she had just
run a mile, but attempting nothing, saying nothing further, awaiting
my attack. What randy, pleasurable excitement she must have been
in, though unconscious of it, whilst only thinking of how to prevent
my fucking her against her will.

"You began piddling." "Didn't." "I felt the piddle on my hand."
She made no reply, but passed on, and wiped her face. When I
said more she merely tossed her head. "Don't be a fool Jenny, —
let us, — you want it as bad as me." Then I rattled out my whole
baudy vocabulary, "prick," "cunt," "fuck," "spunk," "pleasure," "belly
to belly," "my balls over your arse," "let my stiff prick stretch your

cunt," — everything which could excite a woman; to all of which she merely said, "Oho! — oh!" and tossed her head, and never took her staring eyes off me, nor ceased swabbing up her perspiring face, and at the same time looking at my throbbing, rigid cunt-stretcher.

Finding she took to yelling, and even hitting me, I desisted a moment. "Where is the book I sent you last night?" I had till then forgotten it. That opened her mouth. "Have not had a book." "I saw the boy give it you, and you open it." "He didn't." "He did." "I burnt it, — a nasty thing, — I would not let my sister see it." An angry feeling came over me for the moment, for I thought it probable, and should have had difficulty in replacing it. Then came an inspiration to help me, — a man always gets somehow on the right track to get into a woman if he has opportunity. Nature wills it. The woman was made to be fucked, and the sooner for them, the better for them.

"You have not burnt it, — I'll bet it's in your bed-room, — in your box." "It isn't." "I'll swear it's there, — you have been reading it all night, — I'll go up and see." She started as if electrified into life as I made for the door. She got there before me, and stood before me. "You shan't go, — you've no business up there, — I've burnt it, — it's not there." "It's in the kitchen then." "No, I've burnt it," she went on rapidly and confusedly. "I'll go and see," said I pulling her from the door, she screeching out, "No you shan't go up, — that you shan't, — you've no business there." Then I pulled up her clothes to her belly, she got them down, but still she kept her back to the door. I kept pulling her till her cap was off again, and felt sure she was getting weaker and weaker.

Then she turned round suddenly, opened the door, and ran up the stairs rapidly like a lapwing, I after her. Once she turned round, "You shan't come up," said she, and tried to push me back; and then again on she went, I following. I stumbled, that gave her a few steps ahead; I sprang up three stairs at a time, recovered the lost distance, and just as she got into the bed-room, and slammed the door to, I put my foot in it, — it hurt me much. "Damn it, how you hurt my foot, — I will come in," — and pushing the door my strength prevailed; the door flew open, I saw her running round the bed, and there on the very pillow of the unmade bed lay *Fanny Hill*, open at one of the pictures. I threw myself across the bed, and clutched the book. She then stood motionless, panting and staring at me, she had clutched at it, and failed just as I caught it. She would have got it, but for having to go round the bed.

I laughed. "Have you not had a treat Jenny dear!" Her face was a picture of confusion. I was stretched half across the bed, and now went right across. Then to escape me she ran away, and had nearly reached the door when throwing myself over the bed again I grasped her petticoats under her arse, and managed to pull her back. "Damned if I don't fuck you," said I, "by God I'll shove my prick up your cunt if I'm hanged for it," — and pushing a hand up behind I clasped her naked buttocks. She turned round, I pulled her petticoats clean up, she yelling, struggling, panting, imploring. I dropped on my knees, kissed her belly, and buried my nose between her thighs. The petticoats dropped over my head, her belly kept bumping up against my nose and lips, which were covered with her cunt-moisture.

I rose up, pushed and rolled her against the bed, my hand still up her clothes. "Oh! don't, don't now, — you are a great gentleman they say, and ought to think of a poor girl's ruin, — oh! if it was found out I should be ruined." "It won't darling," I had got my fingers well over the whole slit. "Pray don't, — well I'll kiss you, — there." "Feel it." "Will you let me get up if I do?" "Yes." "There then," and she felt me. "Oh! I must fuck you." "Oh! pray don't, — oh! let me go now, and I'll let you another day, — I will indeed sir, — oh! you hurt, — don't push your fingers like that." "Kiss me my darling." "You shan't." "Then there." Another struggle. "Oh! I can't — be — bear it." Her arse began to twist again, her head sank on my shoulder, her thighs opened; then with a start, "Oh! my God it's lightning (it began to thunder and lightning badly), — oh! I'm so frightened, — oh! don't, — another day, — it's wicked when it's lightning so, — oh! God almighty will strike us dead if you are so wicked, — oh! let me go into the dark, — oh! don't, — I can't be — bear it." Her arse was shaking with my groping and frigging.

"Now don't be a fool, — damned if I don't murder you if you are not quiet!" "Oh! oh!" I had got her somehow on to the bed, she was helpless; with fear, liquor, and cunt-heat. I threw myself on to her. A feel between thighs reeking with sweat, with her cunt in a lather, with the sweat dropping in great drops from my face, with sweat running down my belly on to my prick and my balls; I shoved. One loud "aha!" and my prick-tip was up against her womb-door. A mighty straight thrust; and the virginity was gone at that one effort.

Right up there with but a shove or two as far as I recollect, and without trouble, my sperm spouted directly my tool rubbed through the wet, warm cunt-muscles. Then I came to my senses; where was I? had she let me, or had I forced her violently?

She laid quietly under me with closed eyes and open mouth, panting; I was upon her, up her, pressing heavily upon her rather than holding her; then thrusting my hands under her fat bum I recommenced thrusting and fucking. She lay still, in the enjoyment of a lubricated cunt, distended by a stiff, hot prick. Soon she was sensitive to my moments, her cunt constricted, a visible pleasure overtook her, her frame began to quiver, and the soft murmurs of spermatic effusion came from her lips. She spent. On I went driving as if I meant to send my prick into her womb, fell into a half dreaminess, and became conscious of a great wetness on my ballocks; it was her discharge more than mine, the most copious I recollect, excepting from one woman. Then I dropped off on her side. She lay still as death, the thunder rolled over us unheeded by her in the delirious excitement and delight of her first fuck.

She turned on her side slightly, her thighs and backside were naked, she hid her face, and shuddered at the thunder unheeding her nakedness, then buried her face in a pillow, and so we both dozed for a minute or two. Her backside was still naked, when I looked at her in all ways as she lay, and saw traces of sperm on her thighs and chemise. A little lay on the bed, but no trace of red, no signs of a bloody rupture of a virgin cunt. My shirt and drawers were spermed, but had not a trace of blood. The light fell full on her backside, I could see lightish brown hair in the crack of the parting of her buttocks; a smear of shit on her chemise. Her flesh was beautifully white. She had on nice white stockings, and the flashy garters; she had a tolerable quantity of hair on her quim on the belly side. I sat at the side of the bed, got off boots, trowsers, and drawers; then laying down gently inserted my longest finger and delicately began rubbing her clitoris which I could see protruding of a fine crimson color. Then she moved; she was not asleep, but dazed by the fuck, fear of the lightning, the excitement, the heat, and the fumes of the wine combined.

She stared at me, pulled down her clothes, and tears began

to run down her cheeks. What a lot of women I have had cry at such times! "Don't cry my darling." She turned on to her face, and hid it. For a quarter of an hour, I talked, but she did not answer. I told her she had spent, that I knew she had had pleasure. Then I pushed my fingers up her cunt; still she did not speak, but let me do just what I liked, keeping her eyes shut. So soon as my rammer was up to the mark, up her it went fucking, and again I felt its stem well wetted. She was a regular streaming spunker.

After that, "I am going downstairs," said she. "I'll come." "No don't." "You only want to piddle." "Yes," said she faintly. "Piddle here, — what will it matter?" "I can't." "I'll go out if you won't bolt the door." "It's no good bolting the door, — you have ruined me." I went outside, closed the door, and heard the rattle in the pot. When I re-entered she was sitting at the side of the bed crying quietly; she did nothing but look at me, but without speaking. "Arrange yourself in case any one comes to the door." "No one will come." "The milkman?" "He will put it down inside the porch." She sat down the picture of despair. Never had I felt more lewed, I was mad that day with lewedness. "Let's feel your cunt," said I, "I have spent in it three times." "I don't care what you do, you may do what you like, — it's of no consequence." I felt up her cunt, she hung her head over my shoulders whilst I paddled my fingers in the wet. "Don't hurt me," said she. "I have not hurt you." "Yes you have." "Let's look." That roused her. "Oh! no, — no, — no, — you shan't." "Wash your cunt." I fetched the sherry, but she had not washed her cunt. "You should wash it out." "Oh? — oh!" said she. "If I should be with child I shall never be married."

She drank more sherry, and promised to wash. Then I went downstairs, fetched up the brooch and the ten sovereigns, and gave them to her. "How shall I say I got it?" "Does he know how much you have saved?" "Yes." "Is it a year's wages?" "Yes," — and she began to cry again. "What shall I say about the brooch?" "That you bought it, — let's lay down and talk." She yielded instantly, I threw up her clothes, she pushed them down. Then I lay feeling her quim, and got out her bubbies, she submitted, laying with her eyes closed, till my rubbing on her clitoris made her sigh. Then up her, I felt her wetting my prick-stem, and shot my sperm into her at that intimation of her pleasure.

It was about seven o'clock, I had been nearly five hours at

my amusements, and was tired; but had that day an irrepressible prick. It began to stiffen almost directly it left her cunt. I went down with her to tea, there I pulled her on to my lap, and we began to look at *Fanny Hill*. I could not get a word out of her, but she looked intently at the pictures. I explained their salacity. "Hold the book dear, and turn over as I tell you." Then I put my fingers on her cunt again. How sensitive she was. "Let's come upstairs." "No," said she reluctantly, but up we went, and fucked again. Then she groaned. "Oh! pray leave off, — I'm almost dead, — I shall have one of my fainting fits." "Lay still darling, I shall come soon," — but it was twenty minutes hard grinding before my sperm rose.

Then she laid motionless and white through nervous exhaustion, excitement, and loss of her spermatic liquor, which I kept fetching and fetching in my long grinding. She told me afterwards that she could not tell how often she spent. I had never been randier or stronger, nor enjoyed the first of a woman more.

She was a most extraordinary girl. After the first fuck she was like a well-broken horse; she obeyed me in everything, blushed, was modest, humbled, indifferent, conquered, submissive; but I could get no conversation out of her excepting what I have narrated. She cried every ten minutes, and looked at me. After each fuck she laid with her eyes closed, and mouth open, and turned on her side directly, putting her hand over her quim, and pulling her clothes just over her buttocks. Then after I had recovered and began to talk, a tear would roll down her cheek.

About nine o'clock she said, "Do go, my sister will be here, — and the bed wants making." At the door I put her against the wall and rubbed as well as I could my flabby cock between her cunt-lips. She made no resistance. "We'll fuck again to-morrow Jane." "I'll never let you again," said she, "for you shan't come in," — and she shut the door on me with a slam.

CHAPTER XIX

My soiled shirt. — Jenny's account of herself. — Fucking and funking. — Poor John! — Of her pudenda. — Its sensitiveness. — Erotic chat. — Startled by a caller. — Her married sister's unsatisfied cunt. — How she prevented having children. — Doubts her husband's fidelity. — Jenny taught the use of a French letter. — Hikery-pikery, and catamenial irregularities.

When I got home I looked at my linen; never had it been in such a mess after female embraces. I had taken no care about it, it was be-spunked in an unusual degree, and lots of thinnish stains were on the tail which made me think that one or both of us must have spent copiously. Then I recollected that Jenny's cunt seemed very wet to me when I felt it after I had spermatized her. There were no signs of blood, and taking stock of the sensations I had experienced, "Jenny has had it before," I said to myself. Then came a fear that her discharge was from a clap, but I dismissed that from my mind. I had only once had the clap from a woman not gay.

So I washed the tail of my shirt, laid it under my arse to dry, gave it a natural stain of piss, and went to bed reflecting and wondering who had first penetrated Jenny's privates.

A day or two afterwards I went to see her, and shammed a knock. She opened the door. "Oh!," she exclaimed as I entered, "now you shan't, — you shan't again." "I shan't what my dear?" "I know why you come here, — but you shan't." "I want a chat, — don't be foolish, — come here, — I won't do anything, — I don't want anything, — but come here."

I got her into the parlour, and on to the sofa, then talked, then got baudy. "Do just let me feel your thighs, — what harm can it do when I have been between them." "No." "Just a feel, — there

I won't put my finger further, — oh! Jenny you like my finger, — be quiet dear, — just let me feel it." Half an hour after she had said, "Now you shan't," my prick was in her. No woman can refuse the cock which has once stretched her cunt, she is at its mercy. We spent another afternoon in talking and fucking, and she partly in crying and bemoaning her evil deeds.

I had not only opened her cunt, but opened her heart and mouth at the same time. She was the funniest, frankest little woman I ever knew. She told me all her past life, her future expectations, asked my advice, deplored her wickedness to her young man, and all in an hour. She spoke the same incessantly afterwards. In a fortnight I knew everything about her from her birth, and about all her family; it was as if for the first time in her life she had had a confidant.

"What shall I do with your money?" "Put it with the rest." "But he knows what I've got, — we always tell each other." "Keep it to get you a good stock of clothes before you are married." "But he knows all about my clothes." "Put it in a little at a time, or don't tell him till you are married; then say you kept him in ignorance for a pleasant surprize, or tell him nothing at all about it, — you will have more than that." "I don't want your money, I fear it will bring me harm." "Well give it back to me Jenny." But Jenny did not seem to see the advantage of that; so she kept it, and had more besides in time.

"What will become of me and poor John? — he'd die if he knew how ill I behave to him, — now don't, — you do upset a body so a talking, and putting your fingers there, — oh! leave me alone, — no no more." "Once more dear, — how hot your little cunt is, — it's longing for a prick." "Oh! take care of my cap, you will tear it, — I'll take it off." "What a fat backside you've got Jenny, — how wet your cunt is, — shove, shove, fuck, — where is my prick Jenny now?" But Jenny became speechless always after three cock-shoves, and began moistening the intruder with all her cunt-power.

After fucking she was tranquil for a time; sperm seemed to soothe her, but then she had funks. "Oh! dear what have you made me do? oh! if I am in the family way! — oh! if he finds it out, he won't marry me! and he is such a good young man, and so fond of me, — o — o — ho — ho! — I've behaved very bad to him, — and I didn't mean, — oho! — it's all your fault, oho! — I didn't know what I was about, — I never do when it lightnings, — oho! Do you think he will find it out when we are married?" she would ask in her calmer moments, after she had cried herself out. This scene occurred every day I fucked her for a time, then less frequently.

I tried to comfort her, told facts, and many inventions of my own, of how I had had women, who afterwards married and whose husbands had never known that they had been broached.

"Is it true really! — oh! do tell me the truth, — if he finds it out I will drown myself, — I'm sure he will, — it's all your fault, — you must be a bad man to take advantage of a poor girl in the house alone." "But if you're not in the family way, he can't find out until you are married, and then it will be too late. You won't tell him, and your cunt can't speak." "Oh! sir you do say such funny things."

This went on for weeks. "Oh! it's my time, and it's not come on." Then with joy, "Oh! I'm all right, but you can't do anything to-day, — oh! if my mistress should find out, or if my sister should come home and catch you here, — oh! if the next-door neighbours should see you come here so often, and tell my mistress." One or other of these fears was always upon her, but did not prevent our fucking. At that time Sarah was away, and Louisa Fisher still ill, so Jenny had all my essence; and later on as much as Louisa and Sarah spared me. As to my home, I had pretty well done with fucking there.

Jenny's cunt was well-haired, and had rather large inner lips; not so large as I have seen in many women, but larger than I liked. Her tube was easy. What a fight I had when first I saw it. "I won't be pulled about like that, — no it's shameful." "I dare say your John has seen it." That always sent her off howling, and when she had subsided she let me do as I liked. "It's a nasty thing to pull me about like that." But it came soon to the old world-wide habit: a feel and a look before the entry. The same woman who won't let you see the bottom of her belly at first, will hold her cunt open for your inspection in a month. It is breaking in a woman to baudiness which is the happiness of the honeymoon, not the hard burst through a bit of gristle.

It had weighed on my mind ever since I had had her, and about three weeks afterwards I told her my doubts of her then being a virgin. She swore that no man had even put his hands on it till

I did. "Am I different from other women?" She was indignant at the doubt, and honestly and truly I believe. A schoolfellow used to look at her quim, she at her schoolfellow's, she always thought hers was the most open of the two, she always could put her finger up easily. "But you did hurt me through, though I did not bleed. My sister says she did bleed a little when she first had her husband," — and Jenny now described her sister's first night, and her sister's form, and rather wetted my lust for her sister.

I came to the conclusion that she was born loose at her inlet, or had broken through the cover when quite young, and that no prick had rubbed her but mine; but her organ was a peculiar one in its habit of distilling its liquids.

I have told how my shirt was stained at first, and soon found that Jenny was one of those women who spend rapidly, frequently, and copiously. I have met I think two like her in my career, to the time I correct this.

On the second day's poking I noticed this and became fully aware of it afterwards. When I put my prick up her, and began my movements, a shiver and a sigh escaped her almost directly, her bum gave a heave, a discharge came from her, and if I pulled my prick out then, it was perfectly wet. It used in fact to run out a little, and if pushing one hand well under her arse (which was not so easy, for she had a fine backside), I felt the root of my prick or rather the end of the stem, I could feel her moisture running down one of her bum-cheeks, or between them. That over, by the time I spent we usually discharged simultaneously. Her voluptuousness was greater when we spent together, than on her preliminary discharge. She said she could not account for it, but that a delicious sensation crept over her the moment the prick entered; that her cunt tightened and seemed to wet itself copiously; that her spend at the climax was longer, more thrilling, voluptuous, satisfying, and exhausting; that when our spunks had mingled her whole body was satisfied; but that the first spend seemed only to confine its pleasure to her cunt. It is difficult to describe these sensations.

I frigged her several times, and got a copious discharge from her, thin, milky, and barely sticky, yet it left a strong stain on linen. She was astonished when I told her of her peculiarity. Perhaps she wondered what her poor John would think of it. I can't say I altogether admired her wetness; I took a dislike to a tall thin girl

who was much of the same sort as Jenny, but that girl was quite
sloppy-cunted, though not with the whites. This was since.

[Another woman who had this sensitive and sensuous (for it
was both) organization, was the sister of an intimate friend, and
whom I have fucked since the above was written. I don't know
that I shall say anything more about that lady, so tell of her cuntal
peculiarity here. She was plump, fair-haired, had a fine complexion,
and in face strongly resembled the queen. She was to be married.]

When her young man came to town, and Jenny went out with
him, the girl upbraided herself. When I next saw her after his visit
she felt herself a deceiving wretch, and cried. Now would I please
desist, and not make her sin any more. But the persuasion was too
great, the recollection of her pleasure too strong, and never did I
go away without having plugged her.

Did she love her young man? Yes she supposed she did; he
was kind, attentive, and would make a good husband. She wanted
to get married, to have a home of her own; besides he was not a
workman, but a tradesman, and when married they would have a
shop, and be in a higher position. She always spoke more of the
house and shop, and her liberty, than of her young man.

She was of a highly nervous organization, and through me she
was to be shocked severely. She half fainted the first day I took
liberties with her, thunder and lightning gave her an inclination
that way, twice afterwards she nearly fainted, any sudden thing
annoyed her and turned her white. One occasion I'll tell of now,
the other in due course.

We fucked on the sofa after the first day; but though large,
it was not like a bed, so afterwards we used to go to her bed-room.
I used to leave my hat and stick downstairs, so that in case of surprize I might stand in the hall, and say I had called to enquire. It
was a stupid thing to do as I found out, and then I used to take
it into the bed-room. I had fucked her one afternoon, when a double
knock came at the street-door, I knew it. "It's my wife," I said.
Down I rushed for my hat, and returned to the bed-room; and then
Jenny opened the door. She had called to make some enquiry, and
went away. I heard the door close, but no further noise or movement, then crept downstairs. There sat Jenny on a chair, just recovering from a half faint. "Oh!" said she, "I nearly dropped down."
"Ah! she would have knocked you down my dear, if your cunt could

have spoken and said what was inside it." But Jenny never could joke. It was always dreadful, and she was to be punished in some way for her evil deeds with me. A few tears, and then a little baudy chaffing brought smiles again on her face.

I delighted in talking baudy to her, told her smutty stories about the women I had had, described their charms, and any special lasciviousness connected with them. Her astonishment was great, her curiosity intense; she in return told me all she knew about every other woman, and all her own little baudy doings. Never was woman so frank about such matters. When I left her I doubt whether her dear John could have told her half what she could have told him about fucking, and the two articles that copulation is done with.

Her talk was all about her sisters, and principally of the married one who came to sleep with her; a woman about twenty-eight years of age, who had been married some years, and had two children, the last one four years old. She, or rather he, did not mean to have any more, they could not afford to keep them. "How did they stop it?" I asked Jenny. She did not know. But one night the sister wanted particularly to sleep at home, and had asked Jenny if for once she would sleep in the house alone. She consented though frightened. I proposed sleeping with her, and we passed a very delicious night together: a man and woman fresh to each other always do in bed. What a night of feeling, frigging, sniffing, inspecting, and fucking it was!

At all times, no matter what we began talking about, cunt and cock were sure to become the subject. That night I learned that her sister had slept away, expecting to catch her husband out in some infidelities. Since he had determined to have no more children, he made her frig him instead of fucking; so the sister went short of cock and had to frig herself. That annoyed her. Then when he fucked her he did not do it properly, he cheated her sister, Jenny said. I was a long time in getting out of Jenny what the man did, at length she said, that just as the stuff was coming, he pulled it out, and it went all over her sister's thighs or her belly, and often before she had had her own pleasure. Her sister thought it was just as well not to be married, as to go on like that.

That was not all. He used at first to do it every night, and now not once a week, said he could do without it, that he did not

care about it, and so on. She believed that he had other women,
and that was more aggravating because she wanted it herself more
than ever. She was not so well, she told Jenny for want of fucking,
she liked it, and would willingly have more children though she
was so poor. I asked cautiously if she had heard of the skins which
people put over their pricks, and into which they spent their seed?
Jenny had not. I explained what they were. She said she would
ask her sister about it. I cautioned her about showing that she knew
too much. A few days afterwards Jenny told me her sister had
tried them, but they did not like them, besides they could not
afford them. What Jenny's sister paid for French letters I don't
know, I used to pay nine pence each. I fucked Jenny with one on,
just to instruct her.

These two women talked often about such matters; and each
day Jenny told me what her sister had said. Soon I knew all about
her sister's doings, from the night she lost her virginity to the birth
of her last child. The little fucking that the sister had, and her longing for more affected me considerably; I quite longed to see this
hot-bummed, cunt-neglected wife, and soon my curiosity was to be
gratified in a way I little expected.

Jenny and I settled down quite matrimonially, I saw her certainly four days a week, or else every day excepting Sundays. At
times I spent the whole day there, took wine, and meat, and news-
papers. She cooked, and very badly. We eat and drank together,
and fucked, she cried about John and her wickedness, and her fears
of being found out. Then I read to her the news, and also every
baudy book I could get hold of, and explained to her every use
that could be made of our tools, both male and female, from flat-
cocking to buggery, so far as I knew, — but I did not know so much
as I do now.

To prevent its being known I was there, we got quite cunning.
I was not to come at eleven o'clock, because then the butcher came;
nor at twelve, because the girls were always at the window next
door; between one and two o'clock I was safe, because the family
was always at dinner at that time; at three the milkman came, and
I avoided him. So with a little trouble I pretty well escaped observa-
tion, during the eight or ten weeks which I did husband duty, and
perhaps as much as some two husbands would have done.

Once she was awfully uneasy, for her courses had not come

on, and shed floods of tears. She would lose her John, poor fellow! When in that way she was always pitying him, but she was always irregular in her menstruation, which rendered it difficult to judge of her condition. Oh! she was sure she was now in the family way, she had symptoms; she had asked her sister how she had felt when she had conceived, and her own symptoms were the same. "My God what shall I do! — I'll drown myself, I will, — I shall never be able to face him, — poor fellow!" "Go and get something, go and see some one." She went, took a dose of what she called "hikery-pikery," and the ugly red stream came on. I don't believe she was in the family way. Years after I heard she had never had a child, though long married.

CHAPTER XX

A Saturday afternoon. — Copulation interrupted. — Retreat cut off. — Under the bed. — Enter sister. — The new dress. — Heat and sweat. — Undressing. — Jenny's anxiety. — Sweating much, and stripping. — Nature in its simplicity. — Nature in its vulgarity. — Delicious peeps. — A cunt near my nose. — Erotic recklessness. — Fist-fucking.

And now I was to become acquainted with her sister, — the married one. Jenny had no brother, had none of that knowledge about boys' cocks which girls of the humbler classes have when they have brothers. I sometimes think that boys in the humbler classes show their cocks to their sisters; I don't recollect a girl I have fucked who did not say she had seen her brother's cock.

My knowledge of her sister's dissatisfaction with the small amount of fucking she got, her disappointment at having her husband's sperm on her thighs instead of up her cunt, and her very reasonable fears that at times it went into other receptacles besides her own, came forcibly to my mind. It would have been odd if it had not, for every time I poked Jenny we talked about her sister, indeed all our talk, unless about her sweetheart, and her fears was about fucking. I don't recollect any woman I have had who was so anxious to know all, and delighted to hear of my amours, and the descriptions I gave of my various women. If I described their cunts she was amused beyond measure; and to tell all this suited me exactly. For all that she thought it wicked, and that they and I, and she, would be punished by the Almighty (her ideas about the action of Providence were peculiar).

It was the good fortune of her married sister to give me one of the most laughable, but yet natural, salacious, voluptuous treats

I ever had, without her knowing she had done so, — and from that came consequences which affected that lady herself.

I have always been highly delighted to see modest women naked or undress, or doing their toilet and little affairs, when they had no idea that any one saw them. I have looked through dozens of key-holes, bored holes in doors, waited breathless and half-naked for hours at night, have risen by day-light to enable me to get these treats. I had seen as already said, the cunts of my aunt and cousins, young ladies and others bathing, &c. [and as I shall tell of, have since seen a noble lady frig herself]. I have seen in fact modest ladies at their most decent, as well as the most indelicate of their toilet performances, and think I prefer looking at them under such circumstances, rather than at the beautiful voluptuous creatures who undress willingly in my presence, for those are so intent on displaying their charms to the best advantage, to get a male erection and its crisis as soon as possible, make much too evident what they do it for.

Jenny's sister gave me one of those natural displays. Had the lady been drilled in the art of unfolding her charms for the excitement of a male, and driving him into erotic fury, she could not have more effectually done so. Of the many displays of female charms (of modest females) I have seen, I never had one so gradual, natural, voluptuous, and cock-stiffening as she unconsciously gave me.

I called on Jenny one Saturday afternoon, she had said I had better go quite early, but I did not. It was another sultry day, thunder had been heard, the atmosphere was heavy, but no rain had fallen; and the sun was bright and blazing hot. Said Jenny, "I'm frightened to let you stop, my sister is going to leave off work early, and she will be here about five o'clock, — don't come in." I would. "We shan't be half-an-hour, — it's not half-past three." A kiss, and a twiddle on her cunt settled the matter, and we went to her bed-room. She was on the bed, I between her thighs, ready to drop into her, indeed I'm not sure that my prick had not touched her cunt, when a knock and a ring came at the street-door.

To fully understand what follows it should be known that the old lady my friend, for fear that the rooms should be used, had locked up all the rooms but the parlours and a little closet overlooking the street, and the servants' bed-room, and had taken away the keys. I did not know that then, I knew it that day.

"Oh! my God it's my sister, — what shall I do? — I shall be ruined." Pale as death, I thought she was going to faint again.

"Don't be nervous, I'll go and hide in the room below, and when she is downstairs or up here, go out quietly, and leave the street-door ajar." "Oh! all the rooms are locked up." "I'll go into the parlour then, — you get her downstairs." "Oh! she always goes into the parlour first, and sits down a minute, and talks." There was no time for us to talk more, for the woman knocked again. "Fetch my hat and stick (it was in the parlour), — you get her into the kitchen, then I'll slip out leaving the street-door ajar." Down we both went, three stairs at a time, up I went again with hat and umbrella, and had only got to the top when I heard poor trembling Jenny opening the street-door. I leant over the banisters, and listened.

"I've knocked twice Jenny." "Did you? — I was dozing, — the thundery weather makes me so queer. — Have a cup of tea, and take a table out into the garden, — it will be fresher there to have tea."

"No I've got my new dress, it will rumple it if it's long in the bundle, I must open it. Such a pretty one, — you will like it I think. — Tom did when I showed him the pattern, — I'll take it up to the bed-room, and hang it up."

Jenny's voice rose almost to a shriek. "Oh! no, no, don't, — come and have tea first, — I'm so thirsty, so tired, — come down-stairs." "Well you go and make it, I'll only just hang it up in the bed-room, and come down directly," said her sister.

Jenny objecting, the sister answered angrily, "What are you in such a hurry for tea for? — it's not time, — well have it by yourself, I can't drink it, — I had a lot of beer at dinner, and Tom gave me nearly a pint before I left him, — it was so hot, I was so thirsty, — it's on my chest now, — I can't put tea on the top of it yet." "Well if you won't, I may as well go up with you," said Jenny. Footsteps came near, and hat, stick, and self, I threw under the bed. Jenny came in looking like death. "She won't find me here, — get her down soon," was all I had time to say in a whisper before the sister following Jenny entered the room I had quite hidden myself.

The bed had been a good one, the old gentleman and lady had slept on it for years; it was large and handsome, but being shabby and worn out, had that very month only been put to servants' use.

Round it were old red valances hanging to the floor, things not given to servants. No sooner was I under the bed, than I saw there were little openings at the seams, and some moth-holes, which permitted me to see through them. At one spot near to my shoulder as I lay crouching and doubled up, was a long slit where the valance had been torn down. By raising myself on my elbow, and squeezing my head against the mattress I could see perfectly, but no person in the room would have noticed me, even though the room was as bright as day, for the thick red hangings hid me in darkness under the bed, and I was on the side away from the window. I gazed earnestly at Jenny's sister through this opening and others.

She was a well-grown, strong woman, with a handsome round face, and dark hair and eyes; she had shortish petticoats, and thickish ankles in good lace-up boots which made much noise as she walked about. She had a huge paper parcel in her hands, which she placed on the bed; then for a moment she rested her bum on the bed-side, and Jenny did the same by the side of her. The parcel was between them, her ankles were within a few inches of my nose; I gently lifted the valance, and saw up the calf of her legs, her petticoats cut as they were in those days, being drawn up by sitting down. I remember almost every word, every action which took place on that memorable afternoon, and not a movement escaped me.

"I can't untie it, — cut it." "The scissors are downstairs." "I'll go and fetch them." "Oh! no, — where is the knife that I cut my corns with?" "Oh! never mind, — there, I've done it, — I've broken it," — and she rose up as did Jenny from the bed, and both now stood standing facing the side of the bed where I lay.

I heard the rustling of paper, the rustling of a dress, the noise of feet paddling about. "Oh! it *is* nice, — what did it cost? — who made it?" "I made the skirt, and Miss Skinner the body, — she charged me seven and six, — it's not dear, is it? — I'll hang it up, then the creases will come out." "Let's hang it up first." And then on a peg at the back of the door the dress was hung up, and for a moment, both women stood admiring it, their backs towards me and the bed.

"Look," said the sister, "it just wants a little something done to the sleeves, — she said it was not finished there, — oh! yes here it is, — I would not wait for her, I can easily do it myself, — I was glad to get it, and half feared I should not get it for Sunday, — the old beast never keeps her promise, but she has this time, — I gave her sixpence extra. Oh! my gracious how hot it is, — I'm sweating all over, — it's awful, — I'll pull off my frock, then I'll finish the sleeves as it hangs up, — get us the needle and thread Jenny, — just thread a needle dear, while I pull off my frock."

"Don't," said Jenny in an agitated manner, "let's have tea first." "No I must finish it," and as she spoke she undid her dress, and slipped it off. A beautiful, handsome pair of breasts came in view. "Oh! Lord look at my chemise, — look how I've sweated, — see how the stain from the dress has gone through under my arms, — I stink of sweat, — how glad I shall be when the weather is cooler." As she said that with a slight effort she drew her arms through the sleeves of her chemise, and lifting her freed arms showed a pair of black hairy armpits. I began to thrill and cock-stiffen. She lifted her fine arms up, and looked at the stained chemise as it hung over her stays, then with a heave and a push she freed her breasts, so that they were right over the top of her stays showing the nipples; then with naked arms, she began to work at the sleeves of the dress hanging up behind the door.

Jenny was all this time moving about in a restless manner, taking every now and then a hurried glance at the valance of the bed which concealed me; and as it seemed to me placing herself in such a position, as to prevent my seeing her sister's upper nakedness; but it was quite useless, I could see all she had exposed.

She worked a few minutes talking to Jenny, who was making as much noise with her feet as she could. Then the sister looked up, and leaving off her needlework said, "This will make Tom want to do it to me, — a new dress always does, when he sees me in it, — he ain't done it lately, he will to-morrow." They both laughed, and she went to work again.

Again she stopped, Jenny had then seated herself at the edge of the bed over me. "Oh! how awfully hot I am, — what a bore petticoats are, — I declare I've a good mind to leave them off this weather." She stepped forward. "I'll take them off, I can slammack about to-night, — no one will see me." "Oh! no don't," said Jenny in an excited way; but she quickly unlaced her stays, untied her petticoats, and slipped them down to her ankles. Her chemise which was no longer held up to her shoulders by the arms, slipped down with them, and she stood naked before me excepting her boots and stockings. She seemed to have forgotten that her chemise was no longer held up, for just as the petticoats fell below her cunt, she made a slight grasp as if to hold them up, then she gave a laugh. "That's cool enough," said she.

"Don't, — what are you doing?" shrieked Jenny, "put on your chemise, — you're naked, — you're naked," — and she tried to pull up the chemise; but the woman stepped away from the clothes as they lay on the floor, caught up the chemise, threw it on the bed, and placed petticoats and stays on a chair by the wash-hand stand. I saw large hips, a mass of dark hair at her cunt, a large white backside, fine round thighs and limbs; in brief a fine, plump, well-fed woman, a splendid sight. The innocence of the action was beautiful. "Oh! isn't it nice and cool," she said, "I've got so hot walking."

"Put on your things, — what are you doing?" said Jenny. "Oh! isn't it nice! — I wish one could go in one's skin this weather," she replied. She scratched her motte-hair, and felt her arse, and seemed so pleased with herself. Then she looked under each of her armpits. "Oh! Lord how hot I am, — where is a towel?" She took one, and began gently rubbing herself with it under her armpits, put it down, and again scratched the hair of her motte.

"I'm surprized at you," said Jenny walking about, and I'm sure trying to prevent me from seeing her sister, though she always declared to me afterwards that she had no such intention. "Cover yourself, you'll catch cold." "Catch cold? — nonsense, — and you have the window shut also, — what do you shut it for?" "Oh! I can't bear it open in thundering weather." The fact was we always shut it when we went to the bed to exclude noise, and left the door open, to hear if any one knocked at the street-door. "Put something on you at all events," said Jenny, "it's not decent." "Decent? — you *are* modest all of a sudden."

"It's delicious!" She walked round the bed to the window, opened it, came back naked as she was, and went on working at her dress; and so for a quarter of an hour did I see this handsomely-made woman naked, first her side, then her belly, then her bum came in view, till I was driven mad by the state of my penis which was throbbing with excitement, and urging me to frig it.

"Well that will do," she said as she finished, "the creases will never be noticed where they are," — and she walked backwards to the bed, the short distance she was from it, and sat down at the edge just where the valance had dropped. With care I pulled the valance, and the seam opened more, but not much. I raised myself on my elbow, my eyes to the opening. There were the thighs and legs stretching out to the floor, her bum was at the mere edge of the bed, her cunt but about six inches above my nose. I had a wonderfully keen scent for the aroma of a woman, and swear I smelt her cunt distinctly, though I could not see it. She sat there for full five minutes, talking to Jenny about the dress, whilst I kept sniffing up the aroma from her flesh and her love-orifice, and feeling my quivering prick, whilst my greedy eyes gloated on the fat thighs, so far as I could see them.

At length she turned round. "I'll put my slippers on," — and sitting down opposite the bed on the chair on which she had placed her petticoats, she put one leg up, and began unlacing the boot, then between and under the thighs I saw the dark hairy notch. She had scarcely put herself in that attitude before putting her foot down, she came to the bed, put one foot up, and there continued unlacing it, — and there was her cunt just visible, and within a foot of my greedy eyes, whilst she leisurely unlaced the boot on the bed, the other foot on the floor. Had I placed her there for the purpose I could not have done it better.

"Oh! don't," said Jenny, "take your foot off." "What's the matter?" replied she as if just noticing Jenny's excitement, "you've got one of your foolish fits on I think." "You will dirty the bed, — take your foot off." "Nonsense it's quite dry, besides it's on my chemise, — I wish you'd go and make tea, if you are in such a hurry, — one would think you had got St. Vitus' dance," — for Jenny in her agitation, and also to make noise to prevent any indiscreet movement of mine being noticed, had kept moving about noisily and restlessly the whole time.

Silenced, she said no more, but still walked restlessly about, went at the back of her sister, and glared at the valance where she guessed my eyes were peeping. Her face was the picture of anxiety. But I did not look at that long, I was rivetted on her sister's form and dark-haired cunt; that cunt was at times slightly opened by the attitude she was in, and altered its shape as she moved. I saw the thick dark hair curling away until I lost sight of it in the direction of her arsehole, and I could smell her cunt again I swear, my excitement grew intense, I could not keep my hand from my prick, I knew the delicate position I was in, the injury I should do the poor girl if found out; — but a spend in sight of that cunt and splendid pair of thighs I must have. I just touched myself, holding my breath, restraining all emotion, gave one or two frigs, and a shower of sperm fell over my trowsers. If any man might be pardoned for having a solitary pleasure, it was I, placed in such a lust-stirring situation.

CHAPTER XXI

Further undressing. — Slippers wanted. — Toilet operations. — The effects of hash and beer. — A windy escape. — Feeling for the pot. — Sisters exeunt. — A crushed hat, and soiled trowsers. — A narrow escape. — My benevolent intentions towards Jenny's sister.

I thought I had had my pleasure in silence, but I was wrong, I was heard, I had given a slight sigh. The anxious ears of poor Jenny heard it. She made increased noise whilst her sister went tranquilly on, and unlaced her boots without taking any notice or hearing me, whilst the last drop of sperm was running over, and I was still looking at her cunt, and sniffing.

Then she stood looking at her boots. "Ah! this one wants soling, — where are my slippers? — where did I put them?" They were just under the bed, close by me. "Here they are," said Jenny rushing to the side, and pulling them out she gave them to her sister who took them, but instead of putting them on pulled off both her stockings. "I'll wash these to-night," said she, "and darn them the first thing to-morrow, — I'll cut my corns." "Oh! do come down and have tea, — you can cut your corns after you have washed your feet to-night, — oh! put something on, and come." "I won't be long, — you go and make tea." "No I shan't, I know you'll be an hour, — it will be spoiled." "I can cut them so much better by daylight, — I cut my toe last Saturday night you know," and without more ado she walked round the foot of the bed to the other side, where in front of the window was a small dressing-table, a looking-glass, and a chair by the side of it. She was now absolutely naked from head to foot. As she neared the window she said, "Oh! how delicious the air is blowing upon one's skin, — I quite hate putting on my chemise again." Jenny still kept moving about, and shuffling her

186

feet; but the sister engrossed in herself, kept on talking about her dress, her Tom, the place she was going to on the morrow, and seemed to notice nothing. At length she placed one foot on the chair by the window, and began cutting her corns. And now I had a view of her backside and naked form from that side of the bed.

When she had finished one foot, she put it down, and sat on the edge of the bed. "Poof! how hot it makes me stooping, — it makes me sweat, — but I'll do the other, — drat the tight boots, they make corns," — and up went the other foot. Out went my head, and up went the valance, but I was fearful of being seen, so took out my pen-knife, and cut a long slit in the valance. Then my eye was nearer still to her buttocks, but I could not see her seat of pleasure so well, so I took to the floor again, and saw her cunt better.

Then she stood for a minute looking over a little white blind into the gardens. "There is Mrs. B**** and her daughter walking." "Oh! pray put something on, — if they should see you." "Impossible they can't," — and she stooped down, and began operating on the other corn. The cunt opened a little and so did something else, for out popped a pretty loud, short, sharp fart.

"You beast," said Jenny. "I beg your pardon," said the sister, "I'm always windy when I have eaten hash, and drunk beer, — I could not help it." "It's dirty," growled Jenny. "You're far enough off, and it's better out than in," — and ceasing to chuckle, and as if half ashamed of herself she went on corn-cutting without speaking, but that did not suit Jenny who soon began a conversation, and shuffling about. She made no further allusion to the fart.

When she had finished it only seemed as if I had been looking at her there for a few seconds, but on that side of the bed she must have given me ten minutes of that lascivious gratification. I was so engrossed, so delighted that even the fart did not amuse me; it annoyed me; for it made her alter her position, and withdraw from my lustful gaze, that charm which perhaps no one but her husband had ever gazed upon so long and so earnestly.

Then she went back again to the other side of the bed, put on stockings and slippers, and getting up, "Where is the pot?" said she, "is it this side or the other?" — and began feeling under the valance within a few inches of me, but it was not there. Evidently it was usually there, indeed I know it was, but Jenny and I had both pissed before we began to think of fucking, and I had put the pot under the washing-stand.

"Not there," shrieked Jenny rushing to the pot. The sister turned round and saw it. I peeped just in time to see her thighs open as she squatted, then came a heavy thump on the bed. The sister said, "What's the matter? — don't give way, — don't be a fool now." Then without pissing she got up, and came to the bed-side. Poor Jenny excited beyond bearing by anxiety, had fainted on seeing her sister on the point of discovering me in searching for the pot.

She shook Jenny, threw water on her face, and Jenny soon recovered. "What on earth's the matter? — you give way, you do, — a woman need not faint like that, I'm sure," said she angrily, "you scared me dreadful." Jenny said nothing, but repeated that she wanted her tea, that thundery weather always made her feel sick and faint.

"Well we will go down at once, — I did not think you were ill." "You might have seen I was." "I did not, but I'll be ready in minute." Again she squatted on the pot, thighs wide open, belly towards me, pissed like a water-spout, and let one or two little farts of which no notice was taken, whilst I with cock stiff was looking on, and again frigging myself. I could not help it, for every turn, every movement she made was such as if done expressly to show off her naked charms, and drive me randy-mad.

"Give me my night-gown Jenny, it's at the foot of the bed, and I'll only put my dress over it, — it's so hot." Jenny turned to take the night-gown from the bed. "I'll just wash a bit," said her sister, "I'm almost in a lather with heat and sweat." Pouring out water in the basin she placed it on the floor, and turning towards the bed squatted, and sluiced her cunt, then rubbed it dry with the towel. "That has made me comfortable," she remarked, and began putting on her frock.

As she did so she remarked, "You have not emptied the pot to-day, — you should, it smells this hot weather." "Yes I did," said Jenny innocently. "Well then you've peed a lot." "I've done it once or twice since morning," said Jenny hastily.

Then the sister went out first. When halfway downstairs I emerged from my hiding-place and listened, heard Jenny say, "I may as well empty the slops, you go and see if the water boils." Up came Jenny. "Oh! I'm ready to die, — hish! — be quiet." She emptied the pot and waters into a slop-pail, and went downstairs quickly whilst I followed her silently. I was covered with flue, and had managed to crush my hat; my trowsers were partly unbuttoned, and one leg covered with spunk. We got to the ground-floor almost together, and there I stopped. So soon as I heard she was in the kitchen I moved along the passage, and slipped out, leaving the street-door ajar. Luckily a cab was close by, and I jumped into it. The first thing I did was to button up properly. I bolted past my servant as she opened the door to me, took another hat, wrapped the old one up in paper, and the same night tore out the lining, and threw both away in a by-road.

I was in an indescribable state of excitement after this delicious afternoon, and was seized with an almost delirious letch for the woman. I was sleepless for a night or two, scheming how to possess her.

Early on the Monday I got to Jenny's, and spent the rest of the day fucking, and talking of the sight I had seen. My imagination helped to allay my excitement, for the form of her sister though more beautiful than Jenny's, had still a family likeness to her, and as I clasped Jenny in my arms I pictured her as her sister, and enjoyed her as such.

I was cautious in my disclosures, for I found that Jenny who had been most inquisitive about other women, and delighted to hear how they talked, and walked, and pissed, and fucked, was annoyed when I talked of her sister's nakedness. I ought not to have looked, — why I had seen more than she, her own sister, — a poor woman, and married, and she to have her thing looked at by a strange man, — her husband could not have seen more, — and so on. So though I described her sister's charms I took care not to express any admiration of them, nor to say I had frigged myself, and felt desire for her. Jenny had not noticed that my trowsers were undone, and sperm-soiled. I had not noticed that myself till I got out of the house on that eventful afternoon.

On the Monday when I saw Jenny, she declared that another hour's anxiety would have killed her. We found that the time from the minute the sister came into the bed-room, to the time she went downstairs was two hours. Jenny thought that she must have been half-an-hour working at her dress. Jenny had walked round the room trying if she could see me, or if I was looking, but could

only do so once or twice at the holes, or fancy she did; but the
long tear in the valance through which I could see with both eyes
at once, and just above which her sister had put up her legs, she
had never noticed; nor did she believe me when I said that I could
see the cunt when her sister's backside was towards me, when near
the window. So I made her lie down, and look from the floor whilst
I stood naked, pretending to cut my corns. Then she said it was a
shame of me to be peeping. She had a clear inspection from my
bum-bone to my ballocks, and knew I had seen the cunt.

She did not contend any longer. "Do you mean to say, that if
you had been under the bed, and had known a naked man was
cutting his corns, you would not have peeped out?" No she would
not; but had it been a naked woman perhaps she would, Jenny
replied. So after she had heard from me how much I had seen of
her sister's body between her back-bone and her navel, and I had
told her something which made her say, "Law, has she!" though
I can't recollect what it was, the subject dropped. Then I learnt
from her more about her sister's wages, mode of life, and where
she worked; for although the thing seemed ridiculous, I had a letch,
and meant to try to put into that young woman if possible, though
I had not then stroked Jenny many weeks. I liked variety.

CHAPTER XXII

The Sunday following. — Chaste calculations. — The sister alone.
— My embarrassment. — Ale fetched. — Warm conversation. —
Stiffening. — Bolder talk. — An exhibition of masculinity. — A
golden promise. — Lust creeping. — Baudy dalliance. — Cock and
cunt in conjunction.

On the following Sunday her young man was coming to London, and she was to spend the day with him at his relatives. Her sister was to keep the house, the husband was going elsewhere, so the sister would be alone, — all provided it was fine weather. Jenny had promised her mistress that until her return she would never go out with her young man, and that is how Jenny kept her word. She knew I would not tell, would I? — I felt her cunt, and kissed her. "It's not very likely, is it my pet?" Then she snivelled, said she was very wicked, and hoped God would not punish her.

When I heard of this arrangement I lusted strongly. In vain I said to myself, What, again a married woman! In comfortable circumstances for her class, with two children, — a woman you have never spoken to, — can you expect to get her! I did not expect it, but had a burning desire to see and speak to her, to look closely at, and have a chat with a woman whose privates I had seen so nakedly. It seemed to me to promise a titillating treat. Besides I had been so successful with women, — gay women had even been anxious to get me, — that a half-belief came over me, that if I had time, I could persuade even her to let me. Time was the difficulty, for she did not yet even know me by face (so I thought, but was wrong). At all events see her I would, — she was dissatisfied with her fucking, that I knew; she might be randy, and then be much

191

less impregnable than she seemed; so I determined to see her on the Sunday that Jenny went out.

I could think only of one powerful means of getting her, if any thing encouraged a hope, and that was by money. I had not too much then, though getting better off, but determined if ten pounds would tempt her, that she should have it. I was a long time I recollect pondering over the sum. The Sunday turned out fine, I put the gold in my purse, and went to the house just after their dinner-time, and after my luncheon, at which I fed myself up well, and to give me courage took an extra glass, for I had one of my nervous fits of funking come on, mixed with doubts about the morality of deliberately trying a married woman.

She opened the door, I walked straight in. "Who are you?" "Where is the housemaid?" said I, "I have promised Mrs. W**** to call and see from time to time." "Oh! I'm her sister sir, my name is ****, I sleep here every night sir, Mrs. W**** pays me to do so sir, — my sister is out sir, — I'm very sorry, but she is not at all well from being confined to the house so much, — I told her she might go to church, — it would be a change, and give her a little fresh air; — she will be back at half-past four sir." "Oh! so you are Mrs. So-and-So?" "Yes I am." I walked into the parlours. There was a large beer-jug and two tumblers on the table, and ale in one glass. She rushed to take them away. "I beg pardon sir, but Mrs. W**** said we might sit in the parlours, when we have done work, and on Sundays besides, cause it's so dull in the kitchens." The woman was agitated at her sister being out, and at being caught drinking beer in the parlour; she thought I might make mischief, I suppose.

I told her that she need not disturb herself, for I should not stay long, and kept looking, with cock already stiffening, into her face, then at her arms, then at the bottom of her belly, and in my mind's eye seeing the dark hair down there. I had planned conversation, but forgot what to say, through thinking of her nakedness and sexual charms, and stood staring at her till she turned her eyes away confused, and coloured up.

I continued to be embarrassed, and so lost recollection of all I had intended to say and do, that I was actually going away. I asked one or two stupid questions: if letters had come, if any one had been, and so on; all the time thinking that I was looking through her clothes at her naked charms. I was in a sort of a trance of baudiness which muddled me; when noticing the ale-glass I asked, "What are you drinking?" "Fourpenny ale, sir." That reply broke the spell, my senses returned, I thought of an excuse for stopping. "Give me a glass, — I'm thirsty." "That's the last of it sir." "Can't you get some?" "The pot-boy brought that, — it's Sunday, and the public is not always open." I looked at my watch. "It's not church-time yet, send some one to fetch some, — I'm so thirsty, and hot, and so tired," — and I sat down. "I'm alone." "Is not your husband here?" "No, no one." "Do you mind fetching me some?" "If you don't mind waiting, sir." "No." I gave her money. "How much?" "Oh! fill the jug, — not with fourpenny, — with the best ale, — ask them to draw it mild, and get me two bottles of ginger-beer." In a few minutes she was back, — I had given her a five shilling piece. "You may keep the change." "Thank you, sir," said she quite touched and delighted. I always gave the change to girls whom I wanted to poke.

In her absence I went all over the house that was not locked up, even to the privy and coal-cellar, had satisfied myself that she was alone, and was getting quite myself again when she came back.

"Have a glass." "Thank you, sir." "So you are Jenny's sister, — Jane's her name I think." Yes it was. "Aren't you afraid to be in the house of a night?" No she was not. "Sit down." "Thank you, sir," — but she stood. "So you are an upholstress, — sit down," — and after a little pressure, down she sat. We took ale together, and no doubt I spoke with all that kindness which a man shows towards a woman whom he desires to poke, I have heard women say that I have a winning, persuasive manner.

Gradually the conversation became about herself. "You've two children, — why not more?" "Oh! quite enough for poor people." "Well, you see, I can't get any." "Poor people are sure to have lots." "Two is not a lot, — how manage to stop at two?" "Oh! it's all chance." "Is not another coming?" She was getting flushed and excited. "Lord no, I hope not!" "Don't you know?" "I don't." "Yes you do, — how old is your last?" "Four years." "If I were your husband I'd have a dozen." "Well you say *you* haven't any yet, sir," said she. "No, I can't get any." "Ah! if we had your money! — but with we poor people it's different, — it's hard enough to fill the bellies of two." "And so you won't have your belly filled with another little one, — won't you, eh!"

"Oh! Lord," said she laughing spite of herself, "you are plain-spoken." I was in the vein now, did not say an improper word, but gave baudy hints, smutty suggestions about the dullness of sleeping alone, of the results of wives being away from husbands, &c., till her eyes twinkled, and she laughed much. I had now broken down the barrier, had brought myself to her level, and she as every other woman would have done, took advantage of it, and began to return my chaffing and banter. Every woman feels instinctively that when a man is chaffing her (be it ever so decently veiled) about fucking, that she may safely return it: both are at once on a common level. A washerwoman would banter a prince if the subject was cunt, without the prince being offended. To talk of fucking with a woman is to remove all social distinctions, and I had done it without uttering at first a smutty word.

Jenny's sister went on chaffing, and drank ale freely. "Oh! I dare say, but why don't *you* have children?" "I can't get any I tell you, but I try." "Not much at home," said she "from all I have heard." "No, I try out as well, and get none, — I'm a safe man." Then I found she knew a lot about me and my affairs. She had actually worked at my house on some curtains, had seen me once, and knew my voice, though for the moment she had not recollected my face with my hat on when I entered the door that afternoon. But I had never seen her at my house to my knowledge, though if I had I was not likely to have noticed a common upholstress.

We went on chaffing, looking in each other's faces, each knowing we were talking about fucking. "Well Mrs. *** playing at mother and father's a delicious amusement, is it not?" "I don't know." "If you don't know we'd better try, — I'd give five pounds to be your husband for an hour, — and five pounds would buy you a new dress." "It would buy me three," said she without noticing the other part of my remark. "Three?" "Yes three, — I can't afford more than thirty shillings for a best dress." "Really! — such a beautiful creature as you ought to have plenty of dresses, for I have rarely seen a more lovely woman, and so well grown, — I'll bet you have fine limbs." She was flattered, the praise upset her, her eyes twinkled. Yes she might have done better she knew, but it was to be. I went close to her, caught and kissed her. She made not too strong a resistance, but got away. "That's going a little too far." "That's the beginning of a game at mother and father, and you are going to have the three dresses." She laughed in a funny way. "I don't want to be a mother any more, so I don't want any games." But she seemed to me to look as if she did.

What did she get for stopping at the house? Five shillings a week, and her supper and breakfast, — that was an object. "Five shillings? — why my kiss was worth that, — let me give you another, and I'll give you ten shillings for the two." "You don't mean that," said she with a low laugh. "On my soul yes, — but you must give me a kiss as well." She shook her head. "It's going too far," said she. "There it is, I'll trust you, — you won't take it without letting me." She was then sitting. I put the half sovereign into her hand. "Thank you, sir," said she softly. I kissed her rapturously, she let me kiss half-a-dozen times, and whilst doing I so took hold of her hand, and pressed it as if by accident against my cock. She a married woman knew the hard line her hand pressed against, for she moved her hand away. "Now your promise, — kiss me." "I didn't promise." "You took the money." "There then," said she, giving me a kiss, and jumping up sharply, "we are going too far, — we really are now, — we don't either of us know what we are about, I think." "I don't think I do," said I, "for though I never saw you before, I've never been so struck with a woman in my life, I'd give ten pounds to be in bed with you an hour."

I had been putting my cock straight in my trowsers, feeling and squeezing my balls whenever I saw her looking at me. I fancied she kept looking askant at that part of my person. She was getting red in face, hot, and confused in manner. Just then I observed a bed pillow on the sofa; she had, I guessed, been laying down after dinner. "Why here is a pillow, — you've been on the sofa with your husband, — you have been playing at mother and father here." She burst out into laughter. "Why I've not seen him for a week." "Then you've been tickling by yourself." "Tickling?" (it was said quite innocently). "Yes, between your legs." "Oh! really now you are agoing too far, sir," said she, jumping up again, "you speak too freely, — I don't like it." Then she laughed, and said, "Well — this — really is, — oh!"

"Not at all, — you are lovely, exquisite, delicious, — if you've really not seen your husband for a week, let me, — who will know? — we are in the house alone, — let us," — and standing close to her I put my arms around her, but I felt afraid of going too far.

"You must not talk like that." "Oh! nonsense, — I'll give you six pounds." "Oh! no, you don't mean what you say, — it's wild talk." I took out my purse, and putting six pounds on the table in gold, just as I had done to her sister the ten pounds. "There," said I, "that is yours," — and pulled out my prick. She got up, and ran to the other side of the room as if I had pulled out a pistol. "You're talking too plain, sir — it's going too far, — if you expose yourself like that I'll go to the street-door." I'm at a loss to know why I pitched upon six pounds, I had intended ten, but cannot tell why I offered that particular sum. I have often thought since of what made me take that economical figure.

"Sit down." "I won't if you expose yourself, — it's not gentle-manlike." I put my cock into my trowsers, then kissed her again, resistance was not so strong. "Now, sir, don't." "Sit down my darling," — and getting her to the sofa we went on talking. "How foolish, — who would know, — why not delight me, — why not take the money." "No." "Do now." "No." "Won't you?" "Of course not, — no, — no." "Well kiss me." "There then." "Do let me dear." "I won't, — I won't, I shan't, — there."

Just then I noticed one of her garters was hanging down by her foot. "Your garter's undone," said I. I stooped forward, and took it up. "Give it me." I kissed it. "No, — it's been so near where I want to go, — I shall keep it till I've been there." "You will keep it a long time then."

She drank more ale, it was sweet and strong, and I went on talking. Thought I, she must want it if she has not seen her husband for a week. Where did she garter, — below or above knee? "Let me feel?" I felt outside, then pinched the leg, then higher up. She began looking me full in the face, and laughing at my smutty in-sinuations. I pulled her back on the sofa, kissed her, and let her rise up again. I repeated the pull and the kiss more than once, and then as she was rising up and saying, "Now don't pull me about like that," I put her hand on my prick which I had slipped out again. "Oh!" — and she let it go. Quick as lightning I slipped a hand up her clothes to her cunt. "Let me now, — there's a darling." "I shan't." "Do." "I shan't." She repulsed my hand, but did not get away from me. I thought from the way she looked at me, and the quiet manner in which she pushed away my hand, that she was hot with lust, and could scarcely refuse me. I pulled her to me, and got my finger on her clitoris. "Do let me feel your cunt, and fuck, — put my prick in there, — let us, — do darling," said I, twiddling like mad, and rattling out a volume of baudiness.

She bore it all for a minute quietly, wriggling and saying, "I shan't. — I won't, — no, now take your hand away." Then with a sudden impulse she pushed me off, got up, and sat down further from me on the sofa. "Oh! now be quiet, — let me think a minute, — I don't know whether I'm on my heels or my head." She picked up something which had fallen at her feet, as she had doubled herself down when my finger was stimulating her randiness.

Then catching her by her waist I pulled her back on to the sofa, and threw myself on her. "You shan't" were the last words I recollect her uttering; as I threw up her clothes and felt the wet gash. My prick the next instant was buried in it, and we were fucking.

"Don't, — oh! — take it out, — do, — oh! — oh! — ohoe!" she murmured. She had fetched me, and pump, pump, pump, pump, went my spunk up her. Then delicious oblivion. As I came to myself I found her arse still moving. "Oh! do," she murmured. She was besides herself with desire to spend.

But my prick instead of obeying me as it usually did on such exciting occasions, refused, and shrinking left her cunt, to my intense vexation. "I haven't done it," said she softly, and with disappointment as her bum ceased its labors, and my tool lay dripping outside her quim.

We spoke no more, but I lay trying to squeeze it up again. To stiffen it I felt up and round her, rubbed the tip on her spermy nymphœ, she made gentle efforts to second me, but it was of no use, so I rolled off. She sat up, and after looking at me for a minute with eyes filled with baudiness, began like all women, to feel if her hair was all right. "Were you just coming my dear?" She made no reply.

She had not taken any care to arrange her dress, it had dragged up behind her bum, and the petticoats were up to her knees, the leg which had lost its garter was half naked. Taking her round the waist I put my hand on to her cunt, and titillated the clitoris. She let me go on, and continued feeling about her hair. Then looking me full in the face, looking as if she were ready to spend, she pushed me away. "Don't,— don't, — I don't like it done that way."

"You can do it that way yourself, can't you?" "Of course I can."
"I shall soon fuck again." "Oh! I dare say," and she walked to the
looking-glass, then went to the window, and looked out into the
garden without paying any heed to my exciting remarks. I sat on
the sofa feeling my cock, and trying to stiffen it, but it was useless;
so I tried to interest her in something else, feeling annoyed, though
I had nothing to be ashamed of.

CHAPTER XXIII

Jenny's bed-room. — The money hidden. — On the bed. — Fears of maternity. — Inspection of sex. — The use of a husband. — Another Sunday. — Regrets and refusal. — Resistance overcome. — Jenny's ignorance. — Her master returns. — Difficulty in getting at Jenny. — Her sister waylaid. — Against a fence. — Jenny's marriage, and rise in life.

Why don't you take the money?" said I. "You really mean it?" "Of course." She took it up. "It's a real God-send, — it comes just in time, — who'd have thought it?" said she as if to herself. "I must put it where it can't be found, and take it home to-morrow." She went to the door, "Aren't you going?" "No, I'm going to do it again soon." "But you're not." "But I am." Without reply she went upstairs. I had meant to have ready a stiff-stander when she came back, but changed my mind, and followed her. She was nearly at the top when hearing me she waited, and said, "What do you want?"

"I'm coming to see what you do." "You won't." "I will." "I'll come down and wait till you are gone." "I'll stop till your sister comes home." "Do go down, sir," said she in a coaxing tone. "No." She sat down on the top-stairs, I did the same a few stairs below her. Her knees were wide apart, my mind went to the afternoon when I had seen her naked. That glorious two hours. I stared in a voluptuous reverie, her cunt was as visible to me through her clothes, as if she were naked, and my cock began to swell. I stared on without uttering a word.

"What are you staring at?" said she at last, "go down, and I'll be down in a minute." "I'm looking at your cunt, it's open slightly, I can see my spunk in it." "Oh!" said she jumping up, "I never heard such a man in my life." (She had the gold still in her hand.)

199

"You have upset me so, I don't know what I am about." She then turned her bum round towards me, and I put my hand quickly up her clothes, as she went up the stairs. "Oh! you frighten me so I don't know what I'm doing." I followed her into the room, and she locked up the money in a bag that was in a drawer. Turning round she saw my prick out, and as stiff as ever. It was the recollection of what had taken place in that room on the Saturday week previous which had rendered me capable again. I closed on her, kissing and inciting her, pulled her to the bed, and began feeling her. "I don't like that done, — you know you can't, — leave me alone, — go down, — oh! don't."

I coaxed her for a second. She got on to the bed, and opened her thighs wide like a well-trained fuckster to help me, I inserted my penis, and she met me with passion. I was not so rapid, the want of a spend was not now overpowering my senses; whilst she had had two hours' baudy talk, been fucked but cheated of her pleasure, and been left at the critical moment, unsatisfied, with my spunk in her. She was dying for a spend, wanting it like a woman who has been for a week unsatisfied. Her cunt was hungry for prick, throbbing and tightening to pour out its amatory juices, her backside's movements became quick and fierce. "Oh! it's big," she gasped whilst I was still sensible, "oh! — I'm — com — coming," — and gluing her mouth to mine she spent copiously ere I'd well nigh begun to feel the full urging of lust.

The constriction of her cunt, the delight of feeling her pleasure, increased my stiffness. "Let me wash, — do." "You won't come on the bed again." "Yes I will, but let me wash." I clutched her like a vice. "No, I'm coming, — you'll spend again." My prick stiffer and stiffer drove with fury up against her womb. "Oh! don't push so hard." "Fuck my darling, — there, — the tip's only in, — it's in your spunk, and mine together." "Oh! you hurt." On I drove. Her backside's play began, her lips were glued to mine, our tongues played against each other, and we spent together with ejaculations. "Oh! — don't, — you hurt, — oh! oh! — I'm coming." Then we lay palpitating, my prick throbbing and soaking, her cunt squeezing and sucking.

"Let me get up, — let me wash, — pray do." I laid on her heavy, nestled my balls up to her arse, held her as long as I could; but uncunting me she got off the bed, and washed her cunt. I still lay playing with my prick. "You'll have a child this day nine months my dear." "Oh! my God don't say so, — but I believe I shall." "You are all right, I don't get them you know." "Have you never had any children!" "None at home." "Oh! that's nothing, — have you any out, for you are a gay man?"

I got up to piss, and saw my thick sperm in the basin. "You've washed it all out my dear, — you are safe." She shook her head. "This is a strange business," she remarked, "I scarce know where I am, — what I'm about, — it's impossible," — and she stood staring at me playing with my cock. Then she went to the drawer and looked at the money, as if she doubted its being there. "It's a fact," she said locking it up again, "are you not going down?" "No." "I wish you would, — I want to be by myself." "You want to piddle." "You are a strange man," and taking the pot she pissed. "You'd better empty all," said I, "if your sister Jane comes back and sees it she will think your husband's been doing it to you." "She won't think or know anything if she does see," said Mrs. *** "Well I declare I'm atalking to you just like my husband, — I don't seem to know whether I am on my head or my heels.

"Church must be over, — Jane has not come back." "She won't be back till nine o'clock, she is out with her young man." "Oh! not at church?" "No I told you so because Mrs. W**** told her not to go out on Sunday; — but you won't tell?" "Of course not my dear, I dare say Jane and her young man have done what we have been doing." "Lord sir, he is a most respectable young man, and far above her, — they are going to be married, — she is lucky, luckier than I am, — she'd knock his head off if he laid hand upon her improperly, — that she would, she! Lor bless you," — and Mrs. **** laughed with incredulity. I laughed also. "Ah! she looks a quiet young woman." "So she is, and so is he, — his family is well off," — and then she told me all that Jenny had told me.

"I wish you would let me make the bed." "I'm going to have you again." "Oh! likely." "I am." "No you're not, — please go." "No." "Then I shall go downstairs." "Go my dear." She took me at my word, her manner had quite changed, she had been laughing and chaffing, she had blushed, looked at me with fun and lust in her eyes, and at last with full open eyes one moment, followed by the half-closed eye and lanquishing manner of a randy woman. Now she was quiet, almost sullen, and if she looked at me her eyes fell directly, the randiness had been taken out of her. I must rouse it up well if I am to have her again, said I to myself, as I lay thinking about her and the delicious sight I had seen in that room, a sight I never dare disclose to her, — but how I longed to tell her.

Up she came looking glum. "Are you not going?" "No." "Let me make the bed then." "Not until I have had you again." "Then it will go unmade." "That won't matter to me." "But it will to me, — what will my sister say if she sees the bed's been laid upon like that?" "Perhaps she will think a man has been with you." "Well you take it mighty cool, — I do hope you're going." "Not till I've had you." "Now you are atalking nonsense, — you know you can't do it," said she with an incredulous look, and the tone of a woman who knew what a prick could do and what not. "Look at this," I uncovered my prick which was nearly at a full-stand. She smiled when she saw it. "Nonsense, I am ashamed." "My dear I'm proud, and not ashamed, — come." "I shan't." "Then here I'll lay," and I fell back, and pulled balls and cod well out of my trowsers.

I had always a lust stirring tongue, fifty women have told me so. "You'd talk any woman randy," said a gay woman once to me. Brighton Bessie said that in five minutes I could talk her into a lewed state. Others have given me similar compliments. I was not specially conscious of that power that I recollect, but instinctively used it when I had got over fits of modesty, which sometimes prevented my uttering even veiled allusions for a time.

Mrs. ***, like Jenny, was easily flattered. What lovely limbs she had I said; had she much hair on her cunt? my excitement had prevented me feeling or seeing it. "Come and let me feel, — let me look." She coloured and blushed, and at every lascivious remark, "Oh! I never, — no I never did, — oh!" Then she again went to the drawer where the money was, looked in it as if to make sure it was there, and locked the drawer now. "Mine's bigger than your husband's, isn't it?" "Well if I ever heard such remarks." "You said it was big when it was up you." "Oh! you story." "You did my dear, you said when you were just coming, 'Oh! it's big.'" "I didn't." "*Yes you did*, you know you did, — look how stiff it is now, — come." "I won't."

I moved off the bed, caught her, and pushed her against the side of the bed. "Let's see your cunt." "You shan't." "How foolish, — I've fucked it twice, — let me feel it, and you feel my cock, — let me look at it, — I'm sure it's lovely." She got on to the bed after a little resistance, took my pego in her fist, and I got my fingers in her crack. "A delicious fuck you are," — then she let me pull up her clothes and look. "My God what a lovely cunt, — how deliciously you join your wet lips to mine, — how you move, — I shall never forget it to the last moment of my life, — oh! let me." I mustn't, — I would, but I'm frightened." "How foolish, — it's not an hour since my prick was in you, — what is the harm of doing it another time?" "Will you go then?" "Yes." Gently Mrs. ✱✱✱ opened her thighs. Our backsides were soon at the short wriggles. "It's big, isn't it?" "Oh! don't," said she. "I shall spend." My remark, tallying perhaps with something which was passing in her own mind, fetched her, and me with her instantly.

When it was over I would not go. "No I'll do it again." "That's nonsense," said she, "you know you can't, even if you try, and you're only making me anxious." We laid side by side talking, for she liked the subject. I had a most buttock-stirring letch on me, and to her astonishment in about an hour I produced another stiff one. One persuasion is very much like another with the same woman; each time I had less difficulty, for she liked the poking. Dusk was coming on, she got lights, she fetched some liquor, and after the liquor I got her to lay on the sofa (for we then had gone downstairs), and on pretence of kissing her quim I got her to open her thighs wide, and saw in the twilight what I had seen before, large and ugly inner-lips. For all that I fucked her again, after frigging myself up gently to stiffness, and fucked as if it was the last bout with a woman I was ever going to have. Then I left at her earnest entreaties before her sister returned. I had been there six hours.

I called on Jenny next day. She was in a way. Her sister, directly she had returned home, said she must go and see her husband; and spite of Jenny's entreaties not to leave her alone, had gone and never returned all night. Jenny could not make out the reason, but thought that she went away expecting to find out her husband with a woman. She returned to sleep as usual on the Monday night with Jenny, I found subsequently.

That day I went off without poking Jenny, and slunk away ashamed. I was done up with poking her sister. Jenny seemed astonished, but said nothing.

Afterwards I got out of Jenny cautiously all I wanted to know about her sister. The result was, that finding on the next Sunday fortnight Jenny was again going out with her young man, and the sister again would be left in the house, I went there. The woman's astonishment was great, and I believe she was genuinely distressed at seeing me. I attacked her for a time fruitlessly, she would not move from the street-door. "Did you not swear when I let you do it the last time, you would never come near me again, and never tell any one?" said she.

I could not deny it, had great difficulty with her, and thought I never should succeed. For full an hour with her back against the wall of the passage did she stand, refusing to move. I pulled up her clothes, felt her cunt, knelt on the mat, got my head up her petti-coats, my nose on her motte, my mouth on her thighs and cunt, my hands round her marbly buttocks, and held her kissing, sniffing, and groping my fingers between her bum-cheeks, and the red orifice which I wanted to plug. In her struggles to prevent me she once nearly fell, but she got away.

But what woman who has been fucked by a man could with-stand an hour's persistent feeling, cunt-kissing, baudy talk, and be-seeching. I conquered, and fucked her on the sofa. She did not rush out to wash her cunt as she had done at our first meeting, there was no water near. I had her again and again. At each assault when the pleasure overtook her, she had the same mouth-sucking and arse-wagging. When our love-making was over, I gave her two pounds. I had offered it her before in the passage, but she had knocked it out of my hand. When she took it she said, "Ah! it's an awful thing to be poor!" I shall tell of another woman who made the same excuse to herself for getting her lust satisfied, or yielding.

This satisfied me, and I never had her again in the house. A letch for her came again about two months afterwards, — why? God only knows, for then at times I was having her sister, another woman, Louisa Fisher, and lastly Sarah Mavis. The old couple had returned, Jenny had a fellow-servant; I could only get a poke up her with difficulty on the Sundays which her young man did not see her. I took her to a baudy house for an hour or so, then she went to church, and heard the text, because her mistress always asked her what the text was when she went home. It was a sup-position that she went to church on a Sunday.

I knew where Jenny's sister lived, and the place where she worked. It was now dark about six o'clock. I waylaid her on her way home on the high-road which was well lighted and full of people. I walked with her, but she prayed me not to do so, for her husband came partly the same road, and sometimes met her. What would happen if he met her with a swell walking by her side. I could not persuade her to go to a house. No, — she was not a loose woman, though she knew what she had done, — I had done her more harm than I had any idea of, already, — why injure her?

The more she objected, the more I longed for her. At last under solemn promise that I would go away after, we turned up a short street leading into a lane by garden-grounds, and there up against a fence I fucked her. Away she went, and I never saw her afterwards to speak to, though I have passed her without taking notice. I think that in that parting fuck I had all the pleasure, she none.

Jenny's mistress had been taken ill at the seaside, and kept there a month longer than was intended. Owing to this my complete enjoyment of Jenny's charms was prolonged, and to that I owed the second Sunday's fucking of Jenny's sister. Old Mr. W**** came up to London twice, and once nearly caught me in the house. I had written to say I had called at their home, and had never found their servant out. The lady wrote to thank me, and in writing to my mother, said how much obliged they were for my calling; but my wife said she thought the servant (Jenny) was a sly sort of minx, and wondered how they could be so foolish as to leave her in the house by herself.

When they came to town I was for a time very intimate with them, which pleased them much. Jenny used to let me out at the garden-gate, and leave the gate unlocked. Instead of going away, I used to hide in the shrubs, Jenny would came back, close the street-door ajar, and a few minutes afterwards come out again very quietly. Then up against an ivy-covered wall we poked, and she went indoors with wetted privates. Sometimes after waiting I had to go away unsatisfied, she not appearing, sometimes rain prevented us, — all of which was very annoying.

Fucking her in fact became a matter of anxiety. She had to dodge her fellow-servant as well as her master and mistress, and we copulated in fear and trembling. In the midst of the work she has left me because of some scare; once she went off saying, "Oh! there is missus' bell ringing, — oh!" — and uncunting me, off she ran.

One night we went on to the flower-beds between two large trees, and the next day the old gentleman remarked that some man had got over the wall into his garden, and he should tell the police. If there was moonlight we were done. One night latish she was sent to fetch some butter, I waited, and we fucked up against some palings. Unfortunately the butter was let fall out of the basket on to the gravel. We went back for more, but the shop was then shut, so she had to take home the dirty butter, and make the best story she could about it. On Sundays when at the baudy house, the girl was awfully frightened lest she should be seen, and we used to walk there on opposite sides of the way, I going in first. Then we went away with similar precautions, — but I began to get very tired of this, having indeed had enough of her.

Jenny had lost all fear of being in the family way, and poked freely, but she never ceased bewailing her poor young man; though at length my tool had become to her a thing to be longed for. The young man had money left him, quitted his place, and Jenny left to be married. I heard of them for many years afterwards. They opened a shop, then a larger one, and so on, till at length he became (I found this quite recently) the mayor of the town, — if not it was some one of the same name, and in the same line of business. He was much respected; and Jenny his wife was equally so. They had no children up to the time when the old lady, her former mistress, died; and for aught I know they may still be living in the town of ****.

One night some time before she left her situation, we spoke of her sister. "She is in the family way again," said she, "and in such a way about it, and so is he, — the night she left me to sleep by myself, she went home to her husband, because she suspected there was another woman there; — well that night she declared he did not let his stuff go outside, — he says he did, — they quarrel, he says it's her fault, and she says it's his."

Then it seemed evident to me that after the heavy fucking I gave her that day, that she feared being in the family way; so went home, and incited her man to fuck her, and enable her to say that the child was his, and of course it might have been, though it might have been mine.

END OF VOLUME THIRD.

MY SECRET LIFE

VOLUME IV

CONTENTS

PAGE

CHAPTER I. — *Sarah returns.* — *My love revives.* — *Her tour, and poverty.* — *My aid.* — *Old habits again.* — *Sarah jealous.* — *Lewed and lushy.* — *Her shop and her man.* — *A quarrel.* — *Yellow-haired Kitty.* — *At the Café de P**v***e.* — *Kitty's luck.* — *About Bob and Grace.* — *Kitty disappears.* — *Reconciled to Sarah.* — *Sarah with child.* — *Who is father?* — *Hannah's sister.* — *Near it, but not quite.* — *Sarah's luck.* — *A noble friend.* — *The Casino.* — *A failure.* — *Sarah's home.* — *Troubles.* — *Her sister's intrigue.* — *A hard life.* — *Sequel.* 215

CHAPTER II. — *Louisa reappears.* — *Crabs.* — *My despair.* — *A friend's advice.* — *Promiscuous harlotting.* — *Fucked out.* — *My friend's little woman.* — *Lizzie Stanley.* — *The hole by the backbone.* — *The little woman's sister.* — *Many naked ladies.* — *Operations in a four-wheeler.* — *A she on the top.* — *The cunts in two houses.* — *Slandered.* — *A sodomitic offer.* — *Non-acceptance.* 233

CHAPTER III. — *A sailor, a whore, and a garden-wall.* — *The newly-made road.* — *Windy and rainy.* — *Bargaining overheard.* — *Offer to pay.* — *Against a garden-wall.* — *A feel from behind.* — *A wet handful.* — *Blind lust.* — *Into the sperm.* — *The policeman.* — *A lost umbrella.* — *A new sort of washing-basin.* — *Fears of ailment.* 241

CHAPTER IV. — *Mrs. Y***s***e.* — *A neglectful husband.* — *Domestic unhappiness.* — *At a ball.* — *Longings for maternity.* — *The wish expressed.* — *At supper.* — *Hands under the table-cloth.* — *On the road home.* — *The family carriage.* — *Premonitory touches.* — *No coach on the stand.* — *The attempt.* — *On my knees. Jolting difficulties.* — *The trick done.* 248

CHAPTER V. — *The boudoir next day.* — *On the sofa.* — *A dull dinner.* — *Assignations.* — *The linendraper's shop* with two fronts. — The house in T***f***d Street. — Consummation. — A chaste-minded adultress. — The consequences.   258

CHAPTER VI. — Copulation refused me. — Unto us a child is born. — Flight suggested. — Affection unrequited. — Her husband dies. — Narrowed circumstances. — In a foreign land. — She marries again. — Hearsay, fifteen years afterwards.   269

CHAPTER VII. — A big maid-servant. — A peep up from below. — Home late, dusty and stupid. — Chastity suspected. — Consequences. — Dismissed. — My sympathy. — The soldier lover. — Going to supper. — At the Café de l'E*r**e. — In the cab returning. — Wet feet. — On the seat. — Mutual grasping and gropings.   275

CHAPTER VIII. — The next day. — At the Tower. — In tears. — "The wretch is married." — At T***f***d Street. — After dinner. — On the chamber-pot. — My wishes refused. — An attack. — Against the bed. — A stout resistance. — I threaten to leave her. — Tears and supplications. — On the sofa. — Reluctant consent. — A half-virgin.   281

CHAPTER IX. — The big servant's history. — The soldier at the railway station. — Courting. — In the village lane. — On the grass. — At the pot-house. — Broached partially. — Inspection of her privates refused. — Lewed abandonment. — Her first spend. — A night with her. — Her form. — Sudden effects of a looking-glass. — The baud solicits her. — Sexual force and enjoyment. — She gets a situation. — We cease meeting. — The butcher's wife. — An accidental meeting. — She was Sarah by name.   287

CHAPTER X. — Sally at the sea-coast. — Our lodgings. — The landlady and family. — A quarrel, and change of rooms. — My top bed-room. — Advances towards Sally. — Small liberties. — On the sands with her. — Cheap fingerings. — The sands by day. — Ladies bathing. — What the sad sea-waves exposed. — An incomprehensible lady. — Enticed by her, and snubbed. — Wanting fornication. — Masturbation on the sands. — Alone

CONTENTS

in the lodgings. — A journey to town. — Baulked. — From Saturday to Monday. — My return unexpected. — Sally alarmed. — Her cunning. — My caution. — Waiting expectant. — Sally upstairs. — Hesitation and determination. — Whisky and water. — I enter her bed-room.   293

CHAPTER XI. — *In bed with Sally. — The children. — Sally's devices. — Fears of alarm. — An hour's siege. — The citadel taken. — Thirty hours of delight. — Fucking under difficulties. — My devices. — A cunt inspection in the looking-glass. — Sally's account of herself. — The bathing lady again. — Checked and threatened. — I give up the chase.*   303

CHAPTER XII. — *Sally's antecedents. — Her female friend. — How to get shillings on the sands. — How her friend lost her virginity. — Turns gay and goes to London. — Her invitation to Sally. — My advice. — I return to London. — The house in U*p*r N**t*n Street. — Sally's discontent. — Mrs. Melvelle. — I sleep with her. — Confessions of a hot-cunted one. — Sally goes home.*   311

CHAPTER XIII. — *Many miscellaneous whorings. — Mr. McCabe. — The warehouse in the City. — Tenants paying rent. — McCabe's jocosity. — Suggestions for getting bairns. — Mrs. ***. — The Scotch wife. — The four-roomed cottages. — Repairs needed. — At her cottage. — Easy conversation. — The steep staircase. — The bed stood upon. — The hole in the roof. — The hole in the flesh. — Carnal wants and weakness. — Against the bed, and on it. — Against the dresser. — An alarm. — The amour terminates. — Reflexions, regrets, and weakness. — On the sin of adultery. — On the power of lust.*   320

CHAPTER XIV. — *A gap in the narrative. — A mistress. — A lucky legacy. — Secret preparations. — A sudden flight. — At Paris. — A dog and a woman. — At a lake-city. — A South American lady. — Mrs. O*b***e. — Glimpses from a bed-room window. — Hairy armpits. — Stimulating effects. — Acquaintance made. —*

The children. — "Play with Mamma like Papa." — A water excursion. — Lewed effects. — Contiguous bedrooms. — Double doors. — Nights of nakedness. — Her form. — Her sex. — Carnal confessions. — Periodicity of lust.   332

CHAPTER XV. — *Frantic coition. — A priapus. — Purging and resting. — Priapus humbled. — Carnal exercises resumed. — The governess. — A peep through a keyhole. — Bathing. — The after-frig. — My politeness. — The silk mantle. — Travelling resumed. — The new hotel. — Felt, and all but. — Unproductive seed. — A thin partition. — Scared by a laugh. — Unsuccessful. — The mantle given. — Still no success. — I leave.*   342

CHAPTER XVI. — *At the town of A***n*n. — At the railway. — The station rebuilding. — Diarrhœa. — The closet-attendant. — The temporary shed. — Ladies' closets. — A peep-hole. — Women on the seat. — Peasants. — Piddlers outside. — At the peep-hole again. — Onanism. — A male intruder. — The letter-box. — An infantine pudenda. — An impatient male. — The soiled seat. — Sisters. — A succession of backsides. — The female attendant. — Bribed and kissed. — Her husband's occupation. — Next day. — The peep-hole plugged.—Two young peasants.—Private inspections.*   349

CHAPTER XVII. — *The lady's drawers. — Weary of peeping. — With the closet-keeper. — She consents. — The mail-train in. — A rush for the closets. — Piddlers in succession. — The knowing one. — A mother and daughters. — The closet-keeper again. — Connubial habits. — An ugly backside. — Two Americans. — The closet-keeper's anxiety. — In the woods. — "C'est une sale putain." — Punished for peeping. — Unpleasant reminiscences. — A young lady recognized.*   359

CHAPTER XVIII. — *A Grand-Duchess. — At the town of C**s*l. — Travelling with a friend. — Early morning. — A peep through a key-hole. — A big woman and bed. — Naked. — Making up her mind. — Titillation. — Hesitation. — Masturbation. — On the bidet. — Frigging again. — Who is she? — At M****n. — On*

*outskirts of the town. — In search of a harlot. — The
beer-garden. — The peasant woman. — A drink and a
wink. — A kiss and a feel. — A talk and a walk. — The
cottage. — Nein, nein. — Brown legs and white thighs.
— A flaxen motte. — Both gratified.*   367

CHAPTER XIX.—*Clapped, and reflexions thereon.—Change
in taste for condition of pudenda. — Change again. —
Later on in life. — On bricks in a hail-shower. — An
unknown quarter. — A little lady. — 'You can't come
home." — The bricks. — The hail-stone. — A canny
policeman. — A servant for a change. — Sexual charms
of servants. — Catherine. — A stumble on the stairs. —
A well-timed visit. — Unchaste questions, and chaste
replies. — Preliminaries. — Consummation. — Ugly
stockings. — The dining-room table.*   374

CHAPTER XX. — *Catherine at a baudy house. — My anatomical studies. — Catherine's hymen wanting. — Her
explanation. — Servants in bed. — The sham-cock used.
— Gamahuched. — Catherine with kid. — A charming
widow. — The ball. — The cab home. — Rapid persuasion. — At J***s Street. — "Don't rumple my dress."
— Cunt in full dress. — A ginger-coloured motte. —
The tipsy coachman. — Catherine, and widow alternately. — The widow enceinte. — Remedies. —
Catherine goes home. — The widow marries. — Indiscriminate womaning.*   384

CHAPTER XXI. — *Camille the second. — Stripping. — The
divan. — Cock-washing. — Camille's antecedents. —
Face, form, and cunt. — Mode of copulating. — Avaricious. — Free fucking offered. — Gabrielle. — Cunt,
form, and face. — Minette. — My daily dose of doxies.
— At M**g**e. — Lodgings at the greengrocer's. —
Louisa the red-haired. — The lodging-house servant.
— The shop-boy. — My friend's daughter. — Piddling,
and presents. — Loo's bum pinched. — The servant
kissed. — A stroke on the sands. — With Loo on the
beach. — Chaff, and cunt-tickling. — A declaration of
love. — The virtuous servant.*   393

CHAPTER XXII. — *Loo on the beach. — The shop-boy's at-*

CONTENTS

tempt. — Caught at the water-closet. — A knowing one. — The gay sister. — Success despaired of. — Over the china-shop. — Virginity slaughtered. — Alone in the lodgings. — The bed-room on the stairs. — Poking like blazes. — A gamahuche. — Aunt at market. — Clever dodges. — Naked in bed. — Homage to Priapus. — Belly to belly. — Belly to bum. — She on he. — The hand-glass. — Am I with child? — I leave M**g**e. — Sequel.   406

CHAPTER I

Sarah returns. — My love revives. — Her tour, and poverty. — My aid. — Old habits again. — Sarah jealous. — Lewed and lushy. — Her shop and her man. — A quarrel. — Yellow-haired Kitty. — At the Café de P**v***e. — Kitty's luck. — About Bob and Grace. — Kitty disappears. — Reconciled to Sarah. — Sarah with child. — Who is father? — Hannah's sister. — Near it, but not quite. — Sarah's luck. — A noble friend. — The Casino. — A failure. — Sarah's home. — Troubles. — Her sister's intrigue. — A hard life. — Sequel.

During my amours with Jenny I used to call at times to ask after Fisher, and if Sarah had been heard of. Of Sarah they had heard nothing, and if so, they did not tell me. Louisa was still ill. "Mrs. A****y has been asking after you," said Hannah, "she wants you to poke her, — she has a lovely leg, — why don't you have her?" She had a Jewish nose, but indeed a lovely leg, and we fucked once or twice for love.

I also had a woman named Betsy Johnson (of whom I have said more further on), and a very fine tall woman with the loveliest eyes I ever saw, with such limbs and backside, and such a thickly-haired cunt. She was salacious also, and kept me fucking her when I was once in the house with her, whether I desired it or not. In fact she fancied me, and wanted to see me daily. But she was not a clean woman, so I ceased having her, — and years after heard she had been sent to prison for robbery.

At last Louisa came back thin and ill, and I began to poke her. Once or twice or so, she had fits of the baudiest abandonment, at other times was cautious, and would uncunt me, and wash her genitals directly I had spent, just as Sarah used. Again she spoke

215

of my keeping her, and the idea of doing so began to take hold of me; for she was pleasant, a good talker, and I loved her lasciviousness, and wanted a woman to settle to, — when the half-formed intention went to the winds, because Sarah Mavis returned.

Although I then only thought of Sarah with a sigh, I used to ask after her. One morning I went to J***s Street. As I opened the door Hannah looked out of the parlour-door, smiled, put her head back, then closed the door, again looked out, grinned, again closed the door, then opened it saying, "You may come." In I went, and there leaning with one arm on the mantel-piece in the accustomed attitude stood Sarah Mavis.

"How do you do?" said she in her quiet way, as if I had only seen her the day before. With a cry of delight I rushed at her, my heart nearly bursting. All my love returned as I hugged her to my bosom. "Oh! my darling, my darling Sarah, how glad I am to see you again, — my love, my darling."

After I had kissed her till, as she said, I had nearly worn away her face, I wanted her to come upstairs, for my prick was tingling with desire. She would not. "Impossible, — I'm dirty, — almost in rags, — landed from a steam-boat an hour ago, — have tasted nothing but water for twenty-four hours." Her children were with her, tears ran down her face. "Come upstairs, — come my darling." "No." "Go," said Hannah, "I will lend you stockings, and a chemise, — you go upstairs sir, into the front-room, — she shall be with you in ten minutes." "No I can't, — I will in two hours, if I can get my children something to eat." "Come at once, — I'm dying for you," said I, "Hannah shall cook you something whilst with me." "Go up you," said Hannah, "she will follow." Hannah cried at the scene, indeed we all cried together.

Up I went. In ten minutes Sarah came up, a chemise and stockings on only, her long black hair hanging down her neck, a great cloak over all, lent by Hannah. I threw her on the bed, kissed her from head to foot, buried my lips in her fresh-washed cunt, and then ouf! ouf! out flooded my spunk into her, out flooded her cunt-juice to mingle with it. Starved, empty, miserable as she was, how she fucked with me! How she enjoyed me!

Oh! the Elysium as the last drop of sperm sheds into the quim of the woman you love. What is this? Sarah heaving though we had barely reposed, — my prick is still in her. "Go on dear." On

I drove. "Ah! my darling fuck me, — oh! — I — have not — had a fuck — go on — f — for a — mon — month, — my d — darling." My prick was working up into her stiff as ever, her big arse heaving, our tongues meeting, our juices mingling; in another spend, and then was a talk after a long voluptuous silence. Its substance was this.

"I've never been poked for a month, — no six weeks, — we have sold all to keep us, — he is in prison." Sarah was careless, careworn, broken down. Grief and trouble makes any one so. She went downstairs after I had fucked the second time (without washing her cunt), to feed her children. "Don't you come down, — we are none of us fit to look at, — I'll come back when I've got a place to rest in to-night, — oh! how good you are, — thank God I've met you again, — I feared I should not."

I gave her all the gold I had, Hannah gave food, and she went off. I went away, had luncheon, and four hours afterwards we were in bed; and fucked till the poor worn-out wanderer went to sleep with my prick in her cunt, and snored almost whilst I was spending in her. Then laying in semi-nudity afterwards, we fucked and slept till ten at night, when she went away. "If I am in the family way now," she said, "there's no doubt who is papa." It is ridiculous the number of women I have got with child [or who have said so].

I saw her next day, and daily for weeks afterwards. Her account of her doings was this. Everything went well at first, — they made money, then some of the troupe got discontented with their share, quarrels arose, and two left, which spoiled the tableaux. Then Mr. Mavis gambled, then was too polite to Sarah's sister. The troupe got right again, but foreign gentlemen wanted to fuck Sarah. He would have allowed it, but she would not permit it. If she was to get her living as a whore she might as well stay in her own country, she said. A great swell paid a heavy sum to see her nearly naked, with boots and stockings on, and in a recumbent baudy posture. That she allowed, for the money he paid was so great; but her husband was in the room at the time. She insisted on that. The swell frigged himself before them both whilst she laid voluptuously for his inspection.

Then a *large* sum was offered for the whole troupe to perform naked. Some would, some would not, — Sarah would not. Her man should not see her sister naked, she was determined, and one woman would not permit her man to be naked, for he had said jokingly that he should stiffen if he saw Madame W***t*n naked. It ended in a row. One half of the troupe gave private exhibitions naked. "But," said Sarah, "lots of them don't look so nice naked as they may think." Sarah and her man (who was a splendid animal), were the finest made of the whole lot. Sarah, a model to artists from fourteen years of age, knew pretty well what a fine man and woman were.

She and her husband tried to get up poses again, but could not make up a troupe. He gambled "for the best," she said (she always excused him). They got from bad to worse. Their stage and machinery were then seized, which stopped their exhibitions. He got sent to prison for debt. She waited in hopes of his being set free, pawned and sold all she had, and at length came to England with her two children to see what she could do here, where she had relations. She had landed with the children hungry and wet, without a farthing, and had walked with them from Wapping that very morning, after a stormy twenty hours passage from Antwerp. She was haggard, with sunken eyes, her flesh was flabby, and she had every indication of suffering and misery about her when we first met.

Why she never went whoring abroad I can't say. I can't say she did not, but she averred that no one but her husband had done her, and that from the day he went to prison to the day she returned to me, she had not been fucked. "If I must be a whore I'll do it with my own countrymen, and not with those nasty foreigners," she remarked.

We had a honey-moon, and fucked night and day. "I wish I had gone away with you," said she to me one night, "but it was not to be." I believe (you can't be sure of a woman) that she had no man but myself now. I paid for her lodgings, food, and dresses, got out of pawn from Brussels numerous articles, employed an agent to do it, and even helped with money to set her man free.

In about eight weeks he came to London. Then she changed, and relapsed very much into her old habits immediately. Would not do this, nor that, would only meet me this time, or that, as she pleased. It was of no use grumbling. "You know I can't," she would say, "so why bother me." "He won't let you." "Well he is the father of my children, and I must make him comfortable." "You keep him, surely you may do as you like." It was of no use, she would not, and again I submitted.

So things went on. Meetings of a morning, dinners at the Café, just as before. Then, I could not learn why, she would not meet me for a whole fortnight. I got angry, would not see her at all, and by mere chance then met Kitty with the yellow hair. When it was known that I had quarrelled with Sarah, Mrs. Fisher, who had ceased seeing me, turned up. I went one day to learn from Hannah if she had seen Sarah. No she had not, "but there is an old friend of yours in the parlour." It was Louisa. She cried. So did I, but it was about Sarah. After Louisa's vowing that she would never let me again have her, — no never, we had a game of tailing which lasted some hours. "Now you will tell Sarah." "No I won't." But Sarah came to know it. Whenever I quarrelled with Sarah afterwards, I put my prick into Louisa or for a time Jenny, of whom I have already written, and occasionally in a fit of lewdness turned into the first whore I got hold of, out of Regent Street.

Then I saw Sarah again, and we made it up, and she behaved better to me. After a time I found she walked occasionally in Regent Street, began to talk lasciviously, and would drink like a fish. To see her regularly on the streets shocked me. Well, she must get some money, — when she had saved a certain sum she would take a business. Mr. Mavis was by trade a ****, and was determined now to follow it, and open a shop for the sale of his goods, — she would attend to the shop. I gave her much money on condition she would never traipse the streets. If she saw friends, or those who were introduced to her, I could not help it, but I had a horror of the pavement, and of her bringing in any man who took to her. Quiet whoring with me, and a select few if she liked. I agreed to that. So she disappeared from the *pavé* as far as I know.

The shop was opened, and was successful. Poor Sarah was for months in a state of joy, and would scarcely come to me. No, they were getting on, he was steady, they earned a good living, — not as much as she did by her being gay, but enough. It was sweeter and better than money got by wriggling her buttocks. She cooked all the meals, and was always at home, but she came to me occasionally. That for a short time gave a rest both to my pocket and ballocks, and I respected her for her decision, but could not bear the perpetual disappointment at her refusals. At first I used to go home with my heart breaking, and then tried for Louisa Fisher; but she told me once and for all, that she would have nothing more to do with me as long as I knew Sarah; and I saw no more of Louisa for weeks. Jenny was then about to leave her place and marry. I was unhappy, for I was dotingly fond of Sarah, and my misery at home drove me to the company of other women. Cunt certainly saved me from drinking, — but I thought I would go abroad to get clear of all.

I fancy that her man had too much of Sarah's company, or the temptation to let her get money was too strong, for when annoyed in every way, I told Sarah of my determination to go abroad, either what I said, or the fear of losing me affected her; and she said she would see me oftener, and even dine, which she had almost ceased doing.

Dinners then became frequent. "Come at seven o'clock." "I can't till half-past." "Then stay with me till twelve." "You know I must be in at ten." "Then you won't be an hour with me." "Well you can do all you want in an hour." This began to revolt me, to think that my whole object in seeing her was to fuck, yet I submitted. One night she came late to dinner. "I must be home earlier to-night." "When?" "At half-past nine." "Why it's eight now." "You will have time to have me." "Then I won't go in." We were outside the Café. "Nonsense, — come." "I'll see you damned first, — good night," — and I walked towards the cabstand. She stood still for a moment, then came rapidly after me. "Now don't be angry, — do come dear, — I want a poke so, — I can't bear you going away so, — let us go to J***s Street at once, — I must have you, — you shan't go without our having a kiss together." "Will you stop till ten?" "No." "Damned if I'll be humbugged any longer," said I, hailing a cab. "You're not going away, are you, like that?" I drove off, and so we parted, and I would not call at J***s Street for weeks.

While in this state of unhappiness, I was in Regent Street one afternoon when I met an elegantly dressed woman with her veil down. Through it I saw her eyes fixed on mine, and knew her at once. "Kitty!" "Walter!" We stopped. "Don't talk here," said she, walking on till she turned down a by-street, I following her. There we shook hands, glad to see each other. I wanted her to come with me to O*d*n Street. No it was impossible, but she would meet me to dine in Leicester Square in about two hours. She would come if she could, — if she did not it would be no fault of hers.

"But it's of no use your asking me if you expect to have me, for you won't." "Nonsense, — not the man whose prick you first had

pleasure with?" "No, not even you." "Very well, — I'm miserable,
I love a woman who behaves badly to me, — I must dine somewhere, come and dine, and let's talk of old times." "I cannot stop
late." "Go when you like, but come."

At the Café de **** I ordered a room. "No not this, one with a
bed-room where we can wash hands." "They are all let to-day sir,
— we have only one bed-room and sitting-room for travellers who
may arrive to-night." "Well we shall stop all night," — and the rooms
were reserved for me.

Kitty came. She had changed her dress, and was in black silk,
but most elegant it was, and showed her colour off to perfection.
The waiter had gone. "Take off your bonnet, — don't lay it down
there, — go into the other room." In she went, I followed. "A kiss."
"Yes," — kiss, — a hug. "Oh! Kit how lovely you are, — what a fine
woman you have grown, — as plump as ever." "Plumper," said she.
"Yes, I can feel it outside." "Now leave off, — mind what I told you."
"Nonsense, — oh! for God's sake Kit only a feel." I put my hand up
her clothes, and felt the cunt. She struggled. "Oh! Kit let me, —
think how often I have done it." "No, — no, — I have sworn I never
would again, — now pray don't, — I've sworn I tell you." "Well only
another feel." "Will you promise?" "Yes." She let me grope. "Oh!
that cunt, — more hair than ever, — oh! feel *me*, — do." Out I
lugged my prick. "Oh! feel it." "Well there, — there, I have, — now
take your hand away."

There stood Kitty and I leaning against the bed, arms round
each other, kissing, my fingers on her clitoris, she grasping my prick.
"Oh! no, — I've sworn, — I would if I had not, — I dare not, —
there, — oh! now I so wish I had not come, — I'll go if you don't
leave off, — oh! now don't, — I'll go," — but she didn't. There we
stood, silent, lips glued to each other, she sighing, her bum twisting
gently. Then I was on the bed, on her, up her, and the sighs which
began as we stood at the bedside, frantically rubbing our privates,
ended in deep sobs of satisfaction and tranquillity. Suddenly the
waiter knocked. "On a servi, Monsieur."

"In a minute," said I, — and to go into the sitting-room was
the work of half a minute, — Kitty came in directly afterwards. "The
plates are cold," said I. "They have been up five minutes, sir." Kitty
and I looked at each other. "What wine, sir?" I chose it, and he left.
"I must go and wash," said Kit. She had come in to save appearances.

At length we finished dinner in the delightful gaiety of half-satisfied lust, with the tingling of renewed desire in prick and cunt, as we eat and drank, and chatted.

Kitty got at first pensive. "I swore with the Bible in my hand I never would let another man but him, and it will bring me ill luck." But she brightened as she warmed with food and wine. We talked over old times. What a difference between the shabby ill-dressed girl of four years ago, who grabbed a sausage-roll like a coster-monger, and the lovely elegant woman who eat like a lady! I could scarcely believe myself. How glad I was when dinner was over, and we dismissed the waiter. Then our talk ran wild. Our kisses, the feel of my prick, the titillation of her quim soon swept away all scruples. She was proud of herself, delighted to show herself to me who had known her in her poverty, and she stripped to her skin. I found she was beautiful in form, and white as alabaster. I stripped, and both naked we fucked and fucked. My God how we revelled in sensuality, and fucked till my prick would not stand, and till her clitoris was sore with frigging. I think of it now with exquisite delight.

"I swear," said she, "you were the first man who ever gave me pleasure, — I have often thought of that hot summer's afternoon as we lay on the bed together, — how young I was, — I had never had my poorliness, — ah! that first spend, — I shall recollect it to the last day of my life, — I got fond of you from that day, and never had another man till you left England, — money was of no use to me excepting to buy food, and yours was enough, — so I never had another man till you left. Then I had several, and soon went gay." "You spent often enough then?" "It's true," said she, "for a few months I spent with every man I had, — I did not care what they gave me, — if they wanted it twice I let them, for I was dying for it always, but then I pulled myself together. You are the only man I ever told this to, for although my husband of course knows I was gay, he always thinks I had only been out one or two months, — he never asks me anything, and wants to forget all about my past. — And now excepting you, I swear I have never had another man but him since he has kept me."

We talked about the little Pol whom she brought to me. She told me she had been got in the family way by her own brother, and she did not know what became of her. — Cousin Bob, oh! how we laughed about his frig, — that sight seems to have settled Grace.

"It was her ruin," said Kitty. "Grace was always frigging herself, and wishing she could let a man do it to her without fear of the consequences, and after she had seen Bob frig himself, she got spoony on him. Very soon afterwards Bob spent his seed up Grace's receptacle, instead of on the floor, — Grace's belly began to swell, and Bob, instead of helping her, cut her, and got rid of his sperm in some other girl's trap. Then after fretting, Grace took another prick to comfort her, then another, then one for money, and finally went on the town." It was Grace who was walking with Kitty one night when I met her in the Strand, and it turned out that a few weeks afterwards she told Kitty that I had had her; but I had no knowledge of having done so. It occurred thus.

Whilst seeing Kitty and Brighton Bessie I had a stray poke from time to time. Grace had seen me speak to Kitty, and recollected me, but I did not know Grace from Eve. I picked her up, however, one night and had her. "Do you recollect," said Kitty, "one night standing during a heavy storm under the pit-entrance to the Lyceum, and taking a lady from there?" I did perfectly. "She stammered a little," said I. "Yes that was Grace." "She was rather thin, straight, blackish hair on her cunt, cunt with biggish lapels." "That's she, — that's she," laughed Kate. The circumstance was an odd one.

Kitty told me her recent history, it seemed probable to me then, and not improbable now. She met a gentleman, went to a house with him, then saw him again, and again; he offered to keep her and she had been with him ever since. He kept her mother and lived with Kitty, but could not introduce her into society, and was about to sell his commission and take her abroad to marry her. He was an officer, and on talking with her she was certainly well up in army matters.

He had made her swear a solemn oath never to have another man whilst he was away, and to avoid her own relations and every one she had known. "Yes," said Kitty, "I see what you are thinking about, but I declare before God that when I came to dine with you, I was determined not to let you have me. I felt curious about you just as you felt curious about me, and I have still a little liking for you, — see what has come of it, — I believe that I have ruined myself through coming here to-night, — I have a presentiment that great harm will come to me through it."

He had been away for a month, wrote to her every day, and

she to him. She had a nice little house, — not in Brompton, no — perfectly respectable, and had plenty of money. She saw one or two friends, one of whom was his sister. Her great difficulty that night was how to account for being so late out (for we stopped till one in the morning). I dare say she got over the difficulty, for women are clever liars.

"A whole month, Kitty! — and no poking?" "None." "Then you frig." "Of course, — I write a beautiful handwriting," said she, "look, — every one says so." She took down a wine-list, and borrowing my pencil wrote her name. I had been asking her her name, and she had refused it. "Read it." "So that is your name." She howled, and scratched it out with the pencil quickly, — she had forgotten her secret in her desire to show me how well she wrote. I forget the name, and she would not give me her address.

"We may never meet again, Kitty." "I don't think we ever shall." Then with one consent we went to the bed. I laid down my head on her thighs, kissing her pretty quim, she frigging me, till with a chuckle as of old, she delicately took the tip of my pego into her mouth, only the tip, just as she used. Up it came at the challenge. We fucked a long, hard-working, slow-spending fuck, and then we parted. Kitty's cunt was as tight as when she was young, a sweet-looking cunt between dazzling white thighs, yet I always wished it another colour.

"I don't want you to think me a gay woman any longer, but I have a superstition, — give me a piece of gold, and bring a light." Then I went with her to the water-closet, and she threw the sovereign down it, — that was a charm to ward off evil for having broken her oath. "You have enjoyed me, Kit?" "I have not enjoyed myself so much I think since I last met you in Regent Street," said she. With a kiss in the street we parted, and I never saw her since.

I asked her if she had been in the family way. "Yes, you got me with child before you left England, directly after I had my poorliness, — I never had anyone for a long time after you left, so it must have been you. Grace first said I was with child, and helped me by going with me to a woman who lives in a court in Long-Acre."

She had been so since twice by her protector, and had stopped it; but so soon as they were married he said they would have children. It was one of the reasons why he wished to marry her.

All this time I was in full favour with women, was in the prime of life, kind, sympathetic, thought handsome by women, and manly also. I see clearly now, how I could have had no end of other women without paying, but scarcely saw my opportunities then; and though I may have many instances to show, that my love was all that was wanted by some who threw themselves in my way, I can scarcely tell of them here. This luck ran over full ten years of my life, as nearly as I can recollect. During nearly four years of that, I was in love with Sarah who did not return it, but who used her power with moderation on the whole, though she tyrannized over me.

I would not see nor have Sarah for weeks after my last rupture with her, but could not help calling at J***s Street. I liked the scene of so much pleasure to me, to hear the click of the street-door as it opened, the rustle of petticoats going upstairs, the heavy step after them, the demand for a room, the reply, "First-floor front, sir."

[I add now what on reading over the manuscript I do not find, — it is a needful addition written twenty years later.

[When Sarah knew that I was fully aware of her occupations and habits, she changed, talked with me about artists' models, statuary, and so forth, and about her favourite poses as well, for she liked that work. To get me out of ill temper which her tyranny now often put me in, she would pose naked, all but silk stockings and her lovely little kid boots. It was an exquisite sight which almost directly made me mad to possess her. My prick swelled, stood out, lifting my shirt till I raised it, and rushed to feel her. Then laughing at my excitement she would alter her pose, till off went my shirt, she laid hold of my prick, I her cunt, and getting on to the bed I clasped her in my arms, and fucked her. Posing naked before me made her feel lewed and want me, she confessed, slow as she was at such confessions. "There," said she one day when she saw my stiff prick, "that's what would have happened if we had posed naked in Brussels." Every man in the troupe had at one time or another solicited her favours privately, but she never told her own man that, for fear of a row.

[She generally posed thus after we had dined, and when what lust was in her constitution usually came out; I learned how to test her cunt-cravings in a simple way. Directly we got to the bed-room after dining she always piddled. I pushed my prick (stiffening in anticipation) in her face as she sat on the pot. If lustful she laid hold of it laughing, and pulled the foreskin backwards and forwards saying, "ah! — ahah! — look at it, — it's ready"; — if not, and she was thinking only of getting away soon, she pushed it away, saying, "Can't you wait now; — what beasts you men are; what pleasure can it give you to push that ugly thing in my face?" But who can give a reason for any baudy tricks, — they give pleasure, or they would not be done, by all men and women.

[Sometimes when she was posing I used to peep, trying to see more than the hair of the motte, and the dark shadow in the bum-furrow. Quite towards the end of our acquaintance I got her to pose in a lewedly suggestive attitude, but she never would open her cunt-lips herself, nor let me look well inside. She would leave me angry, rather than permit it. "It's not made to look at, — pray go on swearing," she would say as she dressed herself. "I'm going, — it's ten o'clock."

[Indeed her sexual orifice did not even then seem to me so handsome as those of other women. It was fat, large outside, with nymphæ showing from clitoris to the vulva. Perhaps she knew that. It was loose inside, must have been low down, and there was something about it which I never understood, and therefore can't describe. Scarcely any other woman yet that I can recollect uncunted me in the throes of pleasure as she did, when she enjoyed the prick, and was fucking energetically. "Damn it, it's out, — oh! put it in, I was just coming," were exclamations then made simultaneously by us.

[What made me so madly in love with her therefore, it is difficult to say. It must have been the perfection of her form, which enraptured me directly I saw it, and even to the last when she got too fat. Besides she had a quiet, comfortable, companionable manner, unlike a gay woman's; and at that time though I liked a genial lewedness in a woman, open flagrant baudiness rather revolted me, and till lust stirred me fully up I was half chaste in my words, even with them. "Let me look at it, — show it me," were more frequently my words than stronger ones. Nothing I said in those days excepting in highly wrought moments was comparable to my lascivious utterances now, when no language I find too plain to express the wants and acts of those organs which give us all the highest pleasure, both physically and mentally. I had not then learnt all the pleasure copulation is capable of, that unrestrained nature in coition is the best. The absurdity of calling anything indecent or improper, which men

and women may like to say or do together when in private, had not
occurred to me. I now believe that it matters not whether what they
do be called unnatural, or beastly, or not. So long as both like it and
enjoy it, it is natural to them, concerns no one else, is in the instincts
of their nature, and is to them proper.]

And now to my narrative. Sometimes if Hannah was not in the
parlour, I would peep and see the happy couples going upstairs,
the women generally first. If late they were often a little noisy, and
made a liberal display of leg to the men following. Late at night if
women were there, Hannah would then not let me in unless some
of my female friends were there. When Hannah would not let me
peep, I at times threatened not to make up her accounts. That threat
was often successful, I never told any one for many years afterwards
about the accounts.

"Sarah is anxious to see you," said Hannah one night, "so anxious." I saw her, conquered, and we made it up. Soon after she
was in the family way again, she said by her husband; but she
would not be plagued with another child. She let it go on for a
month or so, and during that time fucked freely, keeping my prick
and my sperm up her as long as I wished it. I became fully convinced that sexually she was cold, though a good mother and wife;
but I loved her delicious form, and if she would lay in artistically
free-and-easy attitudes whilst I talked to her, was content. She never
cared about baudy pictures. After dinner when I had poked her, and
we were lying half naked together, she would suddenly feel her
clitoris for a minute, then say, "Come nearer, dear," — that meant
she would feel my prick for minutes, and then, fuck, — fuck was the
order. After her spend she got cold again, the dinner heated her,
and when I had cooled her cunt, she was cool to me.

After a time either they grew tired of the shop or did not make
enough money, for they started on a tour in the provinces with a
troupe. Hannah said Mavis was too lazy to stick to his trade, and
preferred either posing, or living on Sarah's earnings. I was left
unhappy again.

Again Mrs. Fisher appeared, and her modest lasciviousness
again mastered my senses. I was getting accustomed to her, when
Sarah came back. They had made money, the shop business had
gone, but now they attended to that. Sarah was always there, I used
to see her in it, for though its whereabouts was kept secret at first,

it was ultimately told me. I never went into it, but used to linger outside it just for the pleasure of looking at her, even though perhaps the same night I was to meet her. Such was my infatuation. She again met me, but only for as long as she liked. She said she met only me, and I believed it to be nearly true. She was certainly never in the streets that I could discover. He never was in the shop. She told me he was always in the workshop. She might have done a little belly-bumping business by introductions, but Hannah, now quite at my service, declared that *she* never introduced her. Then Sarah was in the family way again. Said she, "I can't tell if it's yours, or his."

Another miscarriage. Then she began to take a great deal too much wine, or anything else. I grudged her not, for she might have swallowed pearls if I had had the money to give them to her; but thought of her health and looks, knowing how liquoring gains on a woman, and how it ruins her. She was annoyed at my remarks. Let her be happy a little when she could. "Aren't you happy?" "How can any one be happy living from hand to mouth as I am?" I began then to think she was unhappy. Now too she began to fuck with fury, when she had a little wine. One night I did not want it but once. "Fuck me again, — you shall," said she. She threw herself into baudy attitudes, she whom I had usually difficulty in inducing to lasciviousness. At length pulling me on to her, she got another fuck, and directly dressed and went away. "Why Sarah, you have not washed." "No I'm going to carry it home with me to-night," she said with a savage sneering smile, "they'll have a treat at home." I never knew what she meant.

I asked her to leave her man; she was half inclined, — she was sick of life, — would I take her children too? Yes I would. A week afterwards: No she must keep to him, however ill he might behave to her, — they were his children, — no one would take care of them but him. "Does he behave ill to you?" "Oh! no, poor man, he has enough to put up with." All this was contradictory.

Then she got so capricious that I quarrelled. I was getting ashamed of allowing myself to be made such a fool of, arranging to meet her, waiting at the house, she never appearing, and so on. Hannah used to come and talk with me because I was so miserable. She was quite friendly, and if she wanted to piss she used to sit down and do it without any apology or remark before me now.

"He is a brute," said she, "do you know he has several times been here whilst she has been with you, and she has at once given him the money you have given to her, — what do you think of him? — isn't she a fool? — poor Sarah! — ah! you are both to be pitied."

Hannah's other sister just then came as servant. She was a pretty creature, had a squint in one eye, but it did not seem to disfigure her. She had been a housemaid, and was found talking to a sailor in the house (she told me he was her cousin), and was turned out at once. I rather suspect she was found with the sailor's belly up against hers, and nothing between their skins. I was such a fool that I could not help going to J***'s Street nightly, asking after Sarah, and crying. This girl seemed to take a fancy to me, and both she and Hannah said I was a goose for troubling myself about Sarah. This was at a time when we had had a quarrel, and I thought I was punishing her; but it punished me awfully.

One night I sent a letter hoping Sarah would come. Word came back she could not, Hannah's sister came in to tell me. I cried. "What a pity to take on so," said she coming near me. I sat her down on the sofa, Hannah had told me she had a beautiful leg (she was about eighteen years old). We talked, I kissed her, she me. "You are plump for your age." "Yes." I felt her breasts. "Hannah says you have a nice leg." "So they say." "Let me see." "No." I began to lift her clothes, she resisted, my cock stiffened, her resistance ceased, she laid her face on my shoulder, I pulled up her clothes to her cunt. She had lovely limbs.

"Let me have you, — let's fuck." "Yes I've been longing for you," she replied, and got up to bolt the door. My feelings then took a sudden turn, a complete revulsion. If Sarah knew it there would be a row, both of us would be sorry for it, I remarked. She made no reply, but left the room. I never had her, for the next day I got Sarah. The girl saw me many times afterwards, and used to look at me, but never referred to that night, and soon left the house. Hannah said she went back into quiet service, — perhaps a lie, but I tell it, as told to me.

Sarah one day said, "You were an hour and a half in the room with Esther (I think it was her name), — did you have her?" "No." "I believe you did." "I did not." "You pulled up her clothes?" "Yes." "Did you have her now?" "No." "What, when your hand was on her thighs?" "No." "I don't believe you." "But it's true," said I. Sarah laughed. "Let's do it," said she.

I could write a volume about Sarah, but it would be tiresome, so will finish about her. After months worrying I heard that one or two officers used to fuck her, she admitted it and that she had been to Aldershot. "I must make money somehow," said she. Then I revolted, but kept on with her for a time, and then the following came about.

Walking in the streets one day, she took the fancy of a nobleman who was seventy years old, they sold their shop, put that money, and the savings she had made by letting out her cunt, to open a Casino with *poses plastiques,* singing, dancing, &c., &c. She told me what they intended to do, — nothing venture, nothing have, — So-and-So had made a fortune that way, why not they? I urged against it, but gave a biggish sum to help. "What is the good? — You will never get enough," said I. Then she told me of the nobleman, and his name. I was staggered, for I knew him and his wife. He had a large family, and had led an irreproachable life, but got so madly in love with Sarah that he wrote her letters, offered to keep her, and actually took her home to see Lady***, an aged woman who cried and said she did not blame Sarah, but did her husband for his folly and wickedness. He helped with much money, they started the Casino, after six months they failed, their money was spent, and they were in debt.

I believe that Sarah never knew my name. I was surprized when she told me the name of the nobleman. I never told her I knew him, though she once asked me if I did. Of course I said no.

I used to go to see her in the poses, go behind the scenes, order champagne, and do all I could to help. The poor woman worked like a slave. Then filled with despair, began to drink deeply, drunk she did not get, but she could swallow a pail full, and she got bloated. Unless she had plenty of liquor she was unable to act. She kept telling me all was going on well, when in fact the affair was going to the dogs.

Then I determined to give her up, I had done my best to help, she had not done much for me, so told her that I should go abroad. "Oh! pray don't, — oh! pray don't, — you don't know what trouble I have, what I have done to keep a home over our head, how I have worked, slaved, whored to do it, for the sake of my children, and to keep him, to keep them all" — but I left off seeing her, and prepared to go abroad.

"Sarah wants to see you," said Hannah to me. "When?" "To-morrow." "I will be here." She came with swollen eyes, slightly in liquor. "Oh! take me with you, take me abroad, out of this cursed place."

Three years before I had offered that first, but had given up the notion, — said so. "It's too late, and yet I could have loved you so, and I loved you, only I dared not show it," said she. "Well I will drown myself, for home I never go again."

Then came a scene. Hannah and her sister were called in whilst Sarah raved about her wrongs. She had kept them all, — all, — all, and now her sister was in the family way, — and by *him*! he had seduced her, — and when poor Sarah talked about sending her home to her mother, No he said, she should not go, but Sarah might, if she liked, — the sister whom she had kept, to be in the family way by *him*! Whilst *she* was walking the streets to get bread for them *all*, he was putting it into *her* sister, — for that sister she was to be turned out.

"I have suspected it for a year, have laid traps for them, but never could catch them, then I could not think after I had got money to set us up fresh three times that he could be such a vagabond. — I have ruined my health by miscarriages, I am out of my mind almost with pain sometimes, and all for him, — and the little bitch, whom I have twice nursed through illnesses that the doctor said would kill her, — oh! I wish I were dead! — but I'll take my time, and do for her and her child too, if it comes to one."

I gave money, and comfort, but she was in despair and mur-derous in intention. She was a cool determined woman, but she fell ill which upset her determination. She kept to her home, and under the pressure of the man, her children, her fears and misery, accepted her humiliation, helped her sister in her accouchement, and by har-lotting kept them all, but was broken-hearted and ultimately kicked out by her man, and by her sister, who took her place. Her sister I don't think was gay, Hannah said so then. I lost sight of Sarah, and no one knew where to find her. I told Hannah I should like the sister, who resembled Sarah, and was fine-made, but smaller. I had seen her in the poses, but never had her.

Then I saw Sarah again well-dressed, and getting money, but heart-broken. The man had her children, and refused to give them up to her. He had knocked her down. She had threatened a magistrate. He had said that he would tell the magistrate that the reason why he refused them was that she was a whore and a drunkard. She had the misery of seeing her man, her two children, and her sister walking out together, and of her own children telling her she was a whore, and that they would be whipped if they spoke to her. She told me this — Hannah said it was true.

Then she left the quarter, and went to live with her mother somewhere in the extreme north of London, and drank very hard, Hannah said.

I met her a few years afterwards in the Euston Road. How she had aged! "You, Sarah!" "My God, you!" She wanted me to go with her. "One kiss for old acquaintance sake, for I loved you more than you thought." "No you did not." "Yes, but my children." I would not go with her, gave some money, and though I yearned towards her, left. (Hannah had left J°°°s Street, and the new keeper knew not my Sarah.) Again after a time I saw her. I stopped her, and gave her money unsolicited, and never saw her again. She told me she was living with a man. She looked poor and broken.

A few years afterwards the trunk of a young woman was found floating in the Thames, there was a peculiar scar below the bosom. I have often wondered if that was the end of Sarah.

I must mention here that after their Casino failed, they acted in *poses plastiques* at a tavern in the City Road. I took a friend who will presently be named to see them act. Sarah was then much fagged and dilapidated.

CHAPTER II

Louisa reappears. — Crabs. — My despair. — A friend's advice. — Promiscuous harlotting. — Fucked out. — My friend's little woman. — Lizzie Stanley. — The hole by the back-bone. — The little woman's sister. — Many naked ladies. — Operations in a four-wheeler. — A she on the top. — The cunts in two houses. — Slandered. — A sodomitic offer. — Nonacceptance.

After calling many times, and not seeing Sarah, Louisa appeared again. We met and poked. She was as lascivious and willing as before, but hurried. She was now kept, and was superbly clothed. Tired of knocking about, I wanted to settle to one woman, and told her so. Said she, "If Sarah Mavis was to come any day, you would throw me over for her, — I would once have lived with you on a pound a week, but you would not have it." That was true. I told her I was going abroad. We met once a week, but I could not reckon on her, and she objected to go to J***s Street; so I used to wait for her with a carpetbag, and go to a hotel, take rooms as if for the night, dine, fuck, and leave. To have this was amusing once or twice, but it did not satisfy me.

She liked me I know, and arranged to stop with me all night at an hotel, which was in Gt. P***l**d Street, but when she came it was impossible, she said, to stay all night. I was excessively angry, and would not fuck her. After dinner she coaxed me, and of course I did, but was sulky. "Don't be angry, — I would like to sleep with you quite as much as you would, but I dare not to-night, — let us do it again." She was laying on the sofa, I would not. How well I recollect her pulling her whole clothes up to her navel, and laying with her big thighs open. "Do it again, there's a darling." I threw myself on to her afterwards. "Is not my cunt wet? — you always do

233

make me so wet, — I always seem to spend twice as much with you as I do with my friend." She kept my prick in her for a quarter of an hour afterwards, kissing me all the time. Then she was obliged to go. She was fond of laying on the bed after I had had her, remarking how wet she was, and then shutting her eyes seemed to be thinking voluptuously of the condition of her cunt.

She went away hurriedly, stooping and kissing my naked prick before she departed. She was going out of town, we were to meet again, but we did not and I never saw her after that night. — Hannah did not either.

[This I note here because it seems to indicate to myself my erotic phase at this period. I never licked the cunt of Sarah or Louisa, nor, to save recurring to the subject, the cunt of Jenny whose doings with me I have already told.]

One day I had Sarah in the morning, had to meet a man at luncheon, and went off hurriedly without washing. I went back in the afternoon, and found Louisa in the parlour. We talked with my hand on her thighs, Hannah said, "You had better go upstairs," just then the door-bell sounded. Hannah looked out, we heard her say, "Go up sir, she will be here directly I'm sure." Coming in she laughed. "It was Louisa's friend." "Hang him," said Louisa, "let's have a poke." "Go on to my bed," said Hannah, and left the room. On the side of the bed I tailed her in no time. She went upstairs, and where she washed I don't know. There was a bed hidden by curtains but no washing materials in the parlour. Hannah performed her ablutions in the back room when it was not occupied. I dined at my Club, and going home, called on Jenny. She was in fear about her sister coming, but I fucked her on the sofa, and left instantly, went to bed tired and without washing, and by daybreak was off on a fishing excursion. In fact I did not wash my prick for about three days, except the tip which I never failed to wash. Then I found I had the crabs. How did I get them?

I had given up Sarah, but still loved her, though I felt I was a madman to encourage it, and that nothing but trouble and misery to me could come of my taking to her again. I had confided my trouble to an old friend, who chaffed me and cheered me. "You fool, to keep to a woman who is only playing with you, — and a fat flabby woman like that." He had gone with me to see her in the poses. "Have them younger and fresher, — you'll get plenty to like you, — but directly you find you are taking too closely to any woman in future, cut her, go out of town, go abroad, try fresh women every night, do all you can to forget her, — change of scene, and plenty of change of cunt, is sure to make you forget any woman."

He was a cold-blooded man, and would have turned off a woman who was in his way with but little ceremony. When he knew of my love-matters he disclosed some of his. I had not the least suspicion before of how much he amused himself with women. His idea of them was that they were only made for amusement, not for affection.

I acted on his advice, and swore I would never have a woman twice. When a woman said after I had stroked her, "Shall I see you again?" "No," I replied, "never." What a lot have stared, and asked me why. Then I told them. "All women are not like her," they mostly replied, but I determined to think they were, and went on changing night after night. Black cunts, brown cunts, little bums, big arses, fat and lean, little and big, I took after each other, just as lust seized me; but however much I enjoyed a woman, go again with her I would not. So I guess nearly a hundred women had my doodle up them, yet I went scaithless, for no ailment overtook me.

This did not satisfy me. I longed to settle at least for a time to a woman, to be a friend to her, to have some one in whom I had some sort of confidence, whom I should always find at home, who would not say she was engaged when I called, would treat me as a friend, and desire again to see me. To feel that I must not have this comfort was doing violence to my best instincts, and I gradually gave up my promiscuous and stern yet lascivious habits. Moreover the variety of cunts had so stimulated my passions that I fucked myself out, and going to a doctor was warned that unlimited indulgence would lead to impotence, and perhaps worse, young even as I was, and not drinking, or doing anything else in excess.

My friend disclosed to me that he had a nice little woman, a gay woman whom he visited, and spoke of her as a beautiful little creature. "Come and see her, — I'm going there," said he when we were dining together one night. We went to Upper N****n Street, then inhabited almost entirely by gay ladies. I found her a poor, thin, insignificant-faced little thing, but with a fine head of hair, and a very sprightly manner. Though I did not like her I commended his choice. "You won't make any attempt to have her whilst I have her?" "Of course not," I replied, and indeed I had no desire for it.

One night when there with him a little woman came down from an upper floor, named Lizzie Stanley. She introduced me to her. I was still fretting about Sarah, and had told my griefs to my friend's woman. "Here," said she to Lizzie, "is a friend of mine who will just suit you, — he has just lost *his* woman, you *your* man, — you're fretting like fools, and are good company to each other." We were both chaffed. I went up to Stanley's rooms and told her about Sarah, she me about a man who had kept her, whom she doted on, and who had gone abroad. We both cried, and then we fucked. She was a very short girl, but plump and exquisitely made, had a lovely face, and the dearest little cunt to look at. Whether it was because she was so anxious to listen to me about Sarah, I know not; but I went to see her again and again, enjoyed her embraces, and she enjoyed mine.

When upon her one night and clasping her backside, my hand, in its rambles in the vicinity of her buttocks, came on a second sort of hole. I thought my finger had gone into her bum-orifice, and withdrew it quickly, having a great dislike to finger that part even of the nicest lady. But again I felt it, and then it seemed to be at the end of the spine. I got curious, and fumbled with my finger all round there. She resisted, and was annoyed. Then, though she had stood quite naked fronting me, I found she would not turn round. What did I want to stare at? No she would not do it dog-fashion, — if I wanted that I might go to another woman, — she hated to be pulled about.

I did not quarrel, for she was a burning-cunted little woman, not more than twenty, and fucked much to my liking; but this sinking on her back-bone which felt like a navel there annoyed me. I began to think it was some disease.

I slept with her again solely to find out all about it, but all night whenever awake I found she was also. I tried to feel when poking her, but she always managed to shift herself, so that my fingers could not reach the spot for long. At last I caught her asleep on her side, and put my fingers on to the sinking, and was turning down the clothes in order to see it (for it then was daylight and summer), when she awakened. We had a row, she left the room, would not have me again, and in a few days left the lodgings. I never saw her afterwards, nor found out what the mark was. My friend's woman said she knew nothing about it. It's a funny incident.

There was a gay lady living on each floor of the house, among them was the sister of my friend's woman, who was gay also. She was a plain, quiet woman, but seemed a strapping, firm-fleshed piece, and older than the little one by two or three years perhaps. She had a very ugly nose. Out of a lot of women I should not have selected her, but yet I had her, — and it came about this way.

I went after dinner with my friend to Upper N****r n Street one night. His skinny little lady was dressing. My friend was very proud of her, — tastes differ. "I can't come out yet, I'm in my chemise," she cried through the folding-door. "Come out, it's only ***." Then out she came. He pulled up her chemise to her quim, and asked me what I thought of her. She really was nice for those who like legs about the size of a rolling-pin, so I admired them. Then he made her strip naked, she nothing loth. I humbugged him by extolling her charms out of kindly feeling to him. "Where is your sister?" said he. "She is dressing." "Tell her, and tell So-and-So, that if they will come down naked, we'll give them a glass of champagne, and pay their cabs to the Argyle." The skinny one went upstairs, there was some debate, — they were not going to strip for a glass of wine, and so on. But at last down three other women came in their chemises, and stripped them off in the room. A female friend was with one of them dressing there. A woman suggested she might also be asked down. Agreed, and down she came. "You should put yourselves also naked, you two men," said one woman, "then we'd have a dance." We did not see that. "Look at his prick," said one woman pointing at me, "it will be through his trowsers directly," — and she came and felt it. I certainly was rising at the sister, whose plain face I had forgotten in admiration of her lovely limbs and body. After lots of pulling up of stockings, adjustment of garters, feeling of cunts, and smutty talk, they scampered upstairs naked, I after the sister, whilst my friend remained with his thin damsel. I was up the big sister's cunt in no time, waited till she was dressed, and going that way, drove her to the Argyle. Before I reached it the spirit again moved us, and to avoid deranging her dress she pulled up her clothes, and turning her arse towards me, impaled herself on my pego as I sat. Then she went into the Argyle with my sperm in her cunt, and carried it with her all the evening, unless there were means of purifying it there, — and I don't think there then was.

I had her once or twice afterwards, and one night when my friend was sleeping with his woman, I had just gone to bed with the big sister, when the thin one came into the room. She began to talk just as we had been thinking of operating. In a frisky way she pulled down the bed-clothes, and discovered my pego in full-blooded erection. "Let's see what sort of a prick he's got," said she, "oh! isn't it a nice one!" We all laughed. "I'll tell your friend." "Oh! no don't," said she, "he is so jealous, and such a bad temper, — there will be a row if you do." Then she whispered something to her sister, and went away, but not till I had asked her to let me see as much as I had shown her. She pulled up her chemise, rolled over the foot of the bed, opened her thighs wide, and then departed to my friend, who was awaiting her in her bedroom.

I had her sister a few times after that, and one night had just gone to bed with her intending to pass the night there, when the thin one who was in her room with some man, appeared again in her night-gown in our room, and laughing said, "Oh! I can't bear him, — I shall sleep here." "Has he had you?" "No, and I don't mean to have him." She got into bed with us, laid hold of my prick after pulling down the clothes to look at it, and getting on the top of me said, "I'm going to be the man, and do it to you." The sister laughed, I resisted, but the little agile devil squeezed her quim somehow on to my tool, and excited by the novelty and by the fresh cunt, I was soon spending up her. She sank satisfied on me. Her sister who had looked on laughing, gave her a loud slap on her buttocks. I think the affair had been arranged between them. My friend did not know of these pranks.

"She has cheated you," said I. No she had not, for she just came on poorly. "I'll come up again soon," said the thin one, — and she did, and I fucked her whilst her sister laid by the side of me. "My sister is fond of you," said the big one, "and she don't like your friend, though he is kind to her." But I did not like the skinny one, and did not like cheating my friend, so never fucked her afterwards. Nor had I the chance, for in a week or so he took her into keeping. That lasted some months, until finding her writing to some other man, he kicked her out and had done with her.

They were at Brighton at the time that took place. He discovered a note of hers in a blotting-book. The very same minute he called up the landlady, paid the bills, and in an hour he had left the young lady with twenty pounds, and never saw her afterwards. He told me all this. The sister told me the same, and that the little thin one cared nothing about it, that she did not like him, that he was ill-tempered, and exacting, had a very little prick, and was a bad poke.

I lost sight of the sister and went with other women, but not until I had fucked every woman in that house. And finding that the girl who had been dressing, and whom I had also seen naked, resided next door, I went to see her, and fucked every woman in that house as well. My price was twenty shillings, and though they were all what is called swell women, I never had my sovereign refused. I think I may say that I fucked a woman in every room excepting the basements in those two houses.

The young woman in the adjoining house was skittish in manner. I neither recollect her name nor her face well, but only that she was a good-sized woman, not too stout, with a very small waist, and an exceedingly large backside. I turned her on to her belly at the bedside, so as to contemplate the beauties of her backside more conveniently. She objected, laughed, said, "Now you shan't do that," but turned round at last, and wriggled her backside about in an unusual manner to me, then she asked me if I liked a tight fit. When I stood up to her backside and rubbed my prick against it, she said it would be a fiver. I was a little ashamed, and said I did not give more than a sovereign. "If you want what Lizzie Stanley would not let you do, I must have a fiver, and you won't tell any other woman, will you?" A light broke in on me. I questioned her, and found that the little bitch Stanley had given out that she had quarrelled with me because I wanted to bugger her. All the women in both houses knew it. My friend's thin woman knew it. I was much annoyed, fearing my friend might have had the lie told him. I swore and cursed at Stanley, — did she (the girl I was with) believe it? She did not know, — some gentlemen had queer fancies. Oh dear no! she had never done it, but she was hard up and would try for a five-pound note, — she heard it gave some women pleasure. I declined the invitation, having not a suspicion of a taste for such a tight fit, so we fucked and parted, nor do I recollect having her again. I told my friend what I had heard at the house some time afterwards. He had then parted with his woman, but he seemed never to have heard of the lie Lizzie Stanley had circulated about me. Altogether that girl Stanley was, and is a mystery to me still.

CHAPTER III

A sailor, a whore, and a garden-wall. — The newly-made road. —
Windy and rainy. — Bargaining overheard. — Offer to pay. —
Against a garden-wall. — A feel from behind. — A wet handful. —
Blind lust. — Into the sperm. — The policeman. — A lost umbrella.
— A new sort of washing-basin. — Fears of ailment.

Amidst all this saturnalia of cunt, I don't believe I ever did
anything with one, excepting to feel and fuck it, though in attitudes
varied. Recherché erotic pleasures were not in my custom, and not
even in my thoughts. Amusements with a man would have shocked
me, had they been suggested. His spunk would have upset my
stomach to look at. To put into a cunt which another man had just
quitted, would have revolted me; yet I was doomed to do all this,
unpremeditatedly, on the spur of the moment and opportunity.

I lived then on the western outskirts of London where they
were building on what had been and were still largely pleasant
fields. About five minutes' walk from my house was a street made not
five years before, and leading out from it a new road, a sixth of
a mile long, connecting two main roads, and made to enable the
fields on either side to be built upon. There were gas-lights at long
intervals, just enough to encourage people to use it at night. The
carriage and footways were of coarse gravel, and quite newly made.

Under wheel and foot these roads crunched as people went
across them. At one end of the road was a new row of houses, the
garden back-walls of which abutted on the open fields, and the side-
walls of two formed the entrance to the road, — both houses just
then were empty.

It was about eleven o'clock at night, windy and rainy at inter-

241

vals, and there was a small moon hidden by thick clouds scudding across it. Sometimes there was a gleam of light, at other times all was dark. It was very windy as I came through the road for a short cut, after thinking whether it was safe or not, and just then I met a policeman at the further end, and bid him good night. The crunching of my footsteps on the newly-laid gravel annoyed me, both by its fatigue and noise, so I stepped on to the meadow-land which lay alongside it, and walked quite quietly. As I neared the street into which it led, I could distinguish what looked like a man and woman standing on the footpath close up against the garden side-wall of the empty house, and well away from lamps. Thought I, "They are fucking or finger-stinking," so walked further from the footpath to prevent noise, and more slowly to see the fun. It excited me lewdly, for I wanted a woman.

As I got near them I was under cover of the back garden-walls. The idea of catching a couple fucking made me more randy. "I won't, unless you give me the money first," said a female voice. I stopped, but heard no male reply. "I shan't then, — what have you got?" the shrill voice said. No audible reply, but I saw a struggle as if a man was trying to lift a woman's clothes, and heard a laugh. Then I stepped on to the path, and walked on. "I shan't then, — if you have no money what did you come here for?" came clearly on my ear, though said in a somewhat lower tone. Just as I came to the angle of the wall I saw plainly a fair-sized woman with her back against the wall and a shortish man in front of her, pulling her about as if he was trying to feel her, or lift her clothes. The amatory scuffling prevented them noticing my approach. The woman said as I neared them, "I won't without the money," — and then was a hush as I walked on.

What then occurred exactly I can't recollect, but I said as I was close to them, "Let him have you, and I'll give you five shillings." "All right, — give it here then," said the woman. I stopped, and saw by the small light of the distant lamps that the man had the cap and open collar of a sailor. A desire sprung up quicker than I write this, and what I meant for a baudy joke became the reality of action, — I followed my impulse without thought of consequences.

"I'll give you five shillings if you let me see you do it." "All right," said she — and to him, "Will *you*?" "I'm right for a bloody spree," said a male voice almost inarticulate either from drink or cold. "Give me the money first." "Certainly, if you let him do it." "Come round the back of the gardens," said the woman, walking off with the man to the rear, and well out of the line of road, I following. We stopped. "Give me the money." "Won't the policeman catch us?" "He won't be back for half an hour," said the woman, "he has just passed." I knew he had, having met him. We were now away from the lamps, it was dark. "Let's feel your cunt," said I getting into reckless baudiness. The man close to us kept chuckling to himself, and I thought staggering, but was not sure. He closed on the girl as I did. "Let me feel your cunt," said I.

The girl lifted her petticoats, her back against a wall; I put my hand between her thighs, and met the man's hand on the same errand, — we were both trying at the same spot. "Bloody spree," said a hoarse drunken voice. We both groped together. "One at a time," said she. I withdrew my hand, and it knocked against his prick, I laid hold of it, and believe to this day that the sailor thought it was the girl who was feeling it. I clutched it, and a strange delight crept through me as I drew my hand softly up and down his stiff stander which seemed longer than mine. "Hold hard you bugger," said he.

Excited beyond all thought, I still clutched and glided it through my hand. "Where is your prick?" said the girl. I felt her hand touching my hand. Letting his prick go, "No sham," said I. "There is no sham," said she, "where is your money?" I put my hand in my pocket feeling for the money, took it out, and gave it her. "Come on," said she to the man. Instantly they were close together. "Bloody spree," I heard mumbled again. "Lift up yer clothes, I can't feel yer arse." I felt that her clothes *were* up. I put my umbrella against the wall, grasped a thigh with my left hand, and my right went towards her quim, but was stopped by contact with the man's prick which was against her belly. "I'll put it in," said she. The next instant the to-and-fro movement had begun, I felt the wriggle of her arse-cheeks which I held with my left hand, his hands were now round her arse above mine, and under her clothes. "It's out," said she, "stop, I'll put it in again" — and all was still. His prick had slipped out through his energy. The woman guided it up again, and the backside jogging recommenced. I know what she said, I guessed much what she did from what she said. The buttock movement there was no mistaking.

It was too dark to see. I heard him breathing hard, and felt her thighs quivering and wriggling. Changing sides and stooping, I pushed one arm and hand right round her buttocks, between her thighs from behind, and under her cunt till my fingers passed her arse-hole, felt his prick, and grasped his balls. I doubt whether he knew it, for his pleasure was making him blow like a man who had run himself out of breath. I felt his prick-stem as he drew back, and that it was wet with the moisture of her cunt. Then with hoarse muttering, of "blood-prick spunk, bloody cunt," I felt him shove and wriggle hard, and then both were stationary and silent. I kept my hand still groping under her cunt, and feeling his prick-stem from beneath, with my thumb and forefinger.

He did not hurry himself to withdraw. "You've done, — get away." "Let's fuck agin," said he. "You shan't." As she spoke, his prick flopped out right on to my hand, wetting it. She moved away, the man swore. Mad now with lust, "Let's feel your cunt," said I lifting her clothes. She let me. "My God what spunk, — how soft your cunt feels, — let him fuck you again, — I'll give you more money, — feel me, — frig me."

I don't recollect the girl speaking, but she seized my prick whilst I groped up her cunt with fingers saturated with sperm. No disgust now. For the moment I loved it. She stopped frigging. "Put it in me, it's nicer." "No." "Oh! it's all right, — it's nice, — put it in." "No." "Do, — I want a fuck." "You've just been done." "You do it." I yielded, and putting my prick into her reeking cunt fucked her. "Oh! I'm coming." "So am I." "Oh! — ah? — ah!" I spent, and think she did, am not sure; but she shagged hard, and squeezed me up to her. The sailor had taken my place, and was looking on I suppose, standing with his back against the wall, mumbling something.

As my pleasure subsided I could just see the man by the side of us working away, I suppose at his prick, with his fist like a steam engine, I felt the sperm oozing on to my apparatus, all round. "Let's fuck yer agin," said the hoarse man's voice. "I'll give you money to let him," said I. Out came my prick. "All right," said she, "let me piddle first." "Where is your prick?" I said, "does it stand?" "Bloody fine." I put my hand on it, and grasped it. A new desire and curiosity about a male organ came over me. The woman had pissed, and was standing up, she caught hold of my prick which was hanging out, whilst I had hold of his prick. Then I took out money, and gave all the silver I had, — I don't know how much.

"Put it into her," I said, frigging it; it was not stiff, and I was impatient to feel him fucking again. He turned to her front. "Let go my prick," said he. The girl took it. "It's not stiff." "Bloody something," I heard him say. Again I heard the rustle of the frig and of her clothes lifted. "Your cunt's bloody sloppy," said the husky voice, and he chuckled. "Make haste," said the woman.

"Oh! the policeman!" Half-way down the road I saw the bull's-eye of the policeman's lantern. I was now standing feeling my own prick with excitement; but at the same instant a glimpse of moonlight came from between the heavy clouds, and showed me the man pressing his belly up against the woman, and her petticoats bunched up high. The policeman's bull's-eye far off was throwing light across the fields. "The police!" I said. "Come further along," said the woman dropping her clothes, and moving off still further into darkness, I moving off in the direction of the road. My lust went off, — what if the policeman saw and knew me! I got to the road, turned to the left along the crunching gravelled path, walking very quickly, and so soon as I turned the corner took to my heels, and ran hard home, ran as if I had committed a burglary.

Letting myself in with my latch-key I found I had left my umbrella behind me. Then a dread came over me. I had fucked a common street nymph, and in the sperm of a common sailor, both might have the pox, — what more probable? I could feel the sperm wet and sticky round my prick, and on my balls. I had then taken to sleeping in my dressing-room. My wife I thought must have been, according to habit, an hour abed. On entering my room there sat she reading, which was a very unusual thing. I sat down wishing she would leave the room, for I wanted to wash and wondered what she would say if she saw me washing my prick at that time of night, or heard me splashing. But she didn't stir, so taking out the soap unobserved, "I've bad diarrhœa," I said, and down I went to the water-closet. Sitting there I washed my prick well in the pan, and went upstairs again. (How many times in my life has a sham ailment helped me? — how many times yet is it to do so?)

Fear of the pox kept me awake some time. Then the scene I had passed through excited me so violently, that my prick stood like steel. I could not dismiss it from my mind. I was violently in rut. I thought of frigging, but an irrepressible desire for cunt, cunt, and nothing but it, made me forget my fear, my dislike of my wife, our quarrel, and everything else, — and jumping out of bed I went into her room.

"I shan't let you, — what do you wake me for, and come to me in such a hurry after you have not been near me for a couple of months, — I shan't, — you shan't, — I dare say you know where to go."

But I jumped into bed, and forcing her on to her back, drove my prick up her. It must have been stiff, and I violent, for she cried out that I hurt her. "Don't do it so hard, — what are you about!" But I felt that I could murder her with my prick, and drove, and drove, and spent up her cursing. While I fucked her I hated her — she was but my spunk-emptier. "Get off, you've done it, — and your language is most revolting." Off I went into my bed-room for the night. What I said whilst furiously fucking her, thinking of the sailor's prick and the spermy quim of the nymph, and almost mad with excitement, I never knew. I dare say it was hot.

For a fortnight I was in a state of anxiety, and twice went to a doctor to examine my prick, but I never took any ailment. I went early next day to see if my umbrella was in the fields, but it was gone, — I wonder who had it. I never saw the woman again that I know of, but had I seen her five minutes after the event I should not have known her, nor the sailor. He seemed to me a young man of about twenty, groggy and hoarse with cold, his prick seemed about the size of my own. She was a full-sized woman with a big arse, but flabby.

Though I could not find my umbrella I saw the spot on which it had stuck into the wet turf; and the place where we had played, for a yard or two square was trodden into mud, whilst all around was green.

After I had got over my fears I had a very peculiar feeling about the evening's amusement. There was a certain amount of disgust, yet a baudy titillation came shooting up my ballocks when I thought of his prick. I should have liked to have felt it longer, to have seen him fuck, to have frigged him till he spent. Then I felt annoyed with myself, and wondered at my thinking of that when I could not bear to be close to a man anywhere, I who was drunk with the physical beauty of women. The affair gradually faded from my mind, but a few years after it revived. My imagination in such matters was then becoming more powerful, and giving me desire for variety in pleasures with the sex, and in a degree, with the sexes.

CHAPTER IV

*Mrs. Y***s***e. — A neglectful husband. — Domestic unhappiness.
— At a ball. — Longings for maternity. — The wish expressed. —
At supper. — Hands under the table-cloth. — On the road home. —
The family carriage. — Premonitory touches. — No coach on the
stand. — The attempt. — On my knees. — Jolting difficulties. — The
trick done.*

Sarah Mavis had gone, Louisa Fisher had disappeared, Jenny
was married to her John. I had gone through the lascivious dissipation which relieved me in my despair after my disappointed love;
and almost immediately I entered into a liaison of an entirely different character. Its seeds were sown even when I visited Mavis,
though I was not conscious of it till I began to write this portion of
my narrative, and to reflect.

[How far chance determined my course in this liaison, how far
an unoccupied mind and a prick with no regular claims on its exertions (for I had all but totally forsaken the connubial couch) combined to bring it about, I cannot say. Certainly my attention seems
to have been led towards the lady instinctively. Perhaps it was because the lady's cunt was yearning for my sperm, a yearning which
the owner of that "nest of spicery" was herself at first barely conscious of, and even when she was, never disclosed it. I believe also
that she never had any intention of gratifying it for lustful pleasure
alone; but that maternal instinct drove her towards me. I shall
always think that some magnetic or odic, or call it what you may,
some subtle, semi-ethereal influence, born of her physical wants,
communicated itself to me, without either word or look of invitation
from her; and generated in me a lust for her. In the end we gratified
our wants together. I for sexual pleasure with a beautiful accom-

248

plished lady, she for a higher and powerful claim (almost a holy one) of her nature. Nothing in my private career presents such a psychological curiosity as this liaison does. It seems to me as I again read the manuscript, almost like a fable, yet it is as true as fact can make truth.]

We were on somewhat intimate terms with Mr. and Mrs. Y***s***e, I had known her in her youth, but her husband only since their marriage of about six years previously. It was a most unlucky union. She was an intellectual, charming, beautiful woman and had married him thinking it a wonderful match, for she was poor, though a born thoroughbred lady. He was a big, handsome man, a manufacturer, and very rich; but within a year after their marriage he had developed a host of vices, among them gambling and drunkenness. He neglected her, though he spoke of her in the highest terms, and kept up a splendid establishment. I knew that he frequented gay women, and that his drunkenness and whorings were driving him towards ruin and imbecility. Things were of course kept as quiet as they could be by the wife, but it became known among friends that he often went to bed drunk, and had even pissed the bed.

His wife took a huge disgust at him. They, I had heard, did not sleep together often, and although they went out together as man and wife, they led an unhappy existence at home. "Poor Mrs. Y***s***e!" were the terms usually applied to her. She kept up appearances, went much into society, gave splendid dinners and entertainments at which her husband was frequently absent. Chagrin told on her, her face assumed a pensive, sad, and even peevish expression; and then some people said she was ill-tempered, and had driven her husband into evil courses. It was false, for I had heard her husband, — whom I could not bear, — say how good she was, and bewail his own bad habits which he said he could not help, — they conquered him.

I met her out frequently, most frequently at houses where she was without her husband, and I without my curse, though sometimes otherwise. My domestic troubles were known to her, hers to me. There might have been some secret sympathy on this account between us. All I know is that I was sorry for her, and wondered how such a lovely creature got on with a man of such brutal, beastly habits. Her manner to me had always been soft and winning, chance had at dinner-parties often assigned her to me. "I'm so glad to take you in to dinner," said I one night just before the time I am going to speak of. "So am I," said she, "I've more pleasure in talking to you than to any one of our acquaintance." Whenever we had met I had seen her eyes following me, yet not the shadow of voluptuousness had been shown, nor any improper advance had been made by her. Delighted with the hug that the waltz gave an occasion for, and the squeeze of the hand which the dance sometimes permits, yet a lustful idea had never entered my head about her, though unconsciously I always was looking at her whenever we met.

We had a habit of asking after each other, as if mutually conscious that in our homes we had troubled lives; yet we never complained to each other, though often we made slightly bitter remarks. There was a veiled meaning in what we said, but nothing in the slightest degree improper.

The following conversation took place at a dance, it is pretty nearly word for word. Said she with a sigh, "Ah! you men can escape your troubles, we poor women cannot." "How?" "You know how, I expect, — or you are very much belied, — nobody blames you men." "But an unhappy home can never be escaped." "True, but you men can get forgetfulness, and keep out of it as you do." "Who says I do?" "Ah!" "What do they say?" "I must not tell you." "Do." "Well, that you are very fond of the ladies." "So I am." "I knew it." "Is there any harm in that?" "You know what I mean." "I don't know, — do explain." "You are a libertine, I expect." "I should like to hear from your lips exactly what you mean." She laughed. "I dare say you would, — but you won't." "Then I am left in ignorance." "Very ignorant, I dare say." "I like them to talk, walk, ride and dance with them, — I love to embrace them in the waltz." "I know you do, and if you dance with me again don't hold me so close." "I love you to be close to me — does it offend you?" "Not at all — but people may talk." "I should like to be as close to you as man and woman could." "Hush!" "I mean nothing." "Of course not." "I like to feel your breath on my face." "They say you are a rake." "Would you be anything else if you were placed like me?" "No, I would do as you do." "Then you like my being a rake?" "No, — no." "Are you a rake?" "I would be if I dared." "Dear Mrs. Y***s***e, let us be rakes together." "Oh! naughty." "You evidently don't understand me." "Too well, and I also often feel quite reckless, for I have nothing to care about, no sister, my mother dead, no child, and such a home-life," — and tears rose in her eyes. "It is sad, — don't cry, — I know also what sadness is, and what you must feel, — I wish you had a child." "Yes, it would make me a home, — and yet a child of his! ah! I thank God we have none." This was said with all the abandonment of an unhappy woman. Then she rose suddenly, and bidding me good-bye, left. I had never before, I think, alluded to her husband when conversing with her.

I met her at a dinner-party soon afterwards, and took her down to table, — she I suppose was then thirty years old. She had a lovely neck, fine hazel eyes, and dark wavy hair. I pitied her. The conversation took this turn. "How strange things happen, some have such flocks of children which they don't want, rich people who want them none." "People without children should change partners," said I. (This was in the drawing-room after dinner.) "Hush!" said she, looking me full in the face. Her own face flushed, she stared at me, her breast gave violent heaves and her mouth slightly opened. I thought I had gone too far, had offended her, and was about to say I hoped I had not done so, when the hostess asked her to play. "Turn over the music-leaves," said she to me, — and I did. She sang divinely, looking up at me as she sang; but although I saw she was agitated, I did not notice anything else, nor did I think about anything but what I said.

I knew that involuntarily I had been guilty of a breach of good manners by those words, was mad with myself, and hoped she would attribute it to wine. Her husband was of the party, but did not come upstairs after dinner. When her carriage was announced I offered to see her to it, but she took the arm of the host, and went off looking at me very kindly. "She has forgotten it," thought I. The husband, who was groggy, was in the hall and went home with her.

Conversation when we met next was about children, but I was unconscious of the tendency of her remarks, nor had I a glimmering of what was in her mind. "Yes, children are a bond of union they say." "How can they be, if husband and wife are apart in taste, habits, and feeling?" "They say however bad a husband may be that a woman loves him if he be the father of her child," I remarked. "I don't believe it," she replied, and became quite agitated.

I met her soon after at a ball, I was there alone and her husband was not with her. We danced together, she was a lovely waltzer. "No baby yet?" whispered I, as I whirled her round in my arms. "No," she laughed. "It's your fault." "It's not." "Should you not like a dear little child?" she asked. This was later on at night, she had had champagne, and the excitement of the scene had told on her. The sweet strains of music, the flushed and happy faces of the women, their white breasts and arms, the ankles and limbs exposed as they circled round, for dresses were then worn which allowed the calf to be seen as a woman waltzed, had excited me; yet up to that moment I had never had a lascivious thought about her. I could smell her sweet flesh as she waltzed, and was suddenly enervated by desire. "Yes," I whispered, "if you were the mother." "Oh! fie!" "Would not you like one?" "Yes, if I liked the father, — but that cannot be." I hugged her to me. "Let us try." She stopped short saying, "I'm tired, — I'm giddy, — let me sit down, — I'm faint." "Come to the dining-room," I said. She came. I gave her wine. "Leave me, — I can't, — I'm better, — leave me." "But I must see you back to the ball-room," I said. "Pray leave me, — I can't speak with you." I left her, and soon after she came back to the ball-room by herself.

Then she danced with others. When I asked her again to dance, her card was full. "At least let me take you to supper, or I shall think you are offended with me." "Very well."

Until supper I looked at her from various parts of the room. Wherever I happened to be, her eyes met mine. The attraction between the man and the woman was complete, both thought of nothing else but, "Yes, if it was by you," — "Yes, if I liked the father." It meant fucking. Was she a loose fish, she who was thought so chaste? — was she in love with me? — was she like her husband, giving way to drinking? Was I in love with her? All this kept running through my brain, and with it a burning, fresh, yet never thought of till that evening, intense desire to have her. "She is married, — never mind, he is a beast, — it's adultery, — never mind, we like each other." In that form of mind I took her to supper, feeling sure that she liked me, even if she did not love me, — but until that night no such idea had ever entered my head.

We talked about different subjects for a minute or two, looking into each other's eyes as we conversed. The champagne flowed. "Don't be offended," I said in a low tone. "What is it?" "My love to you." "Be quiet." "Change glasses." "Why?" "That my lips may touch the glass which your lips have touched, — how I long to touch the lips themselves." "Be quiet pray, — you will be heard." The supper went on, the clink of glasses increased, the pop of champagne-corks, the clatter of knives and forks, the pull of crackers, the peals of laughter drowned all slighter sounds. "Another glass, and look at me." She took a glass. Looking into her eyes, "My love to you, *Mamma*," I whispered. "It's too bad," said she turning away. "Not if I was the father." "For Heaven's sake, cease." "Let me feel your hand — do pray." Just then some lady next to us let fall a lump of jelly into her lap, a lovely dress was spoiled. There was a scuffle, and regrets, and laughter, and "No never mind it," — and the flap of the table-cloth was pulled up over the lady's lap.

Though there were table-napkins, I raised the table-cloth also, so as to keep her dress from the chance of food falling, and spoiling it. I pushed my hand which was nearest to hers under the cloth towards hers. They met, and I gave hers a firm but gentle clasp. What a shiver ran through me as I felt her return the squeeze. I drew it towards me, and pressed it against me just where my prick (which had risen rampant) was shut up. She must have known what I was doing, for turning her face towards me with a wild expression, she withdrew her hand. It had pressed against me for an instant only before she drew it away. She declared afterwards she had no idea for the moment of what I was doing. She got up hastily. "Take me back to the ball-room," she said.

Later on we had a wild tearing gallop, all were excited in the room, and I much with wine and desire. I was holding her to me, whirling her about. "Let's be rakes together, — we shall have a dear little baby," I interjected as the rapid dance went on. "Oh! fie! — oh!" she repeated, "oh! no now, — oh! no, — oh! let me sit down." I danced on with her. "I can't bear this, — I'm getting mad I think, — you are losing all respect for me, — for God's sake, cease."

The dance was getting over. "Good night, I'm going, — my carriage is here." "Let me go with you." "Oh! no, not after your talk, besides I am going to take Mr. and Mrs. ***." "But there's room for four." "No I dare not, — don't come down with me, for God's sake." Her eyes looked wild, but they beamed on me through their wildness.

The carriage (one of the huge comfortable family-carriages of those days, room in it for four large people and six small ones) drew up. I was determined to go home with her, though she had prayed me not. It was a long drive, and on my way home, — and she knew it. It rained, and was past two o'clock in the morning. I handed her in. The lady and her husband whom she was going to drop on her road home, were in the hall. In got the lady. "Would you mind giving me a lift," I said, "for there is no cab to be had, and alas! my carriage is not here." The gentleman was at the back of me, but I stood in the doorway barring his entrance to the carriage. It was impossible to refuse me without rudeness before the other lady. "I shall have great pleasure," said she in an agitated manner. In I got, the gentleman followed, — had I let him in first he would have sat opposite to her, not I. Off we drove.

I was now burning with lust for her, and felt a conviction that she was equally filled with desire for me. For a few minutes I behaved myself, but getting hotter and hotter became at last quite reckless. First I pressed my leg against hers, she moved them away. I followed them till she could move them no further, and still kept pressing my leg against her. I wore pumps and silk stockings, and slipping one foot out of my shoe, and pushing it under her petticoats, rubbed it up against her calf. We were all talking with excitement, she more than any of us, as if she wished to divert attention from what I was doing. "What a lovely ball, — I never enjoyed myself so much, — did you?" "No, nor I." So we all talked and laughed. It was pitch dark, but as we passed the gas-lamps I could see an almost painful excitement on her face. Up went my foot till I touched the under side of her thigh by her knees. She gave a suppressed shriek.

"What's the matter?" said her friend. "Oh! I've got the cramp." "Ah! you have got your satin shoe wet getting into the carriage," said her friend. "No I've not." I had taken away my foot at her cry, but soon impelled by lust again raised it up her clothes. Again she started. "Cramp again? — let me pull your shoe off." "Oh! no." The couple were near home. "Had you not better take a coach, we are near the last coach-stand," said Mrs. Y***s***e, "it's more than a mile from our house to yours." This before her friends. I could not say no, but with anger in my heart said yes, and thanked her for the lift she had given me homewards. She pulled the checkstring, the carriage stopped, I told the footman what to do. Oh! joy there was no coach on the stand. "Never mind," I said, "when you are home, perhaps you won't mind your man driving me back, it is only a mile, — how good of you to let me ride so far with you."

Soon after her friends were set down, and we were alone.

There was not more than ten minutes' drive before me. I knew that well. Though only in the suburbs, we were past gas-lamps. Occasional oil-lamps gave a feeble light. It had now become a slightly foggy night. In a delirium of desire, no sooner was the footman on the box than I placed myself beside her. She was trembling with expectation of what was to come. I hugged her waist and hips, and thrust my hand up her clothes. "Now don't forget yourself, or me, — for God's sake, — what have I done! — what have I said! — it serves me right, — now pray, — if you are a gentleman you won't, — oh! now — don't forget your honour, or mine, — I won't consent, — no never, — never, — oh! this is indecent, — for God's sake don't now, — you sh-a-n-'t, — I'll pull the check-string."

"Kiss me my darling, we are both unhappy, — it is no fault of ours, — let me now, — we love each other, — let us, — how smooth your flesh is, — oh! God let me feel your cunt, — open your thighs, —let me fuck you, — I will, — I swear I will." "What language, — I won't, — no, — no, — no, — I say, — you are taking a shameful advantage of me, — oh! if the footman should look down, — oh! don't, — o — ho! — o — ho!" She thrilled under my titillation of her cunt, her breath came short, her head sunk on my shoulder, and she was speechless. Then her thighs opened quite wide, my lust and passion had entered her, conquered her, she was helpless, defenceless, and abandoned herself to me. Furious to have her at once, I said no more, nor she.

I pulled out my prick, and put her hand to it, — there she left it. A strange idea passed through my brain. "What if I fuck her, and she gets with child!" This whilst I moved her off my shoulder, and leant her back in the corner of the carriage. Rapidly I freed my prick and testicles from my trowsers, and dropped down on my knees between the carriage-seats, threw up her clothes, and kissed her thighs and cunt. The perfume overwhelmed me. I felt its moisture. But she was too far back on the seat for my prick to reach her. Then Heaven knows how I managed it, but I did. Kissing her cunt, I slid both hands round her bum, and pulled her forwards. She let me do it all without a struggle, without a word. Her cunt was soon at the edge of the seat, her thighs wide open. I pushed my prick towards it, and touched it. It was so stiff, I could not bend it, to get it up her. It slipped away as the carriage jolted, and knocked against my own belly. Then I half raised myself, how I can't describe, I don't know, but I was leaning partly over her, and raising one of her thighs whilst I guided my prick right up her lovely orifice, to have it jolted out the next instant by the roll of the carriage. Again I put it in, again it came nearly out, I holding one thigh, my other hand resting on the seat, and half supporting me, my legs cramped, and both of us in such a position as to make fucking as difficult as possible, indeed almost impossible.

But a prick will get itself into a willing cunt, be the difficulty ever so great. Somehow I got her more forward, myself at a better slope. I felt her clitoris, and pressing down my prick so as to move under my fingers, it slid towards her bum-furrow, then back, then forward again as the carriage moved. She let me do what I liked, but did nothing to help me. She was a lifeless log, thighs wide apart, cunt gaping and reeking with the sweat of the dance and lewedness; her passions fully roused, faint with desire, bashfulness, and fear, she yielded herself up, but did not help. At length my prick with one thrust went full up her cunt, I clasped her somewhere like a vice to keep our genitals joined, the movement of the carriage did nearly the rest. It was a rapid wriggle, my only fear that my prick would be dislodged again. "Oh! God I'm spending my d — ar — h — ling." My prick moved vigorously up and down her cunt, she gave one loud prolonged cry, half sigh of pleasure, and with a grip of her cunt, and a heave of her haunches, I knew she had spent with me — and just then an infernal jolt of the coach dislodged my prick almost before I had quite finished spending.

"You've spent my darling, — I've fucked you, — you are delicious, — haven't you spent!" I sat by her side holding my reeking prick, feeling her gluey, sperm-slabbered cunt, and pushed my mouth against hers, my tongue into it. Oh! the exquisite delight of those few minutes. My brain had whirled from the moment her friends had left us alone; it whirled still with subdued delight now that I had had her. I could not forget it, and for a minute went on talking.

I pulled down her clothes, she did not attempt to do so herself. "My darling why did you not help me?" No reply. "You'll forgive me, won't you, — I love you so, — I could not help it." Not a word. She lay with her eyes closed back in the carriage, breathing hard, violently, but speechless, exhausted by excitement, fear, and a medley of sensations which deprived her of movement or utterance.

"We are just home, — for God's sake rouse yourself." With a start she pulled a lace shawl over her head, but made no reply. The carriage stopped, I got out, and saw her to the door. "Can I offer you anything?" said she. "No thank you, — may your man drive me home?" "Certainly." "Good night." "Is Mr. Y***s***e at home?" "Yes Ma'am, and abed," said the footman. Off I went desiring politely to be remembered to Mr. Y***s***e, not forgetting the habits of a gentleman, nor she those of a lady, for she desired her compliments to my wife, and to say she was so sorry she had not seen her at the ball.

The footman closed the door. I had folded the cloak I then wore over my trowsers, which in the hurry were not properly closed. I buttoned them up in the carriage as I was driven home.

That night she slept by herself, her husband had been lifted into bed too drunk to undress himself. He had not fucked her for three months, and had had the clap in the interim; — is it to be wondered that she succumbed to me! I knew all this afterwards from her.

CHAPTER V

The boudoir next day. — On the sofa. — A dull dinner. — Assigna-
tions. — The linendraper's shop with two fronts. — The house in
T***f***d Street with two entrances. — Consummation. — A
chaste-minded adultress. — The consequences.

I passed a restless night wondering at all that had occurred so
unpremeditated, so successful, and yet half a failure at the last
moment; for my spend was scarcely finished in her. The next day
I called. She was unwell, and could see no one. Had she taken cold?
Yes, the servant thought so, she had been ill all night, and could
see no one. It was a maid that opened the door who said this, and
not a footman. Was Mr. Y***s***e at home? No. I did not desire
to disturb her, but I had a pressing message from my wife, and
should much like to give it instead of my wife writing it, if she
would but see me for a minute only, — it was a matter of some
importance. "Mistress has seen no one sir, she has been so ill, —
she has not been long up, — but I will ask."

I waited in a small morning-room. Half an hour passed, the
maid at length appeared, and showed me into the drawing-room.
My heart was beating. Mrs. Y***s***e was seated in an easy-chair,
the fire was burning with a red heat, dusk was coming on. I offered
my hand, she put hers out coldly. "I am ill — what is the message
you have for me?" "None, you know I have none — it was only to
see you, to beg your pardon, to say I could not control myself."
"That will do — not another word about what you have done, I
have permitted enough to be done, to let you think you can do what
you like here." I did not know at this cold treatment what to do,
what to say to her, and was silent.

"I'm distressing you," at length I said, "so I had better go."

"You came to distress me, for you knew you would," she replied. "I never was cruel to a woman in my life," I said. "Indeed, — your wife gives a different version." "Does she? — most likely, — it's to her interest to blacken me, — it saves her own reputation." "All you men are the same, — you might have a happier home if you were truer to your wife." "It's false, she is not fit for a wife, nor could she make any one happy — I might as well say it's your fault that Mr. Y***s***e is what he is." "He! — if I were to tell you all I suffer, it would make your hair stand on end." "And I, if I told you all about my home, you would pity me. Listen."

It was rarely that I told my griefs, but hid them as much as I could. I had told them only to a little gay woman, to one of my servants, and to an old friend's parlour-maid, and had fucked all three women. I was now piqued, was in love with this lady, fancied she had had as much to do with my erotic darings in the carriage as I had, and could not bear to be thought a liar and traitor at home, and to have behaved ill to any woman. "Listen," I said. "Oh! I don't want to hear." "But you must, — you shall, in justice to me, — listen."

Then I told her in a few minutes a history in itself. "Good Heavens, you are jesting." "By the Eternal God it's the truth," — and I burst out crying. How long we sat I don't know, but I heard her saying, "I'm truly sorry for you, — it's almost incredible." I went on to my knees before her. "Kiss me." "Get up for God's sake, — the servant will come in." "Kiss — kiss me." "There, — there, — get up," said she kissing me, "now leave me, pray." "Why I have not been here a quarter of an hour." "You must have been here an hour, — it's dark. — I must ring for lights."

"You are the first woman for years who has kissed me who has not been a harlot," I said, forgetting the servants, the married women, and others I had had, and a lady about whom I shall print nothing. It was an odd thing to say, was quite useless and untrue, but it burst from my lips suddenly, — Heaven knows why.

The story I had told her had stirred her sympathies, for she was a woman in the fullness of her blood, in the hey-day of her lusts. She was a pure woman; but those who have tasted the pleasures of coition with a man, — and she had spent with me, — cannot resist the desire for them again. Hers however was a want which urges many a woman to sexual complaisance without knowing the

cause, although she knew well what she wanted, and was willing
to forget herself, to bring about a result to satisfy the want. It was
not fucking, but the consequences which most women dread, and
try to avoid, when the fucking is illicit. Yes — she yearned for maternity. All her utterances to me, involuntary, irrepressible as they
were, all pointed to it.

The deed of the previous night, and my present disclosures,
had broken all barriers. She had tried at the beginning to fence
herself with coldness — useless. Oh! the mysteries of the cock and
the cunt when once the male and female disclose them to each
other. No fence, no walls, no bolts, no bars, will keep them asunder.
What can a woman refuse a man whose spunk has filled her cunt,
from the portals of her womb to her clitoris, as mine had hers. All
on a sudden I closed on her, kissed her, and put my hand up her
petticoats.

"Now leave off, — if you attempt to repeat last night, I will
leave the room, and deny myself in future when you call." "Nonsense Mary, — let me call you Mary, — dear Mary, — you know
what you told me only yesterday night as we danced, — things have
not changed since then, — let me, — let me be the father."

"Never, — a moment's weakness, — yes I should like a child, —
in my loneliness and misery, with all our wealth, it might comfort
me, — but not one of disgrace, — I forgot myself, and now you
punish me, — forget all about it. As a gentleman, as I know you
to be, — you will forget it, and never disclose my weakness, I am
sure."

"Nonsense, we love each other, — let me." "Now don't, — leave
off, — not now, — oh! don't make that noise, — be quiet then, —
the footman will be in." "He is out, or was when I was downstairs."
She rose up. "Let me feel where I did last night." "No, I forgot
myself once, but never again, — go." "I won't by God, — I will have
you, — I feel mad when I think my prick has been in your dear
cunt, but never spent in it properly, — that my sperm has covered
it, but was half wasted outside it."

Out of the large double drawing-rooms was her boudoir, a sofa
in it. I laid hold of her hands, and pulled her. "Come here." "Oh!
don't make that noise, — the footman may come here." "Well, here."
Gently, and kissing her as I went, I pulled that lady into her boudoir
and laid her on the sofa. Sighs, kisses, murmurs of my love, and we

were spending together on the sofa a minute or two afterwards. The doors were unlocked, any one coming in must have caught us; both must have been delirious with love-passion, to have run such risks. Rising quickly after I had spent, she rang for lights. Then was another ring audible.

"It's his ring, — it's my husband, — he's come home, — perhaps not drunk for once, — sit down there, — no, not so near, — there, — oh! my God what has brought him home!" (He rang a minute after she had rung the drawing-room bell.)

"How are you old fellow?" said her husband, quite sober, entering the room, and shaking hands with me, — "why I thought (to his wife) you would see no one." "I felt better when I was up, and Mr.*** has come to say he has a box for Drury Lane for next Friday, and very much wants us to go with him and Mrs. ***, — I told him to wait a little on chance of your coming home." "Will you join us?" said I. "Yes," replied he, "you stop to dinner with us." I hesitated. "Do." "I'd rather not." "We are all alone, — why don't you ask him, Molly?" No reply. "Why the damned fool has fainted, — it's the second time she has done it to-day, — what the hell's the matter with her?" said he.

[It's singular what a lot of fainting women I had in my youth, — those in after years did not faint during our intrigues.]

To ring, get sal-volatile, spirits, was the work of a minute. She had recovered before they came. Mr. Y***s***e poured himself out three quarters of a tumbler of brandy, and putting a little water to it, swallowed it. "Don't drink all that," said she. "Mind your own business," said he. I rose to go. "I want him to stay to dinner, Molly." "Won't you stay?" "I'd rather not." "Stay, — nonsense," said he, — "she'll be as dull as stale beer to-night, — if you don't stay, come to my club, and we'll dine there." "Pray stay," said she. My seed was up her, that was an attraction, and though kindness would have said go, — I stayed. She left the room. Mr. Y***s***e drank more brandy and water; at dinner he was three sheets in the wind, no one was there but us three. "Who knows if chance may not give her to me again to-night!"

It was the most extraordinary evening in point of strained sensation I ever spent. Shown into a bed-room to wash before dinner, I would not wash the hand which had fingered her cunt; out of a superstition that if I kept it unwashed I should have her again

that night. I had never been at a family-dinner with them before.
My sense of delicacy as a gentleman ought to have made me refuse
her husband's invitation, seeing that she was distressed, and had not
willingly joined with him in asking me. At table he was boisterous
and jolly at first, then heavy and stupid as the wine told on him; she
dull and distressed, though trying hard to hide her being so. "You
are as dull as ditch-water, — you are as cheerful as small beer drawn
yesterday," he kept saying at intervals to her. I had been trying to
engage her in conversation all the evening, but it flagged, although
she drank wine freely. Gradually all the talking fell to him, and as
he was listened to, he seemed contented.

I felt more inclined to think, than to talk; at all events to him,
for my mind dwelt on the changes twenty-four hours had made in
our relations to each other. The night before I had seen her come in
to the ball-room upright, radiant, fresh-coloured, sparkling, proud
in step, composed in demeanour; and I had not had a vestige of a
thought of having her. I had even thought her cold, and should have
said without any sensuality. There she sat now. My hands had
wandered over her soft flesh, from her knees to her navel, I had
titillated her clitoris, spent in her. She was pale in face, dark rings
were round her eyes, she seemed half lifeless, it was painful to see
her. Whenever I turned my eyes towards her, I found hers fixed
on me with a strained expression in them, as if she were hearing
some frightful tale. (I shall never forget the expression in them.)
Her voice quivered, she answered slowly. I kept thinking of my fuck
on the sofa, and all the occurrences. The more I thought, the more
impossible it seemed to me that all could so have come about, — it
seemed a dream.

When she left us, her husband took brandy and water and
cigars and got more fuddled. "Tea is in the drawing-room sir," said
the flunkey. I rose to go. "Wait another quarter of an hour," said
Mr. Y***s***e. I waited "Let us go, Mrs. Y***s***e will think
me rude." "She be damned, — you go, — I'll stop, and have another
glass, and another cigar."

In the drawing-room she poured out my tea with perfect grace.
"Is not my husband coming?" "Soon," I said. Time ran on, she rang
the bell. "Tell your master the tea will be cold." Footman came back.
"He has gone to bed Ma'am." "To bed?" "Yes." "Excuse me," she
said, and left the room. In a few minutes she came back. "Is he

unwell?" said I in all ignorance. She looked at me, to see if I was humbugging her by my question. "No, drunk, — that is my life," — and she buried her face in her hands.

I went close to her, my lust got the better of me, and I attempted to feel her leg. She rose from her chair. "Are you a brute also? — then I am deceived indeed, — no don't touch me, be content, — would *you* break my heart quite? — it is well nigh broken, — if you touch me, I will never see you again." I was awed. She moved her chair away from me, and I did not approach nearer to her.

We talked a short time. "You will meet me, won't you? — our friendship has only begun, — both unfortunate, — why deny ourselves the pleasure our society gives us?" She made no reply for a long time, seemed to be struggling with herself, and buried her face in her hands.

"Where? — how?" she said at last. "Meet me somewhere where we can talk undisturbed." "Where? — how? — so that I may not be known?" The brain of a man works wiles to get a woman, and I thought of a move new to me, perhaps old enough to others; with me it was an instantaneous thought. There were and now are three large linendrapers in London, with corner-buildings, and two frontages. "Call at So-and-So," I said, "stop at the °°° street-side, — make a purchase, — send your carriage away, — go right through the shop to the other street, there I will await you to-morrow." "No." "When?" "The next day at three." "You won't deceive me?" "I have begun, and I'll go through it," said she with a hard look. "One kiss." "Hish! the servants are all about." I kissed her, and left.

The day came. A bitterly cold and rather foggy day, an admirable one for our assignation. I had called at a house in T°°° f°°°d Street, well known in those days to swells. I had never been at it before, but had asked a middle-aged friend if he knew a good house, for I did not like taking her to J°°°s Street. He was a married man with a great liking for intrigue. "You are going to have a married woman," said he (it was an odd shot, but a true one). "No." He winked. "The quietest house in London is So-and-So — there is a back and a front entrance, one in one street, one in another street." I went there, hired the nicest room, ordered a fire, and clean sheets, and paid part in advance.

I waited at the corner looking out for the carriage. No carriage came. A lady got out of a cab, paid and it drove off. "Is it she?" She stood still, looked at me through a thick veil, then went into the shop. I had recognized her, and went round the corner; my cab of course was there. A quarter of an hour which seemed an age elapsed. "Is she never coming?" Then she appeared with a paper parcel in her hand. In a minute she was in the cab; in five minutes at T°°°f°°°d Street, and in a large comfortable, but somewhat dull bed-room.

She took off her bonnet and veil, she was trembling. "Is this an hotel?" "No my darling." "Is it a brothel?" "It's a house where they are not particular." "It *is* a brothel." I did not know what to say, so held my tongue.

She buried her face in her hand, and sat so for a minute. "You have not kissed me darling." She kissed me, got up, and looked at me fixedly.

"Take off your things, — let me help you." She hurried, was quite silent, and soon was in her chemise, but with boots and stockings on. She undressed mechanically, as if she were thinking of something else. "Oh! let me look at you — let me lift your chemise." She resisted. "No, for Heaven's sake, leave me alone." I complied. "Let me draw off your boots and stockings." The next minute we were in bed, and I was up her; getting into the bed with a bound, and mounting her with fury. She had not laid down before I was pressing her. She laid down on her side with her face towards me, but my body met hers, and turned her on to her back. "Wait a minute, — let us talk," she began. "Oho!" she sobbed as with a fierce plunge my prick drove her. The next minute her cunt was deluged.

I was not man enough, or she not appetizing to me enough to make me continue without withdrawing (as I often did with a fresh piece). I uncunted, and began the delights of feeling her all over. That exquisite variety of sensations were mine, which run through a man as he feels a woman in all her nakedness. For the first time, can kiss her mouth, suck her bubbies, rove from her neck to her knees, smooth his lips over her breasts, plunge his fingers up her cunt till they can grope no further. Soon I was in full vigor again, and up her, and then Mary Y°°°s°°°e met me with ardour and in that very fuck was impregnated. She had never spoken from the

time she had got into the bed, till her pleasure came on. Then she
sobbed out, "*Oh! my love!*" — and she was quiet again. She often
repeated the words when spending afterwards. That came naturally
from her, as my prick stiffened to its utmost in her cunt, and she
drew my sperm out of me. She never said any other words when
fucking.

In less than an hour I fucked her again. I could scarcely get
her to talk. After each poke she wanted to know the time, and when
satisfied lay nestling close to me. "You're with child," I remarked
jokingly. "I hope so." I could not realize that she really meant it.
"Don't you wash?" "No, I'll do nothing to destroy the chance."
"Chance of what?" "Of having a child." "Do you really mean it?"
"What do you think I have come here for, if I don't mean it? — do
you think I run this risk for lust? — to have degraded myself in your
eyes for mere lust! — you are in error if you imagine that." "My
darling I am thinking of nothing but the delight I have in meeting
you, in finding a friend and lover in you." "I am not your lover, and
never shall be, though I have been dreaming of such an afternoon
with you for two years past." "Of me?" "Yes, thinking I should like
a child by you." "Why me?" "I don't know, — who can tell why one
likes and dislikes," — and then she explained.

"When grief was upon me I longed to be a mother, and thought
of you. Gradually I came to desire that you should be the father,
and for that I have degraded myself, — yet I swear that this has
come about as if by magic, for I never contemplated having a child
by you, much as I desired it. But from the moment you took my
hand under the table-cloth at the supper, I lost all control of myself.
In the carriage I was helpless as a child, was in a sort of swoon,
though I knew quite well what you were about, and that it was
wrong, I tried to resist you in my mind, but could not stir a limb. It
was the same the day before yesterday. I knew you had sent up a
falsehood, but felt I must see you, and from the moment you pulled
me towards my boudoir, had the same enervation." This was said
nearly as I write it, not as an apology, but as a narrative told in the
most natural way possible, and in a sorrowful tone.

"Did you spend with me in the boudoir?" "Yes. I felt agitated,
alarmed, and almost fainting." "Did you wash yourself, — do tell
me, — do?" I anticipated coyness and evasion, but I did not know

the woman yet, her frankness and determination. "No I did not, —
I thought of doing so, but from a feeling I can't describe I would
not, and I came down to dinner just as you left me."

"Do you not love me? — you could not have thought so of me
without it." I asked her this for I was staggered, and thought spite
of all, that she might be only a frisky one, to whom a fuck on the
sly was a treat. I was too inexperienced to know the varieties of the
female mind, the vagaries that an unsatisfied womb might cause,
the overwhelming passion that a womb hungering for impregnation
might beget.

"I do not love you, — I shall never be a mistress to you, and
from the time I am sure that I shall have a child, you will see no
more of me in the way you see me now, and perhaps not at all."
"I believe you are with child at this moment," I said joking. "I
firmly believe that I became so an hour ago. — I must leave, — how
can I enter my door with the feeling I have hitherto done? — ah!
mine has been a bitter married life!" "And mine my darling also."
"But you men get relief, get even fresh loves, and people overlook
it, — women they crush for less."

She dressed. "You have not washed yourself," I said laughing,
for I had turned away out of delicacy when I saw her put the basin
down. She would not wash at all, not wishing to destroy the good
I had done her. Was it for good or harm? — time was to show. I
saw her to a cab, and we parted. Yes she would meet me again —
to-morrow at the theatre we should meet. She had never smiled,
nor seemed pleased, nor been voluptuous, she only laid quiet, and
let me fuck her as much as I could.

We met at Drury Lane, for I had of course to get the box. That
night Mrs. Y***s***e began to show great attention to my wife,
who in return began to hate her, yet I carefully avoided showing
Mrs. Y****s***e special attention. Mr. Y. went out regularly between each act to drink. I had opportunity to speak to his wife.
"Same time and place to-morrow." The next afternoon we were in
the same bed together again.

And again we met. She came in her carriage, left it at one door,
and passed through the shop to me. We had only time for one
hurried poke. Again the next day, but she had not come in her
carriage to the linendraper's because the coachman was ill. She had
a fit of compassion, would not hear of his coming out in the cold,

nor of a groom driving. She was frightened. He was not a good whip, so she had a cab. It was a piece of luck, I said. "Well it really is," she replied. "I hope he will be confined for weeks." "Poor man, he has a sick wife," said she. How clever are both man and woman in availing themselves of every chance for getting amorous delights, — the old song of my boyhood is right, "cock and cunt will come together, check them as you may."

It was an afternoon of hard fucking. She had a tight cunt, — I told her so. "You ought to know what is tight and what is not, according to all accounts," she said. I had heard similar hints from others within the year before that, and wondered how it came about.

Another and another meeting. She was always quiet, reserved, dignified, even when she pissed, but now was yielding, and taking more her share in dalliance. "Why don't you put your hand down, and feel my prick?" Her hand went gently down, and then it became like mine, inquisitive, and moved under my balls and all about, much more so than the hands of the women did whom I had recently been accustomed to. Satisfying her curiosity stirred her blood, and there was more passion in embrace. Still I felt that I more served a purpose she was determined on carrying out, than that she had pleasure in meeting me for copulation. My vanity was excessive on her declaration that she wished a child by me, but was chilled when she said that so soon as she got one, she would not care about me; and that my embraces were nothing to her, unless they fecundated her egg; that her joy in my arms was only physical, and that when the sperm was laying up against her womb-mouth, she cared nothing for the man from whose prick it had issued. Many as were the cunts I had spermatized, I was too young to have studied their owners philosophically or psychologically, as I since have done.

Gradually she became more free. She had refused my inspection of her, and on any liberty she did not like she mentioned her degradation. "I suppose you think me little better than a prostitute," said she to me one day, "and I deserve it." She was so sensitive about her own sin, as she called it, that when she referred to it I was settled at once, and relinquished my wishes. I had never seen her quite naked even after several meetings, and got wild. "Let me see." "I don't like it." "Well my darling you shan't be annoyed but I have never kissed it, — I will." I ducked down in the bed kissing her breasts, then her belly, and at last lodged my head between her thighs. The smell of her cunt was delicious to me, I opened the lips, I kissed the moist parts. "I'll lay here all the time," I said, but I never licked her, for I had no taste for gamahuching her. "You will be smothered unless you come up." "I don't care, — let me see." I just caught the darkness of the split, and was glad to rise up, and rub my ballocks against it. She would show me no more, but it stirred her up, "Oh! my love," came with more emphasis than ever. I pulled my prick out of her, and stopped her crisis. "What are you doing?" "I won't go on unless you let me look at your cunt," — and then I did. Afterwards I became master, and she no longer refused me.

The coachman was better. Instead of two or three hours she could only manage an hour, — half an hour, — it came to a fuck at the bedside, and a precipitate rush out of the house. We were much vexed. How I hated to see her step out of that big carriage! — how I longed to see her come muffled up out of a cab!

One day she sighed, but smiled. "I am with child," she said. "Are you glad!" "Yes, but I feel sad, and I don't know why." This must have been about a month after I had had her. "Are you sure?" "Yes, — and if in another three weeks my poorliness does not come on, it is absolutely certain, — not but I was certain I should be from the moment we met here, and even before I had you, that you would be the father of a child." I wanted to see her quite naked. "No." "Not to the father of your child? — ridiculous." She reflected. "It is ridiculous, but I cannot bear to be treated like a prostitute." "Nonsense, — does not every man see his wife naked, and have his pleasure with her in every way?" "Do what you like with me, you have the right now, — every right over me, — more right than any one else, — I believe it to be so in the eyes of God."

CHAPTER VI

Copulation refused me. — Unto us a child is born. — Flight suggested. — Affection unrequited. — Her husband dies. — Narrowed circumstances. — In a foreign land. — She marries again. — Hearsay, fifteen years afterwards.

When she had made up her mind to a course good or bad, she did not hesitate. The same determination that I should be the father of her child made her yield to me now. She let me pull her about, lift up this limb, open that, backside and belly, cunt, bubbies, and armpits came under my rapturous inspection. I must have been strong in my expressions of delight, for she took the infection from me. When rushing into her arms, and sheathing my penis in her, "Am I really very nice?" she said. "Divine." "Oh! my love, I am so glad you like me," — and our bodies began to move. The affection which a woman has for him whose seed has given her a child had set in, but I did not reciprocate it. I had not then in my physical love for women learnt to discriminate between lust and love, and thought the former was the latter, until it shifted its object, and then I began to wonder how I had liked the last woman so much, and the one before her so much, and so on.

After that day there was no hesitation. She abandoned herself to me absolutely, I could see and do what I liked, nor was she behind. Though not a sensuous or voluptuous woman, she used to rub her mouth in my balls, and kiss my prick, whilst I fingered her cunt. The way she nestled her nose round my balls was curious — most women have a way of their own in amorous tricks.

She had dark eyes, dark wavy hair, and a pretty nose. Her face was handsome and dignified, you saw at a glance she was a lady. She had lovely shoulders and breasts suggesting much plumpness

below, but it was not so. Although nice and round, she was not
large about her bum and thighs, yet the calves of her legs were
symmetrical. She was prettily shaped, and her bones so fine that
she looked stouter than she really was. She was nice to feel all over,
had exquisite hands and feet, and had all the physical qualities
of good breed. Her cunt had but a smallish quantity of crisp dark
brown hair on it, and the lips and prick-hole were small. It was a
pretty cunt, like a well-grown girl's of seventeen, instead of a
woman's of nearly thirty. When I said she had a small cunt, she
became anxious to know if it was *very* small. She had some fear
that through its size she would have a very severe labour, which
was the case.

In fucking she was charming, but never voluptuous. The tightness of her cunt coming after the capacious well-haired orifices of
Sarah Mavis, Louisa, and Jenny, was a novelty, but I'm not sure
that I enjoyed it so much for poking, though I liked to finger it.
I then preferred the larger cunts for reasons often given. But I loved
to be in bed with her, for it was the first lady I had had for a
mistress, and her manners were different from the humbler sort.
Besides, there was a charm in talking about one's female friends,
and in my disclosing amatory knowledge to a comparative novice.
I had recently had such talk only with women to whom every trick
and dodge of prick and cunt was familiar.

One thing was singular. She had a sweet mouth, and although
not much given to tonguing myself, — indeed not doing so to
women generally, — I began at once to do so to her. She moved
her head away. "No that's not nice." "When you're spending it's
heavenly, — just touch mine, — there, — is it not nice now? — right
into my mouth." Soon she became fond of it. *Her husband had
never done so.* Never? No, never attempted such a thing. Are there
many men who don't use their tongues when fucking, I wonder.

About her husband. By mutual consent we avoided the subject,
yet when I asked a question about him, she took the opportunity
of telling much to justify herself in my eyes, and in her own, for
what she was doing. She had married him for money, hoping love
would come after, — and it never had. Then came his evil habits,
estrangement, neglect, mistresses and casuals, — he had clapped her,
and that was all. There were no rows, no show before people, but
gradual alienation, and rarely coition. He fucked her at times, and

she spent with him at times, though she disliked him. She sought his bed after I had had her first. "He cannot say it is not his child," she said. She had relieved her sexual wants by frigging herself, though but rarely.

The two months proved she was with child. She had said she would cease to have me when assured of that, but had forgotten it perhaps; for instead of ceasing, she seemed more anxious for my embraces than before. She was warming towards me, but I was cooling.

Our meetings had been of the shortest till her husband went into the country, to his mills. I suggested having her at her home, but she would not hear of it. She managed longer meetings, grew more affectionate, fearful of being found out, and of not living through her confinement; then at the dislike of nursing a child in her house when the father was away. She was unhappy, but the child would make her happy when she thought of me. When born: if Y***s***e continued his brutal habits she would separate from him, and live with her child. Why did I not separate, and form another home, — did I love any one? "Do you love me?" I asked, "recollect what you said three months ago." "I love you like my life, my love, my darling, — I did not know myself, and that yearning for a child by you was love for you." She had read in a French novel of a lady who had the same devouring want, and who did as she had done. "I intended when with child that you should never meet me again, — but oh! my God I cannot do it."

A mist fell from my eyes, and I became aware of the true position of matters. This poor lady was deeply attached to me. I cared about her only as a temporary sweetheart, though I began by thinking I was in love with her. I saw misery for her. I never liked adultery. There were enough women to be had without taking the wives of other men. I revolted at the idea of visiting a man, eating his food, drinking wine with him, shaking him by his hand, and when behind his back tailing his wife. Yet here was I without design exactly in that position.

She went to her husband in the North, he remained there, he tailed her when there, I wrung the confession from her. How could she help it, she said. He was pleased as she thought at having got her with child. On her return again came the suggestion, why did I not separate from my wife? "I shall be all but a pauper without her money," I said. "What of that, if you are unhappy." But I was always hoping for happier days, hoping, — hoping, — hoping. "Let us go away together," said she, "my marriage settlement will keep us both, — we can be happy, — a knowledge of our separate miseries will endear us to each other, for I don't think I can bear this life any longer, — the struggle is too great, — let us fly together." This suggestion was hers, and made in a paroxysm of tears.

I did not know what to say, hesitated, equivocated, said my wife was behaving better, that I would leave her for a year, that if we ran away *we* might be unhappy, and so on; that it was best to reflect and not take a too hasty step.

"You don't love me, — you didn't love me," she said, "oh! what will become of me, — what shall I do!" — and we parted in tears.

It was brighter weather now, and we could not get to the baudy house without being seen. She was big in the family way, which made her more noticeable, and she could only stop for one embrace, and was then obliged to get away. Then luckily as I have said the house fronted two streets. She went out on one, I on the other, but it was getting very uncomfortable, to me at least. I did not dare to break it off, I so respected her, and had so much pity for her that I continued to make appointments, though glad when she could not keep them. Again, she was to be the mother of my child. So I let things drift on, but had for some time stroked whores again, not being able to do without women, and having difficulty in getting her. So I was glad when her husband was taken seriously ill in the North, and she was compelled to go there to him.

She was absent a very long time, our letters were sent to post-offices, they were brief, in disguised handwriting, and never signed. How she managed to get hers I don't recollect. When she came back she was an immense size, and told me but little of what had passed whilst she had been away. She feared trouble of all sorts, that misfortune was to be her lot in life, that she had hoped we might pass our lives together, but had made a mistake; her life had been a mistake, a mistake to have married him, to have longed for a child by me, to have loved me, when it was not returned. I declared that I loved her. Nonsense she replied, reflection had convinced her I did not; if I did, why refuse to leave with her.

I repeated what I had said before. She retreated into her cold dignity, the dignity she had before I had fucked her. She used to look at me quietly till the tears brimmed over her eyes, and dry them up quietly without saying a word. She had that strained expression of face which some women have in pregnancy, and had become quite thin. Sometimes an impulse took me by head and heart, and I was on the point of offering to run away with her. Reflection made me know that I did not love her, I did not even love poking her, I only respected and admired her, and with my sensuous temperament, felt that it could only end in misery for both of us, were we depending on each other entirely for our happiness in our double adultery, and with smallish means.

Then on one excuse or another she put off meeting me till I saw that she never meant me to have her again, — and I never did. She was confined with a boy. We visited her. She was affectionate to me when we were alone, but so sad that I could scarcely forbear crying when she spoke to me. She loved the child. When she recovered her health and looks I had a strong desire for her, but she never would let me. Her hand would clasp mine, and tremble in it, but to all my entreaties, it was, "No, — never," — and I never had her again.

Her husband's dissipation had been ruining him, he failed for a huge sum, and instead of spending fifteen thousand a year, came to live on his wife's income of five hundred. Then he had paralysis, and was a repentant, broken, miserable man, lame and ugly, and went with his wife to live in the South of France.

She never wrote to me, but wrote often to my wife, who disliked her for some reason which I knew not; but was obliged to reply because there was a chance always of her coming back again at some time to London. Mrs. Y***s***e it always seemed to me meant to keep me informed of herself through her letters to my wife, for she described everything, their new home, their mode of living, their expenses, the baby, his looks, and so forth, as if my wife had been the person next to herself the most interested in the child. Once she said his eyes were exactly like mine; but the letters at last grew shorter and shorter, and a longer time apart. Then her husband died.

[I may add here after a lapse of seventeen years the sequel of this amour, as far as I know it now. Years rolled on, I was a widower, and went South, called at Montpellier, and made enquiry. She had remained there some time as a widow. An Italian nobleman had married her, and they left for Italy, — I never heard where. She may be living now, so may my child, I should like to know, — but what good would come of it if I did? She and the child had better remain as they do in my memory, — a tender regret, full of respect for her. Her name sounded like Castagni, — but that was not her name.]

CHAPTER VII

A big maid-servant. — A peep up from below. — Home late, dusty and stupid. — Chastity suspected. — Consequences. — Dismissed. — My sympathy. — The soldier lover. — Going to supper. — At the Café de l'E*r**e. — In the cab returning. — Wet feet. — On the seat. — Mutual grasping and gropings.

I have forgotten to say that I had been again much better off, but by extravagance had to draw in, and now lived in a larger house, but kept only three servants. During the latter part of the time of my liaison with Mrs. Y°°°s°°°e we had for a month or so but one servant. A charwoman came to do rough work; but why this temporary arrangement took place need not be told.

She was a big country woman quite five feet ten high, and speaking with a strong provincial accent. When she was alone in the house I used to cross the streets to see her kneel, and clean the door-steps. She had such a big arm, and her bum looked so huge that I wondered how much was flesh, and how much petticoats. She cleaned the windows on the ground-floor, which in the house I then inhabited were got at by an iron balcony with open bars beneath. Seeing her cleaning them one day I went stealthily to the kitchen, and then into the area, and peeping cautiously up her petticoats, saw her legs to her knees. They were big and suited to her buttocks; but though the sight pleased me much, I never thought of having her, for I avoided women in my own house and neighbourhood. She was plain-faced, sleepy, and stupid-looking; the only thing about her nice, was bright rosy flesh. She looked solid all over. Her hair was a darkish chestnut colour, her eyes darkish, and one day she lifted a table as heavy as herself. There was not the slightest amorousness in her face or manner, and she dressed like a well-to-do country woman. Give her lots of nice, good, white underclothing; it was better than a sham outside, I heard she had said. She was about twenty-two years old, but she looked older.

About two months after she came (and just then when without other servants), on arriving home one Sunday night at about ten o'clock, I found she had been allowed to go out as usual, but had not returned. Another hour crept on. Savage, I thought of locking her out. About half-past eleven she returned. I let her in, and asked why she was so late. She looked dazed, muddled, had a very red face, muttered she was sorry, she had fallen down and hurt herself, and without waiting to answer me properly went downstairs. My wife went after her, and when she came up, told me she thought she was in drink, and that her dress and bonnet were covered with dust. "She had been up to some tricks with a man," said she.

Next day I heard she had told as an excuse, that as she was walking along a lane up which she turned to piddle, a man laid hold of her, and had taken liberties with her; that in the scuffle she had fallen down, had screamed, tried to catch him, had failed, and a lot more to similar effect. One or two days later I was told the woman had been dismissed. That I quite expected, for it was the mistress' custom to coax out the facts from poor devils in a kind way, and then to kick them out mercilessly; any suspicion of unchastity was enough for that. Middle-aged married women are always hard upon the young in matters of copulation.

"What is she going for? — a few days ago she was so beautifully clean, strong, and serviceable that none were like her!" "Oh! she has got a sweetheart, and is up to no good with him I'm sure." "How do you know?" "She told me so." "It's hard to dismiss on suspicion only, a poor girl who came up to us from the country." "You always take the part of those creatures." "I know nothing for or against her, nor you." "She is no better than she ought to be. — I have noticed a soldier idling about here for some time past." "As you like, — it's your business — but she came to us with an excellent character."

I pitied the woman, but more than that from the time I heard that a man had assaulted her, a slightly lecherous feeling had come over me towards her. I wondered what he had done, — had he felt her? — had he fucked her? — had she ever been fucked before, even if the man had recently done it to her? I began looking closely at her, getting in the way on some pretext or another, and always wondering if this and that had been done. I looked at the broad backside, so broad that a prick must look a trifle by the side of it. "Have the male balls banged up against it?" I thought. When I heard of her being turned adrift I thought I would just like to have her once or so, and that her leaving us gave me a chance. Curiosity was I believe at the bottom of my desire for her, — it was her huge fleshy form, and that spanking arse. Oh! to look at it naked, and feel it, if I did nothing more.

Finding the charwoman was not coming one day, and that the big servant would be a short time alone in the house, home I went; and on some pretext went down to the kitchen.

"So you are going to leave us." "Yes sir." "Why?" "I'm sure I don't know, — Missus says I don't suit, — yet only a few days ago she said I suited well." Here she broke into tears. I spoke kindly to her, said she would get another place soon, — she must take care not to go up dark lanes again with a man, nor go home late and dirty. She could not help it, — it was no fault of hers. What liberties did he take with her? I asked. The woman coloured up, and turning her head away, said he did what was very improper. "Did he put his hands up your petticoats?" "What was very improper," she repeated. "But how did you get so dirty?" They struggled, and she slipped. "I wish I'd been him, — I'm sure when he felt, he got his hand close up, — I'd give a sovereign to have mine there." That remark threw her into a distressing state of confusion.

I talked on decently, alluding to what I thought had taken place, and wishing I had been the man; but got nothing from her excepting that the man had taken liberties with her, — yes most improper liberties.

I told her I was sorry she was going, and thought she was hardly used, but I could not help it, — how was she off for money?

Very badly off, — she had come straight from the country to better herself, and had bought nice, good, underlinen, knowing she was coming to a gentleman's house, and now before she could turn herself round she was sent off. She had had to pay for her coach to London, and when she had her wages, and paid for a cab to lodgings, she would not have twenty shillings left. What was she to do if she could not get another place? Here the big woman blubbered, left off cleaning, sat down on a chair, and hid her face.

"Don't cry, you're used badly, — I'll give you a little money

until you get a place, — it won't be long." "You're a good kind
master," said she, "everyone says so, — but Missus is a beast, she
ain't no good to any one, — I don't wonder you are out so much,
and don't sleep with her." I gave a kiss and a cuddle. "What lovely
limbs you have, — how firm your flesh is, — you are delicious, — I
should like to sleep with *you*, — come into the lane with *me*, and
tell me when you are going to piddle again, and let *me* take a
liberty."

"Who told you I went up the lane?" "Your mistress," — and
then I left, telling her on no account to let it be known that I had
been home.

After this I heard that she had said it was a soldier. Now I
knew that a soldier who took liberties with a woman, took no little
ones, and generally got all he tried for; so made up my mind that
she had been fucked on the night she came home late.

A day or two after I was surprised with the following. "I've
got another servant, — she will come the day after to-morrow, so I
mean to send Sarah away at once, — of course she will be paid her
month's wages, but I shall get rid of her, for I am sure she is an
unchaste woman."

"Poor devil! — it's enough to make her unchaste, — but it's
your business." "Are you going out to-night?" "Why?" "Because if
you are I'm going round to my sister's." "I am," — and off I went
after dinner; but waited in a cab not far from the end of the street,
watching to see if she really did go out. She did, and directly I
spied her I drew myself back, and told cabby to follow her to the
sister's house. Then I drove back part of the way, and went home.

"So you are going?" said I to the servant. "Yes, I'm turned out,
sir." "A soldier and you went up a dark lane, — what a fool to tell
your mistress." "Ah! she has told *you*, — what a bad un, she sneaked
it out of me, — but I'm not to blame, he is my sweetheart, and is
going to marry me." "Have you got lodgings?" "Yes sir, I'm going
out to-morrow to see them, and I've written telling my sister (a
servant also), and she has taken them." "Wait for me when you go,
and on no account say I've been home, — I mean to help you, —
you are badly used, — what can I do for you?" "If you would help
me to go to the Tower, — my young man's name is ***, he is a
Grenadier, — I've written him, but he has not replied, and I want to
know if he is there." "I will wait for you to-morrow night outside,
when you go to see the lodgings." A kiss, a hug, and out of my

house I went again, after having ascertained where she was going to, and the time she was to go out.

Next evening I waited outside her lodgings, she came in a cab with her box, and told me that her mistress had bundled her out. She had had nothing to eat since mid-day, and was sick and weary. "Make haste then, — arrange your things, and we will go and have something to eat, and you shall see your soldier to-morrow." "God bless you, I do feel grateful sir," said she.

In half an hour she came out. I did not know where better to go to, and knew that it was just the time when the place would be empty, so took her to the Café de l'Europe in the Haymarket. It was a long drive, but I wanted to be with her in the dark cab. She was wonderfully struck with the place, but I was ashamed of being seen with her. She was anxious to go home early, because she lodged with poor people who went to bed early. She had never tasted champagne, so I gave her some. Oh! her delight as she quaffed it, and oh! mine as I saw her drink it, — it was just what I wanted. "A cock has been into her I am sure," I thought, "so another can't do her much harm, — if she'll fuddle she'll feel and be felt, or fuck, or frig, they always go together," my old instructor in the ways of women used to say.

I arranged to take her the next day to the Tower; our talk naturally was about the affair. "He did it to you," I said. She wouldn't or didn't see my meaning. "I could not help it if he did, or what he did, — he took unproper liberties." "He took them more than once, I'll bet!" She did not like such joking, she remarked. All this was when we were going out to supper.

Going home in the cab I began to say a baudy word to her. "He felt your cunt," said I, "did you feel his prick?" She bounced up and hit her bonnet against the top of the cab. "Oh! my! sir," — but she kept on in her excitement, letting out bits of the history, saying at intervals, it was not her fault, — she was fuddled, — fuddled with beer and gin, — a little fuddled her. I saw that pretty clearly from the effect of the champagne; and unbuttoned so as to have my prick handy. It was a wet night, the bottom of the cab was wet straw. "My feet are quite wet," said she. "Put them on the seat, my dear." She did so; I felt them as if solicitous for her comfort, putting my hand higher than above her ankle, just to see if her ankles were wet also.

"Why your ankles are wet." "Yes they are." With a sudden push up went my hand between her thighs, — a yell and a struggle, but I had felt the split before she dislodged my fingers. She was stronger than me, but my hands roved about her great limbs, searching under her petticoats round her huge backside. "Oh! don't, — you're a beast." "Oh! what a backside! — what thighs! — what a lovely cunt I'm sure you have! — let me keep my hand just on your knee, and I swear I won't put my hand higher." To ensure my keeping my hand there, she held my wrist as well as a vice would have done. She had by sheer force got it down to there.

I pattered out all my lust, my desire to have her, incitements, and baudy compliments on her form. "Let me fuck you." "You shan't." "You know what it means." "I know what you mean." "What harm could I do? — who would know?" And then the old, old trick. Taking her great fist in mine, I put my stiff prick into it. What a persuader! Though she kept up a show of struggling she did not get it away from that article instantly.

I suppose unless utterly distasteful to each other, that a man and woman cannot feel each other's privates, without experiencing reciprocal baudy emotions. They get tender to each other. The woman always does, after she has got over the first shock to her modesty, and her temporary anger. If after a man has felt her, a thermometer could be applied to her split, I believe it would be found to have risen considerably in temperature. After struggling and kissing, trying to feel her quim, trying to keep my hand on her thighs, it ended in our having our mouths together and my hand being pinched between her two great thighs, whilst the knuckles of one of her hands, with sham reluctance touched my doodle, just as the cab reached her dwelling, and there we parted. All the rest of our conversation was about her soldier, her being dismissed, and is not worth writing.

CHAPTER VIII

The next day. — At the Tower. — In tears. — "The wretch is married." — At T***f***d Street. — After dinner. — On the chamber-pot. — My wishes refused. — An attack. — Against the bed. — A stout resistance. — I threaten to leave her. — Tears and supplications. — On the sofa. — Reluctant consent. — A half-virgin.

Next day she met me early, and we drove to the Tower. On the road I instructed her what to do when there (it was full six miles off). I tried my best to get her passions up in a delicate way, but amatory fingerings I avoided whilst the poor woman was in search of her lover. The feeling of each other's privates on the previous night, had opened her heart to me. She let out a little more of the history of her escapade with the soldier, and asked my advice how to act in certain eventualities, which could only be applicable to a woman who had been rogered. She was painfully anxious as she approached the Tower. I stopped in the cab just in sight of the entrance, and after instructing her carefully again who to ask for, and what to do, in she went.

In half an hour she came back with wet swollen eyes, got into the cab, and began to bellow loudly. The cabman had opened the door for her, and stood waiting for orders. For a few seconds I could get nothing out of her, then told the cabman to drive to a public house near. There I gave her gin, but still could learn nothing. All she said was, "Oh! such a vagabond!" Into the cab again. I told the man where to drive to, for I had laid my plans. "Tell me, — it's not fair after all the trouble I've taken not to tell me," — sob — sob — sob. Soon after it all came in a gush. "Yes he was there, that is, he was two days ago," but the regiment had gone to Dublin, and would not be back for eighteen months, — a letter would be sent him of course, but his wife would be there in a day, for, — "Oh! — hoh! — hoh! — the wretch is a married man, and he's deceived me." "You should not have let him do it." "I didn't mean to." "You let him do it more than once I'll swear." "He did it twice to me, when in the house, — he swore he'd marry me three days after, if I let him, — and so I d — did, — ho! — her — ho!"

Thus I heard in snatches the whole history, which she told me more plainly afterwards. She had been fucked twice on the eventful night, once on the ground in a lane, and once in a bed-room.

I drove to T°°°f°°°d Street where I used to meet Mrs. Y°°°s-°°°e. It was not much more than mid-day. I got a comfortable little sitting-room, out of which was a large bed-room. A dinner was sent in by an Italian restaurant close by. After her first grief had subsided, the wine cheered her, and she made a good dinner, talking all the time of her "misfortun." When we had finished for a while I sat caressing her. Then I said, "I want to piddle," — and pulling my prick out before her went into the bed-room and pissed.

"Don't you want to?" "No." "Nonsense, — do you suppose I don't know? — now go." She went into the bed-room. I quietly opened the door ajar directly she had closed it. There was she sitting on the pot, one leg naked, adjusting her garter, and pissing hard.

Then raising her clothes that side she scratched her backside in a dreamy fashion, looking up at the walls. The rattle of her piddle went on. She had been out all the morning, had had gin and champagne, and her bladder must have been full. The side she scratched was towards me. She finished piddling, but still she sat scratching her rump. Then rising she turned round, looked in the pot, put it under the bed, pushed her clothes between her thighs, and looking round saw me at the half-opened door. She gave a start, I rushed up to her.

"What lovely thighs, — what a splendid bum" (though I hadn't seen it). "What a shame, — you've been looking at me." "Yes my darling, — what a lot you have pissed, — what a bum, — I saw you scratch it, — let's feel it, — I did last night, and you know what you felt." I got my hands on to her naked thighs, pushing her bum up against the bedside.

"What a shame to think you have been looking, — leave me alone, — pray do, — now you shan't, — no — you sh — han't."

I closed with her. I had pulled my stiff-stander out. I shook it at her. "Look at this my darling, — let me put it in you, — up your cunt." "No, — leave off, — I won't, — I have had enough of you men, — you shan't."

For a long time the game went on, I begging her to let me have her, she refusing. We struggled and almost fought. Twenty times I got her clothes up to her belly, my hand between her thighs. I groped all round her firm buttocks, and pinched them, grasped her cunt-wig, and pulled it till she cried out. All the devices I had used with others, all I could think of, I tried in vain. Then I ceased pulling up her clothes; but hugging her to me besought her, kissing and coaxing, keeping one of her hands down against my prick, which she would not feel, — but it was useless. Then stooping and again pulling up her petticoats, letting loose every baudy word that came into my mind, — and I dare say the choicest words, — I threw myself on my knees, and butting my head like a goat up her petticoats, got my mouth on to her cunt, and felt her clitoris on my lips; but I could not move her. She was far stronger than me. Then rising I tried to lift and shove her on to the bed. I might as well have tried to lift the bed itself. I tried to drag her towards a large sofa, big enough for two big people to lay side by side, and made for easy fucking. All was useless. Her weight and her strength were such that I could not move her. There she stood with her backside against the edge of the bed, her hair getting loose, one of her stockings pulled by me down to her ankle, and the upper part of her dress torn open, but no, she would not let me. She was frightened, — she would not, — I was as bad as the soldier. In the excitement she no longer cared about her legs showing to her knees, but her cunt she fought for, and get my prick against it I could not.

So we struggled I don't know how long, and then breathless, fatigued, I got into a violent rage, — a natural rage, not an artificial one, — and it told as brutality often tells with a woman.

We stood looking at each other. She kept one hand on her clothes just outside her quim, as if to defend it. I with my prick out, felt defeated and mortified. I had been so successful with women, that I could not understand not getting my way now. "You damned fool," I said, "I dare say fifty have fucked you, and you make a sham about your damned cunt, and your fears, — what did you come here for?" She opened her eyes with astonishment at my temper.

"I didn't know I was coming here, — I didn't know you meant me to do that, — you said you'd be kind to me, and give me something to eat, sir, — I'd not eaten since last night, — you said you would be kind to me, sir." It was said in the deferential tone of a servant.

"So I will, but if I'm kind, you must be kind to me, — why should it be all on one side?" "I'm sure I don't know," she whimpered. "You know he fucked you, and I dare say a dozen others have." "No one's ever done it but he, and he only did it twice," said she blubbering. "Let me." "No I won't, — I'm frightened to." "Go and be damned." I put in my prick which had drooped, went into the adjoining room, put on my hat and coat, took up my stick, and returning to the bed-room, there was she still with her arse against the bed, crying. She started up when she saw me dressed to go out.

"Oh! don't leave me here alone sir, — you won't, will you?" "Yes I shall, — you can find your way out." "Oh! let me go with you sir." "I shan't, nor see you again, — why should I? — you won't let me have you, not even feel you!"

"I would let you, but I'm frightened, — I've got my living to get, and I've been ill-treated enough by that vagabond, — I didn't think you brought me here for that." "What did you think then?" "I didn't think about it at all, — I was all along thinking of him." "You didn't think of him when I felt your cunt in the cab last night, — good-bye."

"Oh! stay only a minute, — do stay sir, — don't leave me here." She still stood against the bed. "Will you let me? — what a fool you are." "Oh! don't call me names, — I would, but I'm frightened, — I've got my living to get." "Haven't you been fucked?" "Y — hes, — y —hes," she sobbed out, "but it wasn't no fault of mine, — I was — aho! — fud — dled," — and she blubbered as loud as a bull roaring.

A sentiment of compassion came over me, for I never could bear to see a woman cry. I threw off my hat and coat, and going up to her as she stood, kissed her. "There then, — let me feel your cunt, — that can't hurt you."

She did not struggle any more. I lifted her clothes, and placed my fingers on her quim. I frigged hard at the right spot, but could get my fingers no further towards the sacred hole. Her massive thighs shut me off from the prick-tube as closely as if it had been a closed door — I could not get my hand between them.

But my fingers were between the cunt-lips, twiddling and rubbing. "Don't cry, — you'll let me I know, — who will know but we?" I fetched a tumbler of champagne from the sitting-room, and she took it like a draught of water. Up went my hand again, and with fingers rubbing her clitoris we talked and kissed side by side. Then turning myself more towards her, up went my other hand round her big bum, which felt as hard, and smooth, and cold as marble.

This went on a long time. She began gradually to yield when she felt the effects of titillation. She then grasped my fiery doodle. Then frigging her harder, her head dropped over my shoulder, and I got my fingers under the clitoris, and there to the hole. "Oh! (a start) you are scratching me, — you're hurting me there."

Taking away my hand. "Come here, — don't be foolish," said I, "let us do it, — you will enjoy it, — come," — and I pulled her. Her big form left the bed, and slowly she came with me to the sofa. "Sit down, — there, dear, — kiss me, — put up your legs, there's a darling." Slowly, but with much pushing and begging there at last she lay, and the instant she was down I threw her petticoats up, and myself on to her.

I saw the great limbs white as snow. A dark hairy mass up in her thigh-tops. "Oh! don't hurt." "Nonsense I don't." "You do indeed, — oh!" My hands are roving, my arse oscillating, I'm up a cunt, — all is over, — she is fucked.

"Did you have pleasure (I always asked that if I had doubt), — answer me, — did you? — do say, — what nonsense to hold your tongue, — tell me." "Yes I did, after you had done hurting me." "Did I really hurt you?" "Yes." "Impossible." "You did." What a sham, I thought to myself, a woman always is, — a Grenadier has fucked her twice, yet she says my prick hurts her.

I turned off on my side, the sofa being large enough. We had done the trick, and the recklessness of the woman who has tasted the pleasure, and feels the man's spunk in her quim, had come over her. The champagne added its softening influence. She pulled her dress half-down, we laid and talked. I felt her quim. "Don't." "What is it?" "I'm sore." "Why, you are bleeding." "You've hurt me." Out stood my prick, then rose upright again in a moment. Her blood on my finger and her pain gave me a voluptuous shiver. My trowsers were in my way. I tore them off, and stood by her side. "Let me see your cunt." She resisted, but I saw her big thighs closed, and the dark-haired ornamentation. Then getting between her thighs kneeling, I pulled open the lips from which blood-stained sperm was oozing; then I dropped on to her, and again drove my prick up her. A glorious fuck it seemed as I clutched her huge, firm buttocks, and felt her grasping me round my arse. All women, and even girls without any instruction put their arms round the men who are tailing them, the first time they feel the pleasure, but not before. Then we dozed in each other's arms. Then we got up, she confused, I joyous and filled with curious baudiness. "Wash, — won't you?" "You go then." I did, but back I went soon. She had just sluiced it. "You are not bleeding." "I am a little." "You are poorly." "I am not."

I brought her back into the sitting-room. We drank more wine, she got fuddled, not drunk, or frisky, or noisy, but dull, stupid, and obedient. We fucked again and again, and stayed at the baudy house. drinking and amusing ourselves till nine at night. How that big woman enjoyed the prick up her! And the opening of her cunt opened her heart and mouth to me as well.

CHAPTER IX

The big servant's history. — The soldier at the railway station. — Courting. — In the village lane. — On the grass. — At the pot-house. — Broached partially. — Inspection of her privates refused. — Lewed abandonment. — Her first spend. — A night with her. — Her form. — Sudden effects of a looking-glass. — The baud solicits her. — Sexual force and enjoyment. — She gets a situation. — We cease meeting. — The butcher's wife. — An accidental meeting. — She was Sarah by name.

This was her history. As she came up from the country to us, her box was missing at the station. A big soldier seeing she was a stranger made some enquiries for her, saw her into a cab, invited her to have a glass of gin, which she took, and told him the place she was coming to. The next night he showed himself there, he made love to her, wrote to her, met her on Sunday nights, and at other times when allowed to go out. He offered to marry her, and she had written to her sister to tell her about it all.

On the notable Sunday night, he took her to a tavern, and they had gin and beer till she was fuddled. She knew partially what she was doing, and thought it unwise to go up the lane in the dark with him; yet spite of herself she did. He would marry her that day month, then they would sleep together. He cuddled and kissed her, then began to take liberties. She resisted. Then if she would not let him, she might go home by herself, — why not let him? when soon they would be one in holy matrimony, — and so on. She felt as if she could not struggle. He tried to get into her upright against some railings. Then asking her to lay down on the grass, and she refusing, he pulled her down, and got on to her. She struggled and cried, but felt so frightened, that he seems to have had his way.

287

For all that, he did not, she thought, broach her; he pushed and hurt her; and must have spent outside, she could not be at all certain about that. Steps were heard, they got up, she was crying. Her clothes were, she knew, dirty (though it was dry and fine), her bonnet was bent. She was frightened to go home; he said she must get brushed up, and took her to some low tavern to do so. Terrified at what had been done, and about losing her place and character, she scarcely knew what she did. She had more gin, went into a bed-room with him to wash and brush, and then he persuaded her that now he had done it once, he might as well do it twice. Then he fucked her on the bed. Now the man had turned out to be (there was no possible mistake about his identity) a married man — a sergeant — with two or three children.

"Are you sure he got right into you?" "Quite when on the bed, but I scarcely know what he did or said in the lane, — a little fuddles me, — yes I did bleed, for it was on my smock when I got home, and he did hurt me very much."

I wanted to see her cunt, for her blood-stains made me wonder, and the rather hard pushing I had had, though only for a second or two, set me thinking. I felt her cunt, she winced, — it hurt her. An almost imperceptible stain was on my finger. "You *are* poorly." "I'm not really, — I was so last week." "Let me see your cunt." I coaxed, caressed, tried to pull her thighs open. It was useless. She was much stronger than me, and when she laid hold of my wrist to free herself from my rovings, she removed it easily. Force could do nothing, — she was what had been said of her, as strong as a horse.

So again I got savage. I had conquered by my anger two hours before, and now took to damning and cursing her mock modesty. Then she began again to whimper. "Oh! you do frighten me, — you do 'bust' out so, — I'm quite afeared, — it's not nice to have your thing looked at." "You damned fool, I've fucked it, — I dare say your soldier looked at it." "He didn't, — he didn't, — not that I know of." By abusing I got her consent. Pulling open her thighs I saw her quim. Had she been gay, she would have taken care to turn her bum from the light; but she laid with her arm across her eyes, as if to hide from herself, the sight of a man investigating her love-trap.

There was the ragged jugged-edged slit of a recent virginity, and near the clitoris the jagging seemed fresh, raw, and signs of blood just showing on it. I touched it, she winced, and nipped my hand with her great thighs, which set me damning again. Again they opened, I probed deep with my fingers up her cunt. There was no stain from the profundity, and the blood came from the front. I looked till my cock stood, and then fucked her again.

I could never make this out, and we never met without talking about it. She was perfectly sure the soldier had been up her, and spent in her when in the bed-room. As to his prick, whether it was short or long, thick or thin, she knew not, for she had never seen it, though he had put her hand to it in the lane. His prick must have been a very small one, and only split up enough for its entry, and I had finished her virginity, that is my conclusion.

What is more remarkable, is that her cunt was one of the tightest I ever met with in a full-grown woman. It felt more like the cunt of a girl of fourteen, excepting in its depth. It was a full size outside, and handsome to look at between huge white thighs and huge globular bum-cheeks. It was fledged like a young woman's. I expected to find it hairy up to her navel, but it was only slightly haired, which helped to satisfy me that she was what she said, only turned twenty-one years of age.

She was great in bulk, but poor in symmetry. Her bum was vast, but she was thick up to her waist, and had large breasts as firm as a rock. Her thighs were lovely, but her knees so big, that no garter would remain above them, and she was clumsy in ankle and foot. She had a lovely skin, and smelt as sweet as new milk, sweet to her very cunt. I recollect noticing that in her, because some time before I had been offended with the smell of Fisher's, a woman I fucked, as already told.

I spent the rest of the day with Big Sarah, told her I would keep her as long as she was in her lodgings, and advised her to live well, and to enjoy herself. But she did not need idleness and feeding to make her randy, she was a strong fucker, now that her passions had been once gratified.

I made her twice or thrice stop out all night. She told at her lodgings that she was going to stay with an aunt. I took her to J***s Street, which I liked better than T***f***d Street, for that though the quietest, and only frequented by swells of middle-age, was old-fashioned, dingy, and dull; whereas J***s Street had looking-glasses, gildings, red satin hangings, and gas-lights. We had a supper at the Café de l'Europe, and at nine p.m., we were in the room in which I had poked many a woman. I was delighted to see her white flesh under a bright light. "Now drop your chemise — look at me," — and I stripped to the skin. I exposed her bum, belly, and breasts in turn, whilst she laughing tried to prevent me. Flattery of her beautiful form did it. "Am I so beautifully made?" "A model my darling," — and she stood naked excepting stockings and boots. I had shifted the cheval-glass, and we laid on the sofa. "Look at your thighs and cunt my darling in the glass, — see how my prick looks in it." "Law! to think there be houses with all this, — are there many such?" she asked.

I placed her on the sofa, kneeling, her head against the bed, her backside towards me, and introduced my penis dog-fashion. How randy I had made her! — how randy I was as I felt my belling pressing against those two stupendous globes. "Turn your head there, and look in the glass." "Oh!" said she wriggling her backside, "what a shame for us to be looking like that." The sight made her breathless, and wriggle her cunt closer on to the peg, — how soon a woman learns to do that.

There was a large glass against the wall, so placed that those on the bed could see every movement, — I drew the curtain aside. We fucked enjoying the sight of our thrustings, heavings and back-side wrigglings, and passed the night in every baudiness which then I practised. "Do you like looking?" "Yes I like it, — but it makes me do it all of a sudden." It was true, for I found that when fucking her, if I said, "Look at us, — look at me shoving," directly she looked it fetched her; her big arse quivered, and her cunt squeezed my prick like a vice. It was the same always on future days, or when if not in the same room I placed the cheval-glass at the side of the bed. The sudden squeeze and jerk of her arse as she looked amused me, and I always arranged for the spectacle with her. I did not usually do this with women.

It was a delicious night. We were both start naked. Her lower limbs looked so much better when quite naked, than when she had stockings and boots on. The room got hot, we threw all the clothes off. She was a juicy one, and the sheets in the morning were a caution, — I wondered whether it could have all come out of one cunt and one cock. "What will they think?" said she.

I showed her in the evening where she would find the closet, and advised her strongly if spoken to, not to reply to any one. We had breakfast in bed, then fucked. Her need to evacuate came on, and half dressing herself she went down. When she came back, out I went on similar errand. She had washed, and I found her on my return anxiously looking at the seminal stains on the bed-linen. We got on to the bed again. Questioning her, she told me that the woman of the house had said to her, "What a splendid woman you are, — I wish you would tell me your address. — I could make your fortune." She had made no reply. I had her as already said several times after, at J°°°s Street, but took care never to let her out of my sight.

She went after a situation. Such a strong, big, fresh-looking woman was sure to get one, I knew. The next time I saw her afterwards she was in low spirits. "I've boiled myself a pretty kettle of fish," she said, "I could have married well in the country, but thought I should do better in Lunnun, — and now what am I?" "My dear, your cunt can't speak, and if you hold your tongue, no one will know anything about our little amusements, and you will marry well."

I soon tired of her. She was a good-natured, foolish, stupid, trusting creature, and my wonder is that she had lived twenty-one years in the country, without having had a prick up her. As a lovely-cunted fuckstress she left nothing to be desired. She had her fears about consequences, for her courses stopped, but she somehow managed to set that to rights, and at last went to her situation. Once afterwards I fucked her, — my God how she enjoyed it! She was in service not far from me. A butcher's man very soon after married her. They opened a shop, and did very well, then they moved some distance away, and I lost sight of her for years. Then I met her walking with two or three children, I suppose her own. We passed, only looking at each other.

But I almost spoke, for she came upon me so unexpectedly, and my first impulse was to speak. She stopped short, threw her head back, and her lower jaw dropped, so that her mouth opened wide, and it would have been ludicrous, had it not been for the expression of fear and pain which came over her face. I recovered myself, passed on, and never saw her more.

I paid her expenses at her lodgings, and gave her a ten-pound note as a present. It was very economical, — but I never knew a woman so delighted with my liberality. "I had two pounds, and now I've twelve," said she, "I shall send a pound to my mother." When I gave her the ten pounds she asked what it was, never having seen a bank-note in her life before. One or two country-women of the same class whom I have had, were just as ignorant of a bank-note.

CHAPTER X

*Sally at the sea-coast. — Our lodgings. — The landlady and family.
— A quarrel, and change of rooms. — My top bed-room. — Advances towards Sally. — Small liberties. — On the sands with her.
— Cheap fingerings. — The sands by day. — Ladies bathing. —
What the sad sea-waves exposed. — An incomprehensible lady. —
Enticed by her, and snubbed. — Wanting fornication. — Masturbation on the sands. — Alone in the lodgings. — A journey to town. —
Baulked. — From Saturday to Monday. — My return unexpected.
— Sally alarmed. — Her cunning. — My caution. — Waiting expectant. — Sally upstairs. — Hesitation and determination. —
Whisky and water. — I enter her bed-room.*

In the autumn of the year that Mrs. Y***s***e, then big with child, and thus satisfied, refused further sexual connection with me, we went to a well-known, healthy, but not fashionable seaside town. We took a young lady (Miss E***s) with us as companion, and got lodgings close to the sea at an ordinary lodging-house. For several reasons we would not go to an hotel. There were two rooms on the ground-floor of this house let to a married couple. We had on the first-floor a sitting-room and bed-room, and wanted an old bed-room for Miss E***s; but they would not let a bed-room above us, unless we took both on that floor, which we did. So we slept in the back room first-floor, I taking to the nuptial couch again for a time, and Miss E***s slept overhead. The other room was empty. That constituted the house together with the kitchens in the basement, and a room at the back in the yard.

The landlady's husband was a seafaring man, or was said to be so, and only at home in the winter, — perhaps he kept away in the season, so that the rooms of his house might be let well. The landlady whom we scarcely ever saw excepting to pay her her bills, slept in the kitchen, and so did her two children, whom we did not even know were in existence for some time, so quiet and out of the way were they kept. The servant was a short sturdy girl with lightish brown hair, a very weather-beaten florid face, and merry blue eyes (quite like dozens of girls at that part of the coast), who said she was seventeen years old (she did not seem sixteen). The mistress' sister also waited and assisted when all the lodgings were let, and went home at night. The little servant also went home at night to her father's, a laborer, when the top-rooms were let. If they were not, she slept there. In fact when lodgers filled the house the landlady and her brats pigged together in the kitchen, and when any rooms were empty slept upstairs. We did not however know all this at once; lodging-house keepers carefully hide their mode of living, and so on, for fear that if people knew all they would not take their apartments. Above all they prevent lodgers from knowing there are children in the house, for people don't like them in the kitchen where their food is cooked.

Soon the ground-floor people left, and we were the only lodgers. We had been there but a few days when as usual my wife and I quarrelled. I refused to sleep with her, and went to sleep upstairs. "It's impossible for you to sleep upstairs next to Miss E***s, — what will the people think?" "Think what they like." "Well Miss E***s must come down, and sleep with me." "I don't care who sleeps with you, — I won't." So I slept upstairs, Miss E***s came down, and the two ladies occupied the same bed on the drawing-room floor. Soon afterwards the landlady asked if we would mind the young servant using the odd bed-room until we wanted it, so as to prevent her going home of a night. But my wife would not hear of that, for I had remarked that she was a fresh, active little girl, and that was enough to prevent her being allowed to sleep near me. So the one room remained empty, and the servant still went home to sleep.

I had taken a fancy to the little girl, — Sally she was called (I have known intimately half-a-dozen Sarahs) — the instant I saw her. Within a couple of days I had given her a kiss, and tipped her a shilling, — I had to stoop to kiss her. She resisted with the, "Adun now sir" so common among the country lasses; but as she found a shilling and a kiss went together, it altered in about three days

to, "Oh! don't yer now sir be a doing that, — Missus will be a catching you, and what will I say?" Then being sure *my* Missus was out,
one day I gave a kiss, held her close to me, and gave a nudge near
to her notch. That riled her. She was saucy, so I did not give her
a shilling, and got kiss and nudge for nothing. But as I wandered
about the coast (I was in and out of the house a dozen times a
day), she got frequent kisses, and at length nudges as well. She
responded by pushing me away, but without saying a word when
I nudged her grummit. One day I went in when my people were
out, and having just met the ground-floor lodgers I therefore knew
they were out also. I got her to me with, "Here's a bob for you,"
and said, "I'd give a pound to be in bed with you, and put my
fingers on the naked just there," giving a hard push towards her
notch. This could not have occurred more than a week after I had
taken the lodgings. The lass showed her displeasure by, "Now
don't sir," and pushing me away, but taking my little shilling
nevertheless; and by this time she must have been quite aware,
that I was thinking a good deal about her cunt; and probably she
thought what I wanted to do with it, and with what, — so that I
had set her thinking lewdly.

It was just then that I became aware that she went home after
supper (we had a primitive early dinner, and a slight supper). She
had said, "Please Ma'm do you want anything more to-night? —
if not I'm a going." That roused my curiosity. The next night I kept
outside the street-door, and as she left went up as if by chance to
her. "Ulloah! Sally, going to fetch beer!" "No sir, I'm a going home."
"Home?" "Yes, I goes home to sleep at father's." I walked towards
home with her, flattered her I dare say instinctively, and got her
to walk with me on to the Promenade by the sands. There we sat
down on a seat, had a chat, a kiss, and in the dark I said I'd give
a pound to be in bed with her. "Oh! law I must go, — if I'm not
in by ten o'clock father will kick up a row, and go and ask Mrs. ***
why I'm home so late." I walked towards home with her, and got
her to have some sort of liquor. She would not go into the public-
house, saying they knew her, — so I took a glass outside to her.
Then I walked on outside the town into a dark road. She begged
me to go no further, as her father might be coming along. I kissed
her, stooped and put my hands up her clothes to her quim. With
a cry she pushed me away, and ran off.

The next morning she sulked, — I laughed. "She is a funny little girl," said my wife. "She is," said I. The next night I coaxed her to sit down with me again by the sands. "Oh! now I won't let you do that, — I don't like it, — I don't want yer half-crowns if you wants to do that, — oh! — now, — I won't — now — doan't, — leave off, — I'll call out, — now, — here is some one coming." "So there is, — now don't make a noise, or he will fancy something," said I.

Then I got my hand up her petticoats, and on to her split, I was holding her tight, and she was struggling to get away, when a man approached. I desisted, and she sat quite demurely. When the man's figure had faded away in the distance I recommenced. "I know that man," said she, "I'm sure." "What does that matter?" "If it be he, he'll tell my father I'm on the sands with a man." "He won't know you, — he did not look. I've felt your cunt," said I. "You let me go." "Never mind, make it up, — here is a half-crown." She took the money, and we made it up with kisses, and a promise that I would not do it again. What a wonderful effect kisses have on young women, and so have half-crowns on poor girls. The mistress paid her no wages she said.

Either the larking pleased her, or the money (a half-crown each feel), and one night on the beach I made her feel my cock. "That will go up your cunt some day," said I. I forget the conversation which led to it, but I told her my wife had said she was not eighteen, she was sure. She chuckled. No she was not. How old? "Sixteen and a half." "Why say eighteen?" "Because lodgers won't give you so much if you're young." Though but sixteen and a half the motte-covering (what there was of it) felt wonderfully thick and crisp. The nights were just then moonless, I must add.

It was just before this that my domestic quarrels began; I was asked why I kept out of a night. "Why? — to play billiards." Then there was a row because with opera-glasses when sitting on the beach, I looked at ladies bathing; especially at a fine big woman, who always managed to let the waves wash her bathing-dress so much up, that when the waves retired, she was standing with the dress above her navel, and the dark hair of her motte visible. She did this so constantly (a dozen times in fact each morning), that it became a matter of talk among the men down there. My wife said she was a beast for doing it on purpose, and I was a beast for looking, and we had a hot riot about it. So I went to sleep upstairs, all through a woman showing her belly naked when bathing, — as if a woman would not like to look at a black-haired prick if she got the chance, just as I did at a dark-haired cunt.

"Oh! don't you and your Missus have breezes," said Sally to me one night, "why don't you sleep with her?" I told her that I was miserable with the woman, and that of a night when sleeping alone, I did not know what to do, to put my stiff prick at ease. I made her feel it so, that within two weeks the young one felt it regularly on the beach, till there was moonlight, and afterwards near her father's house, or somewhere; for in the lonely road of a night, there was an opportunity every hundred yards. But I never got my fingers on to the girl's cunt-split further than the clitoris, — a feel, and a shilling; (a finger-stink for a bob, as Fred used to call it). When I had accustomed her to the groping, and feeling, I dropped my half-a-crown to a shilling, but gave more frequently, if she did not resist and make a fuss; if she did, I gave her nothing, and called her a fool.

Just as the time was up for which we had hired the rooms, we one day had a very violent quarrel. The landlady came up to ask if we were going to stop longer, as in the event of our not stopping, she would look out for other lodgers. Said my wife, "We are going." "I shan't then," said I. However she gave formal notice to leave. I immediately gave notice that I should keep the lodgings another month. It ended in she and Miss E***s going back to London, expecting that I should soon follow, — but I had found several friends there, and a good billiard-table, and from temper alone would not have given in. Moreover I thought that by some chance I might spermatize Sally's cunt, and, I fancied, spermatize it for the first time. So there in solitude I remained at the sea-coast.

My letch for the little one increased. For a long time I now had mostly had biggish women, with full-sized, full-fledged cunts, and large arse-cheeks, and the idea of the smaller, half-haired quim of Sally attracted me: yet at the same time by a singular contradiction, I had a longing for the full-fleshed, big-arsed, dark-cunted woman, whose backside and belly the waves seemed daily to expose for my admiration, — for she was still at the coast, bathing daily. Explain this inconsistency who can. One thing is certain, that not having any one to fuck at all, I had sperm ready for any cunt; but

I kept for all that away from gay ladies pretty well, though far from entirely.

I did not want four rooms, but to prevent scandal (for I did not like the landlady to know too much about the disquiet in which I lived), said I expected my wife would return, as she had only gone to see a sick relative; and that so soon as she was better she and Miss E***s would return. The landlady asked if her servant might use one bed-room till they did. I was now sleeping on the drawing-room floor, and gave my acquiescence you may be sure pretty quickly, — and Sally went up nightly to sleep there.

I began to tell Sally when she waited on me, that I meant to go up, and sleep with her. She looked queerly, and said so earnestly that if I did, she would tell her Missus, that I hesitated at doing what I had intended; but kept up the chaffing. "Sally (as I began to call her, — others called her Sarah) I heard you overhead last night." "Did you, sir, — I took off my boots too, for Missus told me." "Oh! not your walking Sally, — I heard the rattle in the pot as you piddled." "O — o — oh! sir, — now you didn't, for I didn't do it." Then she bolted out of the room laughing. When she came in again, "Sally you made my cock as stiff when I heard you piddle as you did when you felt it on the beach." "Oh! here is your herring sir," — and off she ran again. When alone in the house, instead of doing more with her I could do less in the way of fingering her. Money failed to keep her near me then, but I used to pull out my cock, and shake it at her. I had no chance of getting her on the sands now, through her being permitted to sleep in the top-room.

The landlady could not let her ground-floor because the people wanted three bed-rooms, would I give one up, if she made a proportionate reduction in rent? That would not suit me, with my chaste intentions, to have any one sleeping in the next room to Sally; so I refused. Then I made up my mind to go up to Sally's room. For a day or two funked doing so, but at last determined on it, and just then the lower rooms were let, which increased my risk. Luckily the people did not like the lodgings, and left in three days. Then I resolved, come what might, to go up to Sally when in bed, and try my luck.

One night I listened. She stole up quietly. Then when in my night-gown, and just as I was going to open the door, I heard the landlady downstairs, whom I thought must have been fast asleep in her piggerty, with her two young ones. It frightened me back. I did not tell Sally about it.

I had found then (for I could no longer wait for Sally's quim), as I did everywhere, a woman and a baudy house at that coast-town. I was abstinent, not liking the feminine articles there, but I wanted fucking badly. One morning when I had seen the well-bummed lady bathing as usual, I yielded to a most pressing want and a furious lust. Going away from the frequented sands, and nearly out of sight of the bathing-machines, I sat down thinking not of little Sally, but of the fat-arsed, black-cunted one, and frigged myself. This was about twelve o'clock in the day. Annoyed with myself afterwards, I went back to my lodgings, and said I would go to town. I intended to do so, and to have a woman there, but indeed I scarcely recollect exactly what I did intend to do. No packing up of clothes was needful, because I intended going home. I told of my leaving, and went off, but met some friends, dined with them, missed the train (railway only just then opened), and at about half-past eight went back to my lodgings to sleep there. It was a Saturday night, and dark.

I knocked at the door which was locked, instead of being on the latch, as seaside lodging-house doors usually are till bed-time. "Who is that?" said a voice. "I." The door opened ajar, it was chained, and Sally peeping through said with surprize on her face, "You sir!" — "Yes me, — let me in." "Oh! I can't, — I must ask Missus." "What the devil do you mean?" The door closed in my face. I knocked again, and Sally opened the door. "Beg your pardon sir, but we did not expect you to-night." I thought to myself, they were perhaps sitting in my rooms, or they might have let the beds for a night, — who knows what tricks! But I took no notice, finding my rooms all right. Soon up came Sally. "Please sir, Missus gives her compliments, and hopes you will excuse it, but not thinking you would be back till Monday, she let the children sleep in your back room, — but they are not in your sheets, but in our own." I laughed. "Tell her I'll excuse it, — but where do you sleep Sally, — with them?" "Oh! no sir, — Missus said I might sleep in the front, — but not in your sheets sir, — oh! no." "All right Sally," — and after I had given her a pinch on her bum and a kiss, off she went downstairs. The ground-floor rooms were unlet, I was the only lodger that night in the house.

Soon she re-appeared. Did I want anything before the shops closed for dinner to-morrow, because Missus must go and fetch it, — it was getting late. No, I would dine out, but would she fetch me some beer for supper. She would. She did. I had some bread and cheese, and then gave Sally a hug, and put my hands up her petticoats. She declared she would tell her Missus, and then went away with a shilling, a kiss, and a sight of my tooleywagger.

I thought how I should like to fuck the little bitch, — I've felt her, she has felt me, she has seen it, she won't cry out, though she says she will. I thought of my frig that day, of the bathing lady, and of the slight hair on Sally's cunt, till I got reckless with randiness. She was to sleep in the front-room, there was no key to it, — Miss E***'s had complained of there being no key. "I'll go up when the girl's abed," said I to myself. Then I pondered on the consequences. The more a man thinks of such a business, the more randy and reckless he gets. I ceased to think of consequences, and only of the pleasure I should have in broaching Sally's vulva.

"Shall you want anything more to-night sir?" "Yes hot water, — and Sally, as you go up to bed I'll give you a glass." "No thank you, sir." But Sally was fond of whisky, and even took it neat, for I had given it to her. She brought the hot water, I made grog, and she drank some saying, "Oh! I'm afraid she'll smell me of the whisky, and oh! I must go down, she'll be a wondering why I stop so long." "Mind I'm coming up to sleep with you." "Oh! no sir, pray don't, — oh! now I'll tell my Missus, — she says she thinks you ain't up to no good all down here alone without your wife, — she do." "Nonsense, I shan't hurt you, — we'll lay and feel each other, and do what we do on the beach, — nothing more, — and I'll give you half-a-sovereign, and a new pair of boots." "I'd rather not," said she hanging her head. "Did you ever have a sovereign Sally?" "No never, — now leave me alone, sir, — take your hand away, — or! you do talk nasty, — oh! if Missus hears she'll turn me out." "Don't make a noise then, my dear." "Oh! leave me alone, — I don't like your hand there." This was in the first-floor sitting-room.

She had sunk her voice, she wriggled, and writhed till she dislodged my hand from her thighs, and got away. "As you come up to bed I'll give you a glass of whisky and water." "I won't." "Well I'll go up and put it in your bed-room." "Don't, — Missus is sure to come up, and look at the children before she goes to bed, and

if she goes into the other room — oh!" "She won't, my dear, — I'll
put the glass under the bed, just by the pot, — then when you take
it out to piddle you'll find the glass." "I can't wait, — let me go,"
— and off she went.

I waited and waited, took off my slippers, went half-way downstairs, listened, and could hear some one moving about. Then I
heard a noise as of two people talking, and it seemed like a man.
"The devil," thought I, "it's the husband come home," — and I went
back hesitating. "It's risky, I won't go up, — she is like perhaps the
Misses Braham, will feel, and be felt, but no prick shall go near her
cunt, — I don't want merely to frig her, or be frigged," — so I
thought of going to bed, and waiting my chance of getting her to
a baudy house. But I had been delighting in the idea of the thrust
with which I should go up her, for I felt sure she was virgin. Then
after having been stiff for half an hour, down my prick had gone.
"What shall I do," I thought, "if I get into bed with her, and can't
do her?" When I got nervous in that way my prick sometimes
would not stand to its work, try as I might. I have already narrated
an instance.

I fancied still there was a man in the house, but after a while
could hear no one. At all events I resolved to put the grog in her
room, made a tumbler full of water and whisky hot and strong,
and sweetened it well, went upstairs without my shoes, and put it
by the chamber-pot. I knew exactly the spot, though it was in the
dark, having slept in that room. Then down again, and undressing
myself, I put out the lights, and sat down in the room with the door
ajar, and watched. Such a time elapsed that I thought she was going
to sleep with her mistress downstairs, or perhaps had gone home.

At last she came quite quietly upstairs with a jug of hot water
in one hand, and a candlestick in the other, staring at the door of
the drawing-room all the way. When half-way up the next flight,
she turned round, stopped for a moment, and looked hard at my
door, as she wondered whether I was there or abed. Then the door
of her bed-room closed, and her footstep was scarcely audible overhead. I sat waiting such a time as might enable her to wash herself
(the hot water meant that), and get into bed. Meanwhile I could
not keep my cock to the stand at all.

Then, "Shall I go? — what if the mistress finds it out! — what
if she cries out!" I got into bed, for I was chilled sitting in my night-

gown, though it was not cold weather, and laid feeling my prick. As I got warm, that got stiff. "I'll go," thought I, — "if she makes a noise I'll say she asked me to go up." It was a mean thought, and I dismissed it. Then my cock got furious. I went down a few stairs and listened. There was no noise below, all was silent as the grave. Up I went, opened her door, and closed it. The room was dark, only a slight light from a street-lamp somewhere shone through the window.

CHAPTER XI

*In bed with Sally. — The children. — Sally's devices. — Fears of
alarm. — An hour's siege. — The citadel taken. — Thirty hours of
delight. — Fucking under difficulties. — My devices. — A cunt inspection in the looking-glass. — Sally's account of herself. — The
bathing lady again. — Checked and threatened. — I give up the
chase.*

She was in bed, heard me, and sat up. "Oh! now sir, don't you
come, — now I'll call Missus." "Hush! if you do I'll tell your mistress
that you said I might come up, and she'll dismiss you." "Oh! you
won't be so wicked, — now you shan't." "Be quiet you fool, — lay
still, there's a darling, — I won't hurt you." I jumped into bed, and
pulled her down whilst this dialogue was going on, folded her in
my arms, entangled my legs in hers, hugged and kissed her. She
struggled, but her voice dropped. "The children will hear," said
she, — "do leave me, and go, — there is a good gentleman." Then
I felt sure she would not call her mistress. I had won the first move,
when she expressed her fears that the children in the back-room
would hear us.

I cuddled her, swore I would only do what we did on the beach.
Little by little I got her night-clothes up, felt her plump bum and
thighs and firm little breasts, and put her hand to my prick, promising her anything, everything, all in whispers. She kept her knees
doubled up to her belly. Every now and then I pushed my finger
towards her cunt, over her bum-cheeks; then down went her legs
straight. Then my fingers went quickly to the belly-side of her
cunt, and up went her knees almost to her breasts. All the while
she was crying in an undertone, "Now I won't, — oh! I'm so sorry
I ever let you do anything, — I'll call Missus, — I really will if you

303

don't go." But the next instant, "Oh! if Missus should hear us, she'd tell Mrs. ***, — no you shan't feel it, — oh! what a shame to take me unawares, — oh! oh! — now — oh!" I could not succeed, felt wild with desire, annoyed at the resistance; but the prolonged feeling all over her flesh, the keeping it close to mine, rubbing my legs against hers, and the satisfaction of my curiosity, were delicious.

At last I got so close to her belly, that she could not move up her legs. My prick was against her belly, and I held her to me closely by one hand round her bum. "Let me now, — I won't do any harm, — lay so, and I will lay so — feel my prick, and let me just feel there." Sullenly she let me. I rubbed gently over the little bit of her clitoris, that her tightly-closed little thighs let me feel, until she began to feel lewed. "Oh! leave off!" She had now ceased whimpering, her mind was intent on my baudy advances; and she spoke in low tones! "Now don't, — you're a hurting me!" "Nonsense darling, — there." I took then away my fingers from her slit, and my hand roved all over her. "What lovely firm little breasts you've got! what smooth flesh, — kiss me darling, — let's fuck." She kissed me. Then I told her of the pleasures of fucking, of the stiff penis spending its essence in the cunt, of the tightening of the cunt round the prick whilst the pleasure came on. "Let me," — and I felt her quim. "You'll hurt." "Every woman thinks so dear, but every woman wants it done to her. Lay still, — that's it!"

Clasping her still tightly, my prick straight up against her navel, I now lodged it against her clitoris. "Let me rub you with my prick, just where my finger rubbed you, — it will give me pleasure, and you too, — feel, — is it not hot and stiff? — let it go up your cunt!" "No you'll hurt." She was yielding.

I must have been an hour persuading her to this point. How I restrained myself I do not know. Perhaps my morning's frig helped me. My fingers again were on her cunt. She closed together her legs tightly, but my finger could not be kept out. Then with sighs and muttered words her thighs unclosed. I pushed my knee between them. "Let me put my prick there." I raised my body against hers, pressing her on to her back with my belly. Her thighs distended, whilst I felt for the nick, and tried to lodge my palpitating penis. The next minute all thought of the Missus and children went, and I lunged my prick against her cunt.

"Oh! you said you would not hur — hurt me, — oh! — oo — h!

— you shan't." Two or three quick violent lunges, a sharp suppressed cry. "There my darling it's up — your — cunt," — and fucking violently to make sure, the divine pleasure overtook me, and I spent.

It was done, her cunt was spermatized for the first time, she had submitted to the inevitable. "You hurt me so, — oh! I hope the children won't hear," were the first words I recollect her uttering after I had emptied my ballocks into her.

The sensation was over, but the pride of victory remained; my prick was in possession, it was easy to keep it up her, but the usual, "Oh! you're so heavy," was said. She moved, sperm began to dribble out, my tool to dwindle. "Oh! if the children should hear, — oh! if they were to come in!" She feared the children now, as little by little my cock left her cunt. She did not seem to fear her mistress.

I got out of bed, struck a light, and moved gently a wash-hand stand against the door. "There. The children now can't come in without making a noise, — if your mistress comes I'll be under the bed like a shot, — you say you put the wash-handstand there because you heard a noise, and were frightened, — and now my darling let's look at your cunt." She resisted that more than the fucking, and jumped out of the bed to get away. As she did so I saw stains of blood on the night-gown, and did not insist on gratifying my eyesight. Putting out the light we both got into bed again. Soon my prick was churning up the spunk in her cunt, and we spent the rest of the night in dozing, and fucking. Fear, lest the landlady should come up, kept me much awake. Sally never closed her eyes, but she enjoyed the prick, and when it was daylight, what a lovely mess her little cunt, her linen and mine were in, for I saw them all.

About six o'clock I rose. "I'll go down," said I. "Then Mrs. Harris won't catch us, — she won't be up yet, and you'll go down soon to light the kitchen-fire I suppose." "There is no one in the house but the two children and us," said Sally quite quietly.

It was true. The mistress, believing that I had gone to London, had gone to see a sister. Sally was left in the house until Monday to take care of the children; hence the chain up, and the closed door. Sally had kept up the sham of her mistress being within till the last moment, hoping that my threat of going to her bed-room would have the same result as on other nights when I had promised to go to her. She now told the truth, it was useless to tell anything else.

The butcher had brought meat for the Sunday's dinner, he entered by the area — his was the male voice I had heard.

"Oh! don't do it again, I'm so sore." My prick stood stiffer than ever when it touched the sore cunt. Then Sally spent with me and slept, and so did I. I slept a heavy sleep without anxiety now, fearing nothing.

"Oh! it's the children crying, they will tumble downstairs," said Sally. We removed the wash-hand-stand. "I'll lay here," said I. "I'll get them their breakfast," said Sally. "Come up after." "Yes, but I must put my frock on," — and she did, over her nightgown.

In an hour up she came and got gaily into bed, and we fucked again. Then I would look at her cunt, and threw her back violently on the bed to do so. She had not washed. She was a sight, so was her night-gown, so were the bed-sheets. Sarah looked aghast at them.

The children were quite young, but even children talk, and Sally was anxious that no one should know I was in the house. So she took the children up into the bed-room after their breakfast, and then I went down to the kitchen, and got what food I could. Dinner there was none for me, for they had but a pound of steak between the three. I went out and had a repast at a tavern, then took home sausages which I managed to buy, and when the children were put to bed, Sally and I together cooked the sausages, and eat them in the kitchen. She had not had such a feast for some time, for the lodging-house mistress fed her on scraps left by the lodgers. Then we had some mild voluptuous amusements. Then we filled up with whisky and water, and went to bed early.

The next morning I left long before the Mistress returned. The children had never seen nor heard me, and unless the neighbours had seen me, no one could have known I had been in the house. But in the thirty hours I had fucked myself out, and Sally as well. Her prayers "not to do it any more" I shall recollect to the last day of my life, and her swollen, crimson-tinted little cunt was touching to look at. I never had more pleasure in baudiness than I had in hurting her. It made my prick stiffen directly she said she was so sore, and my prick stood in an inflammatory excited state for half an hour at a time, and even when I could get no spend out of it, in Sally's cunt it lingered as if it never meant to leave it.

It was a delicious thirty hours, in which she learned enough about fucking to make her lewed whenever she thought it over in future.

She was in a way about the sheets, but we got over it much in the same way as I did my shirt-tail in my youth. First she washed the patches, ironed it, got out a good deal of the evidence of her lost chastity, and then changed it for one from my bed. I took the dirty one, and my bed on the first-floor was made up with it. The next day after my supposed absence I returned and slept there, next morning laid abed late, took off the sheets, dipped them in water, and told Sally to tell the landlady to come up. "I have been sick and ill in the night Mrs. Harris," said I, "and have taken off the sheets, and put them into the water, — let me have a clean pair," leaving her to imagine whether I had spewed, or pissed, or shit in them. She never made any remark about it, so Sally told me.

A long rest, a day's good food, and ten hours sleep put my doodle into first-rate condition again. My desire for Sally increased; how to get her was the difficulty. She, I am bound to say, did her best to get her cunt amused, and fell in with every suggestion I made, any trick I planned; and they were many. We managed to fuck two or three times nearly every day for a month. The days I was disappointed only gave me breathing-time. I was idle, well fed, and in the finest possible condition. Fucking was my only joy, and I enjoyed myself up Sally.

The children now slept with their mother in what I found was a bedstead in a sort of large closet, in a small room adjoining the back-kitchen, which had only a skylight a few feet above the back-yard. I had looked out of my bed-room window, and not knowing much about the plans of seaside lodging-houses, wondered what the skylight lighted. The little servant now being allowed to sleep in the back two-pair, I used to steal upstairs at midnight without shoes or light, get into bed with her, put a towel under her bum, fuck her, and get down quickly. She had such a fear of being found out, that I believe until she felt the crisis approaching, she never quite forgot to keep her ears open.

But a landlady working hard from morning till night was unlikely to come up three flights of stairs to look after a girl, whom she only hired for the season, and about whose morals she did not care, so long as she attended to the lodgers. Mrs. Harris was respectable, but I believe that had she known that Sally had had a prick up her back, as well as her front-entrance, she would never have troubled herself about it. "If my lodgers are satisfied with the girl," said she to us one day, "it's all I want — she is paid good wages, and must do her duty." The fact being that she paid the girl no wages, expected her to feed herself by stealing lodgers' food, and to keep herself in clothes out of what the lodgers gave her.

When Sally laid the breakfast things I used to pull her into my bed-room, and on the bed, fuck as quickly as I could, and get into bed again to rest. Not so poor Sally. In half an hour she would bring up the breakfast with her cunt still as I had left it. "Have you washed it, Sally?" "Lord no, — what time have I had?" — and she would laugh.

I could not always manage the morning poke. Lodgers came into the downstairs rooms, they rang violently twice one morning when my prick had just gone up Sally, and she was not sufficiently on to disregard it, but uncunted me, and ran downstairs. One day her mistress came upstairs to a closet on the landing, and nearly frightened Sally out of her senses. So we had to keep our wits about us.

Autumn was now closing. It was chilly morning and night. I insisted on having a fire to breakfast by, let it out, and would have it relighted in the evening. That was a long operation, and gave me time to get a poke. One day Sally came up radiant. "She's gone out," said she laughing, "the lodgers downstairs want her to go and buy something, and said I couldn't judge, I warn't old enough." Sally knew that it would give us time for a fuck. She came up for it, though she did not say so. She improved wonderfully. Her mind was dead on rogering ever after the Saturday night, and whenever her Mistress went out she used to come up instantly with a triumphant air to tell me. Towards the end of the month, she pulled up her petticoats herself to expedite matters, instead of waiting for me to do it.

I received letters asking when I was going home, and wrote that I was daily expecting her to return. A reply came, — it was my intention to aggravate, and she should not come. I answered that I should not go home till she did. I knew that would settle it, and that she would not return. So Sally's cunt and my prick got as intimate as they could, what with asking the landlady to go out, and buy chickens or fish; what with coming home without notice, and saying, "Oh! Mrs. H., I'm so sorry I forgot to order dinner, — will you go and get me a lobster for my supper." I was always getting her out of the way, and began to find, that my food cost as much as that of three people. I did not care, for then Sally used to come up as I said unasked, naturally and regularly, and go downstairs afterwards with her cunt spermatized, and a glass of wine, or whisky, or something nice, to comfort her little belly, and prepare her for the next fucking.

Sally did not trouble herself too much with washing her receptacle. "Have you washed?" "Oh! no, I've not had time," was a question and answer often repeated. She carried this negligence too far. "You never do wash your cunt," said I to her one night. "Yes I do," said she indignantly, "I wash it every Saturday night, after I've washed my feet, — if I can't find time I does it on a Sunday." I recollect all this, having for six weeks nothing else to think of but her and her little doings. I have had other girls who said and acted nearly the same about washing cunts.

I tried when bathing to get near the black-cunted, fat-arsed one who let the waves expose her, but saw less than when sitting on the sands. We often met. She looked invitingly at me, and I fancied, as if she were dying for a male, but she never turned her head after she had passed, nor did her little companion; without whom I never saw her. I spoke to her on the pier one day. She answered encouragingly. I met her in the streets afterwards. She smiled and nodded, and passed on. "It's all right," said I to myself. A big arse and a well-haired cunt had again their potent attractions; so I accosted her one evening as she was going to the Assembly Rooms, and was told to go about my business, — that she was a married woman.

I followed her home for several nights after that. She lived a little way out of the town. She knew I followed her. One evening just so far off from the gas-lamp, and from me, as only to enable her form to be seen indistinctly, she sat down to piss by the roadside. Her young female friend, a saucy-looking bitch of about sixteen years of age, standing by her side. I rushed forward thinking it a clear invitation. She got up saying, "Oh! here is the impudent fellow again, — if you come after us so, I'll complain to the police," — and the two hurried off. "I dare say I'll see all you've got to show on the beach to-morrow," said I, and turned away. I heard them laughing in the distance.

I met her the next day, with the same inviting look in her eye as she passed me, just as if nothing had happened. I never saw her with a man, and could never make her out. I think after my remark that she showed her form less, but I saw her belly naked several times afterwards when bathing.

CHAPTER XII

Sally's antecedents. — Her female friend. — How to get shillings on the sands. — How her friend lost her virginity. — Turns gay and goes to London. — Her invitation to Sally. — My advice. — I return to London. — Sally in London. — The house in U°p°r N°°t°n street. — Sally's discontent. — Mrs. Melvelle. — I sleep with her. — Confessions of a hot-cunted one. — Sally goes home.

Curious about Sally, I wanted to know if any one had attempted her virtue before I had. Once only she told me, and not long before I was at the seaside. A young friend of hers walked with her on the beach at dusk, and told her that if she would not mind a man putting his hand up her petticoats and feeling about her bum and quim, some would give her half a crown. "I do sometimes," said her friend, "and sometimes I feel their things, and then run away, — it is in the dark, and they don't know me, — and so no harm's done." Persuaded by this and wanting money, Sally walked with the girl on the beach. One night they met two men, who gave them money, and Sally's sacred split was felt, though the man had said he would only feel her leg. She got frightened and ran away, the man after her, until she got to the road, when he went off. Then Sally heard her young friend calling out, and then screaming, and Sally ran off until the screams were lost in the roar of the waves and distance. Then she stood still on the watch. A man came from the beach running, and was soon out of sight. Afterwards came her female friend with her bonnet damaged, and clothes rumpled, and crying. The man had felt her, then saying they were too near the road, and he would give her another shilling to feel his cock, they went nearer the sea. Suddenly he flung her down, himself upon her, and he fucked her. She had never had it done before, and was a virgin. She did not know the man, and was frightened to tell, because her father would have beaten her. After that Sally had never been on the beach at night until I induced her. That was her story.

She was the daughter of a laborer, had four sisters, and no brothers. Two of her sisters were married. One would tell her what pleasure it was to have a man in bed with her; the other would say, "There now be quiet, — what ideas you are putting into her head, — it's nonsense Sally, — having babies, and all belonging to it, is more trouble than it's worth, — it's no pleasure at all, — don't you get married ever, — men are beasts."

Having Sally thus on the sly and in a hurry nearly always, did not suit me who liked enjoying a woman tranquilly, and playing with her, looking her all over, and feeling her. I had taken also a fancy for putting my middle-finger up Sally's cunt, and keeping it there on account of its tightness, and comparing it with the full-sized vulvas of Sarah Mavis and Louisa Fisher. I can't tell why I took to this trick with her; as for years I had not cared about feeling the inside of women's machines, and rarely if ever did so with casuals. I could not have this enjoyment well in our hurried embraces. Besides Sally's linen was not invitingly white, though she seemed unconscious of it, and pulled it up to her navel unhesitatingly when she saw my prick. "She won't be five minutes gone, — be quick," was a frequent remark, wise and unavoidable, but not pleasant.

I tried for another Saturday, but for three weeks it was unsuccessful. Sally told me the remarks her Missus made from time to time, and as a draw I once said to the mistress, I thought I should go to London, but nothing came of it. Then I did go to London. After that on a Friday the good woman asked if I was going to stop at *** on Sunday. Why? She told me frankly that she could not leave unless there was no cooking to do. Then I said I was going away till Monday, and at eight p.m. that Saturday night Sally and I were again in the house alone with the children.

Instead of sleeping in Sally's bed, we this time slept in mine, and a fine fucking bout we had, after putting a towel under her fat little bum to save the sheets. She was very curious about the altered condition of her cunt, had been so ever since her hymen was ruptured, and had not disguised her curiosity from me. We talked about it; it felt different she said. She described it accurately from touch, and I described the difference from look. She had tried to look at it, but could not manage it. On the Sunday morning I got the hand-glass out of my dressing-case, and what with that, and putting the table-glass on the floor, then on to a chair, then holding it in front of her cunt for her to see; her natural curiosity was gratified, and so was mine. The investigation was a great treat, and the conversation which ensued equally so.

Sally said she had felt five men's cocks on the beach, but had not seen one of them, all was done in the dark. She had frigged none as far as she knew. All the men had felt her, or tried, but she always shut her thighs tightly to stop their fingers going far. The second man had not paid her. She told her friend, who, evidently more experienced, advised her to ask for the shilling first, which she did. "None on em felt so large as yourn." Was she sure? Quite. She was inexperienced, but my belief in the size of my persuader improved. She looked at her cunt by my aid three or four times on the Sunday, saying each time she had had forgotten how it looked. At the last look, I insisted on seeing the piddle come out of it, if I helped her. Point blank she refused that, and I could not persuade her.

I took in on that night bread and sausages, and that is all we had to eat. I cooked them. I had my own tea and wine there, and was sorry when Monday came. I went off quite early, and then came back, as if I had just returned from London, but Mrs. Harris had not returned, so Sally and I had another poke. Then I went to lunch, came back, and professed annoyance at having had to go out, because the landlady was not at home. There never was the slightest suspicion of my game.

Sally was a charming little fuckster. Very soon after I had had her all her modesty went. She was short, and had a girlish face; excepting for that and the small quantity of hair on her quim, she seemed over seventeen. Her form was full and round, her limbs strong and thick. She had largish firm breasts, and a solid backside. She was come of a big family she said, and had had her monthlies two years. She had a small, tight, elastic cunt, and wagged her arse when fucking, after the first week or so, as if she had fucked for twelve months, and had an immense undisguised enjoyment in the operation. She was quite artless, and delighted to talk about the sensations which the prick gave her. That was one of the charms of knowing her.

No lodgers were to be had, so the landlady transferred herself and children to the ground-floor. Being then just under me she could have heard, and caught me had she thought of looking out for my games. This diminished my chances of fucking with ease of mind. It affected Sally worse than me, for she was always in a state of anxiety, and directly I had had her, and her "ah! — er — ha!" which usually accompanied her spending was over, it was, "Oh! let me go, — she'll be a hearing on us," — and she would uncunt me, and set to work cleaning the grate noisily, or removing my breakfast-things, or doing any other work she happened to be engaged on.

My money was running short, my friends had left, and it was dull. I told Sally I must soon leave. She cried. I tried to inculcate morality into her; but it was of very little use. She asked me every day when I was going, — could I not get her a situation in London? — why not let her be one of our servants? — perhaps my Missus would take her, for she had said she was a hard-working girl, — was it difficult to get a place in London? — if she did, would she see me there? She talked much nonsense, and used to cry and mope. The girl who had been ravished on the beach, she told me, had gone to London, turned whore, had written to Sally to go to her, and not be a fool, and stop working hard at a lodging-house. Sally showed me the letter. I would not give it back, and kept it for years, till one day in a fit of virtue I burnt it. Sally was in a bad way about the letter, for her friend begged her particularly to show it to no one, to burn it, and only to keep the address.

It was a funny, ill-spelt letter, and began by asking her how she was, and would she tell her something about the old people, particularly the old man. Did he ever ask about her? — what did they say? — not that she cared, but she'd like to know how her old daddy was. Then she said she had lots of friends, "real gents mind, not shop young men," — she went to the plays, and had lots of what they two wanted, and used to talk about. "Why don't you come? — I'll give you a place with me, — you'll have lots of good grub, and perhaps a gent will take a fancy to you, and make your fortune, — it will be better than scrubbing and cleaning all the winter." — "Why," she went on, "I gets more in one week than your father

and mine gets in a whole year atween em." There was a concluding
line in a postscript which I laughed over, and shall recollect to my
dying day; it was, "Oh! the lots of cocks I've seed since I seed you
at home."

I saw through the whole. The London harlot would have in
Sally a friend, or a servant faithful to her; or who knows, perhaps
had promised a man to get him a girl who was unbroached. Sally
had replied. "You did not tell her you had been fucked," said I.
"Oh! of course not," — she never would tell any one *that*, if they
pulled her tongue out. I told her all that was commonly thought
to be dreadful about the life of a gay woman; but as I had begun
to disbelieve the nonsense which the world said on that subject,
don't expect I made much impression on Sally. She didn't reply to
my advice. I asked her what she meant to do. This was on a day
or two after I had read the letter.

"Why," said Sally, "she says she gets as much money in a
week as father does in a whole year, — do you believe it?" I said
I did not. "She wears nothing but silks." "But she'll die in a hos-
pital," said I. "So did my sister," said Sally, "but she was very comfortable there." Many of Sally's relatives had died in a work-house,
so Sally saw nothing dreadful in that.

Sally was very fond of frigging me. She was not content with
witnessing the ejaculation of my semen once, but seemed to love
the operation. "I likes to see it come," said she, — but I did not,
and would not gratify her. "How old must a man be," she said to
me one day, "before the stuff will come out of his thing?" "Why?"
"Cause I've seed a boy over the hedge next to us rubbing his thing
up and down hard sometimes, as if he were doing it, and he can't
be more than twelve years old, — I seed him sitting on a washing-
tub one day a doin it, and his mother came out and knocked him
off the tub, and said she would tell his father."

Sally, I found, had seen more before she was ten years old,
than a young lady would see all her life if unmarried. She like
other girls I have had since, and before, used to sleep up to fourteen years of age in the same room, and even the same bed as her
parents, and had a knowledge of what fucking was before she was
ten years old. She'd seen her parents at it when they thought she
was asleep. "I know'd," said she, "what they was up to, cos I told
another gal older than me, and she told me all about doing it."

I returned to London, and promised to write to Sally, who gave me an address where letters could be sent her at the coast, but there was great difficulty about that. I gave her one at a London post-office. As the lodging-house keeper dismissed her servants at the end of the season, Sally was soon going home till she could get some other place. We fucked very hard the last week. Sally always moping seemed to think that with me her last chance of having a prick was going. She was not in the family way, and did not upbraid me, nor say I had ruined her; but said I had been very kind to her, and she dared to say I would have another gal; and then she burst out sobbing. I gave her a handsome present and left.

Two or three months afterwards a letter reached me which had been laying a long time at the post-office. She had come to town, and was servant to her female friend in U*p*r N**t*n Street. I went to see her, and we fucked. I could not help fancying that Sally had had a little variety in cocking since I had left her. She could not let me have her when I first called, but made me go there when her mistress was out. Her mistress' rooms were very nice, and we fucked on her mistress' bed on two or three occasions. But it was not to my taste to visit the servant of a N**t*n Street woman. She was evidently anxious that I should not see her mistress; and so I got very desirous to see her, for she interested me, owing to her having lost her virginity on the sea-beach without being paid for it.

Sally was, I found, discontented, and was going to leave. She would go home again. I think she had expected to be set up in silks and satins, instead of which had to make beds, empty piss-pots, and fetch liquor and French letters, about which I found she now had knowledge. But her great grievance was that she was kept up so late of nights. She had improved in looks, had grown much, and the hair on her cunt had increased in quantity. She was very curious about "my Missus" and me, but I told her nothing. I gave her some gold one night, and told her it would be long before I saw her again. Then she said it was all through me that she had come to London, and we parted. Some time after I had a letch for her again, and went to the house. She had gone home, they believed, and her mistress had left, and gone no one knew where to, — or they would not tell.

Her mistress' name was Melvelle I knew, so going to the Argyle
Rooms (which had not been many years opened), I got her pointed
out to me, went home with her, and had her several times after.
She was a fine, fresh, healthy, dark-eyed young woman; vulgar, but
a lovely fucker. My letch for her arose altogether from knowing
the history of her first fucking. The second night I made her tell
me her history. I slept with her that night, and she told me some
wonderful rigmarole about her parents being well off, and her
having been seduced by an officer, &c. I laughed. "You look much
like a girl who lived at °°°town, and who was said to have been
fucked on the beach one night." She looked queer. "So help me
God, it's a lie," said she, "who ever told you?" "My dear," I said,
"I've told you nothing, I know nothing, I only say you look like
that girl." After a pause, "Did you ever come to see my servant
at N°°t°n Street?" "No. Who told you that?" I would not divulge.
She admitted, after some chaffing, that it was quite true, and hoped
I would tell none of her friends. There was no chance of that, for
I rarely let my most intimate friend know what women I had; or
if I could not prevent that, scrupulously avoided telling them anything about them, not liking my friends to fuck my women or
know my habits. I still had a lingering idea that my prick was small,
and did not wish that talked about.

This gay lady told me one night afterwards (for I told her
then what I had heard) how it came about; but she even lied then,
unless Sally had, for she did not say that she was taken unawares
by a man who had given her a shilling to feel her. Her account was,
that she went to piddle, that he being there caught her, and
threatened to throw her into the sea if she resisted him. She resisted
as much as she could, but he was heavy on her, burst up her with
immense strength, and it was all done in two or three minutes. He
hurt her so in every way, both in splitting, stretching, and shoving,
that she was in pain for many days afterwards. I soon ceased to
see Melvelle, not caring about fucking her after I had heard from
her own lips, all about the way she was ravished whilst her backside
was on the sands by the salt sea-waves. She was older than Sally,
and I should not wonder if her cunt had been split before she was
raped on the sands.

"But although you were ravished without pleasure or pay, how was it you came to take to fucking regularly?" That was a question although not put perhaps in exactly those words, to which I gradually got an answer one evening when I slept with her.

For some time after her ravishment she kept away from the sands; but she missed her odd shillings, and went again there, but would not go far from the seats which were not far from the side of the road. There one night a man spent all over her fingers. She remembered how sticky her cunt was after she had been ravished. Then a girl older than she was told her how she had been fucked, and how she liked it. She kept all this to herself, not telling the girl that her quim had also been torn open, but thought and wondered if the pleasure of fucking was greater than she got by frigging, and as she often frigged herself after the event she did nothing but think of how the man who ravished her, rubbed his cock up her. One very dark night a nice young man asked her to come and talk on the sands. She fucked, she spent, and liked it; and again they fucked. After that any man who wanted her had only to ask, and she let him fuck her. She was mad on the nights she could not get out, or when it was moonlight. She wanted fucking; it was not the money, it was the prick which enticed her, any man might have had her, had he asked her. "I was that hot," said she, "that I could have fucked night and day," — and she was hot on me that night, as she told this.

One night it was late before she went home. Her father, who seems to have kept her pretty well in, must have been told where he might expect to find her, and caught her coming up from the beach. He kicked her all the way to her home, and locked her up for days; he called her a whore, and so did her mother. On the first opportunity she ran off to the young woman who had told her she liked fucking. That young woman seems herself to have been found out by her family; so they ran away to town together, and both were gay.

The utmost she ever received on the sands for being fucked was two and sixpence. One night an elderly man gave her a sovereign for frigging him. When she found it was a sovereign she thought he had made a mistake.

"Let's see the friend you came to town with." "Oh! I don't know where she lives now, — we have quarrelled, — oh! it's made me so randy talking about it, — do it again."

I never saw Sally afterwards, but I heard Melvelle spoken about by men. Some time afterwards she became a well-known London harlot, then she suddenly disappeared. Lots of gay women disappear suddenly in similar manner. I wonder where they go to. They don't die I am sure, — most of those I have known have been fine, healthy creatures.

CHAPTER XIII

*Many miscellaneous whorings. — Mr. McCabe. — The warehouse
in the City. — Tenants paying rent. — McCabe's jocosity. — Suggestions for getting bairns. — Mrs. ***. — The Scotch wife. — The
four-roomed cottages. — Repairs needed. — At her cottage. — Easy
conversation. — The steep staircase. — The bed stood upon. — The
hole in the roof. — The hole in the flesh. — Carnal wants and weakness. — Against the bed, and on it. — Against the dresser. — An
alarm. — The amour terminates. — Reflexions, regrets, and weakness. — On the sin of adultery. — On the power of lust.*

From the time I left Sally at the sea-coast till the spring my
connections were purely with the venal ones. With the exception
of having a few times fucked Sally, and her friend and mistress,
Mrs. Melvelle in London, the ladies were mainly selected at the
Argyle Rooms, which is the resort of the handsomest and best-
dressed gay women. Many swell-women also are there with, and
at other times without, their protectors. With several of the sweetest
of these creatures I have had intimacy, and often passed the night
with the choicest of them. I did not take a permanent fancy to
any one of them, though one did to me. This variety is charming.
To take home lovely women in the bloom of youth, and in the
hey-day of their lust, to speculate on the charms yet unseen, to
kiss and feel their thighs on the road home, to see them undress
leisurely, their breasts appear, their naked arms, the limbs show
one after the other; to lift the diaphanous chemises, see the round
columnar thighs, smooth bellies, and coloured hairy mottes; to note
and compare mentally the variety in form and development of the
various splits, lips, and clitoris, filled me with voluptuous and ever-
varying delight. And now I was able to afford to have these char-

320

mers; for though not at the prices paid by their rich admirers, I
rarely was refused by them. This charming variety in copulation
was only broken, or rather varied by the following little incident.

I had at that time an old friend who had known me from my
birth. A Scotchman, rich, and a widower, liberal in some things,
but grinding in making money, though he was childless; and had
none to whom he cared much about leaving his money to. He was
about seventy-three years old, but a splendid big old man, with a
head of thick reddish hair and fine false teeth. Though living in
London most of his life he had never lost the Scottish dialect, indeed was proud of it, and of his nationality. He was a wholesale
****** merchant, which business he carried on in the heart of
London in huge old-fashioned premises. I may add now, that he
left me a largish sum of money when he died, and I spent it in
travelling and whoring.

He had some funny whims and habits, among which was
making some of his town-tenants go to pay him personally. He did
this to save the expenses of an agent, he said, though I believe it
really was for his amusement. I have heard that the tenants could
with the greatest difficulty induce him to do anything to a house
when once they were living in it. One of my sisters and I used to
stop often at his country-house from Friday till Monday, on which
day he came to town as he said for his tenants. He had several
clerks, but they had nothing to do with his property. He was fond
of consulting me about some of his houses, and often I was present
when his rents were paid.

Within a stone's throw of his counting-house were several
courts. One court containing about a dozen small houses of four
rooms each, and mostly let to weekly and monthly tenants. They
were poorish but respectable; people of the foreman and shopman
class, a class among which the wife does her own work, cooks her
husband's food, &c. The old boy (Mr. McCabe) used to say this
property should be mine. He did not leave it to me, but left me
something very much better. Several of these houses were inhabited
by his own assistants and men, but he made even them or their
wives attend and pay weekly, or monthly, together with other
tenants, on Tuesday mornings.

He was a dear old boy who could laugh at a smutty joke,
though he never told them himself; but he would chaff a man or

woman with double entendres, with hints, and suggestions perfectly unmistakable, and to the very limits of decency, without
uttering an indecent word, or showing an indecent gesture. He was
always ready to let this off at me for having no children, and
specially this when any goodish-looking woman was present, before
whom he dared venture on it.

One morning I was with him on rent-day, when in came a
stout, fully-developed woman, middle-sized and full five-and-thirty,
clad in the neatest and cleanest light colored cotton gown, and a
nice white cap on her head. She was the wife of a man renting one
of the houses in the court, and looked like a very well-to-do, neat
little tradesman's wife.

She was indeed handsome though of a coarse class, had chest-
nut-brown hair, and bright dark roguish eyes. I was smitten with
desire the moment I saw her. Perhaps I wanted a woman, I can't
say, but recollect taking a letch. She also did nothing but look at
me, turning quickly away her eyes whenever she found mine upon
her. "Set ye doon Mrs. Byron," said the old man, which she did.
Whilst he settled with some one else, we two looked at each other
for some minute, till my cock stood, and the woman who seemed
cheeky flushed crimson. I'll bet she had got randy too — it was a
case of cock-struck and cunt-struck. Her big, round, plump, fleshy
form was greatly to my taste just then. At length McCabe being
ready, the woman rose and came to his table, just in front of which
was a chair. I was sitting on the other side of the table near to
him with a newspaper in my hand.

"Set ye doon Mrs. Byron, — and how's the bairn? — has it left
off suckling?" said he. "Now you're at me again, sir." The old man
chuckled. "What, not a babe yet!" "Why you know there is not, —
here's the month's rent, and you really must say what you'll do to
the house, — it wants a lot, — my husband says he won't stay unless
you do it up a little, — seven years, and you've never even done a
bit of whitewash." Whilst saying this the woman's eyes kept glancing
at me at intervals.

The old man took no notice about the repairs. "Why ye should
be baith ashamed of yesels, you can't understand the business, —
have ye put the pillow at the other end of the bed, and tried it
there?" — and he chuckled. I began to laugh. "Aye, aye, we understand all aboot it," said she with a strong Scottish accent, "it's nae

gude, — but about the repairs, — won't you paper the bed-room? — it won't cost much." McCabe turned a deaf ear. "Aye, aye, I'll see about it, after next quarter, —when you've had yer fust bairn. There's a bonny lassie," said he turning to me, "isn't she and been married ten years, and no bairn, — isn't she bonny," — and he winked, — "a wish I war young again," — and the old man laughed and chuckled. "Aye ye've been a weekend one in your day I'll bet," said she, "none but yersel knows the capers you've cut." "You should make your husband sleep by himsel for a month, then go to bed some Saturday, and not get up till the Monday." "He'd be tired o that," said she laughing.

I could keep my tongue no longer still. "I'd like to be him," said I, "and I'd go to bed on the Monday, and not get up till the Monday after." "Aye, — oor, — aye, — there, — lawk," said she trying to look modest, yet looking hard at me and laughing. The old man laughed loud. "Try him, Mrs. Byron, — he won't hurt ye, for he can't get any bairns of his own." "Is the gentleman married?" said she. "Yes, worse luck for him" (he hated my wife). He gave a receipt for the rent, the chaffing mixed with business went on. McCabe got serious when the woman said, "Weel take this as a notice to leave." "Go and see," said he turning to me, "but I won't pay much." He had sent me before on similar errands to one or two other houses, why? God only knows. Not wanting to offend him, "I'll go at once," said I delighted at the idea of getting near her by myself, and with a vague notion that some fun would come of it.

"No dinna coom yet," said she, "it's no fit for ye to see, — I'll mak the bed and clean up, and tak oop the carpet, and ye'll see better," — and off she went. "I won't spend more than one quarter's rent," said my old friend, "though they are gude tenants, and I dunna wish them to go." Winking his eye and chuckling, "Tak ye care Walt, she's a frisky one, though I won't tell your wife." I fired up, hoping to hear something warm about her; but there was nothing against her. She was a good, clean, industrious, sober wife, ten years married; "but," added the old man, "I think she'd like mair than her husband can do for her, — he's six feet high without his shoes, — but a poor creature — a poor creature."

"I'll come back to my lunch with you, I am going to my stock-broker's," said I, "and I'll go to see the house in the afternoon."

Having thrown this dust in my old friend's eyes, I went straight to Mrs. Byron's, ten minutes after she had left us.

She opened the door. I entered a little sitting-room, all in it bright as a new pin, humble, yet with every comfort, — wonderful for her class of life it seemed to me. She showed me what she wanted done, whiting the ceiling, this and that. I said "yes" to everything, but was thinking of nothing but getting into her. Lust struck me all of a heap, our eyes were meeting each other, my lewdness was increasing. There she was in the house alone with me. "So you have no children," said I, and we entered on the same strain that my old friend had. "Nor you?" Then we compared notes. We had been both married for a number of years. I told her I hated my wife. "Oh! what a pity," said she, "and such a fine mon as ye be."

Then we went into the kitchen. A little place with lots of tins as bright as silver, and a little table white as if just made. I complimented her on the beautiful cleanliness; she was much flattered. Yes she prided herself on it, cleaned everything herself every day, had nothing else to do; then had her dinner, and laid down and had a nap, then got ready for her husband's supper. "Won't he be home to dinner?" I asked. No it was too far off, — he never came home till half-past six, — just now he had gone a little way off for his firm, and would not be home for three or four days, — he was foreman somewhere.

I jumped at the news. "I think we had better do what Mr. McCabe told you, go to bed at once, and not get up till your husband comes home, and see if we can get a bairn." "And much good that will do me," said she, "won't it, if we did, — aye, that would get me into trouble," and she laughed. "No it won't, — we should have the fun, and no mischief after, — you know I can't get bairns." "Ar dunna know, ar dunna know," said she shaking her head very slowly, looking at me, and turning scarlet. "Damn it," I cried, "give me a kiss, — I've been longing for you from the moment I saw you," — and I gave her a kiss or two without much resistance from her. She broke away, but I clutched her, and kissed her again and again, rubbing my belly up against hers in a baudy way.

Then we fell to talking about not having children, and how funny those things went. Some women the first time a man was in bed with them, it was done. Others might sleep with any man, and have none. "How did I know?" she asked slily, then turning off said, "Well now have the floor mended, — look at that hole, — I've stopped it up, the mice come through, — the other night one came out, and ran up my clothes whilst sitting at the fire." I was ready with a baudy suggestion for that, or anything else she might have said, for I was now randy to recklessness.

"You had your feet on the fender?" "Yes." "I was sure, and your clothes well up, warming it, weren't you now? — it is so nice to warm it, isn't it?" She laughed. "The mouse peeped out, and seeing it looked so warm and cosy up between your thighs, ran to get between them. I wish I'd been that mouse, — I'd have got right in." She laughed, and gave me a hard slap on my shoulder. "Oh! you're a bad un," said she, "I thot ye war when I saw ye fust." My cock was standing, I began to pull it about outside my trowsers to let her see that I was randy. I always did that instinctively when trying to get over women, fancying that seeing me fiddling there, and knowing what it meant it made them randy too. She eyed me laughing, checking herself, then laughing again and said demurely, "Then there's the roof, the wet comes in both back and front, and just over the bed — tell Mr. McCabe that, won't you, and he'll repair it if ye say he must."

"I've not seen where the roof leaks." "Come up," said she. I followed her to the narrow staircase, scarcely wide enough for a stout man, and steep as a ladder. She went up first. Directly I had got up a stair, I laid my head down on them whilst she went up unsuspectingly, leaving me to look up her short petticoats. A jolly thick pair of legs I saw, thick and clumsy, but in such white stockings. As she got to the top, not hearing me she turned round, saw my game, and disappeared into the room. I followed quickly, she was covering up the bed. "It's all in a muddle," said she, "excuse it sir, I had not time — ye coomd sooner than ye said." She looked at me as I thought invitingly.

I'm sure she was lewed at that minute. A strong, hale, half-fucked woman of thirty-five who had been half-an-hour talking baudily, though in guarded language, with a young man in whose ballocks the sperm was boiling. I caught her, and kissed her again. "There man, — that's all, — that's all," said she.

"I can't see the wet," said I. It was a large four-post bedstead

of common make, but with as nice white hangings as I had in my
own house. The bed nearly filled the little room. "I must pull off the
top," said she, "don't you see where the wet has come through?"
I did, but said I didn't. She put a chair by the side of the bed, and
stepped from it on to the bed, pulled back the linen-head, and
showed the stained ceiling. I put my hand up her clothes. With a
cry she flopped down on to the bed, showing her limbs. "Adun
now, — adun, — ye'll get me into trouble, — ar dun sir," — but I
pushed my hands all about under her petticoats, pushed everywhere,
and felt warm flesh and hair, whilst she squirmed about and
squealed gently. I then shoved her violently back, pulled out my
prick, and tried to feel her cunt. What I did feel I don't know; but
she slid off the bed showing her limbs, and crying, "Har dun now."
I clutched her close as she came to the floor, my prick still out. "Let
me fuck you." "Ah! hish! mon." I put both my hands round her, and
kissed her, pulling her close to me. "Now dunna, — ar won't, — na,
— na, — now leave me alone, — ye'll be getting me into trouble."

What next I scarcely know, but I talked, persuaded, and told
her I'd have her with a condom. She did not know what it was. I
then often carried French letters in my pocket; so I pulled one out,
explained it, and showed how it came over my prick. She was all
curiosity. No it was beastly, fit for whores, said she, "them beasts."
"No ye'll get me into trouble, — no ye shan't, — I wonna," — and
then leaning her back against the bed; one of her legs on the chair,
one on the floor, in that ambiguous, uneasy position, with a strip
of carpet slipping about under my feet, I got my prick into her.
How the devil one leg was on the chair, one on the floor just then,
I can't to this moment understand. Did she lift it up? did I? But in
that posture my prick made acquaintance with her cunt, and pushing hard the carpet slipt away, my feet and me with it, out coming
my prick whilst I stumbled against her in slipping.

Incensed and swearing, "Let's do it properly my love," I pushed
her back against the bed, and clutching her thighs with both hands
heaved them up to my hips. I could not guide my pego, but pushed
at random, its instinct directing, and I dare say her quiet help, soon
got me to the nick after a few battering shoves against her buttocks,
and cunt-wig; and then Mrs. Byron and I being joined together in
holy copulation, moistened each other's privates copiously and
speedily.

Well primed that morning, I stood a long time with my prick well up her after spending. She laid motionless. Then letting one of her legs drop on to the chair, and still holding up the other, I pushed up her drooping petticoats so as just to see her belly, and slowly withdrew my pego, full-sized though not in full ramming condition. As it left her cunt I saw the sperm draw out with it, and sat down on the chair. Then with a violent start, as if just awakened, and just as I had the merest glimpse of her split, she came to her feet, and pushed down her petticoats. We looked hard at each other for a moment, then without uttering a word she walked to the window and looked out. It was a bright, sunshiny day late in the autumn.

I sat feeling my pego for a minute, still in want of a fuck, then went to her. "Oh! don't look out, — if they should see you." "I've come to see about the repairs, if they do." "Oh! but they had better not." Then I brought her to the side of the bed again. It was about two yards from the window to the place where the impress of her heavy arse was still visible on the bed. We looked at each other; she could not look me in the face long. "Fucking's nice, isn't it? — and you're a charming fuck." "We are a wicked pair," said she. "Not at all, — we both wanted it, — neither your husband nor my wife will know, — they won't be the worse, and we are all the better, — let's do it again — feel, my prick, it's quite stiff," and I put her hand to it. She took it kindly, and held it softly, and we looked at each other again, my left arm round her waist, my other on her thighs.

"Let's feel your breasts," said I. "Nay, nay," — but she did not hinder me. I pulled open her dress, and felt the globes (each as big as a half-quartern loaf), and round to her armpits. A strong fleshy smell met me as I kissed them. I liked it, and remarked it. She thought it offended me. "Every night and morn I wash from top to toe," said she. Then kissing her breasts, one hand round her, I tried to feel her thighs higher up. She would not let me, struggled, and got up; but I got a feel, felt the sperm on her thigh, and touched the split. Then standing together, I excited her by talk, and touch, and kisses, and got her on to the bed.

Both laid quiet a minute, not more. Then with a rapid push down of my trowsers, and a pull up of her petticoats, I turned on to her belly. My prick struck into the right path without guidance, a soft and gluey path. I clasped one side of her bum with one hand; with the other I played with her bubbies. Then we had that gloriously prolonged fuck, which a healthy couple in the prime of salacity have for their second spend, a fuck slower, more thoughtful, but in its voluptuousness better than the rapid spilling out of spunk which comes with the first fuck of the night. Ten minutes had not passed I think between our first and second crisis.

I dozed on the top of her, then slipped off to her side. Down she pulled her petticoats. We talked. "I'm afeared ye'll get me into trouble," said she again, "air ye sure you've got no bairns?"

I talked a history of smuttiness and love-making. I could always keep any woman listening when I began, gentle or simple, doxie or virgin. She wondered. "Aye I knew ye were a gay one, — we're a bad couple." In half an hour I wanted her again. She did not refuse, but would I go downstairs a while, "a wee time?" I guessed she wanted to piss, or something. Down I went. "An any one knock, coom up gently, and don't go near the winder," said she. I waited a few minutes, heard movements overhead, knew the jerry had been called into requisition, then up I went. She had locked the door, but let me in at once.

I had a feel up her fresh-washed cunt, and round her buttocks. My God, what spankers! and her breasts, what a pair! firm too, though so heavy. We fucked again. "It's time I had my bit of dinner," said she, "we are a bad coople." Then she began to talk about repairs. "I'll come back in an hour," I said, "don't you say I've been here." "Dunna come back, — dunna," said she. "I wun't let ye mair."

"I've not seen what the house wants," said I. I went back to McCabe, and told him I had been to my solicitor's, then had luncheon with him, and bid him good-bye. "But what about the good woman's house?" he asked. "Lord I've forgotten all about it, — what's the number? — I'll go at once." He told it me, and back I went. She opened the door.

"Come in, come in, the neighbours will see ye," said she, "but dunna gae further." I gave her a prod with my finger in the region of her cunt, and shut the door. "Now ye'll get us both into trouble, I'se sure ye will — I could na eat my dinner for thinking about it, — I've had awful dreams last night, and your face was in them." Luncheon had set me up, I was baudy in mind, randy in body, spite

of my fuckings before luncheon. I went into the kitchen, and pulled
up her petticoats. "Why you've a clean chemise on." Yes she had,
she said, "there be the other," pointing to a large tub with linen in
the water. I could not move her lust, and spent some time in
violently pulling up her petticoats, she in pushing them down. Then
out I pulled my pego, and as she obstinately refused to leave the
room, and struggled; after dropping on my knees, and kissing her
cunt under her petticoats, I finished by shagging her as she stood
with her backside up against the dresser. Whilst we stood wriggling
gently after our full pleasure came a knock. "My husband," said
she, "get in the yard, and over the wall." I buttoned up my cock,
and opened the back-door. Another knock. It was nothing of importance. How often I have been flurried in my fuckings by a
knocking at a street-door. "It's a warning," she said hurriedly, "I
wish I never set eyes on ye."

The knock startled and upset me. I thought I had better go.
Perhaps I had had enough of her; for I took out my pocket-book,
and whilst she sat down on a chair, she told me all she wanted
done. I made note of it, and prepared to go; but the baudy devil
was still strong in me. "You've spoiled another chemise sitting
down," I said. "Nae, nae," she replied, "yer nae so full," — and then
I went away, gave McCabe an account of the house, and he said
I might tell the "gude woman," that she might have it all done up
to ten pounds worth. "I'll write it to her," said he. I agreed that
was best.

The next day I was with him. I had awakened in a liquorish
frame of mind about the "gude woman." He had written, but not
sent the memorandum which was on a very small slip of paper as
usual. "You haven't explained very clearly what you mean," I said
when I had read it. "Ye tak it," said he, "and tell her what I mean."
So I did, got into the house with her after a little persuasion and a
wrangle, and then assaulted her. She was strong, and for a time,
though pulling up her clothes successfully, I could not get my hands
more than half way up her thighs. But such baudy attacks at last
so heat a woman who knows it all means fucking, that there comes
a point when lewed feelings overcome her, and she can resist no
longer.

It was so with Mrs. Byron. I pushed her at last on to a chair
breathless, and had both hands up her clothes, one round her bum,

the other between her thighs, and moved my fingers about so
enticingly on the slit that she opened, and let me grope. "If I let
ye this once, will ye gang?" said she, "ye wunna wish to harm a
body I'm sure, — if Jack should come home, or the neighbours see
ye coom in, and wonder what ye ar aboot sae lang, mischief will
come oot of it." I promised, of course. We went upstairs. We fucked
on the bed, but I would not get from between her thighs till I'd
done her a second time. Then with unwashed cunt she saw me to
the door. I gave her a kiss, and departed.

I was not that way for some time afterwards, and then passed
the cottage to try to see her, for I have always been pleased to
see the woman who has given me pleasure up her. She was at the
window, and bobbed away. I did this two or three times with the
same result, and once thought of calling. It was as well I did not,
for McCabe said her husband was at home ill. Then I had other and
better fish to fry, and never had the "gude woman" afterwards,
though she lived there for years. Once my old friend asked me to
go to see if the repairs he allowed for were really done; but for
some reason or other I did not.

I called on McCabe on one rent-day a month or two afterwards, forgetting she had none to pay till the ten pounds were
worked off, and expecting to see her; but of course she did not
appear. About nine months after (I think) I went there. In she
came. "How d'ye do?" said I, "have the repairs been done?" "Thank
ye, yes sir," she replied looking awfully confused. I went to the
back of the old man, and from there began feeling my cock, and
making signs with my tongue. It was so delightful to see the
woman I had enjoyed; but I did not follow the intrigue up, and she
gave no signs of encouragement.

And here I must add a few reflections. Although I always have
had a great dislike to stroking married women, regarding it as an
improper, — perhaps the only improper path in fornication, as un-
fair to married men, and a social sin to be carefully avoided, —
yet fate seems to have determined that I shall err in that direction.
My second woman was a married one, though I did not know it till
late, my first I had again after she was married, and I have had
several since. Was it the fault of the women, or myself? — did they
intend me to fuck them, or not? Certainly I never deliberately set
to work to tempt them, but the letch when it took me seems to

have overcome all my moral objections. Has the devil determined to tempt me in this direction? If so, am I to blame for not being gifted with control of myself and my cod-piece? In my recent illness I have thought much on this, — with what practical result, who can tell?

[The foregoing paragraph printed in the original words exactly, was not written until many years after the affairs with the Scotch woman. This one is written as I send the narrative to press.

[It is useless for me to attempt to write the Scottish dialect, equally difficult is it to write the vulgar tongue of some of the women I have had, though I have written the characteristic remarks in our conversations.

[Now occur events which took place during the time when I had one woman all to myself, but to whom I found it utterly impossible to be faithful sexually.]

CHAPTER XIV

A gap in the narrative. — A mistress. — A lucky legacy. — Secret preparations. — A sudden flight. — At Paris. — A dog and a woman. — At a lake-city. — A South American lady. — Mrs. O*b***e. — Glimpses from a bed-room window. — Hairy armpits. — Stimulating effects. — Acquaintance made. — The children. — "Play with Mamma like Papa." — A water excursion. — Lewed effects. — Contiguous bed-rooms. — Double doors. — Nights of nakedness. — Her form. — Her sex. — Carnal confessions. — Periodicity of lust.

I pass over many incidents of a couple of years or more, during which I was well off, had a mistress whom I had seduced, as it is stupidly called, and had children; but it brought me no happiness, and I fled from the connection. All this was never known to the world. My home life at length became so unbearable, that I at one time thought of realizing all I had, of throwing up all chance of advancement and a promising career which then was before me, and going for ever abroad I knew not where, nor cared. My mother had died, one sister was married, and was not much comfort to me; the other was far off, my brother nowhere. Just then a distant relative left me a largish sum of money, it was scarcely known to any one of my friends, quite unknown at home, and to none until I had spent a good deal of it. I kept the fact to myself till I had put matters in such train that I could get a couple of thousand pounds on account, then quietly fitted myself out with clothes. One day I sent home new portmanteaus, and packed up my clothes the same day. "I am going abroad," I said. "When?" "To-night." "Where to?" "I don't know, — that is my business." "When do you come back?" "Perhaps in a week, — perhaps a year," — nor did I for a long time. I never wrote to England during that time, excepting to my solicitors and bankers who necessarily knew where I had been at times.

I went first to Paris, where I ran a course of baudy house amusements, saw a big dog fuck a woman who turned her rump towards it as if she were a bitch. The dog licked and smelt her cunt first, and then fucked. He was accustomed to the treat. Then I saw a little spaniel lick another French woman's cunt. She put a little powdered sugar on her clitoris first, and when the dog had licked that off, somehow she made it go on licking, until she spent, or shammed a spend, calling out, "Nini, — cher Nini, — go on Nini," — in French of course.

I could make a long story out of both of these incidents if it were worth while, but it is not, and only notice that the Newfoundland, whose tongue hung out quite as long as his prick as he was pushing his penis up the French woman's quim, turned suddenly round when it had spent, seemed astonished to find he was not sticking arse to arse with her, and then licked the remains of the sperm off the tip of his prick. It was not a nice sight at all, nor did I ever want to see it again.

There were few large cities of Central Europe I did not see, and think that the best baudy houses in most large cities saw *me*. It was a journey in which my amatory doings were especially with the priestesses of Venus. Beautiful faces and beautiful limbs were sufficient for me, if coupled with ready submission to my wishes. Although I learnt no doubt a great deal, and had my voluptuous tastes cultivated in a high degree, yet they developed none of those outside tastes which ordinarily come with great knowledge and practice in the matters of cunt. I shall only tell the most remarkable fornicating incidents.

I was at the Hotel B*** in a Swiss town by a great lake, had arrived late, and was put into the third story, in a room overlooking a quadrangle. It was hot. I threw up my window when I got out of bed in the morning, and in night-gown looked into the quadrangle, and at the walls and windows of the various bed-rooms opening on to it on three sides. Looking down on my right, and one story below me, I caught sight over the window-curtain of a bed room, of a female head of long dark hair, and a naked arm brushing it up from behind vigorously. The arm looked the size of a powerful man's, but it was that of a woman. She moved about heedlessly, and soon I saw that she was naked to below her breasts; but I only caught glimpses of that nakedness, for seconds, as she moved backwards and forwards near the window. Then she held up the hair for a minute, and seemed to be contemplating the effect of the arrangement of it, and showed what looked like a nest of hair beneath one armpit. Her flesh looked sallow or brown, and she seemed big and middle-aged. My window was near the angle of the quadrangle, so was hers, on the adjacent side of it. Perhaps from the window where I was, and that above mine only, could be seen all what I saw.

The armpit excited me, and I got lewed, though the glimpses were so few and short. Now I only saw the nape of the neck, and now her back, according to the postures which a woman takes in arranging her hair, and so far as the looking-glass and blinds and my position above let me. Once or so I saw big breasts of a tawny color. Then she looked at her teeth. Then she disappeared, then came forwards again, and I fancied she was naked to the waist. Then I lost sight of her, and again for an instant saw just the top of her naked bum, as if she were stripped, and in stooping down had bent her back towards the window. When she reappeared she was more dressed. She looked up at the sky, approaching the window to do so, caught sight of me, and quickly drew the blind right down.

I went down to breakfast, met some friends, and sitting down to table with them in the large breakfast-room, saw close to me this very lady. I had seen so little of her face that I did not recognize her at first by that; but the darkness of the eye and hair, the fullness of bust, and the brown-tinted skin left me in no doubt. We were introduced to each other. "Mrs. O*b***e, a lady from New Orleans, a great friend of ours, — been travelling with us for some weeks, with her two little children," — and so on.

I found out from my friends as we smoked our cigars in the gardens after breakfast, that she, with another American lady, and themselves, were going for a long tour, and had been touring for some weeks in Europe. She was the wife of a gentleman who owned plantations, and had gone back to America; intending to rejoin his wife at Paris at Christmas. The lady with the very hairy armpits and her husband were intimate friends of my friends.

I found this party were travelling my road, and I agreed to wait at **** as long as they did. We met at meals; I joined in their excursions, and took much notice of her children who got quite fond of me. She seemed to avoid me at first, but in two or three days showed some sympathy. I guessed that my history had been made known to her, and found out at a latter day that it had. "A married man travelling without his wife is dangerous," said she to me one day when we were a merry party. "A married woman without her husband is a danger to me," I replied, and our eyes met, and said more than words.

I objected to my room, and in a few days the hotel-keeper showed me some better rooms. I had then ascertained which hers were, and pointed out the room next to them. "That," said he, "won't do — it's large, and has two beds." "Oh! it's so hot, I want a large room, — show it me." He did. "It's double price." "Never mind," — and I took it at once. Luck, thought I. Her own room was next, and adjoining it a room in which her two children slept. A half-governess, half-maid who travelled with her, was on another floor, — why I don't know, — perhaps because the next room to the children's was a sitting-room.

My new room had as usual a door communicating with hers. I listened one or two nights and mornings, and heard the slopping of water and rattle of pots, but with difficulty; and nothing sufficiently to stir my imagination or satisfy my curiosity. There were bolts on both sides of the doors, and double doors. I opened mine, and tried if hers was fastened. It was. But I waited my opportunity, intending to try to have her, thinking that a woman who had not had a man for months, and might not for some months more, would be ready for a game of mother and father if she could do so safely.

She was not very beautiful, but was fine, tallish, handsomely formed, with a large bust, and splendid head of hair. Her complexion had the olive tint of some Southerners. One might almost have supposed there was a taint of Negro blood in her, but her features were rather aquiline and good. The face was coldish and stern, the eyes dark and heavy, the only sensuous feature of her face was a full, large-lipped mouth, which was baudy in its expression when she laughed. I guess she was a devil of a temper.

After a day or two I gave up all hope, for she would not understand double entendres, coldly returned my grasp when I shook hands with her, and gave no signs of pleasure in my company, excepting when I was playing with her children. Yet when she looked into my face when laughing; there certainly was something in her eye, which made me think that a pair of balls knocking about her bum would delight her. I used to think much of what a friend of mine, a surgeon in a crack regiment in which I had some friends, used to say, which was this.

"All animals are in rut sometimes, so is a woman, even the coldest of them. It's of no use trying the cold ones, unless they have the tingling in their cunts on them; then they are more mad for it than others, but it doesn't last. If you catch a cold woman just when she is on heat, try her; but how to find out their time, I never knew, — they are damned cunning." So said the surgeon.

I must have caught Mrs. O°b°°°e on heat I suppose, and it came about soon. We went out for some hours on the lake in a boat. She was timid, and when the boat rocked I held her, squeezed her arm, and my knees went against hers. Another time my thigh was close against hers. I put one of her children on to her lap. The child sat down on my hand, which was between her little bum and her mother's thighs. I kept my hand there, gradually moving it away, creeping it up higher and higher, and gripping the thigh as I moved it towards the belly, but so delicately, as to avoid offence, and I looked her in the face. "Minnie is heavy, isn't she?" I said. "She is getting so," she replied, looking with a full eye at mine.

Now I felt sure from her look, that she knew I was feeling her thigh. I had stirred her voluptuousness. The water got rougher. "I shall be sick," said she. "What! on such a lake!" "Oh! I'm a bad sailor." Placing my arm round her for a minute I pulled her close to me. It became calm, and lovely weather again. The water always upset her, it seemed to stir her up, she said. "I'd like to see you stirred up," said I. Then to avoid remark I changed sides with a lady, and sat opposite to Mrs. O°b°°°e. We faced each other, looking at each other. I pushed my feet forward, so as to rub my foot against her ankle. She did not remove her foot, but looked at me.

Arrived at °°° we dined, and sat afterwards in the garden. It grew dusk, and we separated into groups. I sat by her side, and played with her children. One child said, "Play with me like Papa, — play with Mamma like Papa does." "Shall I play with you like Papa?" said I to Mrs. O°b°°°e. "I'd rather not," said she. "I'd break an arm to do so," I replied. "Would you?" said she. "Oh!

put the children to bed Margaret," — and the governess with the children and Mrs. O°b°°°e walked off. I for a minute joined my friends smoking, then cut off by a side-path leading to that through which Mrs. O°b°°°e would pass, She had just bid the children good night. "I shall come up to see you directly," said she to them, — and to me, "I thought you were going into town." "Yes I think I'll make a night of it, — I'm wild. — I want company." "Fine company it will be, I dare say." "Let me keep you company then." No one was near, I kissed her. She took it very quietly. "Don't now, you'll compromise me." It was now quite dusk. I kissed her again. "I'm dying to sleep with you," I whispered. "You mustn't talk like that, — there now, they will see you," — then I left her.

I had noticed her habits, and knew that usually she went up to her children soon after they had gone to bed, so I waited at the foot of the stairs. Soon she came. "What, you here?" "Yes, I'm going to bed like you." It was a sultry night, everybody was out of doors, the hotel servants lolling at open windows. No one met us as we went upstairs. "Why that's not your room, — it's next to mine." "Yes it is, — I've been listening to you the last two nights." "Oh! you sly man, — I thought you were sly." "Look what a nice room it is," said I opening the door. There was a dim light in the corridors, none in my room. She looked in, I gave her a gentle squeezing push, and shut the door on us.

"Don't shut the door," said she turning sharply round. I caught and kissed her. "Stop with me, my darling, now you're here, — I'm dying for you, — kiss me, do." "Let me go, — there then, — now let me go, — don't make a noise, — oh! if my governess should hear me, what would she think!" "She is not there." "Sometimes she stays till I go up to the children, — oh! don't now, — you shan't." I had her up against the wall, my arm round her, I was pressing my hand on her belly outside her clothes. She pushed my hand away, I stooped and thrust it up her clothes on to her cunt, and pulling out my prick, pushed her hand on to it. "Let me, — let's do it, — I'm dying for you." "Oh! for God's sake don't, oh! no — now, you'll compromise me, — hish! if she should be listening." For a moment we talked, she quietly struggled, entreating me to desist; but my fingers were well on to her cunt, frigging it. I don't recollect more what she said, but I got her to the side of the bed, pushed her back on it, and thrust my prick up her. "Oh! don't compromise me — don't now." Then she fucked quietly till she gasped out, "Oho — oho," as a torrent of my sperm shot into her cunt.

Excepting from the clear light of the night, which came from the sky through the window in the quadrangle, the room was in darkness. I don't know that my prick ever lingered longer up a woman after fucking and declare that whilst up her, I told how I had seen her brushing her hair, and so on. She said that I should compromise her, — and oh! if she should be with child, — "what will become of me." Feeling the sperm oozing out over my balls, and my prick shrinking, I uncunted. "Oh! what have you made me do, you bad man?" said she sitting upon the side of the bed. "Oh! if they should see me going out of your room, — oh! if she has been listening."

I drew down the blind, and lighted a candle, much against her wish. She sat at the edge of the bed just where she had been fucked, her clothes still partly up. I listened at the door between our two rooms, but heard nothing, then told her again how I had watched her from a top-window, and seen her breasts and armpits. My prick stiffened at my own tale. Sitting down by her side, "Let's do it again my love," I said, and pushed my hand up her clothes. I shall never forget the feel. The whole length of her thighs, as she closed them on my hand felt like a pot of paste. Only a minute's pleasure, and such a mass of sperm! She repulsed me, and stood up.

I stood up too; kissing, coaxing, insisting, she looking at me, I fingering, pulling backwards and forwards the prepuce of my penis. No, she would not. Then I threatened to make a noise, if she would not, and swore I would have her again. She promised to let me if I would let her go to her bed-room first, — she would unlock her side of the two doors, if she could. She was not sure if there was a key, — if not she would open the door on to the corridor, but only at midnight, when the gas was turned out, and few people about. She promised solemnly, and sealed it with a kiss. "Oh! for God's sake be quiet." I opened the door of my bed-room, and saw no one in the lobby. Out she went, and got into her own room unnoticed. Then I opened the door to her room from my side. There were double doors.

She seemed to keep me a long time waiting, though she had

scarcely been in her room five minutes. I stripped myself to my shirt, then knocked at the door gently, then louder. A key turned, the door opened. She had only gone in to be sure that the children were in their bed, and the governess not with them. "Oh! I have been so fearful lest she should have been there," she said.

The children were asleep, she had bolted their door. "And now go to bed, and let me also, — there is a dear man, and don't ask anything more of me." "To bed yes, but with you." She begged me not, all in a whisper. My reply was to strip off my shirt, and stand start naked with prick throbbing, and wagging, and nodding with its size, weight, and randiness. "Only once, one more, and then I will be content." "No."

"Then damned if I won't," said I moving towards her. "Hush! my children will hear, — in your room then," — and she came towards my door. "Oh! nonsense, not with your clothes on, — let us have our full pleasure, — and this hot night too, — take off your things." Little by little she did, and stood in her chemise. I tried all the doors, they were securely fastened, and then I brought her quite into my room. "Leave me alone a minute," she said. But as randy as if I had not left my sperm up her fifteen minutes before, I would not, and pulled her gently toward my bed, tore the clothes off, so as to leave the bottom sheet only on, and got her on to the bed. "Do let me see your cunt." "No, — no, — no." As I pulled up her chemise, down she pushed it. "Oh! no, — I'm sure I shall be with child," said she, "and if I am I'd just best make a hole in the water." Her big breasts were bare, her thighs opened, a grope on the spermy surface, and then fucking began. "Oho!" she sighed out loudly again, as she spent.

Off and on until daybreak we fucked. After the second she gave herself up to pleasure. The randiest slut just out of a three months quodding could not have been hotter or readier for lewed fun with cunt and ballocks. I never had a more randy bed-fellow. She did not even resist the inspection of her cunt, which surprised me a little, considering its condition. Our light burnt out, our games heated us more and more, the room got oppressive, I slipped off her chemise, our naked bodies entwined in all attitudes, and we fucked, and fucked, bathed in sweat, till the sweat and sperm wetted all over the sheet, and we slept. It was broad daylight when we awakened. I was lying sweating with her bum up against my belly, her hair was loose all over her, and the bed. Then we separated and she fled to her room, carrying her chemise with her.

Oh! Lord that sheet! — if ten people had fucked on it, it could not have been more soiled. We consulted how best to hide it from the chamber-maid, and I did exactly the same trick as of former days. Have not all men done it I wonder?

I got a sitz-bath in my room, which was then not a very easy thing to get. I washed in it, wetted all my towels, then took off the sheet, wetted it nearly all over, soiled it, then roughly put it together in a heap, and told the chamber-woman I had used the sheet to dry myself with. She said, "Very well." I don't expect she troubled herself to undo or inspect the wet linen, or thought about the matter.

I went to breakfast at the usual time. "Where is Mrs. O*b-***e?" I asked. The governess appeared with the children saying the lady had not slept owing to the heat. She showed up at the table d'hôte dinner. I avoided her, knowing I should see her soon afterwards, and said I should go and play billiards; but instead, went to my bed-room and read; nursing my concupiscent tool, and imagining coming pleasures.

I heard the children, having opened the door on my side and found that the key of her door was luckily so turned as to leave the key-hole clear. The doors connecting all the rooms were as is often the case in foreign hotels, opposite each other, and I could see across into the children's bed-room. They were putting their night-gowns on in their own room. Then the governess came into her mistress' room and I heard her pissing, but could not see her. To my great amusement, for the slightest acts of a woman in her privacy give me pleasure, she then came forward within range of my peep-hole, and was looking into the pot carefully. Then Mrs. O*b***e came in and the governess left. Mrs. O*b***e went to look at her children and returned, opened our doors, and then we passed another amorous night, taking care to put towels under her bum when grinding. We did not want the sheets to be a witness against us again.

Mrs. O*b***e was not up to the mark, and began to talk that sort of bosh that women do, who are funky of consequences. After a time she warmed, and yielded well to my lubricity. I would see her cunt to begin with. It was a pretty cunt, and not what I had expected, large, fat-lipped, and set in a thicket of black hair, from her bum-hole to her navel; but quite a small slit, with a moderate quantity of hair on her motte, but very thick and crisp. I told her again how I had seen her from the window. The recital seemed to render her randier than either feeling my prick, or my titillation of her quim. The hair in her armpits was thicker, I think, than in any woman I ever had. Her head-hair was superb in its quantity. I made her undo it, and spread it over the bed, and throw up her arms, and show her armpits when I fucked her. She was juicy-cunted, and spent copiously; so did I. The heat was fearful. We fucked start naked, again.

Later on she told me that she cared about poking but once a month only, and about a week before her courses came on. At other times it annoyed her. Going on the water always upset her stomach, and made her lewed, even if in a boat on a river, and however smooth it was, it upset her that way. At sea it was the same. It made her firstly feel sick, then giddy, then sleepy, but that always two or three hours afterwards, randiness overtook her. After a day or two, the lewedness subsided whether she copulated, or frigged, or not. She told me this as a sort of excuse for having permitted me to spermatize her privates, the night of her excursion on the water with us.

She was curious about my history. I told her I had women at every town I came to. She declared that no other man but I and her husband had ever had her.

CHAPTER XV

Frantic coition. — A priapus. — Purging and resting. — Priapus humbled. — Carnal exercises resumed. — The governess. — A peep through a key-hole. — Bathing. — The after-frig. — My politeness. — The silk mantle. — Travelling resumed. — The new hotel. — Felt, and all but. — Unproductive seed. — A thin partition. — Scared by a laugh. — Unsuccessful. — The mantle given. — Still no success. — I leave.

On the third night which I had her, she had undressed to her chemise, and had lifted one leg to pull off her boot. It was a small foot, and a fine fat leg. A letch to have her with her boots and stockings on struck me. She was now complaisant in everything, and I fucked her thus at the side of the bed, and then with her bum towards me I had her again. She was tired, and prayed me to desist. I felt tired, but so heated, and irritated in my privates, and so furiously lewed, that though my sense told me I had done enough, my prick refused to be quiet, and kept standing. It was still fearfully hot. I had been abstinent from women for some time, until I had seen Mrs. O*b***e's armpits, and had since been idling, eating, drinking, smoking, and thinking, almost dreaming, of nothing but baudy things and of fucking her.

At last I let her go to her own bed, and laid down outside my own. My prick had come out of her stiffish, and soon got as hard as iron, and kept so till I could bear it no longer, and went into her room. She was asleep, and outside her bed with her boots and stockings on still. She had laid down fatigued, and fell asleep thus. I think I see her now as I pulled up her chemise, and felt her still wet cunt. I made her angry, but she came to my bed. Again my pego pushed up her. Now she had said "Oh! I'm so tired, — pray let me go." "I will my darling after this." "Oh! I'm spending again," she almost shrieked, and so did I. Then I let her go. I tell all this with minuteness, for the circumstances were so exceptional, that they are impressed on my memory in the minutest detail.

I fell asleep and awakened with prick harder than ever, heard her snoring, and not liking to disturb her, pissed, thinking that that might reduce my concupiscent machine to a wagging size. It did not, and thinking about her bum, armpits, and all her charms, I got furious. My prick had none of the soft voluptuous sensation in it, which comes from sperm-charged balls, but ached from its roots to my arse-hole; yet the tip was sensitive to pleasure. Rubbing my finger on it made it throb, and my whole body quiver, though I had none of the incipient pleasure of a spend.

I awakened her. No I should *not* do it any more. But I threw myself on to her, and fingered her cunt with passion. Her thighs opened again, and I drove up her with violence and baudy ejaculations, for my brain seemed on fire. "Oh! pray, — oh! if the children should awake." "Come to my room then." I uncunted, and she came. Ram, ram, ram. "Oh! I'm doing it," she cried, but it took me a mile of shoving to spend. She spent twice before I did, and when I uncunted my prick was still stiff. I would not let her leave, but lay fondling her (almost sticking together in our sweat), and making her feel my iron-bound prick till I mounted her again.

"Oh! what a man, — you're hurting, — why it's stiff still, — don't push up so hard, — I feel as if my womb was falling, — oh! I'm spending, — oh! you'll kill me, — don't, — leave off." At daylight I was still feeling her cunt, kissing, and pushing my prick up her, almost as soon as I had uncunted. Then she refused angrily to let me do it any more, — and no wonder, but I held her to me.

Now I could not spend at all, yet had pleasure in the fucking. She on the contrary spent quicker, and quicker, had got inflamed and excited both in mind and cunt. She kept begging me to stop after each of her spends, and saying I should kill her. At the last spend she gave a scream, and began to sob, uncunted my penis by a violent jerk, and there was blood on it. I think some of it was mine. How often I spent that night I never could tell. I was fucking for about eight hours, off and on almost without stopping. Then I slept, and when I awoke, had still a prick stiff, but it was aching fearfully.

She had locked herself in, never answered my whispered calls, nor my discreet raps, and did not appear that day. She was ill. I looked a scarecrow, and told a man of our party that I had been at a baudy house all night. My prick all day kept standing at intervals. Seeing in the afternoon the governess take out the children for a walk, I went to my room, saw Mrs. O*b***e, and promised not to exact anything that night; but at bed-time insisted on plugging her cunt again. She said I was a brute, that I only cared about my own pleasure, and refused me positively, entreating me not to make a noise and compromise her, but I fucked her till she screamed, and so did I, with mixed pain and pleasure.

My stiffness without much desire, still continued and much annoyed me. Such a copulative fury had never occurred to me before. At last I began to think that there was some ailment coming on. I had heard of such things, of men going mad through it, and got alarmed.

Then I frigged, hoping to reduce it, and after immense trouble got a pleasure, but so mixed with pain that I groaned. I could scarcely see any sperm, felt burning hot all over me, my mouth was parched, I was trembling, and thought I had better see a doctor. I carried medicine in my trunk, took a violent dose, in a few hours nearly shit my guts out, then took more medicine, and laid a bed, all day, eat nothing, and my prick gradually became tranquil. Mrs. O*b***e's cunt was mulberry in colour, my prepuce was raw, we rested from our amatory labours for several days, but we talked about it a great deal.

Then both with re-invigorated privates, we fucked, and covered again some towels with sperm. She was sure she was in the family way. Again I got symptoms of a priapus, and wore her out by ramming, and making her spend. At last she spent thrice before I did, I felt a peculiar wetness on my prick, pulled it out, it was covered with her courses. "Thank God," said she.

Then I had a weakness which I thought was clap. It was nothing but the result of over-fucking. She got her courses over, and refused to let me have her again. My gleet cured itself by quietness and careful living.

We kept as secret as we could that my room was next to hers. We always looked into the corridor before leaving or entering our rooms, and never did so at the same time. She had special fear

of the governess finding her out. I thought that she need have no
fear on that head. But one never knows.

One evening she said to the governess, "Give the children their
bath just warm." The girls had a bath once or twice a week,
before going to bed. Instinct which has always helped me so in
these affairs, made me go directly afterwards to my bed-room. Instinct was right. The bath was in front of the key-hole in Mrs.
O*b***e's room. I saw the girls washed, could just see where their
little hairless splits began (it was daylight still), and then oh!
luck! The governess, a dark-eyed, short young woman about twenty-
four years of age, an American, gave herself a bath, and soaped and
rubbed herself from the nape of her neck to her toes. She rubbed
her cunt dry in a most irritating, cock-stiffening manner, within
two yards of my eye, and then dressed herself again, and sat down
on a chair.

Scarcely had she seated herself, than she began to pull up her
clothes in all manner of ways, as if hunting for a flea; then got a
book, and turning her back to the light began reading, keeping her
right hand up her petticoats. Then she went and pulled down the
blind. She lighted candles, and sat down reading again, nearly
facing me. Her hand after a while went up her petticoats on to her
quim, and moved gently. She put the book on a little movable table,
one of her legs on the edge of the bath, the other on the floor, and
pulled her petticoats a little up to ease her hand, showing her legs
a little above her knees (she had not put stockings on after the
bath). Then her legs opened wide, her hand moved, she frigged
hard and quick, I saw the shake of it, her legs quiver, stretch open
then close, her bum wriggle, her legs open, her head fall on one
side and her eyes close. Her hand then appeared from under her
clothes and hung lifelessly over her petticoats, which fell down,
and so she sat for a minute as if asleep. Then she put her hand under
her petticoats, withdrew it, looked at it, washed it in the bath, and
moved away. Then I heard her pissing. Then the chamber-maid
appeared, and took away the bath. When doing so Mrs. O*b***e
came in and asked why the bath was still there, and if the children
were asleep. I closed my door, and slipped downstairs, not desirous
of having it known that I had been in my bed-room.

It was a delightful sight. Nothing gives me more pleasure
than seeing a woman dress and undress, wash, piddle, and do all

she wants, not thinking any one is looking at her. I'm not sure that it is not as exciting as the baudiest sights a woman can give a man. Three women, — chaste women, — have I seen frigging themselves, when they could not have thought they were observed, and the sights will never fade from my memory. I have seen and heard full twenty chaste women dress, undress, wash, brush, piddle, without their knowing I did so.

Later that night I had Mrs. O*b***e and fucked her thinking of the governess. How strange it seems that when my genitals have been in a woman, and the sperm rising to moisten her cunt, I have at times thought of some other woman, and copulation with them.

Mrs. O*b***e and I did not allude to our married condition. One evening laying face to face, kissing, I fingering her clitoris, she holding my prick, I put a question. She said no, her husband's prick was not quite as large as mine, very nearly she thought, and then, "Oh! don't let us talk about such things," — and we never as far as I can recollect referred again to similar subject.

Her first night with me seemed the highest development of randiness and sensuous enjoyment I ever witnessed in a woman, who was what may be called chaste. Her long abstinence from a doodle, the effect on her physical organization of the rocking of the boat, and my stimulating words acting upon her mind caused it. She seemed almost mad with pleasure. When fucking, her sighs were continuous, though she was quiet in tongue, until the crisis came on. The copious discharges she made were like a flood, but it was that night alone, afterwards she was different. Towards the end of our acquaintance, she said she was worn out, and did not care about it. She was a strong-scented woman. When she got hot, a sort of baudy, cunty, sweaty exhalation evolved from her. I shall always think it was that among other things, which got me such an attack of stiff-standing, and that the aroma of her body excited me, though it somewhat offended me.

I had been at the Lake hotel some weeks, and the party were about to move off. I was going in the same direction, but expected a friend to meet me, and they left a day before I did. The last night I begged her to let me have her and she consented under a solemn promise not to spend in her. I always loved to spend hard home, but kept my word, and spent outside her cunt, pulling out my prick just when the ejaculation of sperm began, and letting it fall on to her buttocks. Then we parted. She said if ever we met again we must try to forget what we had been to each other, and that I was to blame more than she was. We saw each other two days afterwards, but I never had her again, and she did not go to Paris at Christmas. I did, and heard she had gone back to America.

From the night I saw the governess frig herself, I lusted for her. Talking about her to one of the party, he told me he thought she knew the feel of six inches of stiff up her; but I got no more out of him. I met her walking in the town, and looking at a mantle in a shop-window, and asked her if she were going to buy it. "Oh! no I can't afford it, though it would just suit me." "I'll give it you if you will let me —" "Let you what?" Her eyes met mine. "Let me bring it to you some evening when they are all a bed." She shook her head, and walked away. I bought the mantle, and took it to the hotel.

I took it with me three days afterwards to the town of ***. There we were all again together at the same hotel. She was not far off from Mrs. O°b°°°e's room this time. I got a bed-room as near to hers as I could, but was bothered because my friend with whom I was going to travel had a bed-room very near to mine.

I told her I had bought her the mantle. No she would not take it, nor let me take it to her, Mrs. O°b°°°e would ask her where she bought it, would wonder how she could afford it. Spite of all her objections I knocked at her door one evening just before she could have undressed, and after Mrs. O°b°°°e had gone to bed, "only to show it to you." I saw her, and got into the room. There was as occasionally happens, no door between hers and the adjoining rooms, but the partitions were so thin that you could hear through them easily any one cough, snore, or fart. I begged and besought her to feel me, to let me feel her. I threatened to make a noise and compromise her. She did not want the mantle, if she was to be ruined and insulted for it, — she had not asked me for it, which was true enough. But little by little we kissed, I pulled up her clothes, saw her thighs, and got the smell of her cunt on my finger; but she would not let me do it, though she felt my prick. "Oh! do leave me, — I'll do anything but let you do that, — I mustn't, — if Mrs. O°b°°°e found anything out, I should be ruined and turned off in a strange land." And in the midst of this I spent whilst her hand was round my prick, one of mine on her thighs, and I was vainly trying to push her on to the bed. Then I desisted.

With her hand covered with sperm she stood looking at it, and at me, and saying, "Do go," I tried for another hour I suppose, and was about to conquer, had got her on to the bed, and was just getting on myself, when we heard a loud burst of laughter in the adjoining room. That disconcerted us both, for it seemed as if they were laughing at us, and she jumped up in terror.

She recovered herself, when we heard the talking and laughing continuing, but it had spoiled my chance, though I tried for hours afterwards. Then angrily leaving her, I left her the mantle; but the next morning I asked her for it, which was mean. She sent it into my room. I felt a little ashamed of myself for taking it. I never got into her room again, so I amused myself by talking the hottest and lewedest I could to her, for the three or four days I remained there; principally asking whether she would like any of my sperm on to her cunt and if she had frigged when I had left the room. She took it very quietly, but used to colour up and look randy. Then I was obliged to leave, so I sent the mantle to her with a note saying it was hers, and departed without having fucked her, nor do I know whether a penis had ever probed her or not, but I think that had I remained longer, I should have found that out. A woman who has had a man's sperm on her fingers must feel yielding afterwards.

CHAPTER XVI

At the town of A***n*n. — At the railway. — The station rebuilding. — Diarrhœa. — The closet-attendant. — The temporary shed. — Ladies' closets. — A peep-hole. — Women on the seat. — Peasants. — Piddlers outside. — At the peep-hole again. — Onanism. — A male intruder. — The letter-box. — An infantine pudenda. — An impatient male. — The soiled seat. — Sisters.— A succession of backsides. — The female attendant. — Bribed and kissed. — Her husband's occupation. — Next day. — The peep-hole plugged. — Two young peasants. —Private inspections.

Then I saw a sight that I never wish to see again, for though it was exciting, it was nasty, and for some time afterwards came offensively into my mind, even in my most voluptuous moments with women; destroying the sense of their beauty, and what of romance there is in the conjunction of cunt and prick. However my mind came round to its right balance at last.

I was at A***n*n in the south of France, and went up with my luggage to the station which was being rebuilt. A branch-line had been opened the day before, and all was a chaos of brick, mortar, and scaffolding. The water-closets were temporarily run up in wood, in a very rough manner. A train had just brought in many passengers. I was taken with violent belly-ache, and ran to the closets. They were full. Fearful of shitting myself I rushed to the women's which were adjoining the men's. "Non, non Monsieur," screamed out the woman in charge, "c'est pour les dames." I would have gone in spite of her, but they were also full. Foul myself I must. "Oh! woman I am so ill, — here is a franc, show me somewhere for God's sake." "Come here," said she, and going round to the back of the wooden structure, she opened the door of a shed.

On the door was written "Control, private, you don't enter here." In I went rapidly. "Shut the door quite close," said she, "when you come out." It had been locked. I saw a half-cupboard, and just in time to save my trousers made myself easy on a seat with a hole in it.

It was a long compartment of the wooden shed and running at the back of several privies. No light was provided for it, excepting by a few round holes pierced here and there in the sides; but light came also at places through joints of the woodwork roughly and temporarily put together. There were chests, furniture, forms, cabinets, lamps, and shelves and odds and ends of all sorts in the shed, seemingly placed there till the new station was finished. The privy seat on which I sat was at one end. The privy enclosure had no door, and looking about when my belly-ache had subsided, and I could think of something else, I heard on my right, rustlings, and footsteps, as of females moving, and a female voice say, "Make haste." Then doors banged and opened, and just beyond my knee I saw a round hole in the woodwork through which a strong light came into my dark shed. Off I got in a trice, and kneeling down looked. It was a hole through which I could have put my middle-finger, a knot in the wood had fallen or been forced out, in the boarding which formed the back of one of the women's closets, and just above the privy-seat. What a sight met my eyes as I looked through it!

A large brown turd descending and as it dropped disclosing a thickly haired cunt stretched out wide between a fat pair of thighs and great round buttocks, of which I could see the whole. A fart followed, and a stream of piddle as thick as my finger splashed down the privy-hole. It was a woman with her feet on the seat after the French fashion, and squatting down over the hole. Her anus opened and contracted two or three times, another fart came, her petticoats dropped a little down in front, she pulled them up, then up she got, and I saw from her heels to above her knees as she stood on the privy-seat, one foot on each side of the hole. Off the seat then she got, pulling her petticoats tightly about her, and holding them so. Then she put one leg on to the seat, and wiped her bum with two or three pieces of paper which she held in one hand, taking them one by one from it with the other, wiping from the anus towards her cunt, and throwing each piece down the hole

as she had done with it. Then looking at her petticoats to see if
she had smirched them, she let them fall, gave them a shake, and
departed.

She was a fine dark woman of about thirty, well dressed, with
clean linen, and everything nice, though not looking like a lady.
The closets it must be added, had sky-lights and large openings
just above the doors for ventilation, so they were perfectly light.
The sun was shining, and I saw plainly her cunt from back to
front, her sphincter muscle tightening and opening, just as if she
had arranged herself for me to see it. I recollect comparing it in
my mind to those of horses, as I have seen many a time, and every
other person must have seen, tightening just after the animals have
evacuated.

The sight of the cunt, her fine limbs, and plump buttocks made
my cock stiff, but my bowels worked again. I resumed my seat,
and had no sooner done so than I heard a door bang. Down on my
knees I went, with eye to peep-hole. Another woman was fastening
the closet door. It was a long compartment. When near the door,
I could see the women from head nearly to their ankles; when
quite near the seat I could not see their heads, nor their knees which
were hidden by the line of the seat; but I saw all between those
parts.

It was a peasant-girl seemingly about twenty years old, tall,
strong and dark like the other. She took some paper out of her
pocket, then pulling her petticoats well up, I saw the front of her
thighs and had a momentary glimpse of the motte. She turned
round, mounted the seat, and squatted. She then drew up her
petticoats behind tighter, and I saw buttocks, turds and piddle.
She did not lift up her petticoats quite so much in front, yet so
light was it that the gaping cunt and the stream were quite visible.
She wiped her bum as she sat, then off she went, leaving me delighted with her cunt, and annoyed at seeing what was behind it.

Then I found from looking around and listening, that there
were several women's closets at the back of all of which the shed
ran. It was a long building with one roof, and the closets were
taken out of it. Through the chinks of the boards of one closet I
could see the women enter, and leave, could hear them piss, and
what they said in all of them; but in the one only could I see all
their operations. I kept moving from one to the other as I heard

their movements, their grunts, and their talk, but always to the
peep-hole when there was anything to see, — and there was plenty.

I had now missed my train, the two women I expect must have
gone off by it, and for quite an hour the closets were all empty.
I began to think there was no chance of seeing more unless I stayed
longer than an hour when I knew an express train arrived. I resolved to wait for that, wondering if any one would come into my
shed for any purpose, but no one came in. I had eased myself, and
covered up the seat; but a strong stink pervaded the place, which
I bore resolutely, hoping to see more female nakedness.

There had been a market at A***n*n that morning. Some of
the farm-people had come by the train for the first time, the
junction railway only having just been opened. I had heard them
say so on the platform before I was taken short. Hearing voices just
outside my shed, I cautiously opened the door ajar and peeped.
Groups of market people had arrived, and were standing outside
the station, mostly women with baskets. The eaves of the shed-roof
projecting much, gave a little shade from the sun, and they were
standing up against it. That told me there would be another train
soon; so I shut the door.

In a few minutes close to my door I heard two female voices.
"I want to do caca," said one of them (in French of course). "They
charge you a penny," said the other. "I won't pay a penny, — we
shall be home in twelve minutes when the train starts." "I shall
piss," said one in broad French. She was close up against the spot
where I stood, a board only between us. I heard a splash, then two
splashes together. I opened the door ajar again, and peeped. They
were both standing upright, but pissing. Both laughed. "I must
do it somewhere," said one. "Go over there then, — they won't see
you." "No I'll go to the woman, and say I haven't any money when
I come out." The next minute she came into the privy with the
peep-hole. On my knees I went, and saw the operation complete.
Such a nice little girl. She sat some minutes after she had dropped
her wax, pulling her petticoats well up from time to time. I had
such gloat over her cunt. Once or twice she put her hand under,
and felt it.

Spite of my diarrhœa, my prick got so stiff, and I was so
randy, that with my eye to the hole and gazing on her round bum
and gaping cunt, I frigged myself. My sperm fell on the partition

in front of me. I sat looking at it, when I was shitting again. The
girl went back to her companion by the shed, and said she had
been obliged to pay, and it was a shame. I opened the door, feeling
as if I must see the girl's face again. They saw me. "There's some
one in there," said one, and they moved away.

After that the woman in charge wiped the privy-seat, which
I suppose was dirty. Then two or three women came in. Old, and
dirty were one or two of them, who sat on it English fashion. I
saw their skinny buttocks, and the back-view of their cunts. It
sickened me, for they all of them shit, which revolted me. Yet the
fascination of the cunt made me look at all of them, — I could not
help it. One woman had her courses on, and moved aside a rag to
do her needs, — that nearly made me vomit. That woman squatted
on the seat.

For a quarter of an hour or so no one came. A trumpet, a
railway-bell, and a hubbub, then told me the express train was
coming in. Then was hurry, and confusion, a jabber of tongues in
many languages. All the closet-doors banged at once, and I heard
the voices of my country-women.

Pulling her clothes up to her hips a fine young English woman
turned her bum on to the seat. It came out of a pair of drawers,
which hid nearly her buttocks. As she sat down her hand eased
her drawers away from her cunt. Splash, trump, and all was over.
The hair of her cunt was lightish. She was gone. Another came who
spoke to her in English, and without a moment's delay pissed, and
off she went.

Then a lady entered. As she closed the door I saw a man trying
to enter. She pushed him out saying in suppressed voice, "Oh! for
God's sake are you mad? — he can see from the carriage-window."
"Not there sir," I heard the woman in charge cry out. The door was
shut, and bolted.

The lady, young and handsome, stood quite still, facing the
seat, as if overcome with anxiety; then feeling in her pocket, took
out some letters, and selecting some, tore them in half, and threw
them down the privy. That done she daintily wiped round the seat
with a piece of paper, lifted up handsome laced petticoats, and
turning her rump towards the seat daintily sat down. She had no
drawers on. She must have fancied something, for she rose again
directly, and holding her clothes half-way up her thighs looked

carefully at the seat. Then she mounted it, but as if she scarcely
knew how to do it, stumbled and bungled. She stood upright on
it for an instant, and then I could only see half-way up her legs. At
length the bum slowly descended, her petticoats up, and adjusted
so as to avoid all chance of contamination. I saw the piss descending,
but she was sitting too forward, and the piss fell splashing over the
edge of the seat. She wriggled back opening her legs wider, and
a pretty cunt with dark hair up to her bum-hole showed. My cock
stood again. She jumped off the seat, looked down the privy, gave
her clothes a tuck between her thighs, and went off.

Then came others, mostly English, pissing in haste, and leaving,
and bum after bum I saw. Then came a woman with a little girl.
She was not English, she mounted the seat, and cacked. Whilst
doing so she told the child to "pi-pi bébé" on the floor, which she
did not. When she had finished she wiped her arse-hole with her
finger, — how she cleaned the finger I didn't see. She then took
up her child, held her up over the seat with her clothes up to her
waist, her cunt towards me, and made her piss. The tiny stream
splashed on the seat, and against the hole through which I was
looking — a drop hit me on the eye. How funny the hairless little
split looked to me. To think that her little split might one day be
surrounded with black hair like her mother's, and have seven
inches of stiff prick up it! Her mother's hair was black, and she had
a moustache.

Again a row. "Not there Monsieur, — l'autre côté." "It's full
God damn it, — I am not going to shit myself," said a man in
English. "Vous ne pouvez pas entrer," — but he would. A big
Englishman — a common man — pushed the woman in charge
aside, and bolted the door muttering. "Damned fool, — does she
think I'm going to shit myself!" He tore down his trowsers, and
I moved away, but heard him let fly before he had sat on the seat
(he had the squitters), and muttering to himself, he buttoned up
and left. I heard him wrangling with the woman in charge.

Instantly two young ladies entered, — sisters seemingly, and
English, — nice fresh-looking girls, both quite fair. One pulled up
her clothes. "Oh! I can't sit down, — what a beastly place, — what
beasts those French are," said she, — "dirty beasts, — call the
woman, Emily." Emily looked outside. "I can't see her, — make
haste, or the train will be leaving." "I can't sit down." "Get on the

seat as those dirty French do, and I'll hold your petticoats up. Take care now, — take care."

"I shall get my feet in it," said she. "No you won't." She stood fronting me, and pulling up her petticoats till they looked as if tied round her waist in a bundle, showing every part from her motte, to her knees, (my eye just at the level of her bum), and saying, "Don't look and laugh" — but laughing herself, she got on the seat. A prettily-made creature, not stout, nor thin, with a cunt covered with light-brown hair. She squatted. I saw the bum-hole moving. "I can't do it like this," she cried, "with all this nastiness about me, — are my clothes falling down?" "No, — make haste, — you won't have another opportunity for two hours." Out and in went the anus again, the pretty fair-haired quim was gaping, the piddle began to fall. She wanted to piddle badly enough. I said aloud in my excitement at seeing her beauty, "Cunt, cunt."

The girl got upright, I could now only see half her legs. "Hish! did you hear?" said she. Both were silent. "It must be the woman in the next place." "It sounded like a man." Then she spoke in a whisper. "No it can't be." She squatted again laughing. "It's no one." Her evacuations dropped and off she got. "You go, Mary," said the other. "I only want to pee, and I'll do it on the floor." "The dirty creatures, why don't they keep the place clean?" Squatting I watched her face. It was all I could see then, and suppose she pissed. I only saw her hitch up her clothes, but nothing more.

Then the closet-woman came, and wiped the seat grumbling, women opened the door whilst she was doing so, then others came in, and for half an hour or so, I saw a succession of buttocks, fat and thin, clean and dirty, and cunts of all colours. I have told of all worth noting. The train went off, and all was quiet. I had again diarrhœa, and what with evacuating, the belly-ache, and frigging excitement, felt so fatigued that I was going away. As I opened the door the woman was just putting the key in. She started back as she saw me.

"Are you ill?" she said. "Yes." "What a time you have staid, — why did you not go?" Then all at once, as if suspecting something, she began looking at the backs of the women's closets, and found the hole, and looking half smiling, half angry, "You made that," said she. "No." "Yes you did." I declared I had not. "Ah! méchant, — méchant," said she (looking through the hole), and something

about the chef de la gare. "You have been peeping through." "Certainly." I was so excited, so full of the adventure, that I had been
bursting to tell some one, and talk the incident over. So in discreet
words I told her about the man, and the woman, and her letters,
and other incidents, till she was amused, and laughed. Then spite
of my illness my lust got strong as I looked at her, for she had a
cunt. She was a coarse sun-tanned, but fine stout sort of tall peasant
woman about thirty-five years old. So I told her of the pretty little
splits, and nice bums I had seen, all in select language. And I so
longed, Madame. "Oh! if I had had them in here." "Ah! no doubt."
"Or if you had been here, for I wished for you." "For me? — ah! ah!"
— and she slapped both her thighs and laughed. "Mais je suis
mariée, moi, — ah! méchant, — méchant." "Here is another five
francs, but I must have a kiss." She gave it seemingly much flattered.
I said I should come the next day. "Ah! non!" she must tell the
Chef, it was her duty, — it would be useless if I came for that hole.

We talked on. She was the wife of a workman who it seems
travelled up and down the line almost continually with officers of
the railway, and only came home about once a week, or ten days.
She had no children. Whilst talking my diarrhœa came on. My
paper was gone, she produced some from her pocket, and simply
turned her back whilst I eased myself (the enclosure had no door),
as if it was the most natural thing in the world. Finally after saying
that she would not dare to let me in the next day, yet on a promise
of ten francs she said she would, and volunteered the information,
that by an early train many farmers' wives would probably arrive
for the market, that many would come by the line just opened. She
must report the hole to the Chef, — it might cost her her place if
she did not, and it would be stopped. I kissed her again, and
whispered in her ear, "I wish I had seen you sitting, and that you
had come in here afterwards." "Ah! mon Dieu que vous êtes
méchant," she replied laughing, and looking lewedly in my eyes
and I went off. I had been there hours.

I took my luggage back to the hotel, eat, got refreshed, went
early to bed, awakened quite light and well, and got early to the
station. She was awaiting me and directly I approached, took no
notice of me, but opened the door, looked in, closed it and walked
away. I guessed what the game was, loitered about till no one was
on that side, then slipped into the shed, the door of which she had

left ajar. Soon after in she came, and gave me the key. "No one is likely to come," said she. "It's only the Chef and Sous-Chef whom the seat was made for, and now they have new closets on the other side of the railway; but if they should, say that you saw the door open, and wanting the cabinet used it." Then off she went, but not till I had kissed her, and asked her to go and sit on the women's seat. I found the peep-hole plugged up, and could not push the plug out. I hesitated, fearing to make a noise; but hearing a woman there, my desire to see cunt overcame all scruples. With my penknife I pointed a piece of wood, applied it to the plug, and taking off my boot to lessen the noise, hit it hard with the heel, and at length out tumbled the plug. I expect it fell down the seat-hole.

Two well-to-do French peasants came in. One got on to the seat, and to my annoyance shit and farted loudly, both talking whilst stercoratious business was going on, as if they had been eating their dinner together. She had huge flappers to her cunt, — an ugly sight. The next pissed only, and I was rewarded by a sight of a full-fledged one, and a handsome backside. One had a basket of something for the market which they discussed. One said they must give the caretaker a halfpenny, and they evidently thought that a great grievance. What had they been in the habit of doing in such necessities previously I wonder. One said she would take care not to pay it again. The closet accommodation at railways in France was at that time of a very rough primitive kind, seats had not long been introduced.

For half an hour all the women were of that class, many quite middle-aged. More women came into that privy, than into the others I could hear. (I had given the keeper the ten francs.) They were mostly full-grown, and had thickly dark-haired cunts. Almost all the women mounted the seats, some pissed over the seat as they squatted. I was tired of seeing full-grown cunts, disliked seeing the coarser droppings, and left the peep-hole weary, but the cunts took me back there.

Two sweet-looking peasant girls came in together, they must have been about fourteen or fifteen years old only, and both had slight dark hair on their cunts. When they had eased themselves they stood and talked. One pulled her petticoats up to her navel, the other stooped and looked at her cunt, and seemed to open it, then the other did similarly. They spoke in such low tone, and in patois, that I did not understand a word they said. Both girls wore silk handkerchiefs on their heads, had dark blue stockings and white chemises. They were beautifully formed little wenches, and I longed for them with intense randiness, but restrained myself from frigging, determining to find a woman somewhere to fuck, and I felt again an overwhelming desire to tell some woman of the sights I was witnessing.

I missed a good deal of the talk when women were together, owing at times to noise in the station; yet the women who came by express trains talked very loudly, nearly always. They seemed in a scuffle of excitement, ran in, eased themselves, and ran out quickly; and if two together, spoke as if they had not the slightest suspicion of being overheard. [Travellers were not so cautious or particular as they now are.]

CHAPTER XVII

The lady's drawers. — Weary of peeping. — With the closet-keeper. — She consents. — The mail-train in. — A rush for the closets. — Piddlers in succession. — The knowing one. — A mother and daughters. — The closet-keeper again. — Connubial habits. — An ugly backside. — Two Americans. — The closet-keeper's anxiety. — In the woods. — "C'est une sale putain." — Punished for peeping. — Unpleasant reminiscences. — A young lady recognized.

No one had yet noticed the peep-hole, though so large. The women seemed mostly in a hurry, pulled up their petticoats, and turned their rumps to the seat directly they had shut the door. At length a splendid, big, middle-aged woman came in, and was most careful in bolting the door, then turning round towards the seat, she lifted her clothes right up, and began feeling round her waist. I wondered what she was at. She was unloosing her drawers. She was dressed in silk, had silk stockings on, and lace-edged drawers [drawers were only then just beginning to be worn by ladies]. Peeping out from between the drawers every now and then was the flesh, but nothing more suggesting what was behind.

Apparently unable to undo them, she broke the fastening with both hands, and the drawers fell down to her knees. What a pair of lovely thighs she had, but I only saw even those for a second, for her petticoats fell. She disengaged her limbs from the drawers, pulling the legs one by one over her boots, rolled up the drawers tightly, and put them into her pocket. Then pulling up her petticoats as she stood sideways I had a glimpse for a second of a splendid bum, and the edge of the hairy darkness. Then she dropped them, stood still and looked. I felt sure she was looking at the hole, and drew back. When I looked again the hole was plugged with paper. I did not move it till I heard she had gone.

Although now growing tired of seeing backsides, and cunts gaping in the attitude in which cunts look the least attractive; yet I felt annoyed at missing the sight of this lady's privates, and could scarcely restrain myself from pushing the paper through. I thought she told the closet-woman, for I saw that woman look in directly she had left.

For a full hour I then saw nothing. I had not heard a train, and looked at my watch. It had stopped. I peeped out of the shed-door, saw no one, went out, put my head round the corner, and saw the care-taker knitting in the shade. She saw and followed me at my beckoning. The train had not arrived, it was one hour behind time.

She came into the shed. "Talk low," said she, "for some one may be there and hear." I told her of the lady and her drawers. She said the lady had told her of the hole. We both laughed, she called me, "Sale, — méchant," but did not stop my kissing her. I got more free, and from hinting got to plain descriptions. She took no offence. I told her of the two girls looking at each other's cunts, that I longed to be kissing one of them; that the sight of their pretty slits made me long to have one of them (I used chaste words). "Or both," said she. "I'd sooner have you, for I like plenty of hair." In the half-light I saw her eyes looking full into mine. She laughed heartily, but stifled the noise, and I was sure that she felt lewed. I kissed her, and pinched her. "What fine breasts you have." Then her bum. "Laissez-moi donc." Then my hands went lower. "My God let me feel your cunt." "Hish! talk low," said she. The next minute I was feeling her cunt. "What hair, — delicious, — ah! foutre, — faisons l'amour." But she coquetted. "Now don't, — if any one should come, — I won't," — whilst gently I edged her up against the side of the shed, one hand full on her cunt all the while. "You must not, — mais non." Then out came my prick, and she felt it. Another minute's dalliance. "Let me put the key in the door," said she, "and then no one can let himself in." She did, and in another minute standing up against the shed, we were fucking energetically. Didn't she enjoy it!

We had just finished when we heard the train-signals, and off she went. "Come back." "Yes, yes presently." Down to the peep-hole I dropped, holding my prick in my hand; there already was a cunt pissing in front of me. English I guessed, for she was half sitting on the seat. Then for half an hour was a succession of backsides and quims, mainly English and Americans (a first-class train only). I knew them by face and dress, and nice linen, and because they nearly all sat or half-sat on the seat, whilst others mounted it. I wished my country-women had mounted also, to enable me to see their privates better. They nearly all piddled only. There was a restoration at the station. Nearly every woman of other nationalities shitted, they wanted I guessed, full value for their ten centimes.

Another woman plugged the hole with paper, a knowing one who did it the moment she entered the privy. I pushed it away directly she had left, she grunted much, and was a long time there.

Then I saw the cunts of an English mother and four daughters, just as the train was ready to go. They had from what they said been eating and only just came in time. The girls looked from fourteen to twenty years of age, the mother not forty.

Luckily some one before must have fouled the seat. The mother entered first with the youngest. "Stop dear," said she in a nice quiet voice, "the seat is filthy." She opened the door, put her head out, and I expect called the woman. Returning, "Get on to the seat dear." "How Mamma?" "I'll show you," and she got up, but daintily hid her limbs from her child. "Look the other way dear." The girl turned her back, and then she pulled up her clothes, and I saw the maternal quim and piddle. Then she helped the girl up. "I'll tell Clara what to do," said the mother, "take care of your clothes dear," and she left the privy. The girl did take care, and showed her nice little bum and unfledged cunt charmingly. Piss only again thank God.

The other girls entered afterwards. Each smiled as she mounted. Would they have smiled, had they known my eye was so near their bum-holes? Piddle only. Then the fourth followed and piddled. The train moved off, directly they had left.

The care-taker soon came round to the shed. I told her all, talked baudy, soon at her I went, we fucked, and after our privates had separated we talked. There would not be another train for some hours, she usually went home to dinner, any one could go to the closets then without paying. I wanted to go home with her, but she refused it. She would be there at *** o'clock, an hour before

the *** p.m. train. Yes on her honour. I gave her a louis. "How
good you are," said she. She was surprised. I had promised her
nothing for fucking her. We both wanted that, and therefore did
it, — that is all.

I went to my hotel, eat and drank, and before the time, let
myself into the shed with a key she had given me. She came back
early, and dropped her eyes. She was a stout woman with large
waist and haunches, a sturdy, plump, well-fed peasant with good
eyes, and bronzed cheeks, a good bit of flesh for a fuck. I wonder
how I had cheek to attack her for all that. Now however I had felt
her hard buttocks, and in my randiness her cunt had seemed divine.
I had whilst waiting, pulled down a dusty, long, cushioned seat
from the miscellaneous heap of things, and we sat down on it. I
began feeling her. "Let me see your cunt." "Haven't you seen
enough women's?" "No I must see yours." "Tell me about the two
girls again, — I think I know them," she said. On being asked I
told her, and a lot more. "Que vous êtes méchant, you men, — do
you so like looking at women when they are doing caca?" "No I did
not, — I could not bear it, — but their thighs, their lovely round
bums, their cunts, anything to see those parts, — I will see yours,"
I got her to stand up; and then with the modesty like that of a
newly-married woman permitting her husband, she let me see. It
was not a bit in the manner of a harlot. I looked at her wet quim in
the dim light, and soon we fucked again.

Then we questioned each other. What she had to say was soon
told. Her husband had for many years held his post, he was here,
there, and everywhere, and came home once a week if lucky, but
generally once in ten days, and then had an entire day to himself.
She had the post of privy-opener given her, because of her husband,
and made more money than he did though only in pennies. It would
be a good deal more now, if they let her have it all, for there would
be more trains, but they would divide it, for there were to be
closets on both sides. "Then you only get fucked (not mincing words
now), once in ten days." "That's about it," said she laughing. "You
long for him to come home?" "That's true." Just then we heard
some one in the privy. I looked, she would not, and went off with
a moistened quim to attend to the people. A train was coming in.

Back came she afterwards, and we talked for two hours. My

cock was ready. I laid her on the form, and straddling across the seat, and holding her legs up across my arms, entered her quim. But she nearly fell off the seat, it was so narrow; so again up against the wood-work, we copulated. She was well grown, so it was not difficult. She took to the fucking, as if I had a right to it, and she liked it, but I always disliked uprighters.

Again we sat down and talked. "You won't want your husband now." "He comes home to-morrow," and she showed me a little scrap of dirty writing-paper with, "On Tuesday" written on it, and a mark at the bottom with a date. "That's his mark," said she, "he can't write, — I've been frightened to-day, for sometimes he comes without writing, — I'm here to meet him." We then kissed each other. "You are very handsome," she said. "You are beautiful," said I. "Am I really?" "Yes, and fuck divinely." "Do I really?" said she in a most flattered manner.

"Directly he comes he fucks you here?" "He's never been in here in his life, but he makes love directly he gets into our rooms," she replied in a quiet tone, as if she'd been telling a doctor her ailments. Still we sat and talked. The shed had been only built for storing things quite temporarily, the privy was for the Chef, but it had not been used by any one for some time. The hole in the wood could not have been there long. How made, she knew not. She must have noticed it, had it been there long, for she washed the seats continually. Holes were often made by men in the sides next the women's closets, they bored holes to look at the women, she wondered "pourquoi mon Dieu," why they wanted to see women, when they were doing their nastiness?

Again through the peep-hole I saw such a nasty, dirty, frowsy, beshitten backside, and the chemise of an oldish-rabbit-arsed female, that a disgust which had been gradually intensifying, made me indifferent to seeing any more, and females came and went without my even looking. I now sat on the cushioned though dirty form comfortably (before I could only sit on the privy-seat), waiting for the privy-woman to come back. But curiosity still got the better of me. An express train came in with English and Americans, and I looked. People who come by train are always in a hurry, sometimes they have wanted to ease themselves an hour or more, and then let fly before almost they get their breeches down, or their petti-

coats up, very often indeed they let fly at random over the seat.
Then those following them finding the seat dirty, mount it to avoid
fouling their clothes.

"It's beastly," I heard in a high pitched American tone. Two
nice, young, shortish girls, were there. "Let's go to the next one."
"There is some one there, — there is not time, — get on the seat."
Up got the girl with her face towards me. "Not so Fanny, — turn
round stupid." "I can't, — this will do," said Fanny, and pissed out
of a dear little cunt covered with lightish brown hair, set in delicious
buttocks. I put my eye close to the hole, and the piddle spashed into
it, for she peed on to the back of the seat, and how she wanted it!
"Make haste Fanny." "Oh! I did want so, — I've not done it all day."
Then up got the other in other fashion, close to my peep-hole, and
watered! In shape of bum, thigh, and cunt the two were as like as
two pins, pretty, fleshy little bums, round little thighs, plump as a
partridge. I was so lewed I could scarcely resist a desire to call out
to them, and say I had seen their charms. The last one turned
round when she had done, and got down. "Oh!" said she, "there is
a hole in the wall." "Oh! if — " said the other. That was all I heard,
for they quitted the privy like lightning, putting their heads together, and lowering their voices to a mumble, and talking earnestly.
Afterwards when the train had left, back came the keeper to me,
and said the young ladies had told her of the hole.

She begged me not to go there the next day, for her husband
might arrive by any train; but I did, and had her. I dined at the
hotel, and at night having nothing better to do, strolled towards
the station smoking a cigar. — The attraction of cunt I suppose did
it. She had said that she left directly after a particular train, and
some other woman took her place for night-work. There she was, —
no her husband could not arrive now till next morning. Let me go
home with her, on no account would she. Between the station and
the town were some woods being made into public gardens. Walking there against her will and in the dark, I talked lewedness to my
heart's content, and at length had her with her back up against a
tree. "Lay down, — it's quite dry," said I, and on some coarse sort
of dryish herbage, — I could not see what — I fucked for the last
time and on the top of her. We got up whispering adieu, when we
saw dimly a man and woman who began the game. She was scared
"Let me go, and you stay," said she. Just then their vigorous love-

making made a great noise. Off she went, I in a second or two followed, and overtook her. "C'est une sale putain," said she, "she has commenced coming here of a night to meet men going to the station, — it is disgraceful, — I shall inform the Chef to-morrow." Then the closet-keeper kissed me, and went off with her cunt wet, and a Napoleon which I insisted on her accepting.

The next morning I left A***, but could not keep my promise, and went to her at the station. The blood rushed into her face, she looked scared, and shook her head seemingly in a funk, and I departed by the next train.

I have often wondered at the affair, and at that woman. Had she been a whore? did she in her husband's absence usually have a bit of illicit cock? My impression is that she was steady and honest; that I caught her just when she was hot-blooded, that my doings were so baudy, that her lust was roused, and so she was helpless at my first attempt, and then having slipped, thought she might as well have all the pleasure she could. She had no children. French women don't see so much harm in an outside fuck or so. I had promised her no money, had offered no inducement whatever but my prick. It was lust which stirred lust, and we gratified each other. What more natural?

The adventure left me in an unpleasant state of mind, for I could not bear at that time anything connected with the bum-hole. With women, if I thought of that orifice, it destroyed voluptuous associations. Now I could not look at the prettiest woman without thinking of her shitting and farting. The anus came into my mind when dancing, dining, or talking and whether randy or not; and when the tingling in my prick made me look, and long for a woman, thinking what a leg she had, what thighs and quim perhaps, my mind went to her bum-hole spite of myself. I was punished heavily for my peeping. It was a year or two before my mind recovered its balance, and I was able to think of their sexual organ and its beauty and convenience without reference to its unpleasant neighbour!

One of the first I saw bogging, was a pretty shortish English girl perhaps seventeen years old, but with a backside that many a woman might have envied. She had also a lovely skin and complexion. She neither got on the seat, nor quite sat on it, but rested in a half-standing position, and turned out a light-brown turd a foot long. I saw also her hand feeling once a plump little cunt. She could not find the paper to wipe herself with, felt in a pocket, took out her handkerchief, felt again, found nothing, put her hand in her bosom, took out a letter, and after opening it, tore off a piece about three inches square, replaced the letter in her breast, and wiped her bum with the torn fragment.

When I got back to my hotel that day, the first female I saw was the young lady. I could not keep my eyes off her. She was a sweet-looking creature; but all that I could think of, was that great turd. I thought of it till mad with myself, I left the table, and got out of her way.

Fortunately the greatest number only piddled, — I shall always like to see a female at that function. The attraction to the peep-hole was of course to see the hidden charms, the fat round buttocks, the lovely columns of flesh which support them, the split, the love-seat, the seat of pleasure, the cage for the cock, the cunt, that mysterious aperture leading to the organs in which a future human being is formed and secreted, and to which man gives life by fucking, — fucking, that divine orgasm, that creator which ought to be praised daily in our prayers and hymns, and which a false refinement (born of lewedness) calls indecent and beastly, if it be alluded to.

[At this time I had already written much of my early life. This episode of the temple of Cloacina dwelt so much in my mind, that although I disliked it, yet at the first hotel which I stopped at for a few days afterwards, I wrote this out, and a great deal more. I recollected the face, form and performances of every woman I had seen; but the repetition of similitudes was wearisome, and I obliterated quite one half, if not more. I had doubts if I should not omit the whole, but a secret life should have no omissions. There is nothing to be ashamed of, it was a passing phase, and after all man cannot see too much of human nature.]

CHAPTER XVIII

A Grand-Duchess. — At the town of C**s*l. — Travelling with a friend. — Early morning. — A peep through a key-hole. — A big woman and bed. — Naked. — Making up her mind. — Titillation. — Hesitation. — Masturbation. — On the bidet. — Frigging again. — Who is she? — At M****n. — On outskirts of the town. — In search of a harlot. — The beer-garden. — The peasant woman. — A drink and a wink. — A kiss and a feel. — A talk and a walk. — The cottage. — Nein, nein. — Brown legs and white thighs. — A flaxen motte. — Both gratified.

Some time after this, I was travelling for a while with a friend, a rich but mean old man. We arrived at the dull, out-of-the-way though renowned old town of C**l, in Germany. We saw the Palace and grounds one day, and rose at day-break the next morning, intending to post to *** before the heat of the day. I was in a big room, the bed was in the corner against the wall. On the opposite side of the room was a door communicating with the adjoining room. For a wonder I had never thought of looking through the key-hole when I went to bed. When I arose I did, and saw (it was quite light, though the outer-blinds were partly closed) a big room with two windows, and between them a large wash-hand-stand and looking-glass over it. On the further side, and placed in similar position to mine against a wall was a bed, and in it a woman with dark hair. The door between us no doubt was locked, the key was in the door on *her* side; but so turned that it left a large hole through which I saw with ease the whole side of the room next the windows and the bed in which she laid. I was delighted, and in my night-shirt, put a pillow on the floor, knelt on it, my eye to the hole, and watched the woman, my heart beating with excitement, and dreading each moment that she would turn the key, and stop my view. The whole spectacle I shall never forget.

Seemingly she had just awakened. She put hers arms out, laid a moment still, then threw the clothes off of her, on to the side of the bed next the wall, as if too hot (it was a sultry morning). Her night-dress had rucked up all round her waist, and exposed her naked limbs, and I saw the hair of her quim sticking up, though she was laying on her back. Then she turned on her right side, and laid her head on her arm, her naked buttocks being then towards me, — and a big pair they were. Thus she laid such a time, that I thought she must be asleep, so rose, and began to dress myself, but fear of losing a sight soon made me cease. Looking again, she had moved on to her back, and soon turned on to her side, facing me, and I saw she was a middle-aged woman, strongly and big built, with a mass of dark hair at the bottom of her belly. For a minute or two she turned about restless, then put one knee up, and felt her quim, and lying on her back kept her hand between her thighs so long, that I thought she was frigging; but she took it away, looked at the finger which had been on her quim, and got up, drew up the blind nearest to her bed, looked out for a minute (the windows were closed); then stepped back, slipped off her night-gown, threw it on the bed, and stood start naked, pulled out the pot from the bedside-stand, and pissed, got up, looked out of the window again, and then looked at herself in the large looking-glass, cleaned her teeth, then walked back (start naked still), and sat down by the side of the bed, felt her cunt again, left off, and after sitting quite quiet (for a minute I suppose) looking on the floor as if reflecting, reclined on the bed, and putting both hands under her head on the pillow, lay on her back naked, showing a black armpit, and so for some minutes. Then again a knee went up, and a hand went to her cunt. "She is frigging herself now," I thought, and perhaps she was. But she ceased directly, got up, and after putting on her night-dress, got into bed again, and rang a bell. She had gone out of my sight in the room, I suppose to unlock the door.

She looked five feet ten high, and say between thirty-five and forty years old, with massive thighs and big arse, dark hair and eyes, thick dark hair on her cunt, and dark masses in her armpits, her breasts were large, hanging and flopping about.

Then I heard her say something in German, and a female

servant came in, who drew the other blind, and opened the jalousies of both windows. A flood of light came in, but no sunshine. Then she brought in coffee, and gave a cup to the lady in the bed. I heard a man's voice as I thought in the lobby, and looked through my door. It was a man-servant. Just then out came the female servant, and I heard both were Germans. The female went back to the room, and I to the key-hole. Then the servant came straight towards the door that I was peeping through. "She will stop it up," thought I. But I was wrong, she only took up some articles of female clothing, and there must have been a sofa, or bed, or table on that side of the door and close to it, for to my disgust as she put it down, it blocked my view. I heard the two women talking, and the servant say in German, "Your Grace." Looking again through the key-hole a minute or two after, it was clear. I expect the apparel, or whatever it was, had sunk down, or been moved. The servant went out I think into an adjacent room, the lady got out of bed, and sat on its side drinking her coffee, again looked out the window, again dropped her night-gown off as if hot, and stood naked to cool herself; came up to the glass, looked at herself, turning all round as if admiring herself, then to the bed, sat down on the edge as if thinking, and again laid down lazily, first putting up one leg, and letting the other rest on the floor. Then putting the other up, she began whilst lying on her back, to feel her cunt quietly, and then frig herself vigorously.

There was no mistake now. The right hand with which she was operating was the furthest from me, but I saw it half hidden in the cunt-wig and shaking with the unmistakable frigging motion. She was some time at it. A length I saw her thighs moving restlessly, one went up, then down again, then the other, the knees opened and shut, then her buttocks gave two or three wriggles, just as she might have done had she been fucking. Then all was quiet, and she turned on her side away from me, giving the sheet a tug which just sent it carelessly over her back and shoulders, leaving her arse and thighs fully exposed, and must have gone to sleep. A full hour must have elapsed since I first saw her in bed, I looked and looked from time to time, fancied I saw black hair up the chink of her arse-cheeks, but don't now know if it were fancy or not. She was hairy enough elsewhere to have had hair round her arse-hole.

My friend knocked at the door, and asked if I was ready for

breakfast, — when should he order the carriage? I wished him at the devil, but was obliged to talk with him, determined not to miss seeing all I could of the lady. So I told him not to order it at all, that I had been up all night, and much wanted an hour's sleep. I could not get rid of him, he would keep at the door (I holding it ajar) for some minutes. Should he get me anything? would I have some coffee? — he would have it with me in my room, — and so on. At length he went away, I saying I would be down in a couple of hours. Then back to the key-hole I went; there still she lay. I dressed, peeping at intervals, but for a long time she never moved. When I looked again she had seemingly just got up and was putting the piss-pot back. Then she went up to a bidet which the maid had uncovered, and put water in, and straddling across it, sluiced her cunt and rubbed it dry with a towel, and afterwards, began washing her neck and face. That done she put on her night-gown, the maid came in again, and the lady sitting down in front of the glass, the maid dressed her hair.

That took a long time. I grew tired of looking, so finished dressing and packing my trunk, but peeping at intervals. The maid put on the lady's slippers or shoes, and left the room, for I heard her outside my room talking. The lady again took off her night-dress and walked about naked, then took up a pair of stockings which were on the bed or table near my peep-hole and seemed to be comparing them with some dress or petticoat, went back near to the bed, and sat in a large armchair which was there, took off her stockings and put on the other pair, then put on her chemise, sat in the arm-chair, and put her fingers on to her cunt. She was now facing me, she put one thigh over the arm of the chair, and I saw the split. She felt it only for about a minute, twiddling it gently with her finger, and then laying herself on the bed again, her chemise on now, she frigged as hard as she could. Directly after she began to dress herself, and the maid came in.

I could not stay longer from my friend, besides the lady was dressed, and a fine big woman she looked. Off my friend and I drove. When we had got some distance he told me that the Grand-Duchess Stephanie of *** with her suite had arrived the night previously. He described her as a big, fine, dark woman, and so on. "I should like much to see her," I said, "let's go back and leave to-morrow, — it will be all the same to us." He would not, and to this day I don't know whether it was the Grand-Duchess or her sister the Princess of ***, or one of the ladies of honour, whom I saw frigging herself twice, but it was one of them. I did not tell my friend, keeping such little adventures to myself, but when in the middle of a hot day our Lohnkutscher rested his horses, and we had luncheon, my friend went to sleep, and I rushed round the streets of the town to find a baudy house. I could not, but I found a stout peasant woman who seemed to have been working in the fields. She had nothing of the appearance of gaiety, but I fucked her twice on a poor bedstead in a cottage with a tile floor, thinking of the frigging Duchess all the time. Then on we went to our evening's destination.

I first saw the woman sitting down outside a beer-garden on the outskirts. I was in a sweat with walking and randiness combined, and had a tankard of beer. I looked at her, and she at me. I asked her to have some. She accepted, and had two huge glasses full. She said, "Thank you Your Grace," and walked away. She had some field implement in her hand, but I don't know what. I followed and talked imperfectly in German with her. When she came to a cottage, one of two in a lane (one cottage had no roof on, and was empty). I said, "It's hot, — let me sit down." She nodded, and in I went. I had been looking at her as we came along, and she looked to me handsome; but in my lewed state, perhaps any woman would have looked handsome to me.

She had flaxen hair, and a highly sun-burnt face and lightish eyes. The impetuosity of lust alone often carries a man to his goal. I gave her a kiss. "Nein, nein," said she, and what else I don't know, till I found my hand on a wettish cunt, and the next minute was up her. I had closed the door. She lay quite quietly with my prick in her, till I uncunted it, so expect she had spent. Then without saying a word she opened the door, went to the road, and looked up and down it.

As she did not come back I looked out. She was pulling about some chemises and women's linen which were on some bushes, and some on a line. She saw me, turned away her head, and kept going from linen to linen, and turning it over in the sun, looking furtively to see every now and then if I was looking after her. She had no shoes and stockings on. Until then I had not noticed that — if she had had no arms, I expect I should not have cared — cunt, cunt,

cunt was just then all in all. I called her. She shook her head, her
back was towards me, then again she looked up and down the road,
and came to me at the door saying, "Aren't you going?" I pulled
her in. "Nein, nein," said she again, "oh! nein," — and a lot more
in German. I gave my cock a frig, and it stuck out stiff from my
trowsers. I shook it at her. "Oh! nein, nein," but she laughed.

I pulled her towards the bed, of straw I think, though on it
was clean, coarse, home-made linen, and pushed her back to see
her cunt, but she got on to the bed. I saw the dust-stained dirty
feet gradually merge into ankle and calf of a deep mahogany brown,
and then the calf gradually grow whiter and whiter, till her thighs
showed up as white as snow. Obstinately she pushed down her
clothes to prevent me seeing her cunt, and I did not. I dare say it
did not look too inviting with my spendings about its flaxen-colored
hair, for I could pretty well guess its colour. So I dropped on to
her, and fucked right off. "Sein Sie schnell!" said she, liking the
exercise, and murmured out her ecstacy in German. I then buttoned
up as quickly as I could, and gave her I think a Thaler. "Ich danke
Ihrer Höheit, — oh! thank you," said she, seizing my hand and
kissing it. And we parted.

What made that woman let me have her? She was not a gay
woman, that is certain. It might have been money, but I never
offered her any, though I gave her some when my pleasures were
over. Was she flattered by my wanting her, — "Your Grace?" —
was it my civility in giving her beer? — was she randy when I met
her? Many a modest-looking woman has a randy cunt when no one
knows it but herself. Did I make her randy by my advances? — I
know she spent. Was she married I wonder, — there was male linen
about.

Many a time since when I have seen German peasant women
working in the fields, stooping, jutting out their bums, their thick
brown naked ankles and feet showing under their petticoats, have
I thought of the German woman I fucked, and her white thighs and
brown legs, and wondered if the other women's were as white.

At night we got to the town of ***, and my companion went
to bed. Then out I went, and seeking a baudy house, emptied what
remained of my semen into one or two cunts, for the frigging
spectacle in the morning had thoroughly roused me and I could
think of nothing else. A voluptuous sight at that time remained in

my mind for weeks. I thought of it when my prick was in a woman, even if one of the loveliest. I delighted in taking a woman into my confidence, and telling her what I had seen, and when my body was joined to hers, the recollection coming over me, would suddenly fetch my sperm before I wanted it. At the time I speak of I was travelling easily from place to place, without trouble or worry, eating, drinking, and living in the open air, and getting the chance of women every three or four days only. Then I could fuck them every two hours comfortably, and even five times in a night, but never more. Three times was my usual number, twice at night, and if I slept with them, once again in the morning. I did nothing, or but rarely anything to exhaust myself, and was always ready for a woman. What a delightful time it was. Soon after I returned to England.

CHAPTER XIX

Clapped, and reflexions thereon. — Change in taste for condition of pudenda. — Change again. — Later on in life. — On bricks in a hail-shower. — An unknown quarter. — A little lady. — "You can't come home." — The bricks. — The hail-stone. — A canny police-man. — A servant for a change. — Sexual charms of servants. — Catherine. — A stumble on the stairs. — A well-timed visit. — Un-chaste questions, and chaste replies. — Preliminaries. — Consum-mation. — Ugly stockings. — The dining-room table.

Then I again took the ladies' fever, and was again obliged to have recourse to surgical appliances to keep my urethra open. This suggested some serious reflexions, and in a degree modified my habits with women in one particular.

I had delighted in a cunt with its natural juices in it, and dis-liked one recently washed. I could find out one when too clean, though I could not detect one which had been recently washed and rinsed with astringents as well. I did not know much about the chemical aids ladies used, though I had heard of such things, indeed had heard of most things, and have put into cunts which felt to me like a nutmeg grater, though I then did not know the cause. The extreme delicacy and sensitiveness of my prick-tip made me 1 expect discriminating, and susceptible of sexual pleasure in the highest degree; and I had found that it was greater in a cunt in its natural state of slimy lubricity. Hence my choice of that condition.

Now thinking it would give me greater immunity from clap, I became very careful in investigating, and insisted on the ample washing of every cunt before I took cock-exercise. I began to look at cunts carefully, even after washing, and before I would put into them; but either my gland had become less sensitive, or what is more likely looking at my age, that my lust was so strong and impetuous, that I did not after the washing mark the difference in the lubricity, excepting at times.

About this time also, I cannot tell why, I became indifferent to looking at the cunts, and especially at the overflow of what I had left in coition up those paphian chambers. I had even at times a dislike to looking, and would withdraw my prick from her into my hand, roll off the lady, and turn my head away from her quickly. All this was so entirely contrary to what had been my custom, that it is worth noting as illustrative of my character and taste in sexual matters, from time to time during my life.

[After some years my sensitiveness returned. I had really never lost it, and I reverted to my former taste in this particular of copulation. Lubrication, and even an excess of lubrication, of the right sort, became absolutely needful to my pleasure. I add this now before it goes to press, and many years after the foregoing was written.]

The next thing which happened to me and is worth telling, was quite early in spring. I was going home from a party just at midnight. At the junction of two streets I saw a very little woman, bidding a man good night, and kissing him in the street. It was done quite in a modest, affectionate way. I passed them. A few seconds afterwards I heard the feet of the lady coming quickly after me. She seemed to be pretty as she passed me by a street-lamp. She took no notice of me, but I hailed her, for I was lewed. "My dear I wish you would give me a kiss like the other man." She looked round and laughed, but walked on. I saw she was game. "I'll give you a glass of wine for a kiss." "How much is that?" said she. "A shilling." "Give it," said she stopping. "Then you will let me have a feel," said I. "You want enough for a shilling," — and she went off quickly. "Stop, — don't run off, — half-a-crown." She laughed, hesitated, and then we turned down a side-street, and up against a wall I felt her cunt. I had to stoop to get at it, she was so short.

I was just in the mood for a woman, and enjoyed the feel. It was a tight little cunt, and a young one I knew from the small quantity of hair on it. I felt it for two or three minutes, whilst she remained quite quiet. "I'll frig you," said I, "here is the money."

She took it. "Let me feel your cock then," said she. So I turned
half round, took her round the waist conveniently and began frigging, and she laid hold of my prick which had got quite stiff, and
which I had just extruded from my trowsers. "I shall come soon,"
said she, "do it to me, — let's go to some house, and do me properly,
— oho! leave off! — I shall spend, — let's go somewhere," — and
she pushed my hand away. Just then came near to us a policeman.
I dropped my great-coat over my cock, and let fall her petticoats.
He must have known what we were about, but took no notice. "A
preciously cold night," said I to him. "Aye it is, sir." "Here is a
shilling for a glass when you're off duty." He thanked me, and was
soon out of sight round the corner, never looking back.

It was a bitterly cold night, though not freezing. The wind
was blowing a gale and dark clouds most of the time hid what moon
there was; but it showed every two or three minutes for half a
second, and then all was quite dark again. The streets were deserted, the public-houses closed. I began frigging her again, again
she felt my prick unasked by me, again she suggested my having
her. "I don't want a poke," I said, "and I've no more money." "Never
mind the money, — let's fuck," said she randily. I began to want
to put my prick up her, but didn't much like risking it, so I ceased
frigging her, and with resolution drew my cock away from her
fingers, for she was manipulating it very rapidly, and dropped my
great-coat over my open trowsers. "Why won't you?" said she. It
was all she said.

I walked on with her to a lamp-post, stopped under it, and
looked well at her. She I then saw was very pretty, and I began to
long for her. "I'll go home with you, — is it far?" "Oh! you can't
go home with me." "Go to a house then." "I don't know one, I have
only just come to live at this side of the water, — don't you know
one?" I was out of my beat, and did not know a house. The more
I talked and looked at her, the more randy I got. "I'll bet the man
you kissed has been home with you." She laughed out. "Well that's
true enough, but he is my brother." It had struck me from the
manner in which it was done, that it was not a fucking-friend she
had kissed.

Nearly close by where we were standing they were rebuilding
the front garden-wall of an empty house. Bricks were stacked
against it in the street, a heap of rubbish was close by the bricks.

"Let's fuck here," said I. We were both a little timid, but the place seemed deserted, so we tried. Her back was against the wall, but so short was she; that though I bent my knees, and she almost tiptoed, I could not get into her. My prick when I bent it down ran past her cunt towards her bum-furrow.

Then I moved her nearer to the empty house, pulled down three or four bricks from the edge of the stack, and placed others, so as to leave a good footing and level, and which stood her up six inches or so (a convenient height), and we fucked with much gratification. She was very randy, so was I, and we were soon in sexual ecstasy.

Whilst fucking, huge hail-stones, as big as filberts, began to fall. They rattled on my hat, hitting hard, and bounding off on to the pavement. Suddenly I felt a chill at the root of my prick-stem. "Oh!" said I as we both felt its chill. A hail-stone had got between our bodies, and stopped us for an instant, but we both guessed what it was, and finished our pleasure. The hail-stone must have just lodged between her motte and my belly; it was chilly and melting, and still held in the mingled hair of our privates when I pulled my prick out of her. A hundred thousand people might have been fucking in the open that night, without such a thing happening to them. It amused both of us mightily. "Nobody would believe it if I told them," said she. "Nor if I do," said I, "but I shall tell some one." "So shall I," she remarked laughing.

Still we talked together. She had been gay she said, but had been kept by a commercial traveller for a year — a good fellow. They had only just come to live up there. The landlady thought they were married. Of course she could not take me home, besides her friend might return. He was in the woollen trade, and was often away a week or ten days, she never knew when he might return. He knew her brother well. He had now been away ten days, and she hadn't been fucked for that time. She was lewed, and she wanted it, but if any body had told her half an hour ago, that she was going to do it with me, she would have said they were mad. She could not tell what made her let me feel her, it certainly was not for half a crown. My voice and manner was nice, and when I felt her it made her randy at once. She had never been felt in a public street before.

Just then the policeman came round again, took no notice of

us, and passed out of sight. One solitary man passed us walking rapidly. I was getting cold standing, I kissed her. "Here is another glass of wine," said I giving her another half-crown (she had not asked me). "Thank you," said she, "every little is useful." I turned to go, and then turned back. "I should like to do you again," said I. "I'm ready," said she, "come on, — let me piddle first, — you have made me so wet." "No don't do that." "But it's all running down my thighs." "I like that." The idea stiffened me. She mounted on the bricks again, and we had another most lovely fuck, — she was at the exact height for me. "You've enjoyed the fucking," I said. "Yes, I haven't had it for ten days." "But you have frigged yourself?" "Not once," she said, "though I sometimes do when my friend's away."

Again we talked of fucking. She seemed to like talking as much as I did. Her friend was a strong man, and did it as often to her as any woman could want. She would not give me her name or address, or say where I could meet her. She pissed, and with her hand washed her cunt with her piddle. It was possible her friend might be home when she returned, though not likely, she said. "Aren't you just a lewed man," said she as we kissed and parted. She would have let me do it again if I could. When we parted she ran off like mad, and I saw her no more. She was very nicely and quietly dressed in silk, and seemed a superior sort of person of her class. It was a most pleasing, most gratifying incident. Such accidental copulation I have always found most delicious, — and I have had scores.

Then I had had so many gay women, that I wanted a change in the class. I enjoyed their lubricity, their skilled embraces, their passionate fucking when they wanted it themselves, and liked me (I had had many such). Yet I was tired of their lies, tricks, and dissatisfied, money-grabbing, money-begging style. I wanted a change, and began to look out for a nice fresh servant. I have now had many servants in my time, and know no better companions in amorous amusements. They have rarely lost all modesty, a new lover is a treat and a fresh experience to them, even when they have had several, and few have had that. They only get the chance of copulating once a week or so, they are clean, well-fed, full-blooded, and when they come out to meet their friend, or give way with a chance man on the sly, are ready, yielding, hot-arsed, lewd, and lubricious. Their cunts throb at the first touch of a finger, and moisten, and they spend freely and copiously. No women's cunts are wetter, than a young healthy servant's is after the first fuck on her night out. No one will take more spunk out of a man, and give more herself than the lass who says, "I couldn't get out before, — I'm sorry you had to wait, — I must really get back by ten." How they kiss in silence, — how they feel the first lunge of the prick up them, — what pleasure they quietly show, — how they love you, and die as your hot spunk spurts, and their cunt liquidizes. So I longed for a servant, and soon found my chance. I suppose all men do if they set their mind upon women, for there are thousands of cunts waiting to be fed, and ready to open to opportunity and male importunity.

We were very friendly with a nice family, a widow with three daughters, living in quiet comfort at R*****. They only kept two servants. The parlor-maid was a well-grown wench about twenty-one years old, fleshy and round, dark-eyed, dark-haired, fresh-coloured and healthy-looking. She opened the street-door. She had not been there long before I tipped her a shilling occasionally, and one night kissed her at the street-door, which she took quietly. Next time I pinched her bum, she gave a suppressed squeal, and then my letch for her came on. As usual I had luck. Calling a day or two after, I made a smutty remark, and pinched her thigh outside her clothes. It was day-time, and risky.

She was flurried by it, but made no noise, and running upstairs to deliver my message to the lady in the drawing-room, her foot slipt on a loose stair-carpet, and she fell on her knees on the stairs, the carpet slipping with her, and a stair-rod rattling down. The calf of one of her legs was exposed by this nearly to her knee. This was at the bottom of the flight and close to where I was standing. I put my hand on her calf and pinched it. Recovering herself she shook her head at me, went upstairs, and came down with, "Will you walk up, sir." Up I went, whispering as I neared her, "I saw your thigh" (which was a lie). She gave me such a look as she closed the drawing-room door. On leaving I said, "I wish I had put my hand higher." She gave me a sulky look as she closed the street-door.

To get at her I took to calling frequently on my friends, and often saw Catherine, and tipped and kissed her whenever she opened the door. If sure that no one was near, I whispered smutty double entendres to set her thinking about cock and cunt, and rubbed my belly up against hers when I caught and kissed her. At length I got her to take a walk with me one Sunday night. Then being near gardens, at a quiet place I put my hands up her clothes, felt her thighs, but missed her cunt. She ran off home, I after her, but without catching her, and thinking from her manner that I had made a muddle of it.

A day after, I called at the house in the afternoon, a time the family would usually be out, taking some Devonshire cream with me as a present to the lady, but really as an excuse for calling. "Out, — are they? — this must be kept in the cool, or it will soon turn sour." "Give it me, sir," said Catherine. "No, I'll give it to the cook myself." "She's out," said Kit. Here was an unexpected chance.

"I'll write a line to Mrs. ***," said I, stepping in, and I began a note. The girl waited. When I had written it, I asked if Miss Lucy (a daughter) was in a hurry to get married (she was engaged). Kitty didn't know. "What do they marry for, Kitty?" "To be husband and wife," said she. "But what do they go to bed together for." She didn't know. "Yes you do." "Oh! don't bother." I had begun kissing, and had got her to kiss me. "They kiss, Kit, like this, and feel each other all over, and then — what do they do then?" "I don't know." "I'll tell you." "Don't want to know." "Well I won't tell, — sit down." I pulled her on to the sofa, for she had got familiar, — a woman soon does if you talk smut. We sat and chatted till my randiness made me reckless. "I'll tell you what they do when they are married, and in bed." "I won't hear." "You shall, — they fuck." I had her by the waist, and she could not escape me. She made a very slight attempt to do so, but I held her tightly whilst I let out my baudy talk.

What else I said exactly God only knows, but it was all about newly married couples. "He pulls up her night gown, feels her cunt, rubs his prick against her thigh, puts it in her cunt, &c." Kit kept saying, "I won't hear, — I won't hear," put both hands up to her ears, but did not move away from me. I pulled out my prick red hot, "That's what he shoves up her cunt, — and oh! God, don't they have pleasure, — let's put this up your cunt, Kit."

"Now don't," said she, starting up, but not moving away. I pulled her down to a sitting posture again, and with a dash got my hand up her clothes. She cried out, and put both hands down (they all do that) on to her thighs, closed her thighs on my hand, wriggled to get away and for some minutes struggled, and cried. "It's a shame, — you shan't." "Let's fuck." "I won't now, — I won't, — oh! dear," — but I exhausted her. She was half sitting, half leaning on me with my fingers pinched tightly between her thighs, so that I could not get a good feel of her cunt; but my forefinger was well between its lips and on her clitoris titillating, and making her randy. She seriously, now begging me to leave her alone, I swearing I would fuck her, give her pleasure, promising bonnets, clothes, money, and everything else, and uttering all the voluptuous words my imagination could muster.

Nature helped me. She could bear no longer the friction on her clitoris, her voice fell to a whining tone, she breathed short, "Oh! — do — now — leave off — do," she wined out in broken utterances. "Kiss me," said I, "and I will." She put her mouth to me, and kissed me excitedly. I held her head to mine, shoved my tongue in her mouth and frigged harder. With a sigh and a sob, "Oh! I c — hant — b — hear it," her thighs opened. "Oh!" she howled loudly and sharply as my finger slipped on to the prick-hole entrance. But now quite overcome with voluptuous sensations, she was nearly spending. I pressed her back on the sofa, pulling up her clothes. "Oh! don't," she said faintly. I pulled up her legs on to the sofa. "Oh! don't," but with excitement and lewdness she made no further resistance. I covered her rapidly, and with one strong lunge buried my prick up her, fucked for a minute, and spouted a deluge of hot spunk into her cunt. Just as I finished I heard her sighs of pleasure, and felt her sympathetic bum-movements.

Under the excitement of fresh cunt, I kept up Catherine a long time, laying on her, kissing, endearing, and enjoying her. At length it began to shrink, I put my fingers down to feel between our coupled genitals, and cunningly I looked at them to see if there were signs of a virginity, — there were none. "Let me get up, — oh! do." I got off her quickly, she pulled her clothes down, and sat up, I by the side of her. Both were quite quiet, I quite surprised with the quickness and ease with which I had won her person.

"Wasn't it nice? — didn't you like it?" "No," said she, "it was a shame," and she was going away, but I caught hold of her. "Let's do it again." "No, no, — oh! let me go," she cried, but she let my hands go up her clothes. I felt the sperm all over her thighs, as I thrust my hand up between them. "I must go," said she; but fiercely pushing her down without her struggling, I was soon up her, and again we fucked. She took my prick up her with the greatest pleasure. Thought I as I pulled out, she had had more than one prick there, I felt sure of that.

Nothing is so delicious as the intimacy established between man and woman by a fuck. When once he has moistened a woman's cunt with his sperm, they seem to have known each other for years. You may know a woman socially, closely; live under the same roof for years with her, know her habits, when she eats, drinks, sleeps, and piddles, and she may know as much about you; but if you are caught looking up her petticoats as she goes upstairs, there will be a row; and a hint about the make, shape, &c., of any part of her body between her ankles and armpits, must not be referred to. You really know nothing about her that is vital, and you and she are virtually strangers. A quarter of an hour before I could not feel Kitty's knee without a struggle, now I lay smoothing her backside with my hands, wriggling my shrinking prick in her, talking soft baudiness, and she lay listening to it, kissing me in return, her arse as quiet as if it were a lump of lead.

There is an end of all things. "Oh! if the cook should come back," said she, "she's no business out, and won't be long." "Damn the cook, — isn't feeling nice?" "Yes, — but let me get up." "Feel how my prick's in you, and I'll get off." She felt it. "You've got black stockings," said I, noticing them for the first time, as I once did with Mabel years ago. "Yes, — don't you like them?" "No." On the narrow sofa I could not lay by her side, so I dropped outwards, and off of her, but lewd still I put my hand on her cunt just as my prick came out of it. It was gruelly, but there was no blood. "Wash," said I. "I'm going," — and she left.

I wished to see her cunt when she had come back, I had not even had a glimpse of it. She let me feel it, still wet from the washing. I saw her thighs, her motte, but the crack she kept her thighs closed on. Then returning to the sofa, kissing, and feeling her cunt, the time passed. We talked about the family, but talked much more about fucking, that eternal subject, until I had twiddled her quim into a fever. Then tonguing her, "Let's do it again," said I. "Let me go and see to the kitchen-fire first," said she.

This took place in the dining-room. She wasn't gone long. When she came up she was a little coy. "No not again," — as she stood with her bum against the dining-table, with my hands round her thighs. "No, no, the cook may come in at any moment." But I put my hands round her bum, and lifted her up with some effort suddenly on to the table. I have done so with other women.

She fell back on it. I looked at her thighs, and in a jiffy my prick was into her. I saw the dear girl's face as she spent. "You will think of this as you lay the cloth for dinner," said I still holding her thighs over my arms, my prick still up her. The bell rang. "Oh! good gracious, it's cook." Out came my prick. "Oh! how do I look? — will she notice anything? — is my hair all right behind?" She was all right, and downstairs she ran to let the cook in.

I buttoned up, and directly almost rang the bell, and up she came. "Cook's not noticed anything," said she in a whisper. Then with the cream downstairs she went, and returned. I had a rapid feel, and went off, agreeing to meet her out on Sunday.

CHAPTER XX

Catherine at a baudy house. — My anatomical studies. — Catherine's hymen wanting. — Her explanation. — Servants in bed. — The sham-cock used. — Gamahuched. — Catherine with kid. — A charming widow. — The ball. — The cab home. — Rapid persuasion. — At J***s Street. — "Don't rumple my dress." — Cunt in full dress. — A ginger-coloured motte. — The tipsy coachman. — Catherine, and widow alternately. — The widow enceinte. — Remedies. — Catherine goes home. — The widow marries. — Indiscriminate womaning.

That day I took her to my favorite house. It was about five in the afternoon. I'm sure she had never been in one before from her curiosity. "Undress, and let's go to bed," said I. Persuaded at last, and creeping on to the bed in her chemise. "Let's look at your dear little cunt," said I, for I was curious about the virginity. I knew how a quim recently broken looked, I had broken many, had studied them, and recently had been abroad, and at an anatomical museum, had seen models of the hymen and of its ragged slit when broken.

She refused. "You've been fucked before last Tuesday," said I. No she never had, — how could I tell? — I was cruel. "Let me see then, — if you don't I'll go away, and see you no more." She didn't care if I did, she hadn't asked me to meet her. But gradually she yielded, and I saw a pretty quim looking as if it had only recently been broken, so jagged was the orifice. I was puzzled, knowing that I had not broken it. Then all but naked, we fucked with all the delight which nakedness and randiness without fear of being discovered, could give a couple. We fucked ourselves out, and left at nine o'clock.

Then came the difficulty in getting at her, which is one of the drawbacks with servants. She could not get out often and was one Sunday out in the morning, the next at night. So we arranged that if the family was out, and the cook were also out, she should put a card up angleways in the window, just above a wire-blind (they used in that house to put a card up to give notice to some tradesmen if wanted or not). The ladies usually took their walk at about the same hour daily, the cook disobediently often then went out, and I went in when I saw the card, but it was very risky. I have gone in, fucked her, and been out of the house in ten minutes; and I liked the excitement of the intrigue for a little time, for the change from women who pulled up their clothes, directly I was in the bed-room with them, was pleasant.

I had her against a wall, and against a tree in the Park, and got her on one holiday for some hours in a baudy house. On my hinting that she had had something stiff up her quim, before I put anything there, she denied it. How did I know? — would any man know if a girl was virgin or not? That question she put to me every time, and when I said "yes," she whimpered. Then she put the question to me in various indirect ways, and was evidently in a great state of anxiety about it. What if a man did not look? — if he had not felt first with his fingers, would he know? Whilst in bed together, and I kissed her, and titillated her quim, I got the grounds for her anxiety out her.

She was engaged to be married, and feared her young man would not be deceived, for she knew she was broken. What should she say if he found it out when married? — her fellow-servant, a widow, told her she had had several men before marriage, and her husband had not found out the want of virginity. She used to sleep in the same bed with that servant; they got from talking to feeling, and then to frigging each other. Did I see any harm in that? No I did not, I told her.

Encouraged she then told me more. One night her fellow-servant produced something like a man's thing, and put it up herself, saying it gave her more pleasure than frigging. Another night, when Kitty was made over-randy by talking, and feeling each other, she let the woman put the thing up her. It was up her before she was aware of it almost, and did not hurt her much. She spent, it gave her pleasure, but she was bleeding, and she cried. "It was a dildo," said I. Kitty had never heard the word, the cook called it a sham-cock. I comforted the girl, and told her I had heard that women managed to humbug a husband on the marriage-night. "But I'm afraid I'm in the family way," said she. That was annoying news to me. "Let's fuck as much as we can then before your next monthly time my dear," — and we did. Afterwards she told me all about the lewed tricks the two women played together. The cook had gamahuched her, and always wanted to do it. Kit liked the pleasure, but had never done it to the cook. Such confidences I always got after a time from women. I know they will lay in my arms, and tell me all about themselves after a little. I don't know how much to believe of this tale of Kitty's, but write it just as she told it to me. I think it true.

She was a nice girl. I greatly enjoyed fucking her, and oh! didn't she! but in a few weeks I had had enough of her. During that time I never touched a gay lady, and had quite a dislike to their ready voluptuousness; but it became very difficult to get a grind with the girl, which was annoying. She had asked to go out as often as was possible, but the family was much at home, through wet weather, and I wanted a spend daily. But I think I should have continued longer my attentions exclusively to her dark-haired motte, had chance not thrown quite a different coloured article in my way.

I was out at a dance. A very pretty, quite light, fair-haired woman whom I had known some time was there. She had been a widow about three years, had three children, was about thirty years old, and was soon going to marry again. She bore an excellent virtuous character among our mutual friends. I had since her widowhood once or twice, when a little warm, dropt a double entendre, but she never took it up, and I had not thought about having her, nor indeed much desired her.

On the night in question a strong letch for her came over me, perhaps I was over-fed and heated. It was a very warm night for early spring. I danced with her several times, and at intervals asked her if she did not feel frightened in bed by herself, and other suggestive questions. She parried them by evasive but rather warm replies, and we in fact egged each other on, both getting randier and randier I expect. At last I said in the middle of a quadrille something very strongly suggestive. She replied that if it would not look strange, she would leave off dancing with me at once. But I kept on same sort of joking, and warmed her up till she replied much in the same spirit. She must have been awfully lewed by the time the quadrille was finished.

I did not take her into supper, but was near to her, drank to her, and kept looking at her, and she at me. Then I danced again with her, hugging her in a waltz. About half-past one in the morning we were both in the hall leaving, and her carriage had not come. She got tired of waiting, and would wait no longer, so had a cab called. No she would not give me a seat, — of course not. I left, and walked on, leaving her in the hall. It was a lovely night. I intentionally did not go out of sight of the house, and when the cab neared me, boldly called to the man to stop, on seeing the lady inside. "Now do give me a lift, no one will know or can say anything," — and into the cab I got with her. She did not resist, though she objected.

I can't tell exactly the order of what followed, it was all rapidly done. We must have been both stewing in lust, she perhaps worse than me, from not having had a prick up her for three years. In a minute I was kissing, in another my fingers were on her cunt, in another her hand clasped my prick, and I was entreating her to let me have her. We were crossing London, and I suggested a house. She was in a state of voluptuous silence. "Oh! — no — oh! — n — ho," was all she said as I kissed, frigged, and entreated her, not heeding her refusal. "Café de l'Europe," said I to the cabby, who turned his horse's head, and drove there. She had consented in a passive manner. At the Café we got out, I drew the hood of her cloak over her head. Off went the cab. We stopped in the café-lobby, and directly the cab was gone I walked her into J***'s Street close by, and up into a room I had occupied a hundred times. In a minute I pushed both hands up her clothes, feeling her bum, thighs, and cunt. "Let's fuck my love, let's fuck." I never minced words at that stage, and was kneeling on the floor feeling her, whilst she stood in silence permitting it.

"Take off your dress love." "Impossible, — how can I fasten it again?" "The chambermaid will." "Oh! don't let her come in, and see my face." I pulled her to the bedside, and threw her back. "Oh! my head-dress — what will my maid think if it's undone?" In my fierce lust I thought of nothing but fucking her, but she was in ball-dress, a feather in her hair, jewels round her neck, bracelets and ornaments about her everywhere. Her fears were wise. Hastily I pushed pillows under her back to keep her head up. "Don't rumple my dress." "I won't." "Oh! don't get me with child," said she as I pulled up her clothes. "No I'll not spend in you" (I had said that when in the cab). The next second I saw a pair of lovely plump, white thighs and a sandy-haired quim, my prick was up it, we were both wrought up to the highest pitch. "Kiss me dear." "O — h — o kiss me," said she. I was fucking upright by the bedside, for fear of deranging her clothes. Now I closed on her, thrust my tongue into her sweet mouth, and forgetting all about dress or children clutched her tight, and spent up her, and she with me.

It's delicious when one's passion has been cooled in a woman, to hold her thighs up round you as I did those of Mrs. X. I never saw a woman lay so tranquil with eyes closed so long. She was a lovely sight as she lay with diamonds, and gold, and feathers, her full breasts showing nearly to her bubbies over her satin dress; silk stockings on her plump legs, white satin boots on her feet, all upon her of the cleanest and richest. My cock at length began to dwindle, I felt the moisture running onto my balls, and cooling round my prick where her cunt-lips closed round it, and then she opened her eyes. "Take care of my clothes." "Hold your thighs well up, and I will." I placed my hand under my prick, drew it out, and caught the sperm which followed it. She rose holding her cunt, and rushed to the basin like mad. I poured out water. "You've got me with child," said she. "Nonsense." "You have, — you have, — I'm sure you have," she replied as she squatted, washing her cunt.

After a long slopping she rose looking confused, then in the glass to see if her head-dress was all right. "I'm frightened," said she, "I'm sure I shall be with child." "Nonsense." "I'm perfectly sure," — and she sat down in a thoughtful state. "Oh! why did I let you get into the cab with me!" I dropped on my knees in front of her, my prick still hanging out. I felt grateful to her for her sacrifice. I have always liked a nice woman more after I have fucked her than before, and she looked such a lovely blonde though of a colour I did not admire. Then I found a lot of our spending had dropped on my black trowsers. Getting a towel to cleanse them, thinking of the moisture and its cause, I stiffened, and my cock stood in front of her like a bowsprit. "Let's do it again." "I must go, — I must get back," — but I had had neither a feel nor a sight of her charms. In my rutting fury I had driven my prick up her directly I felt her nakedness. Nor had she in her maddening want of prick impeded me. Now both were inclined for the soft voluptuous amusements, that gentle examination by sight and touch, those delicious kisses which are nearly as nice as the crisis that follows them. She was overcome, and yielded readily, spite of her anxiety.

Without coyness, yet with perfect modesty, she let me see her charms. She was beautifully made, with thighs of dazzling whiteness, — most light-haired women have, — her cunt well-covered with hair of the colour of dark ginger, had darkish red, and largish nymphae showing through it. A prettier light-haired cunt I never saw. The slight aroma from it, mingled with the perfume of her moist skin, of flowers, clean linen, and silks, drove me wild again. Never but twice before I think have I seen a lovely, modest woman in exquisite clothing, exposing her charms to me, and both the others had dark-haired cunts. "Oh! let me see you from a distance," said I retreating to the other side of the room to look. She laid exposed, but I could not wait to contemplate long. Dropping on my knees again, I buried my tongue in her cunt, tickled it in ecstacy, kissed, smelt, and licked slightly her quim all over. Then at the edge of the bed again, placing pillows for her head, and folding up her dress above her navel, so as not to rumple it, I fucked her. Both embraces must have been done in a quarter of an hour. My excitement was intense. With her it was almost a wedding-night, and she was overcome with sexual pleasure.

"The mischief's done," said she as she washed again. I laughed at her, but she persisted. Her first child was born nine months to a day after her marriage. They would have had more than three children had they not taken precautions to prevent them. She told this to me rapidly whilst preparing to leave. She was of a breeding nature, and all her family were. She pressed me to leave at once, but I was mad about her. I longed to get picturesque views of her hidden charms, surrounded as they were by lace and jewels. Her coachman was her anxiety, — was he drunk? — had he gone to fetch her or not, and when! — what if he had gone, and returned home, — found her not returned? — what should she say? We were puzzled, but arranged that her cab was to have broken down, and she had difficulty in getting another, — a lame story, but the best we could compose. Again I wanted her. "Oh! think of me, — think of the consequences, — let me get home." I had been furiously frigging my prick whilst talking, hoping to make it stiff, knowing that nothing persuades a woman like a stiff-stander. Many a woman will say, "no, no," till she sees the red-tipped cunt-stopper ready,

and then can say it no longer. It has been my experience with
women of the modest class.

Her cloak was on, the hood well over her head. "Let me have
you." "Another day perhaps, but let us go now." I kept on frigging
myself. "Let us do it again, — look it's stiff, — we shan't be five
minutes." "Oh! yes we will." "One look then at your cunt, at those
lovely thighs again," said I frigging on. Dropping on my knees,
pulling up her clothes, I began kissing her motte. Nothing makes a
modest woman more randy than a man looking at her nakedness,
the idea of it stirs her lust. Then my tongue played on her lovely
little clitoris, she fell back on the bed, then I arranged her head,
and gamahuched her for a minute, and then put into her. Once
my cock seemed inclined to shirk its duty, but I drove it up her
fast and furious, her cunt clipped, my spunk shot up it, and we had
copulated again, but I was a long time at it. She spent again. Then
without either of us washing we left. I had a four-wheeler, and
she drove away, but not from the baudy house door. "Pay him
well," said I.

I called the next day, how we looked at each other! — a lady
was with her. "Think," said she to her, as though for her information,
"how my coachman served me last night." Then she told the lady
that on getting home in a cab, she found him slightly tipsy, but
putting in the horses to the carriage, and swearing she had told
him three a.m., and not one a.m., — she would dismiss him. How
I blessed that tippling coachman, — all was safe.

Gentlemen never visited at her house without their wives, her
and children were always present or friends with her, she was most
particular in her conduct. So I wrote asking her to meet me in the
B**l***t*n Arcade. She did meet and promised to go with me
"Once, only once mind, — at some hotel in the day-time, to a house
of another class, never." So I took a sitting-room and bed-room at
the *** hotel, and slept there one night as a blind. She came the
next day, and I had a lovely three hours with her. I gamahuched
her, — but not till she spent. I never have been able to say why I
at times did this to a woman when I passed scores over. She had
never been cunt-licked before. I had her several times afterwards,
and did the same. Again I took her to my house in J***s Street,
telling her that it was a sort of private hotel. Perhaps she believed
it, perhaps not, but she came a few times there. We neither entered
nor left together, and she asked no more questions about the house.

I was thus having her and Catherine alternately and my mind took a voluptuous twist. When I was with Kitty I would think of Mrs. X's flaxen-haired cunt, and fancy I was fucking her. When up Mrs. X. I thought that Kitty's black-haired motte was twisting and twining with my prick's surroundings. Then the two got mixed in my voluptuous imagination, and I felt as if I were in both cunts at the same time. So I enjoyed the two females immensely, but for a short time only. Mrs. X.'s courses came on, they did so one afternoon when I was stroking her. "Thank God," said she, and she never let me have her afterwards. I have kissed her, and she me, slyly shown her my penis, have felt her quim, but she could not be persuaded to more. Some months afterwards she married, and has had several children since. She is alive now as I write this. She asked me to avoid speaking to her as much as I could, when she was married, if ever we met at friends' houses.

[I did meet her several times for years afterwards, but never by look, or otherwise, showed any intimacy with her.]

I knew a little of her second husband, but as on her marriage they did not send us cards, we did not visit them, which was as it should be. After her fucking she used always to say, "Oh! what madness, what wicked madness of me, to let you do this."

I lost Kate nearly at the same time as I lost Mrs. X. She was impudent to her mistress, who dismissed her, and she went home. I never heard if she married, or what took place after. She was in lodgings for about a week before she returned to the country. During that time I took her to J***s Street nightly, and had delight in shagging her in exactly the same way at the bedside as I had Mrs. X. I told her I had had a lady on that bed with ginger-coloured hair on her cunt. "A light-haired thing like that must look very ugly, — doesn't it?," said she. Now I never gamahuched Kitty, nor thought of doing it to her, and yet I did it to Mrs. X. Why to one, and not the other I never could tell, when I thought of my selection.

I was glad both liaisons had terminated. The "family way" annoys me always and I suppose both women spoke the truth. Mrs. X. was frantic when her monthly period approached, and there was nothing to show for it. "My God if this should cause my marriage to be broken off," &c., and I could not marry her. — She had always liked me she said. Good God what madness had come over her on that unfortunate night, when she let me get into the

cab with her. She took however her fucking readily enough as long
as her courses stopped. We never were actually in bed together,
though we were undressed, and on it. Curiosity, opportunity, and
a randy cock and cunt brought the affair about, — I expect there
are many such cases. I have at J***s Street when Hannah was
mistress, seen once or twice, ladies come in fine evening dresses,
hiding their faces, and going upstairs with gentlemen, and once
she told me that a lady came there, stripped herself naked, covered
her face with gauze, and then was fucked by men she got for her;
but she never would tell me who the men or the lady were.

Kitty took her "family way" more coolly. She had not her
courses on, even when she left, but she had been to some woman
who gave her something, sure she said to set her to rights, though
it would make her very ill. So she resolved to take it when at home
with her mother in the country. I gave her ten pounds at parting,
and the fullest advice I could, as to her behaviour on her wedding-
night, and fucked her just before she got into the cab to depart.
She met me under the portico of the Haymarket Theatre, leaving
her cab with her box outside close by. She was behind time, and
I thought she had humbugged me. I had just only time to throw
up her petticoats, have a last look at her male-cage, and plug it.
Then looking at my watch I doubted if she would catch her train.
Off she went with my spunk in her cunt. I had her address, and she
a post-office where she could write to me, — but neither of us did
write.

Then I took to indiscriminate whoring, and having for the
time plenty of money, soon tailed about three dozen of the finest
women of the Argyle set. I was surrounded by them so soon as I
showed myself there, — they were the palmy days of the Argyle.

I don't think I have said that Hannah had been dismissed
from J***s Street. I have never seen her since.]

CHAPTER XXI

Camille the second. — Stripping. — The divan. — Cock-washing. — Camille's antecedents. — Face, form, and cunt. — Mode of copu- lating. — Avaricious. — Free fucking offered. — Gabrielle. — Cunt, form, and face. — Minette. — My daily dose of doxies. — At M**- g**e. — Lodgings at the greengrocer's. — Louisa the red-haired. — The lodging-house servant. — The shop-boy. — My friend's daugh- ter. — Piddling, and presents. — Loo's bum pinched. — The servant kissed. — A stroke on the sands. — With Loo on the beach. — Chaff, and cunt-tickling. — A declaration of love. — The virtuous servant.

Since I had finished with Camille, her sister Louise, and the French artistes in letchery whom she introduced to me when I was twenty-one years old, I do not recollect having gone with a French woman excepting when abroad, my tastes ran on my own countrywomen. Now in the year 18**, a year of national importance, and one in which strangers came from all parts of the world to London, I was to have a French woman again.

Was it for the sake of change only, or because they were more willing, salacious, enterprising, and artistic in Paphian exercises? — was it my recollection of having that when I did not want it? — I cannot say.

At quite the beginning of the month of June, about four o'clock in the afternoon, I saw a woman walking slowly along Pall-Mall dressed in the nicest and neatest way. I could scarcely make up my mind whether she was gay or not, but at length saw the quiet invitation in her eye, and slightly nodding in reply, followed her to a house in B**y Street, St. James. She was a French woman named Camille.

I named my fee, it was accepted, and in a quiet, even ladylike

393

way she began undressing. With a neatness unusual in gay women, one by one each garment was folded up, and placed on a chair, pins stuck in a pin-cushion, &c., with the greatest composure, and almost without speaking. I liked her even for that, and felt she would suit my taste. As each part of her flesh came into view, I saw that her form was lovely. When in her chemise, I began undressing, she sitting looking at me. When in my shirt, I began those exquisite preliminaries with this well-made, pretty woman, feeling her all over, and kissing her; but my pego was impatient, and I could not go on at this long. Smiling she laid hold of my prick. "Shall we make love?" this was in the bed-room. "Yes." "Here, or in the salon?" "I don't like a sofa." "Mais ici," said she pushing the door open wide, and pointing to a piece of furniture which I had not noticed, though noticeable enough.

In the room was a sort of settee or divan, as long, and nearly as wide as a good-sized bed; so wide that two people could lie on it side by side. It had neither head nor feet, but presented one level surface, covered with a red silky material, and a valance hanging down the sides. At one end were two pillows, also red, and made flat like two bed-pillows. "There, on that," said I at once.

I never saw any divan or piece of furniture like it in my life since, neither in brothel, nor in private house, here or on the Continent, excepting once when quite in the extreme East of Europe.

It was a blazing hot day. "Shall I take off my chemise?" "Yes." Off she took it, folded it up, and took it into the bed-room. "Take off your shirt." Off I drew it, and we both stood naked. She laid hold of my stiff prick, gave it a gentle shake, laughed, fetched two towels, spread one on the divan for her bum, laid the other on a pillow for me, went back to the bed-room, poured out water in the basin, then laid herself down naked on the divan with her bum on the towel. I kissed her belly and thighs, and she opened them wide for me to see her notch, without my having asked her to do so. To pull it open, have a moment's glance at the red, kiss and feel her rapidly over, mount her, fuck and spend, was only an affair of two or three minutes, so strongly had she stirred my lust for her.

I laid long up her, raising myself on my elbow to talk with her whilst my prick was still in her sheath. At length it slipped out. Gently she put her hand down, and caught it, taking off the excess of moisture. Delicately she raised the towel, and put her hand on her cunt, and saying with a smile, "Mon Dieu, il y en a assez," went to the bed-room, I following her.

She wiped her cunt with the towel, half squatting to do so, then rose up quickly saying, "Shall I wash you?" I had begun, but the offer pleased me. I have no recollection as I write this, of any gay woman having made such an offer since the first French Camille, and one or two of her set, excepting yellow-haired Kitty, who liked doing that to me. "Yes wash it." "Hold the basin then," — and taking it up she placed it under me, so that my testicles hung into it whilst I held it. She washed me. "Soap?" "Yes." "Inglis sop" (laughing), — the first English words I heard her speak. My prick washed, she performed a similar operation on herself. All was done so nicely, cleanly, and delicately that I have never seen it excelled by any woman.

"Causons-nous?" said she leading the way to the divan. Then both laying down naked we gossiped. She was from Arles, in France, eighteen years of age, had been in London a fortnight, had been tailed six months and lived with her father most of that time. A month ago had been persuaded to go to Lyons by an old woman who there sold her pleasures, and kept her money. Another old one snapped her up there, and brought her to London, to a house in B**n**s Street, where a young French woman more experienced than Camille induced her to work on her own account. They two got away, Camille set up in B**y Street, her friend elsewhere. That was told me laying naked with her on the divan.

[She was alone in London, and still exercising her occupation the other day, thirty-one years after I first had her. I have known her, and had her occasionally during all that time, though sometimes two or three years have elapsed between my visits to her. She has been in poor circumstances for years past, and oftentimes I have gone out of my way purposely to meet her, and give her a bit of gold, out of regard for her.]

We lay during her narration (which was soon told) naked. Hot as it was I felt a slight coolness, and drawing myself closer up to her, "It's cool," I said. Without reply, she put one hand over me to help my embrace of her, with the other handled gently my prick, the next instant kissed me, and I felt her tongue peeping out of her pretty lips, seeking my tongue. My fingers naturally had been playing gently about her cunt all the time of our talk, and her hand rubbing gently over my naked flesh. So for a minute in silence our tongues played with each other, and then without a word and with one consent, and like one body we moved together gently, she on to her back, I on to her belly, my prick went up her, and with slow probing thrusts, with now and then a nestle and a pause, till the rapid clip-clip of her cunt drove me into more rapid action, to the rapid in and out and the final short thrusts and wriggle against her womb, till my prick with strong pulsations sent my sperm up her again. "Ah! chéri, — mon Dieu, — a — h — a!" she sighed as she had spent with me. "You fuck divinely," said she, but in chaste words, afterwards.

A wash as before, and then with chemise and shirt on, we talked about France, London, beer, wine, and other topics. "Let me look at your cunt." I had scarcely looked at it. Without reply she fell back, opened her thighs, and then I saw all, all, — and so for two hours we went on, till it was time for me to dine, and with a parting fuck which we both enjoyed, we parted. I added another piece of gold to what I had already put on the mantel piece before she began to undress. A custom of mine then, and always followed since, is putting down my fee, — it prevents mistakes, and quarrels. When paid, if a woman will not let me have her, be it so, — she has some reason, — perhaps a good one for me. If she be a cheat, and only uses the money to extort more, be it so. — I know my woman, and have done with her henceforth.

Camille was a woman of perfect height, about five foot seven, and beautifully formed, had full, hard, exquisite breasts, and lovely legs and haunches, though not too fat or heavy. The hair on her cunt, soft and of a very dark chestnut colour, was not then large in quantity, but corresponded with her years. Her cunt was small, with small inner lips, and a pretty nubbly clitoris like a little button. The split of her cunt lay between the thighs with scarcely any swell of outer-lips, but had a good mons, and was altogether one of the prettiest cunts I have ever seen. I am now beginning, after having seen many hundreds of them, to appreciate beauty in cunts, to be conscious that there is a special, a superior beauty in the cunts of some women as compared with others, just as there is in other parts of their body. She had pretty hands and feet.

Her skin had the slightly brown gipsy tint found in many women in the South of Europe. I never saw a woman in whom the colour was so uniform as in her. From her face to her ankles it was the same unvarying tint without a mottle, even in any cranny. It had also the most exquisite smoothness, but it neither felt like ivory, satin, nor velvet, it seemed a compound of them all. I have scarcely felt the same in any other woman yet. That smoothness attracted me at first I expect, but it was only after I had had her several times, that I began to appreciate it, and to compare it with the skin of other women. She had with that, a great delicacy of touch with her hands.

Her face was scarcely equal to her form. The nose was more than *retroussé*, it bordered on the snub. She had small, dark, softly twinkling eyes, and dark hair; the mouth was ordinary, but with a set of very small, and beautifully white, regular, teeth. The general effect of her face was piquante rather than beautiful, but it pleased me. Her voice was small and soft, — an excellent thing in a woman.

[Such was the woman I have known for thirty-one years, but of whom there is scarcely anything to be told. No intrigue, nothing exciting is connected with her and myself. I cannot tell all the incidents of our acquaintance right off as I do those of many of my women, who appeared, pleased me, and disappeared; but she will be noticed from time to time as I had her, or sought her help in different erotic whims and fancies, which took hold of me at various periods. I write this now finding that her name appears in my manuscript a long way further on. She was moreover a most intelligent creature, clean, sober, and economical, and saving with a good purpose and object, to end alas! for her in failure.]

I never had a more voluptuous woman. Naked on that divan, or on the bed when the weather was warm, I had her constantly during that summer. I know nothing more exciting, than the tranquil, slow, measured way in which she laid down, exposing her charms; every attitude being natural yet exciting by its beauty and delicate salacity. She always seemed to me to be what I had heard of Orientals in copulation. She had the slowest yet most stifling embrace. There was no violent energy, no heaving up of rump, as if a pin had just run into her, nor violent sighs, nor loud exclamations; but she clung to you, and sucked your mouth in a way I scarcely

ever have found in English women, or in French ones; but the
Austrians and Hungarians in the use of tongue with tongue, and
lips with lips are unrivalled in voluptuousness.

Beyond a voluptuous grace natural to her, she had not at first
the facile ways of a French courtesan, they came later on. I saw
the change, and from that and other indications feel sure she had
not been in gay life long before I had her. I could tell more of her
history, but this is a narrative of my life, not of hers.

[I have destroyed some pages of manuscript solely relating
to her.]

She soon got a good clientele, picked up English rapidly,
dressed richly, but never showily, and began to save money. She
made affectionate advances to me which I did not accept. After a
time she used to pout at what I gave her, and got greedy. So one
day saying, "Ma chère, here is more, but adieu, — I don't like you
to be dissatisfied, but cannot afford to come to see you," — she
slapped the gold heavily down on the table. "Ah! mon Dieu, don't
say so, — come, — come, — I am sorry, — you shall never pay me,
— come when you like, — I did not want you to pay me, but you
would, — come, — do come, — that lovely prick, — do me again before you go, — don't go, — my maid shall say I have not come
home" (she expected some man), — and she never pouted about
my compliment, till many years afterwards.

I suppose that having had this charming fresh French woman,
made me wish for another; for spite of my satisfaction and liking
for her, I made acquaintance with another French woman, as unlike Camille as possible. Her name was Gabrielle, a bold-looking
woman with big eyes and a handsome face, very tall and well-made,
but with not too much flesh on her bones, with a large, full-lipped,
loud-looking cunt in a bush of hair as black as charcoal. I never told
Camille about her, and think it was the great contrast between the
two which made me have her. That woman also seemed later on
to have taken some sort of fancy to me.

She had all the ready lechery of a well-practised French harlot,
I saw it from the way she opened her thighs, and laid down to
receive my embraces. About the third visit she brought water, and
made me wash my prick, on which the exudation of healthy lust
was showing whitish, before she let me poke her. I liked her
cleanliness, but to my astonishment no sooner were we on the bed,

than she reversed herself laying side by side with me, and began sucking my prick. I had no taste for that pleasure, nor since a woman in the rooms of Camille the first did it to me, had my penis been so treated that I recollect, though I had made ladies take it into their mouths for a second. I objected. "Mais si, — mais si," — and she went on. My head was near her knee, one leg she lifted up, showing her thighs, which opened and showed her big-lipped cunt in its thicket of black hair. She played with my prick thus till experience told her she could do it no longer with safety, then ceasing her suction, and changing her position, I fucked her in the old-fashioned way.

The amusement seemed not to have shocked me as much as I thought it should have done, and it was repeated as a preliminary on other days, without my ever suggesting it. After I had had my first poke, the delicate titillation of the mouth seemed vastly pleasant, my prick then being temporarily fatigued by exercise in its natural channel; but I felt annoyed with myself for relishing it at all.

I had not overcome prejudices then, though evidently my philosophy was gradually undermining them. Why, if it gives pleasure to the man to have his prick sucked by a woman, who likes operating that way on the male, should they be abused for enjoying themselves in such manner? A woman may rub it up to stiffen it, the man always does so if needful, — that is quite natural and proper. What wrong then in a woman using her mouth for the same purpose, and giving still higher, more delicate and refined pleasure? All animals lick each other's privates, why not we? In copulation and its consequences, we are mainly animals, but with our intelligence, we should seek all possible forms of pleasure in copulation, and everything else.

With these two women I was satisfied till towards the end of August, both of them trying to make me see them much. Gabrielle for some fancy of her own took to calling me Monsieur Gabrielle. I did not see her nearly so often as Camille, but one or other I saw almost daily, Camille generally between luncheon and dinner, Gabrielle after dinner. I have seen both on the same day, and then both were fucked; but I usually copulated but once daily. I was in good health, and one daily emission of semen kept me so, and seemed as needful to me as sleep. I had much lewed pleasure in comparing mentally their two cunts, their being a most striking difference in the look of the two.

I was so amused with them that year, that I would not leave till near September. Then, "You've stopped all the long days, and the hottest weather, when I wanted to be by the seaside, — and now I won't go at all." I was glad of it, and without waiting for change of intention in that quarter, had my things packed up, and without delay, took myself off to the healthy, but vulgarish town of M°°g°°e. It was a place where I expected a little fun, a few kisses from healthy lips, and a little intrigue perhaps, and the chance of getting some young healthy, unfucked cunt. I know pretty well now that with town-women out for a brief holiday like most of those who go to M°°g°°e; that idleness, better air, more and better food than they are accustomed to, heats the cunts, and makes many a modest one long for a male, and discontented with her middle-finger.

I had not been at my hotel a day, before I met an intimate friend with his wife and eldest daughter, — a girl of fourteen. He had taken the upper part of a house over a shop, being a man of but moderate means, and intended to have brought two other children, and a maid, but something prevented that. I liked both him and his wife, and at his suggestion went to occupy one of his rooms, and live with them (paying my share). I found the rooms were over a greengrocers, which I didn't like, and think I should have cried off, had I not seen that the servant was a healthy, full-fleshed bitch, and I thought there might be a chance of prodding her, like Sally on a previous autumn.

The house newly built, and evidently for lodgings, was bigger, more comfortable than most of its class, and had a side or private entrance-door, opening on to a passage separated from the shop but with a door into it at the end where also was a kitchen with a bed-room over it, and a water-closet, all looking into a little garden with one or two trees in it. The sitting and bed-rooms over the shop were occupied by my friend and wife, and of two rooms above, one was mine, and one his daughter's; the attics the landlady and the servant I thought occupied. There was also leading out from the staircase, the bed-room over the kitchen which my friend had also hired, to avoid having strangers in the house with them. This was entered from the staircase-landing, as was the lodgers' water-closet, a convenience which few such houses had then.

The shop seemed flourishing. Any one going in at the private door could not fail to see the whole of the shop, down to a small parlour having a window on to the garden. The first thing I noticed was a strong, healthy, red-cheeked, saucy-looking girl about sixteen years of age, with a curly but dishevelled head of deep-red-coloured hair, — a very unusual and peculiar deep-red, and but rarely seen. The girl standing at the shop-front stared hard at me when I arrived, and nudged a big boy about fifteen years old who was half-sitting close by the girl, upon a sack of potatoes. The girl called the woman of the house "Aunt." She attended to the shop I found when the aunt was away (cooking chiefly when so). The boy took home the goods purchased, and left nightly after closing the shutters. Red-Head slept in the attics over me, and took off her boots at times as she went upstairs, so as not to make a noise over the lodgers' heads, — the aunt slept there also. They two eat in the kitchen or the shop-parlour.

I was at once cheery with the servant, but it did not promise much. The red-haired one (another Louisa, and called Loo), pleased me, though I did not like her hair. She spoke so loud, laughed so heartily with customers, took chaffing, lifted such heavy weights, and then flung her short petticoats about so much in moving her haunches, that I longed to pinch her. She looked so hard at me (and also my friend), when we passed the shop, for she was generally at the door, and often outside it, goods being placed there, — that I made up my mind she had just come into the first lusts of womanhood, and was pretty strongly in want of a man.

In a day or two I was buying fruit two or three times daily. "Keep the change Loo (I hear that's your name), — it will buy you some ribbon." "Oh! thankee sir," — and she put it quickly into her pocket without hesitation. Emboldened I gave her half a crown. "Keep the change, and you shall give me a kiss for it." Into her pocket it went. She looked quickly towards the back of the shop, — there was the boy. She slightly shook her head. "I can't," said she in a low voice, taking the change out of her pocket and tendering it to me. I winked, pushed out my lips as if kissing, and left the shop, leaving her the change. The boy was out of sight somewhere when I was buying the fruit.

Between eleven and one o'clock she was mostly alone, her aunt in the kitchen, the boy out, and the same for an hour or two in the afternoon. Unfortunately those were the bathing and prome-

nading hours, so there was difficulty in getting at the girl unobserved, but nothing stood in my way when cunt-hunting, and
never had. From always thinking how, and where, I all my life
have got my opportunities with women. I also found that of an
evening, her aunt just at dusk went out at times to get, I heard her
say, a mouthful of fresh air. Then the girl was alone with the boy
till he left.

About the fourth night, the boy had left, Loo was alone in
the shop-parlour, my friends upstairs. I went out (as I said), to
have a cigar, and a stroll, but when just at the bottom of the stairs
the shop-door in the partition opened, and Loo appeared. "Hist, —
hist," said I. She stopped, I caught hold of her, and kissed her.

"Oh! don't, — Mary [the servant] is in the kitchen." I kissed
again. "Oh! don't." "You owe me a kiss." "Oh! not here, — go to
the front-door," said she. I did. She came there, just outside the
door, but up against it, she kissed me, and went rapidly back. "I'll
wait for you as you go to bed," I said, and did so with slippers off.

About half-past ten she passed my bed-room. I heard Miss
**** moving about in the room opposite to me, but on the landing
I pinched Loo's bum hard, — very hard as she passed. She winced,
and passed on very quickly, shaking her head and smiling, candle
in hand. I put my head down shamming to look up her clothes.
We were intimate already, I had begun double entendres which
she took, and I began to think that the fresh-looking, saucy one,
young as she was, knew a prick from a cucumber. Then I found
that the servant went home each night to sleep.

I hadn't been at M**g**e a week before I wanted female
assistance, and picking up a casual, and thinking of my intention,
gave her five shillings to show me a baudy house or two, which
she did. One, a very quiet one, was in the old part of the town, over
a china-shop.

Parting with the woman I strolled on to the beach, and met
her there again, and felt her cunt, I sitting on a seat, she standing
by the side of me. My cock stood, and I gave her money for a
poke. It was not a dark night. "There is sand low down," said she,
"no one will notice us when we are lying down." But a fear came
over me, — I told her so. "Well I've got your money, and if there
was anything the matter with me, I'd hardly ask you to have me,
— I'm here every night, and live up at *** with my mother." Then

near to the waves, she laid on her back on the soft dry sands, and
I fucked her, and enjoyed her very much. "How do you wash your
cunt?" "I piddle now, and wipe it with my handkerchief, down
there (nodding her head) — there are rocks and pools of water, —
I'm going to wash it there, — I always do after gents," — and she
went off to do it.

Next day buying something, "Come Loo, and kiss me in the
passage." "I can't — he'll be going out at half-past eleven." Excus-
ing myself from accompanying my friends, I was at the lodgings at
that hour. The servant above had then all the beds to make, and
the aunt was cooking. It was risky, yet I had a brief talk with Loo
in whispers in the passage, and kissed, and hugged her, and told
her I had fallen deeply in love with her. I had not begun smut,
but her bold manner made me wonder why I had not. That afternoon I overheard a quarrel between her and her aunt, and saw Loo
wiping her eyes. Loo said to me when I told her what I had heard,
that she wished she'd never come, and would sooner go to service.

I noticed also, for I was dodging in and out all day, and listening in the passage where I could hear much said in shop and
parlour, what seemed to me a very familiar manner between the
girl and the boy. One day he took her round the waist. She, seeing
me enter the shop, pushed his hand away and boxed his ears. He
stooped, pulled her petticoats a little way up, and then suddenly
appeared very busy. Evidently she had given him a hint. It annoyed
me, and I wondered if the boy had felt her.

I did not quite give up hopes of the maid, who looked five-
and-twenty. I kissed her, and gave her a little present for cleaning
my boots nicely. She took that fairly well. Then I felt for her notch
outside her clothes. She repulsed me violently, and with a look
which I didn't like. So for a time I desisted, but recommenced, and
at length kissed her every time I got her alone. My friend's daughter
caught me at it, and her father spoke to me. *He* didn't mind, but
his *wife* did, — I must take care, — it wouldn't do to let a young
girl see that game going on. Nothing more was said, but I noticed
that he and his wife looked after me. One night when we were
walking out alone, he said, "You want that woman, — and a damned
nice woman she looks, — if my wife wasn't here I'd try to get her
myself, — but for God's sake don't let either of the ladies catch
you, — it won't do."

The young lady's room was opposite to mine, and such was my insatiable desire to see females in déshabillé or nude, that it passed through my mind to bore a hole (which I had done at foreign hotels) through her door, to spy her. I could have done so, but I did not, though I could not restrain myself from listening to hear when she piddled and a few times succeeded. Then I thought of her piddle and little hairless cunt, which gave me such pleasure, that I quite felt a liking for the girl, but not sexually, and brought her presents which pleased both her and her parents.

In a fortnight I had often kissed Loo, and pinched her bum till she said it was blue. I told her I should like to sleep with her, for I loved her, — this was on the first night she got out for a walk at dusk. I had heard her aunt say she'd keep a tight hand on her, and I found Loo was fast almost to a gallop. We walked and sat down on a beach-seat. "How can you love me? — you're married, — Mary heard Mrs. L**g saying so." "I never said I wasn't, but I hate *her*, and do nothing to her, and love *you*." "Oh! gammon," she replied. I had now a little changed my opinion about the girl. She wanted to know the meaning of my "doing nothing," was free in manner, and any delicate smut which I began using she answered frankly to. "Oh! I knows what you means well enough, but don't you go on like that." I concluded she had been brought up with coarse people who spoke of all their wants, and acts openly, so that the girl saw no harm in such things. She had only been with her aunt that summer. She told me of her relatives, and where they lived in Northumberland, — there was a large family, — but that was all I could get out of her. "Yer don't want to call on em," said she laughing.

All was soon finished with the servant. One morning I waited indoors in hopes of getting at Loo, and spied the servant as she brought a slop-pail to the closet which as said was close to the bed-room over the kitchen. When she came out I asked her into that room which I had never entered before. "Come here, I've something particular to tell you, — come." Reluctantly she came in, then I kissed, and gradually getting to the unchaste, got my hand on to her cunt. "Be quiet, — you shan't, — oh! don't, — Mrs. Jones will be up to see if all's right." "No she's out — oh! what lovely thighs, — what hair on your cunt — don't make that noise." She resisted hard, and pushed down her clothes, at first spoke in suppressed tones, then louder. "You shan't, — oh! you wretch, — I don't want a dress, — you shan't, — oh! oh! leave off, — I'll tell Mrs. Jones, — I will."

I desisted for the moment, but only to pull out my prick. She had taken up the slop-pail looking very angry. With prick out I rushed at her, she banged the pail down, I pushed her against the bedside, and got my fingers on to her cunt again. "Let me have you." "Oh! — you — shan't, — I'll call." "I'll say that you asked me in here." "You liar, you beast, — I won't, — oh! hi!," and she cried out so loudly that I desisted.

"I won't stop here any longer, and I'll tell Mrs. Jones." She went out of the room crying and nodding her head furiously at me. There will be a row, thought I. Later on I offered her two sovereigns. "Don't say anything, — you'll only lose your character if you do, — I've done you no harm." Indeed I rather funked the affair. She took the money without a word, and pushed me off when I tried to kiss her, and I never got at her again. Two days afterwards she left, — she was only a weekly servant. I don't think she ever told about me, — she said she didn't like the place.

CHAPTER XXII

Loo on the beach. — The shop-boy's attempt. — Caught at the water-closet. — A knowing one. — The gay sister. — Success despaired of. — Over the china-shop. — Virginity slaughtered. — Alone in the lodgings. — The bed-room on the stairs. — Poking like blazes. — A gamahuche. — Aunt at market. — Clever dodges. — Naked in bed. — Homage to Priapus. — Belly to belly. — Belly to bum. — She on he. — The hand-glass. — Am I with child? — I leave M**g**e. — Sequel.

I had no one now but Loo. She had gone out one evening without leave, and met me. Her aunt scolded. I got very warm in my hints and words. She laughed at them, but still I hesitated, she was such an odd, unusual girl. I did not know what to make of her, and my failure with the servant made me cautious.

It was slow I found being always with my friends, the lady didn't like my taking her husband out of a night without her, so though dining with them I went out by myself, but usually came back just when the shop was being shut up, to catch Loo, — even if I went out afterwards.

The night after the new servant came, I left my friends at a concert, and went home. Entering I heard voices wrangling, and stealthily crept as near the partition-door as I could. Loo and the boy were scuffling. One second I couldn't hear a word, the next minute everything. "Don't, — leave off, — I won't let you," — then a chair or something made a noise. "Oho," cried she, — "shan't." "I've felt it, — aint it hairy?" chuckled the boy quite loud. Another scuffle. "I'll tell aunt, — don't, — oh! — the lodgers will hear." Again a scuffle. "Oh! — now — you — shan't." "Cunt," — "Oh" — "Prick," — a slap. One of them banged right up against the partition, something dropped, and all for a moment was silent. I mounted the stairs out of sight, and listened. The door opened, the two came out at the same moment, and the servant, who had not gone, came out of the kitchen. "I dropped the candle, and couldn't see, and jumped agin the door," said the boy. "You're a stupid clumsy," said Loo. The boy went out of the house like a shot, the servant and Loo into the kitchen. He's been feeling her cunt, — perhaps she him, — the little bitch has been fucked, thought I.

A day or two before I made a hasty offer to take her to London for a week, — would she go? — "Oh! won't I just, — I'm longing to see London." Then, "How can I get away? — aunt would tell father." No she could not. "Take a walk with me when the shop is shut up." But the aunt rarely let her go out in the evening, nor in the day, except on Sundays. Put up to it by me she told her aunt she would. "We'll go out together," said aunt, — but it rained a little, aunt said it would spoil her clothes, and would not go.

Next night the aunt was out, the girl had the shop shut directly it was dark, and spite of aunt came out to meet me on the beach. I told her what I had heard. She admitted the boy had tried to feel her, but had not succeeded. "But I heard him say it was hairy." "He's a liar." "I don't believe you've got any hair there," said I. "Oh! ain't I though," said she laughing. "Let me feel." Then in the dark, little by little, I managed to feel a fat pair of thighs, and the tip of a cunt. She sat quiet, at last kissing me, and I her. One of her legs was over the other, so that my finger could only just rest on her clitoris. Then she felt my prick. It was a lovely hour I passed on that seat by the shingle. I whispered in conversation, "prick," — "cunt," — "fuck," — that magical triad. "Oh! I knows what yer means." "Open your thighs now," "there then, — oh! you hurt," — and she got up. "You wicked little devil, let me." I thought her cunt seemed open enough. There was a row when she got home, but she cheeked her aunt boldly.

Next morning I went to the closet, some one was there, and wanting to bog badly I went down to the closet in the yard, pulled open the door sharply (it was not bolted), and there stood Loo with petticoats up, showing both legs nearly to her backside. She was just turning to seat herself. "Oh!" she shouted dropping her clothes. "Oh!" said I banging the door to, startled as much as she was. I went off, but an hour afterwards bought some fruit, — no one was in the shop. "I saw your bum." "You didn't," said she without a blush. "I did." "It was no fault of mine if you did." "Show it me now, — there is no one here." "Shan't." She really blushed, and sat down, but could not contain herself from laughing. I showed her my prick, and was nearly caught doing so, by some one entering the shop.

She got out another night to walk with a female friend whom the aunt thought Loo could be trusted with. Directly clear of the house, that girl went off with her lover, — five minutes later I was with Loo on the beach. It was moonlight. How I cursed the moon, then luckily heavy clouds hid it. Now I talked about copulation openly. She knew all about it she said, and at last admitted laughing that she had felt the shop-boy's prick. "No," no other man's excepting quite small boys, — she had felt those. "Let me do it to you, — fuck you, — it's such pleasure, — you know all about it, — why not?" "I would, but I am frightened, — suppose I had a child." I told her how I would prevent her having one. No, she was frightened. We felt each other well. How I restrained myself from frigging God only knows; but we were only about an hour gone.

Next day I felt her quim in the shop and again as she went up to bed, and showed her my prick. What risks I ran, and how I escaped! Had my friend opened his door, or the girl opposite opened hers, I must have been caught.

I found she did not like being in the shop, did not like her aunt, and soon after said she would go away with me to London, if I liked (I'd now offered to keep her). That bothered me, I had only just got rid of a woman, and did not want another. "But in London you'd come to grief, — perhaps go on the town, and be miserable." Well she didn't care, she wouldn't stop with her aunt, didn't want to go home — had had enough of *them*. She had a sister who was gay at ****, who told her she was very jolly. The murder was out, her cheek and frank acceptance of baudy suggestions, her knowledge of fucking, were due to her gay sister. At once I said, "What's the good of sitting here by the sea where we may be known? — let's go and have a chat and a glass of wine in a house." "No." "Why you know you've been fucked, Loo," said I angry, not mincing words now, and believing she was shamming for a purpose. "I'll take my solemn oath on any Bible, I ain't had it done to me," said she earnestly, — but I didn't believe her.

There were constant quarrels now between her and her aunt, — we heard them upstairs. Mrs. L**g, my friend, complained of the noise. Then I found that Loo had been sent there by her father, to keep her away from her gay sister. All this time my friends had never noticed my goings on with the girl, all having been done by us two with such stealth.

After that night I talked open smut to her, and felt her, and she felt my prick on every opportunity. We discussed fucking, and getting with child, as if we were married. She a girl of sixteen would look me in the face, and laugh about it without the sign of a blush. It was the most extraordinary state of things I ever have experienced; but matters stopped there. A month nearly had passed, I had shagged the woman (already named) on the sands two or three times, to keep myself from fist-fucking, and liking the novelty of the place; but I was very lewed on Loo. She liked the spooning, and liked my feeling her cunt, but, "No, I'm frightened, — I won't go anywhere with you, — I won't let you do it." "I fucked a girl on the sands, as you would not let me," said I in just those words. "Lor you didn't." "I did." She became quite silent.

My friends were now leaving. "I'm going away with them Loo, as you won't meet me." I said that on two successive days. She made no reply. Sunday came. "Come out this evening." "I'm going to church with aunt." "Well, meet me instead." She did, and I got her without any trouble to the china-shop, and five minutes after that, we were sitting close together, her hand round my prick, I titillating her clitoris, our mouths glued together, speechless. Oh! those lovely five minutes. Her thighs and bum gently moved. "Oh! don't." "Get on the bed Loo, — don't be foolish, — we'll feel each other better there." She rose. "Take off your gown, you will rumple it." She took it off in silence, and got on to the bed herself without help. We laid down. "What a lovely fat bum you have. — I must kiss it." I loosened my trowsers. "There now, let my prick just touch your belly, — feel me." My fingers slipt along her cunt, and I tried to put one up it. "Oh! you hurt." Is she virgin? Then without any resistance I laid on her. She sighed, her thighs opened, I adjusted my prick, grasped her buttocks firmly, and thrust. "Oh — ohoo! — har!" one loud cry only. I had shattered it in three or four hard thrusts. She was a virgin, and a tough one. My sperm was filling her cunt the next minute. She had meant fucking some hours before, I am sure of it, and almost fancy now, that she had made up her mind to have it done to her, long before that Sunday.

Coming to my senses, "Did you like it? — did it give you pleasure?" "No it hurt," said she with perfect tranquillity. I laid still, kissing her, nestling up her my still stiff prick, put my fingers down, and found them red. I had put a towel on the bed, and now pushed it under her buttocks, and uncunted, — I thought soiling her linen might cause her difficulty. For a moment to my delight, I saw the unusual sight of a virgin cunt just fucked, and then pushed the napkin between her thighs. "You never have had it before," I remarked. "I told you so," she replied. She laid still till I suggested her washing. As she washed, "You've made me bleed," and she laughed. The affair did not seem very serious to her. Then we talked, I saw her cunt, and fucked her twice more, — the second poke I stopped in the middle. "Don't you feel pleasure now?" "Oh! yes — oho, ah!" She did not get home till past ten o'clock. I went home first. Her aunt rowed her in the passage. Walking with a friend, — walking with a friend was her only reply. My friends heard the row in the passage, as well as I, and next morning remarked, they were afraid that shop-girl was giving her aunt much trouble, — Mrs. L**g said she looked an impudent minx.

Then came that delicious time when a couple both on heat scheme how to fuck on the sly. It seems to me the most delicious gratification of sexual passion, when it is done thus successfully. To kiss, and finger your privates, whisper as you pass, give signals to each other, cunt in one's mind, cock in the other's; to think all day when, where, and how the copulation is to come off; to watch this one who is in the way, scheme to get the other out of the way, hatch excuses for getting out of the house, tales about where you have been, and reasons for coming in late is delightful. I love the secret joys of success in deceiving, the passionate fuck here, there, anywhere, just as the opportunity offers; the rapid spend from genitals in which from thinking constantly of it, with lewed desire for hours, the sperm and sexual juices have been accumulating, ready for mingling. I had all this with Loo, have had it with many other women since the age of sixteen, and know nothing in life so soul-absorbing, so delicious.

Next day we felt each other in the shop, on the staircase, and going up to bed. Next day promised to be unsuccessful for us, but

I was so lewed that I was ready for any risk, — she much the same. We could think of no place, till suddenly, "There is the bed-room on the stairs, — it's empty, — no one will think of your being in there." I went in the evening to a bazaar with my friends, left them there; and then slipped into the house, and into the bed-room unobserved. The servant had left, the aunt went out, and Loo slipped into the room.

She had left the boy in the shop. I fucked her quite in darkness on the bed-side, — the boy thought she had gone up to her bedroom. I sat patiently half an hour, then up she came, and we did it again. Nearly another hour, and again she came, and was fucked. "You haven't washed your cunt, have you?" "No, — ought I?" said she. "Isn't fucking nice?" "Oh! ain't it just!" The boy wondered at her keeping the shop open so late. "The bed (a feather one) will show," said I. "As I come down in the morning, or directly Tom's gone, I'll set it to rights," said she.

For the rest of the time of my acquaintance with this red-haired damsel, my dodges and devices to get her were mostly like those with little Sally, already told of. The circumstances were nearly the same. A sea-coast town, a lodging-house, a landlady, a young lady anxious to get her cunt buttered, a man in full health, intent on buttering it for her. Who could under those circumstances prevent copulation?

The next night she went out without asking leave, and I had her in the china-shop. "My darling let's look at your cunt." She opened her thighs quite freely. "Does it look much different to what it did?" She had been trying to look at it in the glass, but couldn't see, — she hadn't a hand-glass. "But it feels quite different," she remarked. We fucked like blazes for a couple of hours. There was a great row, and threats of the aunt about her absence, when she got back.

She was biggish, almost a woman in form, but with girlish expression in face. Excepting for that she looked eighteen. She had large thighs, a fat backside, and nice plump, but little breasts. Her flesh was beautifully white. She had a pretty cunt, a very fully-developed clitoris, and the hair on it was more carroty than that on her head. I had never yet seen a regular carroty cunt, but there was not much hair, — in that respect it looked sixteen. The edge of the split hymen was well jagged, any one could have seen that it had not been split up long. I looked at it till the exceptional letch seized me. I tickled the clitoris with my tongue till she gave a sigh, then the idea of giving her full pleasure enchanted me. I closed my mouth on it, and licked and licked, and thrust my tongue in and out, till she writhed. "Leave off, — oh! — it's dirty, — oho!" My jaws ached, my tongue was weary, I thought it was impossible to finish her, till with a strong effort, gliding my tongue over her clitoris, with all the rapidity that fatigue would let me, her thighs opened, and with a low yawling, half-moan, half-sigh she spent, clutching my hair spasmodically, and her thighs nipping. I don't know how long I had been operating on her, and wonder why I did not fetch her sooner. I never did it to her again, and can't account for this sudden letch, — I never can give reasons for gama-huching one woman, and not another.

Next day my friends left, I stayed, and hired their two rooms, and the odd bed-room, — the old landlady said she could only let them together. The weather was getting cold, no other lodgers were expected, the shop-business fell off. The landlady next day asked if I would mind her waiting on me, as she and her niece could do all I wanted, unless other lodgers came. Though delighted I said in a dissatisfied manner that I expected to be properly cooked for, and waited upon; that I didn't like persons above their positions about me, and so on. Oh! she'd take care, and her niece should wear a cap. Soon after she returned. Would I excuse the cap, — her niece would not wear one; — she added that the girl had given her father lots of trouble, and now gave her trouble, — and she should send her home. How I laughed in my sleeve; the servant left, the shop-boy remained, a charwoman came for an hour daily, and the land-lady, Loo, and I were alone in the house at night.

I gave lots of trouble, sending the landlady out to buy this and that. Whenever I wanted her out of the way I sent her to buy something. I kept her hard at cooking, and did not care what it cost to get her out of the house, nor did she, for she got profits. When she was out up came Loo. In a trice I had her on my bed, and shagged her. The landlady laid the cloth, my beefsteak was burnt, and I grumbled. She was very sorry. Then she laid the cloth an hour before my meal, so that she might cook. I wasn't going to have a table-cloth on in the room all day, — I should dine out. Oh! she was so sorry. "Get a servant then." Well she would, — but would I mind her niece without a cap laying it? "No, let her," — and up came Loo. What a lark! the woman was cooking whilst I was pulling up Loo's petticoats, slapping her backside, kissing her motte, she laying the cloth. Then I slipped into my bed-room. Then knock, knock, "Your dinner's on table sir." In I went. "I see the young woman has laid it all right." "Yes sir, I'll see that she does." I rang, and up came Loo. "A bottle of pale ale." The shop-boy fetched it, Loo cleared the table, and had a glass of ale, her aunt had gone out to buy me something, so we fucked. A randier little bitch never had a prick up her. At a late dinner it was the same game, and Loo's cunt had another seminal libation. What a jolly day! Is it my luck, or my clever maneuvering? I think the latter, for I have had much practice in this sort of thing.

For a week, twice a day, and mostly three times I had the girl. She gave me hints when to get her. "Aunt will go out at such a time." "Where will the boy be?" "In the shop, — I'll tell him I must be in the kitchen, — he daren't leave the shop, — if he goes into the parlour even, aunt would send him about his business, — he puts any money he takes down on to the counter, till aunt takes it." Then up skipped Loo directly she thought it safe, got on to my bed, and almost pulled her own petticoats up, so longing was she for the prick. Directly afterwards, and often with her carroty quim unwashed, off she went. I grumbled about her want of attention to her aunt, to keep up the deception. The old woman let out about the girl being a wild one, and giving her trouble, and then for a couple of days the woman attended to me herself, and I had no poke.

"Aunt goes to market herself to-morrow," whispered Loo grinning. During the season a relative went to the market for her. At six o'clock next morning off aunt went, Loo partially dressed, let her out. The boy was to have been there to open the shop. He entered by the private door to do so, and Loo had cunningly told him to come later. The lock was always bolted back when the door was opened in the morning, so that lodgers could let themselves in and out. The lass omitted this, and there were we in the house alone and secure, I in bed ready.

Upstairs she ran like a hare, "Pull off all your clothes, — yes, naked." "No I won't," — the only objection I ever heard her make. But I stripped her and myself, and in a minute we were both

start naked in my bed together. What a delicious cuddle we had
on that chilly morning! Then I gratified my eyes, never having seen
her naked before. A little reddish hair was just showing in her armpits. A kiss on her pretty little breasts and her red-haired motte,
a peep at the ragged, jagged opening to her cunt. I knelt over her,
and she kissed my prick, — never before, and she did it with such
delight. Then ouf! in tight libidinous naked embrace our genitals
coupled. Oh! what a divine fuck it was, — luckily with a towel
under her backside, I don't spoil sheets, and give trouble now, —
I deluged her cunt. Everything is nice to people in copulation. "Put
your hand down darling, and feel my prick in you." "Oh! isn't it
wet!" "Do you like fucking naked in bed?" "Oh! yes, it *is* nice, —
do married people do it naked?"

Then lying coupled, nestling our bellies, talking of fucking,
instructing her (half the delight of having a virgin is in instructing
her in libidinous acts, and instilling into her mind ideals of copulation), kissing, tongue-sucking at intervals. We passed a time. "Can
you feel that my prick's getting smaller in your cunt?" "Yes it is."
"Do you like the feel of the spunk in it?" "Oh! yes I do" (a question I have put to all my virgins before, but ever fresh it comes).
"Feel my prick now it's out. Isn't it small!" "Yes, — I shall try to
make it stiff." "Do love, — let me look at your cunt." Thighs wide
opened I saw the offering my prick had left there. "Would you like
to see your cunt now?" "Yes, — but it looks nasty, don't it?" "No
dear." I stiffened. "Look love, look at my prick, — let's fuck before
your aunt comes in, — get up, — kneel, — there, that's it," — and
then with her white, smooth, hard backside against my belly as I
knelt at the back of her, I had another glorious fuck in her smooth,
sperm-lubricated vulva.

"What am I doing dear?" "Oh! — ah! — a doin it to me — ah!"
"Say fucking." "Fuck — hing, — ah! — ah!" We are quiet, I am
bending over her, hands quiet on her buttocks, motionless all but
in the last throbbing of my prick, and the gentle clipping of her
cunt round it, as my ejaculation finished.

My prick kept in its channel, her bum close into my belly.
What delicious tranquility, and soft baudy dreaming. "Is it nice this
way dear?" (the first time I had done it so). "Oh! yes, — do married
people do it this way ever?" A silence. "How long's aunt been gone?
— oh! that's the boy ringing." "Don't move Loo, — my prick's stiff

yet." A pause. "Oh! I'd better, — he'll keep on a ringing, — what a nuisance." "Let him ring." "Oh! take it out, — he might tell aunt, — and I've got to dress." Out I pulled it, she dressed (a frock over her chemise). "I shall tell him I fell asleep." Then she let him in, and again came to me. We kissed, felt each other's genitals. "Don't wash your cunt, Loo, and we'll do it again at breakfast." Off she went, dressed properly, and lighted the kitchen-fire.

When she brought my breakfast, "I wish we could sleep together." "So do I," she replied. "We'd sleep naked." "Yes," said she grinning, but we never did. We could not manage a poke till after luncheon, and then did it on the sofa, backside to belly again, because it took so long to make the feather-bed look square, after we had rumpled it. How quickly she rumped up to my prick! — how gloriously she fucked! She was made for fucking, and loved it. I guess that in a year or two, when full-grown, it will take a strong man to do all her carnal work. Her exact age was sixteen years and one month the day I broached her.

We were baulked all the next day, for the aunt attended to me, but the next morning went to market. The boy's mother was ill, so Loo told him he might come late, and again in bed naked we strummed. I put her on the top of me. Libidinous devices, played with the young lass, pleased me fifty times as much as with an accomplished courtesan. "Are you coming Loo?" "Y — hes, y — hes," — our salivas were mingling. "Do married people do it like that?" said she as she lay on the top of me after her spend.

I had every meal at home, and had cooking and things fetched at intervals all day long, to get the aunt out of the way. To my annoyance she said she must get a servant, for it was too much for her. "Why don't you make your niece do more?" "She don't like waiting [all arranged], — the girl's a rare trouble to me, and to her poor father; but I must send her home." "As you like, but I am not likely to dine at home so much." No servant was got, — one would have spoiled all, — so I did not lose my lass. Every other morning the aunt was away for about two hours, and did not know the boy came late (he was glad to come late), for the shop was always open before she returned. We lost no time, my prick was in Loo's cunt five minutes after her aunt went out, and generally in it a quarter of an hour before she came back. Between our carnal exercises, she with only a frock on lighted the kitchen-fire, and let the boy in, stripping and getting into bed with me like lightning between those performances. She now kissed and toyed me most lasciviously directly she got into bed.

One morning I lent her a hand-glass, and helped her to inspect her cunt. She contemplated it with great satisfaction. I pointed out to her the edges of the ruptured hymen, — it almost looked like a cock's-comb on each side, she said.

"I wonder if I'm in the family way," said she one day just after we had fucked, and whilst she was taking away my breakfast things. She had had no symptoms, no sensations that she knew of, but she wondered, — she would know by the following Monday. On Monday she was all right, the redness showed, and for three days she was untouched. Then we resumed our fornication, and for nearly a month more carried on this sweet little game of copulation, and I believe unsuspected excepting by the boy.

It was close to November, all visitors were gone, and I told her then that I must leave, and then for the first time she showed anxiety about her future, and shed tears. But from conversation, though she had now got very close, I firmly believe she had made up her mind to turn strumpet. Her aunt and she quarrelled daily. Aunt was always threatening to send her home, she threatening to run away. I urged her going home, and one morning feeling uneasy about her, I gave her twenty pounds in sovereigns. That set her crying violently (she had never asked me for a farthing). As I could not take her to London (which it was impossible for me to do), perhaps she'd go home. "If you don't go home, stay here, — you're handsome, — you'll get a sweetheart, and marry if you're careful, — he won't find out what you've done." Only common shop-people spoke to her she remarked with a toss of her head, as if she thought them not good enough.

Two of her monthly periods had passed since I first had her, without signs of pregnancy. I felt quite comfortable about that, and after a heavy day's fucking, and three fucks on the last morning done with great risk, to my astonishment she suddenly cried bitterly, and just before her aunt came home, put her bonnet on, went out, and I never saw her more. The aunt was in a state of anxiety when I left, and so was I, the girl being so peculiar in character. I feared she would come to London, but I never saw her, if she did. The following spring, being about twenty miles from the town, I went there purposely to enquire. As I saw the aunt in the shop I went in, and bought something.

The aunt knew me, smiled, and asked if I were coming to M**g**e again. "Where is your niece?" said I casually. "Oh! gone home — or somewhere." After a pause, "She gave my poor brother lots of trouble." I asked one or two fishing questions, but learnt nothing further. I am convinced that she turned gay, and would have done so whether I had had her or not. She was made for much fucking, was ready for it, waiting for it. I believe she often had felt the shop-boy's prick though she denied that. She admitted once having done so, but they were always scuffling.

It is funny that I should so soon after I had a lady with a ginger-coloured motte, have fallen upon a red-haired motte. Liking neither of the colours I yet much enjoyed both women, but Loo far better than the other, owing to her youth, freshness, and inexperience. But each woman as she succeeds another, seems fresh to me, and brings her own peculiar charms and enjoyment. The delights of women are inexhaustible.

[I was alone nearly all this time at M**g**e, the season was over; what acquaintances I had had left, and these notes were written partly whilst there, and the rest soon after, for I had just then strongly on me the desire of describing the incidents of my private life, and writing them gave me the greatest pleasure. The account cf my doings with Loo the red-haired, are word for word as I then wrote them.]

END OF VOLUME FOURTH.